Europe's Promise

EUROPE'S PROMISE

WHY THE EUROPEAN WAY IS THE BEST HOPE IN AN INSECURE AGE

Steven Hill

UNIVERSITY OF CALIFORNIA PRESS

BERKELEY   LOS ANGELES   LONDON

University of California Press, one of the most
distinguished university presses in the United
States, enriches lives around the world by
advancing scholarship in the humanities, social
sciences, and natural sciences. Its activities are
supported by the UC Press Foundation and by
philanthropic contributions from individuals
and institutions. For more information, visit
www.ucpress.edu.

University of California Press
Berkeley and Los Angeles, California

University of California Press, Ltd.
London, England

Library of Congress Cataloging-in-Publication Data

Hill, Steven, 1958–
    Europe's promise : why the European way is the
best hope in an insecure age / Steven Hill.
        p.   cm.
    Includes bibliographical references and index.
    ISBN 978-0-520-24857-1 (cloth : alk. paper)
    ISBN 978-0-520-26137-2 (pbk. : alk. paper)
    1. Europe—Social conditions—21st century.
2. Europe—Politics and government—21st century.
I. Title.
    HN373.5.H55 2010
    306.2094'09051—dc22   2009022718

Manufactured in the United States of America

18 17 16 15 14 13 12 11 10
10 9 8 7 6 5 4

This book is printed on Cascades Enviro 100, a 100%
post consumer waste, recycled, de-inked fiber. FSC
recycled certified and processed chlorine free. It is
acid free, Ecologo certified, and manufactured by
BioGas energy.

To Lucy. Without you, none of this would have been possible.

Contents

Preface

On January 8, 2009, French president Nicolas Sarkozy mounted the speaker's podium at a two-day summit in Paris that had been called to tackle the ongoing collapse of the global economic system. Occurring less than two weeks before the inauguration of President-elect Barack Obama, alarm bells had been ringing in the world's capitals as the impacts of the economic crash from the previous fall ricocheted around the world. In all the world's major and developing economies, unemployment was rising rapidly, the global banking system had frozen despite various interventions, the stock market had fallen off a cliff, and most nations had tilted into severe recession. The Paris summit was packed with other political heavyweights and heads of state, notably German chancellor Angela Merkel, former British prime minister Tony Blair, Nobel Prize–winning economists Joseph Stiglitz and Amartya Sen, World Trade Organization head Pascal Lamy, and European Central Bank president Jean-Claude Trichet, among others. The stunned world leaders realized they were staring into the face of the worst economic calamity since "the one whose name must not be mentioned"—the Great Depression.

Unlike Sarkozy's predecessor, the elderly Jacques Chirac, who had led European opposition to the Bush administration's Iraq invasion and was scornfully labeled as a washed-up remnant of "old Europe," this French president was viewed approvingly by many Americans as the type of European leader they could trust. In his 2007 campaign for the presidency, the conservative Sarkozy had gone out of his way to break with the perceived French tradition of U.S. bashing, pronouncing himself pro-American and even reaching out to President George W. Bush. He advocated for a "rupture" with France's top-down, *dirigiste* economic model in favor of a more U.S.-style free market economy. In the ongoing Rorschachian transatlantic dance in which Americans and the French seem to see in each other what they don't want to see about themselves, Americans refreshingly saw Sarkozy as an "outside the box" thinker and a "force of nature," and ultimately *Time* magazine selected him as a runner-up for its Person of the Year, 2008, just behind President-elect Obama himself.

So with most of the world blaming the U.S. financial system for the global meltdown, Uncle Sam was happy to have a friend in the office of the French presidency. America thought it had nothing to fear as President Sarkozy stood at the podium at the Paris conference, projecting his usual energetic dynamism at the eye of the tempest. Until he started to speak.

"I've always in my political life been a supporter of a close alliance with the United States, but let's be clear: in the twenty-first century, a single nation can no longer say what we must do or what we must think," said Sarkozy. Questioning the morality and logic of American-style capitalism, Sarkozy called capitalism based on financial speculation "an immoral system" that has "perverted the logic of capitalism."

"It's a system where wealth goes to the wealthy, where work is devalued, where production is devalued, where entrepreneurial spirit is devalued," said the conservative French president, practically sounding like a French Marxist. And then he uttered the line that sent shock waves across the Atlantic and caused Wall Street CEOs to quake in their $1,500 Testoni shoes. "In the capitalism of the twenty-first century, there is room for the state," he declared, standing at a podium sporting a banner that read in French, "New World, New Capitalism: Ethics, Development, Regulation."[1] In a previous speech he had earnestly pronounced, "Laissez-faire is finished. The all-powerful market that always knows best is finished. Self-regulation as a way of solving all problems is finished."[2] In a clear warning not only to Wall Street but also to the Washington consensus of economic philosophy that had dominated the post–World War II era, he promised to bring a new European agenda to the world's stage.

German chancellor Angela Merkel, another conservative European leader also seen as being more pro-U.S. than her German predecessor, went even further. In a clear rebuff to American economic leadership, the chancellor called for an "economic council" at the United Nations that would function alongside the U.N. Security Council, as well as a "world charter" on economic sustainability that would foster "a long-term reasonable economy" based on new regulations for global financial governance. There's no returning to laissez-faire approaches by governments once the crisis has passed, said the center-right German leader. "Our response must be more than a few rules. . . . Once everything is going better, the financial markets will tell us: 'You politicians don't need to get involved because everything is working again.'" But "we must not repeat the mistakes of the past. . . . The crisis is an opportunity to create an international architecture of institutions."

Less than a month later, at the annual gathering of world leaders in Davos, Switzerland, Chinese premier Wen Jiabao and Russian prime minister Vladimir Putin gave headline speeches in which they blamed a freewheeling U.S. financial system that had produced a contagion of toxic financial products as the source of the 2008 crash. Their jeremiads found an attentive audience, its concentration focused by the depth of the economic crisis. The so-called Washington consensus, which for years had dogmatically called for deregulation of just about everything in the name of free trade and economic growth, suddenly had its back to the wall. In what some have been calling a new "post-American world," American professors Bruce Jentleson and Steven Weber pronounced in an important article in *Foreign Policy* magazine that "the rules have changed, and the biggest and most basic questions of world politics are open for debate once again."[3] Influential American economist Joseph Stiglitz agreed, writing that the legacy of this economic crisis "will be a worldwide battle over ideas—over what kind of economic system is likely to deliver the greatest benefit to the most people. . . . [A]mong the big losers is support for American-style capitalism" ("Wall Street's Toxic Message," *Vanity Fair*, July 2009).

Indeed, one of the unexpected consequences of the financial crisis was the emergence in April 2009 of the Group of 20 (also known as the G-20), a bloc of both developed and developing nations formed to promote dialogue around common global issues, as a new and important forum at which the world's most pressing economic problems would now be addressed.[4] Unlike the G-7, G-8, or U.N. Security Council, which has been dominated for many years by a handful of the world's major powers led by the United States, the G-20 represents 85 percent of the world's gross domestic product, most of the world's population, and many of the world's largest emerging market economies, including China, India, Brazil, and Saudi Arabia. In this new, more inclusive forum, neither the U.S. nor any other nation has veto power. "That means that the G-20 is likely to be a more competitive platform for diplomacy, ideas, and intellectual leadership," says Douglas Rediker, a former investment banker and a codirector of the Global Strategic Financial Initiative at the New America Foundation, a Washington, DC, think tank.[5] Wrote Jentleson and Weber, "It is fundamentally wrong to believe that the world wants to 'go back' to 2007 or even 1999."[6]

Since World War II, American power and leadership mostly have gone unchallenged, especially since the implosion of the Soviet Union in 1991, which left America as the world's lone remaining superpower. But as world leaders have grappled to find a way out of the economic crisis, the European model of capitalism suddenly has risen in importance. Says Rediker, "Europe seems poised to exert increasing influence over the next generation of global financial supervision and architecture. With so many basic questions back on the world's table, the impact of European ideas and proposals will likely be more significant and global than it has been for decades." In part, says Rediker, this is because the European Union, given its complex structure requiring balance among the diverse interests of its twenty-seven member states, has been a testing ground for how to forge consensus among dozens of nations, balancing the need to regulate and supervise cross-border interactions with the need to recognize the interests and culture of each individual country. Those are precisely the skills that the world is looking for now—not those of a single hegemon who can be the world's RoboCop and fix it all single-handedly, but ways to bring the world together around the common challenges of our times.

It's not just in the financial sector that the world is taking a closer look at the European way of doing things. In the new post-collapse era, state regulation of economies is back in the game as a real alternative. In a historic turning of the page, President Ronald Reagan's pronouncement in 1981 that "government is the problem" has been replaced by a more Franklin Roosevelt–like "Government is part of the solution." And Europe has had lots of practice at this, ever since the end of World War II, when it began crafting a new version of "social capitalism," balancing regulation with competition and striking a more functional and less volatile equilibrium than the world or the U.S. has experienced in the last decade and a half of bubble economies. In a time of great economic insecurity and imbalance, the European way of doing things is projecting a more humane and efficient brand of economics that has displayed a striking ability to harness capitalism's tremendous wealth-generating capacity and foster not only a more broadly shared prosperity, but one that better buffers families and individuals against the risks of an economic downturn. And it accomplishes all that in a way that is seeking to be ecologically sustainable. That combination is exactly what the world needs at this time.

"In Europe, we have a social market economy," said European Commission president José Manuel Barroso during his comments at the Davos, Switzerland, meeting of world leaders, almost like a salesman touting the superiority of his product—in this case, a development model that differs from its transatlantic cousin's in crucial ways. "We have universal health care, a more generous system of social security, a general principle of almost free university education." Warming to his subject, President Barroso became more bold. "President Obama," he said, "is moving toward a European-style model," citing the then-new administration's aims to boost health care coverage, access to student loans, and public infrastructure spending as examples of America's emerging European tilt. Obama also had announced plans to spend more on renewable energy and conservation, as Europe had been doing for years.[7]

Indeed, in an age of globalized capitalism that threatens to turn us all into internationally disposable workers, this may end up being the European century. Imagine a place where doctors still do house calls, or where everyone has quality, affordable health care and child care is affordable, professional, and widely available. Or where all new parents are paid to stay home and care for their newborns, and receive a monthly stipend to pay for diapers, food, and other daily needs. Or imagine a place where a young person doesn't have to mortgage her or his future by going into debt to pay for a college education. Or where all workers receive two months' worth of paid vacation and holidays every year, and paid sick leave too, as well as generous retirement benefits, and if laid off receive helpful levels of unemployment compensation and job retraining.

To most Americans, such a place sounds like Never Never Land. But to most Europeans, as well as to the Japanese, Canadians, Australians, and New Zealanders, most of those supports for families and individuals are commonplace. America is the outlier here. It is important for Americans to keep this in mind as President Barack Obama advances the goals of his administration in the wake of the crash of 2008–9. If the Obama administration manages to resuscitate the American economy but leaves most families and individuals still lacking in the type of institutional support and social infrastructure that is crucial for providing economic security in this uncertain age of global capitalism and worldwide climate change, then Americans will remain stranded by the same "ownership society" ideology that has been part of the problem.

A more comprehensive solution has been crafted in Europe. Post–World War II Europe has pioneered an efficient, comprehensive social capitalism that lays a much stronger foundation for its people than the Wall Street casino capitalism that has dominated the United States provides for Americans. After two decades of being lectured to about the superiority of Wall Street and preached to on the merits of untrammeled Anglo-American free markets, most of the world is recognizing the advantages of the European way. Today, Europe, as well as Japan, Australia, Canada, and others, is showing a different path forward with a brand of economics that is quite distinct from the American version. Europe's capitalism does not require roaring Chinese-like growth rates but instead relies on a balanced, steady state economy that grows not too fast but not too slowly, making it sustainable ecologically as well as economically.[8]

Many Americans, even President Obama, seem to mistake the world's call for America to get our financial and economic house in order for a renewed call for U.S. leadership and dominance. The world wants a partner, not a preeminence, in Uncle Sam. At a critical juncture in international affairs, Europe is proposing a bold new vision for global development. A unique European Way has become the world's leader during this make or break century, challenged by a worldwide economic crisis, global warming, and new geopolitical tensions. The current global order is about to be remade, with most of these changes taking place over the next two decades almost as imperceptibly as the polar ice caps are melting. What will emerge on the other side will be a new world based on the European model that is not only more economically balanced, but also more environmentally sustainable and more egalitarian and democratic than the Washington consensus that dominated the post–World War II era.

Since the dawn of civilization, humans have sought better ways to organize and protect themselves against their own innate frailty, the capriciousness of nature, and their own species' tendency toward tribal-like violence. For those Americans and others around the world who are anxious about the insecurity of our age, the European Way has much to offer. History is in the making, and those paying attention have ringside seats.

Steven Hill
San Francisco
August 2009

INTRODUCTION

A Quiet Revolution

A quiet revolution has been occurring in Europe over the past sixty years. A world power has emerged across the Atlantic that is meticulously recrafting the rules for how a modern society should be organized and how it should provide economic, political, and personal security, as well as environmental sustainability, for its many peoples. This is no small feat. In an era of globalized capitalism and worldwide climate change, when breathless media offer constant reminders that China and India, with their roaring economic growth rates, teeming populations, and spoiled environments, are supposedly the harbingers of everyone's future, Europe's crafting of a development model that has the potential to take us forward rather than backward raises a beacon of hope. Yet these changes mostly have taken place under the radar, misreported by the media and misunderstood by the American public and its leaders.

One of the reasons Americans have not grasped the magnitude of what is occurring across the Atlantic is rooted in the way we define "power." During the U.S.–Soviet superpower tussle of the Cold War, power and leadership were heavily dependent on military might. The Bush-Cheney years from 2001 to 2009 saw an aggressive reassertion of this muscular posture, and President Barack Obama has yet to turn this page, maintaining significant troop levels in the Middle East and elsewhere around the world. Yet for all the talk of America as the world's lone remaining superpower, the events since September 11, 2001, have demonstrated the limits of that power. Meanwhile, Europe's power and influence have been manifesting in myriad ways, some of them traditional and others unconventional:

Economic strength. The European Union, with its twenty-seven member nations and half-billion people, has become the largest, wealthiest trading bloc in the world, producing nearly a third of the world's economy—almost as large as the United States and China *combined.*

Competitive businesses. While its critics have derided Europe as a land of "creeping socialism," in fact European economies are unapologetically capitalist, with way more Fortune 500 companies than the United States, China, or Japan. The World Economic Forum's rankings of national economic competitiveness regularly list European nations in most of the top spots, and European companies are corporate America's biggest target for foreign investment, far more than businesses in China or elsewhere in Asia. But it's not a one-way street: in 2004, European businesses accounted for nearly 75 percent of all foreign investment in the United States, being the top foreign investors in forty-five states, with more than $1.4 trillion in investments.

Real family values. Yet Europe's brand of capitalism is increasingly different from that of America's. Europe has led the way in figuring out how to harness capitalism's tremendous wealth-creating capacity so that its benefits are broadly shared. To do this, post–World War Europe transformed its nation-states from the war machines they had been since the sixteenth century, redirecting huge amounts of resources away from military expenditures and plowing them into universal health care, education, pensions, various family-support measures (such as paid parental leave, sick leave, child care, and "kiddie stipends"), housing, and transportation. American detractors have decried this as a "welfare" state, but nothing could be further from the truth. A better name for this system is a "workfare" state, since all of these supports are part of a comprehensive system of institutions geared toward keeping individuals and families healthy, productive, and working. Instructively, this approach was conceived as a *security* revolution, not a socialist revolution, by the *conservative* politicians of western Europe—men like Winston Churchill, France's Jean Monnet and Robert Schuman, and Germany's Konrad Adenauer—following the devastation of two world wars. In the ensuing years, it has contributed greatly to Europe's success, helping to enact a broadly shared prosperity and to minimize personal risk for individuals and families in an age of globalized capitalism and rising economic insecurity.

Better health care. European nations are rated by the World Health Organization as having the best health care systems in the world, spending far less per person for universal coverage and quality results than is spent in the United States. France has the highest-rated health care system, while the United States's is ranked thirty-seventh—just ahead of those of Cuba and Slovenia. Yet contrary to stereotypes, France and numerous other European countries do not use government-run "socialized medicine," nor do they use a U.S.-style for-profit system. Instead, they have figured out a "third way," a hybrid with private insurance companies, cost containment, short waiting lists for treatment, and individual choice of doctors, most of whom are in private practice. And, it turns out, this third way is good for European businesses, because it doesn't expose them to the soaring health care costs that have plagued American businesses.

Readying for global warming. Europe also has taken the lead in readying its mass economy for the advancing crisis of global warming. The continent's landscape is being transformed slowly by giant high-tech windmills, vast solar arrays, underwater seamills, hydrogen-powered vehicles, "sea snakes," "wave dragons," and other remarkable renewable-energy technologies. Europe is implementing conservation and "green" design in everything from skyscrapers to automobiles, trains, lightbulbs, and toilets. In the process, Europeans are creating entire new industries and tens of thousands of new jobs. Consequently, Europe's ecological "footprint" (the amount of the earth's capacity that a population consumes) is about half that of the United States for the same standard of living. The Obama administration has taken badly needed steps in this direction, but its proposals have been timid compared with Europe's innovations.

Robust democracy. After centuries of kings and dictators, the European nations have forged political institutions and electoral methods that have resulted in the most advanced representative democracies the modern world has ever seen. European democracies foster inclusiveness, participation, political debate, multiparty representation, and majoritarian policy based on a consensus of viewpoints and broad public support. Their institutions and methods are quite different from the antiquated, eighteenth-century winner-take-all methods still used in the United States. Europe's robust, consensus-seeking democracies are the single most important reason they have been able to harness their capitalist economy to create such a broadly shared prosperity.

Multiheaded hydra. Europe enjoys many of the advantages of a single nation, such as a vast common market of five hundred million people and a single, supranational government led by the European Parliament (representing the second largest democratic electorate in the world, after India). But it also enjoys the advantages of "more heads than one" — having so many powerful nation-states allows each nation to act as a laboratory for the others, learning from one another's successes and shortcomings. In addition, when it's time to cast votes in multilateral organizations such as the United Nations, the World Trade Organization, and other global institutions, Europe suddenly splits into separate countries with over two dozen votes to cast on behalf of the European position, compared with one for the United States, China, or Japan. During the crucial Group of 20 meeting of developed and developing nations in April 2009, which refocused the global response to economic recovery, European nations had over a third of the G-20 seats. Trick question: Who won the most gold medals in the 2008 Olympics, the United States or China? Answer: Europe, and the tally was not even close. The U.S. won thirty-six gold, China won fifty-one gold, but Europe won eighty-six gold. Is Europe a single nation or a union of individual nations? Increasingly the answer is: both. And that duplexity can provide distinct advantages.

Innovative foreign policy. Europe is leading the way not only with some impressive foreign policy accomplishments but also in reevaluating how we define "power" in the twenty-first century. America's aggressive brand of unilateralism and military "hard power" has suffered unexpected setbacks in recent years. But Europe's "smart power," which is based on multilateral diplomacy and regional networks of trade, investment, and Marshall Plan–like foreign aid that link one-third of the world to the European Union, has produced more concrete results than its critics are willing to admit. For starters, this velvet diplomacy has been instrumental in bringing greater peace, democracy, and prosperity to the former communist countries of eastern and central Europe, as well as to neighbors such as Turkey, Ukraine, and others in its periphery. It also shows the right temperament for slowly nudging

Russia, China, the Middle East, and other hot spots toward rapprochement with the West.

Contrary to its reputation as a military weakling that "punches below its weight," Europe has the second largest military budget in the world after the United States,[1] with two countries possessing nuclear weapons (France and Britain), over two million European soldiers in uniform (more than the U.S.), and as many boots on the ground in peacekeeping missions around the globe in Afghanistan, Lebanon, Kosovo, Bosnia, the Congo, and elsewhere. But Europe's real strength is that the European Union has had lots of practice at forging consensus among dozens of players, and that gives it a skill set that is more effective than America's hard power at bringing large segments of the world together over the many challenges we collectively face in the twenty-first century. Indeed, the top analyst in the U.S. intelligence community wrote a report in September 2008 in which he concluded that U.S. superiority in military power will "be the least significant" asset in the epoch that is unfolding.[2] In an emerging, multipolar world, Europe is transforming our very notions of "effective power."

In short, the Europe that Americans thought we knew doesn't exist anymore. Under the decades-long protective umbrella of the Pax Americana, our old transatlantic ally has quietly evolved beyond a mere tourist destination and junior Cold War partner. A distinct European Way has emerged, and it has launched a transformation on five major fronts— the economy, workfare supports and health care, political democracy, energy/transportation, and foreign policy. In the process, Europe is reshaping the world, becoming a global leader that is illuminating the path forward in this make or break twenty-first century.

THE GLOBAL IMPERATIVE

Europe's leadership has arrived none too soon. Behind the headlines generated by the global war on terror, economic downturn, and climate change, a gradual shift in geopolitical power has been occurring. *Newsweek* columnist Fareed Zakaria's *The Post-American World* and other books have chronicled this realignment of power, loyalties, and coalitions. President Bush's and President Obama's secretary of defense Robert Gates acknowledged late in 2007 that American primacy is over and the world is suddenly multipolar.[3] The United States is still a mighty power, but more than ever in the post–World War II era we are now sharing the stage with others, with upstarts pounding on the door. This shift has been a stunning shock to the American system. It wasn't that long ago that Bush administration nationalists and unilateralists who championed the Iraq war were crowing that this was to be a "New American Century."

Instead, a "Made in USA" contagion of toxic financial products based on shaky mortgages spread like a cancer around the globe, bringing the world economic system to the brink. Any nation whose economy was integrated with the U.S. economy was sucked into the vortex, including the European countries, Japan, and China. The resulting economic downturn has caused millions of people all over the world to lose their jobs, their homes, and their future prospects.

In the United States, the wealthiest 1 percent of Americans now earns a greater share of the nation's income than it did in the previous two decades and possibly since 1929, according to the *Wall Street Journal*.[4] Affordable health care and guaranteed pay-out pensions, two of the great foundations of the post–world war social contract and middle-class prosperity, are being methodically deep-sixed by U.S. employers. As American economists Robert Frank and Philip Cook have pointed out, in the age of Wal-Mart and "Chindia,"[5] the lives of millions of breadwinners and their families have been made less secure by the creation of a virtually unlimited global labor pool, which has tended to drive wages, benefits, and quality of life toward the lowest common denominator. By concentrating most economic gains among just a handful of winners, the U.S. development model has dramatically widened the gap between the wealthy and the vast legions of everyone else, consigned to the treadmill of a "winner-take-all society."[6] Combined with America's foreign policy failures, this has caused the U.S. to lose much of its global credibility and, with it, its allure to the world.

President Barack Obama has attempted to make up for lost ground, but his efforts are in their early stages, and success is by no means assured. That's because the world has moved on; the world when George W. Bush left the Oval Office was a very different place than when he entered it. Many aspiring nations today are not quite sure of the best way forward: Is it China's state capitalism and "deliberative dictatorship," or America's deregulated, hyperdrive Wall Street capitalism? Or Russian petro-dollar authoritarianism, or Japanese *zaibatsu* cronyism, or extreme Islamic fundamentalism?

It is into this breach that the European Way has stepped. Considering this insecure age of globalization and worldwide climate change in which we live, Europe has fashioned the right institutions and practices at the right time. The overarching challenge today is to advance the institutions and practices capable of enacting a desirable quality of life for a burgeoning global population of 6.5 billion people, and to do all that in a way that is ecologically sustainable. That is a tall order to fill, yet it is the defining task of the twenty-first century. The European Way offers great hope because it proposes a coherent system that utilizes a robust capitalist economy to produce the wealth that underwrites both the workfare supports for individuals and families and the technologies that have the potential to make this dynamism ecologically sustainable. And from Europe we see the style of leadership necessary to bring the world together over its many challenges rather than watching nations divide into warring camps over finite resources while the planet's atmosphere overheats. Truly we are all in the same boat now, and the European Way comes closest to manifesting that awareness.

Unfortunately, much of the detail and nuance about Europe has long been missing from American reportage and commentary. In fact most journalists, pundits, and analysts seem to have been infected by patriotism or ideology or both. Just as the American media tragically misreported the reality of Iraq and weapons of mass destruction leading up to the 2003 U.S. invasion, and failed to uncover the housing bubble and impending economic collapse, so have they been misreporting the reality—the totality—of Europe.

CHALLENGES TO THE EUROPEAN WAY

When I first began traveling to Europe for research purposes in the late 1990s, I was trying to understand differences between the political systems and democratic institutions of the United States and Europe. I interviewed all sorts of people: politicians, elected leaders, journalists, bureaucrats, political party leaders, union officials, and business leaders. I also had conversations with shop vendors, business owners, CEOs, taxi drivers, young people, people on buses, in elevators, restaurants, and cafés, in their homes and in the street, sometimes whether they wanted to talk or not. I began to realize it's not only our political systems that are quite different, but most of the other key institutions as well, including economic and corporate structures, health care, pensions and other workfare supports, media, energy, transportation, foreign policy, and more. I began to hear about quintessentially European institutions and practices with funny-sounding names such as codetermination, works councils, supervisory boards, flexicurity, proportional representation, and more. Europe's institutions had been slowly taking shape during the Cold War years, a fertile incubation period thanks to the Pax Americana.

But recognizing Europe's emerging leadership and America's slippage is not to say that Europe is some utopian paradise that has reached its "end of history" moment, far from it. Like many other regions of the globe, Europe faces challenges and threats—economic uncertainty, unpredictable energy prices, global climate change, immigration, integration of ethnic minorities, its aging and (in some countries) declining population, geopolitical tensions (with Russia, Central Asia, the Middle East), and competition from Chindia. If Europe fails to navigate those waters it will find its leadership short-lived. And despite the creation of a European "union," the continent is hardly without internal discord. Several failed attempts to enact a constitutional treaty that would bind the E.U. member states even more closely point to the "one step backward" that accompanies their "two steps forward." If it were a symphony, Europe would sound more like the atonal early Bartók than the melodious Beethoven, with a creative tension composed of bickering and dickering which, if not properly understood, can look and sound like pandemonium to the point of perpetual crisis.

But unmistakably the trajectory of Europe has been steadily upward, toward a greater realization of its unique continental identity. The economic crash of 2008 served to heighten this awareness, as American-style casino capitalism came crashing down while Europe's social capitalism and its safety net kicked into a higher gear to better protect families and workers against the rising floodwaters. Times of crisis can sharpen the mind, both for individuals and for nations; the crisis accentuated fundamental transatlantic differences, opening many eyes to the virtues of the European Way.

Some will object that there is no such thing as a "European Way," since Europe is composed of numerous individual nations that show differences among themselves. Certainly there is some truth to this, with those nations displaying variations in domestic and foreign policies, culture, wealth, democratic development, size, and language, which often correspond to certain basic cleavages: north-south, east-west, Protestant-Catholic, Anglo-Saxon–Continental, pro-U.S.–neutral, and more.

But despite these differences, certain predominant elements and tendencies can be distinguished among all the European countries, especially when compared with the United States. That's because under the cohesive force of the European Union, all member nations must accept some eighty thousand pages of laws, regulations, and directives as a condition of membership. Those eighty thousand pages change a country from the inside out, fostering common fulcrum institutions and making the European Union more than a loose-knit coalition, like NATO, the United Nations, or the pre-Constitution Articles of Confederation. The member states of the E.U. elect a common parliament, have a common executive branch and other continent-wide institutions, and dispense hundreds of billions of euros in development aid to domestic projects. They have similar approaches to their national economies, health care and other workfare supports, energy, transportation, and democracy and generally have bound their destinies together in a way that transcends national sovereignties or geographic borders. While some European nations hew to this "way" more than others, the overall trend line is unmistakably clear. As political scientists Sven Steinmo and Jeffrey Kopstein have observed, the differences between E.U. member nations increasingly are not that much greater "than the differences among Alabama, New York and Minnesota."[7] Considered together, the similarities in their basic fulcrum institutions compose a European Way that is distinct from the American Way.

In this book, my central aim is to describe to my fellow Americans and interested others the essential components of this European phoenix that has arisen from the gray, bitter ashes of horrific war—centuries of it—having learned important lessons about peace, prosperity, and sustainability. I hope in this book to begin a dialogue among my fellow Americans about these portentous changes, since the transatlantic relationship between the United States and Europe has been one of the most important and successful in the post–World War II era. Together, though not always perfectly, America and Europe have advanced a human potential that has flowered in the form of economic opportunity, a vibrant middle class, democracy, human rights, civil society, and dignity and worth of the individual. It has been a transformative partnership, one that has marked a new era in human history. But Americans have failed to recognize that Europe no longer is content to sit in the back seat while America sits up front driving. Europe has something important to share with the world.

In terms of the flow of the book, in chapter 1 I provide an overview of the European Way, outlining its major components, institutions, and practices, as well as a brief history. Then in subsequent chapters I drill down and explore these individual components and institutions in more detail. In chapters 2 through 8, I explore different aspects of what I call Europe's social capitalism—the powerful economic engine and successful industrial strategies that have been deployed to harness capitalism's tremendous wealth-creating capacity; and its comprehensive workfare supports for individuals and families, including universal health care, generous retirement, paid parental leave, free or inexpensive university education, affordable housing, and more. In chapter 6, I delve into the impact of the economic crash of 2008–9 and show how the different governmental and business responses to the crisis were fundamentally a reflection of America's Wall Street capitalism vs. Europe's social capitalism. In chapters 7 and 8, I examine the formal and informal health care systems in several countries, showing how they produce quality health care for all, even as they spend about half of what the United States spends on our broken, patchwork system. Many Americans have heard something about Europe's generous system, but it usually has been derided as "welfare" or "socialism," and so we Americans have little realization as to the breadth and depth of it or to the economic strategy behind it. Europe's hybrid social capitalism provides important advantages, especially during these times of economic uncertainty.

In chapters 9 and 10, I explore how Europe is leading the world in figuring out how today's mass societies can enjoy prosperity and quality of life in energy efficient, environmentally sustainable, and business-friendly ways by implementing renewable energy technologies and widespread conservation. In chapters 11 and 12, about European foreign policy, I look at how a continent that for centuries was wracked by bloody and bitter war has become a model of economic and political integration for entire regions, turning former combatants into "peace and prosperity" partners. I also look at how this European Way of foreign policy is being applied to the world's hot spots, including Russia, the Middle East, and China. In chapters 13 and 14, I delineate the unique political, media, and communication institutions that form the basis of European Way democracy, which has resulted in the most inclusive, advanced, representative democracies the modern world has ever seen. In chapter 15, we reach back into history, back to the seventeenth and eighteenth centuries and the times of John Locke and the Puritans, to understand how the present-day gap between the European Way and the American Way is rooted in diverging branches of a common philosophical and Christian heritage, resulting in capitalist Europe striking a new, twenty-first-century balance between individual property rights and the common good, between liberty and equality, and between government regulation and the free market.

Like any model of development, the European Way has its inconsistencies and aspects that do not live up to its own lofty rhetoric and expectations. The continent faces numerous challenges and threats to its future, and in chapters 16 through 18 I examine in detail two of the most significant: on the one hand, immigration, Muslim extremism on the continent, and Europe's mixed success at integrating its ethnic minorities (in chapter 16), as well as the recent civil rights solutions that are being tried (in chapter 17); and on the other (in chapter 18), Europe's aging and (in some countries) declining population, which threatens to destabilize its generous workfare support system.

To illustrate many points in these chapters, I often provide cases and examples from particular countries, which is certain to involve some selectivity and thus influence the portrait presented. Although other examples might present a somewhat different portrait, I have tried to select those cases that I thought were most representative of Europe's current trajectory and to look for examples that contradict it. In a book of this nature, such selectivity is unavoidable since citing examples is how we add to knowledge. While my specific examples, as well as this book in general, will no doubt provoke much argument, my objective is to describe a place, a process, and a development model, not to pronounce the final word.

That's because the future always has the final word, and certainly the most looming question for Europe's future is: Can the European Way last? Given the looming pressures and geopolitical jousting of the twenty-first century, is the European Way with its social capitalism, comprehensive workfare system, ecological sustainability, and international leadership viable over the long term?

The short answer, I believe, is a cautious "yes," and in this book I will endeavor to show why. Today, as one passes through the European port of call, one stands on the threshold of an evolving landscape that, with fits and starts, is emerging slowly into its own global identity, displaying a new approach for a modern mass society that is beginning to influence other nations. That European Way has the potential to lead the planet toward its best possible future in the twenty-first century.

Some have predicted that China, or perhaps India, Brazil, Russia, or Venezuela, by virtue of their large populations or abundant energy resources or both, are destined to rise to global prominence, perhaps even supplanting the United States and Europe. But these are still developing countries with low per capita incomes, low energy productivity, high pollution, and inefficient economies that produce but a fraction of Europe's or the United States's wealth or productive capacity. None of these other countries so far have demonstrated an economic model capable of fostering a middle-class quality of life that can work for vast populations of people. China's growth and evolution since Mao have been most impressive, yet as we will see it remains in essence a subcontractor to the West, wracked by internal contradictions, its leaders lacking the confidence to tolerate even a whisper of public reflection, let alone protest, during the twenty-year anniversary in June 2009 of the Tiananmen Square crackdown. Japan, Australia, New Zealand, and Canada have a large middle class and certainly display exemplary aspects of their national "ways," but compared with Europe or the United States their economies are too small to lead by example. Only Europe has demonstrated how a capitalist economic system can be harnessed for the good of a half billion people and also has the sheer economic muscle to be globally influential.

I know it is difficult for many Americans to believe that the continent that spawned two world wars in the last century and has always seemed to need America to prop it up could somehow be a beacon for humanity's future. Nevertheless, it is true. A visible outline of Europe's impact on the world is emerging, and it looks robust and transformative. The greatest potential for the planet lies with that clanking, conglomerating, cacophonous confederation on the other side of the Atlantic, even with all its faults.

Alexis de Tocqueville, writing in *Democracy in America* in 1835, said, "The greatness of the Americans does not simply consist in their being more enlightened than other nations, but in their being able to repair their faults."[8] One can only hope that Tocqueville's observation is still operational today, in the twenty-first century. Toward that hope I offer this book.

PART ONE

SOCIAL CAPITALIST EUROPE

ONE

THE RISE OF THE EUROPEAN WAY

"WELCOME TO PARIS, THE LOCAL TIME IS . . ."

Arriving at Terminal One of Paris's Charles de Gaulle International Airport, one is struck immediately by a distinctly European mise-en-scène. As in a modern-day Tower of Babel, the languages of the world spike the air with an incessant buzz. The smooth nasality of French intermingles with the guttural "*ich*s" and "*ach*s" of Dutch and German speakers. On the periphery are Italians speaking in a lilting aria, with some halting English tossed in. Nearby stands a fashionable Polish couple in shiny black leather, sipping espresso, and Spanish speakers (probably from Spain, but maybe Argentina or Chile) are browsing the crowded news racks. Clumps of Asian businessmen, looking well dressed and sleep deprived, are sniffing for bargains in the airport shops. In a nearby bar, with a blaring TV tuned to a football (that is, soccer) match, a knot of Russian businessmen elbows for space near the bartender. Ebony Africans saunter by in colorful traditional dress or business attire or both, reminders of Europe's colonial past (eons ago or not that long ago, depending on who is doing the reckoning). There are clusters of men wearing Muslim head wraps or Hindu turbans, women whose saris and burqas flow to the floor, veils covering attentive female eyes and obscuring the ginger skin and wary faces of the newest Europeans. Several dialects and accents of English punctuate the cacophony, including one from a good ol' American boy with a

Texas drawl. And Euro-accented pop disco blares from an unseen speaker, the whole screaming effect sounding like a postmodern version of a Wagnerian hip-hop opera.

Paris and other European cities from A to Z—Amsterdam, Barcelona, Berlin, Brussels, Budapest, Frankfurt, Geneva, London, Kraków, Madrid, Oslo, Prague, Rome, Stockholm, Vienna, Zagreb, Zurich— long have formed some of the most important crossroads of the world, historical capitals of commerce with records of trade dating back to ancient times. It is a tribute to their durability and that of their people that these old, old cities have not only survived but thrived, grown, and modernized. In fact, *BusinessWeek*'s ranking of "the World's Best Places to Live 2008" listed thirteen of its top twenty cities as European (the highest U.S. city was Honolulu, in twenty-eighth place). Today, Europe has about thirty cities with populations greater than a million people, compared with only ten in the United States (and more than a hundred in China).[1]

Despite its ancient roots, much of what we know today as modern Europe arose only sixty years ago from the ashes of the most destructive war humans had ever known. Tens of millions of people died during World War II, most of them civilians, and entire cities were reduced to rubble. Following the annihilation of two world wars within the span of thirty years, Winston Churchill and others began calling in 1946 for a "United States of Europe." In the incubation period of the postwar Pax Americana, an entirely new Europe began to emerge, one less founded on the militarization of economies. It was as if the horror of the bombs and concentration camps had wiped much of the historical slate clean, leaving a tabula rasa onto which Europe could redraw itself, influenced greatly by the American ideal.

Postwar Europe embarked on a series of treaties that, over the next five decades, remade the European continent and, by extension, the world. In 1949 the Council of Europe was established as the first pan-continental organization to try to reassemble the jigsaw puzzle of Europe from the pieces into which it had been smashed. Guided by the vision of French political leaders Jean Monnet and Robert Schuman and German leader Konrad Adenauer (three of the fathers of modern-day Europe), it was followed, in 1951, by the formation of the European Coal and Steel Community, whose six member countries agreed to share control of their coal and steel industries; notably, two of its members were the formerly warring nations of France and West Germany. Monnet's strategy was simple yet brilliant: since coal and steel were the principal resources for waging war, pooling these resources into a regional network rendered hostilities between the signatories much more difficult. It also avoided creating any grand blueprint for Europe that might fail, opting instead for a series of smaller-scale, concrete proposals with practical outcomes which would serve as a gradualist vehicle for engaging the former combatants. The European Coal and Steel Community was the auspicious start of a successful strategy that Europe would employ many times over the next six decades, using incremental steps of engagement to foster multilateralism and consensus building between nations. The Community's founders declared it "a first step in the federation of Europe," and the Treaty of Rome in 1957 extended this strategic pathway via the creation of the European Economic Community, with six original member states: West Germany, France, Italy, Belgium, the Netherlands, and Luxembourg.

In 1973 the European Economic Community was enlarged to include Denmark, Ireland, and the United Kingdom. Greece, Spain, and Portugal joined in the 1980s. The first direct democratic elections of members of a European Parliament were held in 1979, the first pan-European elections ever to be held (as well as the first international elections of this magnitude). In November 1993 the Maastricht Treaty went into effect among the European Community nations, launching the supranational body known today as the European Union. Austria, Sweden, and Finland joined in 1995, and in 2004 the European Union saw its biggest single enlargement when ten new countries, most of them former communist states in central and eastern Europe, joined the union.[2] Three years later, two more eastern European nations joined, bringing the number of member nations to its current level of twenty-seven and reaching a geographic conclusion to the formal·effort to reunite western Europe with the east, this time not as conquerors but as hopeful partners in peace and prosperity.

Today, the terms *Europe* and *European Union* are nearly but not exactly synonymous, since Switzerland, Norway, and Iceland are part of Europe, both historically and culturally, and participate in numerous treaties and pan-European organizations, but so far have declined to join the European Union. Many of the small Balkan countries—Croatia, Serbia, Bosnia, Kosovo, and others—are part of Europe and hope to join their fellow Balkan country Greece as members of the European Union sometime within the next five to ten years. Beyond those borders, definitions of what is considered "Europe" begin to diverge into various and sometimes heated opinions. Some consider

Ukraine, Belarus, Turkey, Moldova, and even eastern Russia to be part of Europe, though few of these nations—possibly none of them—will become member nations in the European Union anytime soon.

So the current twenty-seven-member configuration of the European Union, populated by half a billion people, is only a few years old, and the founding of the union itself is less than twenty years away from its Big Bang. The first modest attempt at forging a European "community" from former combatants is a mere sixty years out of the cradle, having arisen from the volcano of the most devastating conflict, followed by the ice age of Soviet communism, which covered half of Europe and froze its development. Europe had to decide if it was to go capitalist or communist, and it took decades to cut one cord and grasp the other. But finally, with the help of its powerful friend, Uncle Sam, that course has been set.

"The E.U. is riding high," says Professor Andrew Moravcsik, director of the European Union Program at Princeton University. "Over the past decade, Europe has completed its single market, eliminated border formalities, launched the Euro, and strengthened foreign policy coordination."[3] Professor Charles Kupchan of the U.S. Council on Foreign Relations has pointed out that it took roughly a hundred years after its founding for the United States to congeal and nurture a strong identity that transcended state and local loyalties and histories.[4] Given that time frame, Europe—whatever it is becoming, whether an eventual single nation or a more unified superagency—appears to be ahead of schedule. Europe is united—politically, economically, and, increasingly, culturally—in a way it has not been since the Roman Empire, and a distinctive "European way" has become discernible.

Amidst all the drama of today's headlines, it is easy to lose sight of how significant a tiding this is. The European Union is an entirely new species of human organization, the likes of which the world has never seen. It marks a new evolutionary stage in supranational development in the way it links and closely integrates entire regions of nation-states economically and politically, even as it allows the nations within that region to preserve most of their national sovereignty and culture. As the world attempts to forge multinational agreements among dozens of nations over pressing matters like financial re-regulation, economic integration, global warming, nuclear armaments, geopolitical tensions, and more, Europe's long experience in fostering trust and engagement among diverse players via small, concrete steps that nurture a consensus will be invaluable.

THE EUROPEAN MODEL OF SOCIAL CAPITALISM EMERGES

Europe will not be conjured up in a stroke, nor by an overall design. It will be attained by concrete achievements generating an active community of interest.

Jean Monnet, father of modern-day Europe

A compromise is the art of dividing a cake in such a way that everyone believes he has the biggest piece.

Ludwig Erhard,
German economist and chancellor, 1963–66

Parallel to the ebbs and flows of these political peregrinations, the shattered nations of postwar Europe engaged in deep bouts of soul-searching. With its people and major cities devastated, the antagonist Germany was ready to beat its swords into plowshares. In the mid-1940s a group of economists based in Freiburg and Cologne, led by Walter Eucken, Alfred Müller-Armack, and Ludwig Erhard, proposed a new type of capitalist blueprint. They criticized the inefficiencies of both U.S.-style laissez-faire "free competition capitalism" and communist state command economies, and devised a third way they called the "social market economy." The social market economy was founded on the principles of both pursuing a free market and serving humanity. This set the nations of Europe in motion on a decades-long journey of economic restructuring, reducing military budgets, increased social spending, and maturing of their political democracies, led initially by conservative leaders such as Winston Churchill, Monnet, Adenauer, and Schuman, joining with leftist leaders like Italy's Altiero Spinelli and Belgium's Paul-Henri Spaak—the founders of modern-day Europe.

Just as astounding as Europe's postwar economic rise was its accomplishment of all this while deepening its values of fairness, equality, and solidarity. Unlike in China today, where an impressive economic rise has nonetheless left the vast majority of people poor and the gap in inequality growing, and unlike in America, where a more hyperdrive, deregulated capitalism has resulted in rising inequality, a lack of health care for millions, retirement insecurity, and unaffordable higher education, the European economic engine has been harnessed to create wealth that has been broadly shared. These values first were fostered in the late nineteenth century by German leader Otto von Bismarck and others who, trying to ward off the growing influence of trade unions and calls for communist revolution, granted concessions and forged the beginnings of social democracy. But after the horror and trauma of World War II, European recovery and redevelopment could have taken any of several disastrous turns; following World War I, its redevelopment had teetered and finally plunged into fascism, national socialism, darkness, and eventually another catastrophic war. But in the aftermath of World War II, a miracle happened. The various western European nations embarked on a journey together that has led to the most egalitarian and democratic societies the modern world has ever seen, all the while producing robust capitalist economies with competitive businesses and a productive workforce.

Over the decades, Europe's political and economic integration has grown steadily, increasing people's personal wealth and security year after year (though always subject to the recurring ups and downs of the economic cycle). At the same time it has made fair and more equal distribution of that wealth a hallmark of its raison d'être. To an American, looking at the comprehensive and universal nature of the supports enjoyed by Europeans is truly a strange wonder to behold. Europeans, on average, are enjoying the highest of living standards and the most economic security, with health care for all, paid parental leave (following the birth of a child), affordable child care, monthly kiddie stipends, paid sick leave, free or inexpensive university education, ample retirement security, supportive elderly care, generous unemployment compensation, vocational training, efficient mass transportation, affordable housing, and more. They have an average of five weeks of paid vacation (compared with two for Americans) and a shorter work week, plus a plethora of holidays thrown in. In some European countries, workers on average work a full day less per week than Americans do, yet enjoy the same standard of living.

Instead of figuring out an American version of these comprehensive supports for individuals and families, U.S. critics and Euroskeptics have dismissed Europe's way as a "welfare state" and "creeping socialism." But as we will see in chapter 4, Europe can be more accurately described as a "workfare support state" rather than a welfare state. (European-style workfare should not be confused with the stigmatized American workfare; it has a different meaning from that in the United States and is grounded in a different philosophy. American workfare is targeted exclusively at the poor and government welfare recipients, making it politically vulnerable. But Europe's workfare support system is for *everybody*—middle class, rich, poor; its application is universal.)

It is part of the overall capitalist matrix in which Europe's powerful economic engine produces the wealth needed to underwrite its comprehensive workfare supports, which in turn maintain a healthy and productive workforce that keeps the economy humming, like a well-tuned Swiss clock.

In short, Europe's workfare system has been grossly mischaracterized by Americans in thrall to a fundamentalist free market ideology. U.S. politicians are known for invoking the importance of "family values" and a "work hard, get ahead" creed. Indeed, the United States is known as the inventor of the middle class, the attractive ideal that a good life is within reach for the vast majority of people. But if America invented the middle class, Europeans have taken that good idea and run with it one giant step further. They have figured out how to set the middle class on a more solid and secure footing and put some meat on the bones of their family values. They also have fewer poor people; indeed, "old Europe" shows more economic mobility and more poor people joining the middle class than does the American "land of opportunity," completely turning convention on its head.[5] Europeans have constructed their system so as to support families better and to minimize the personal risk for individuals in an age of globalized capitalism that has brought increasing economic insecurity.

THE "STEADY STATE" ECONOMY

The European model is, first, a social and economic
system founded on the role of the market, for no
computer in the world can process information better
than the market.

Jacques Delors,
former French president of the European Commission

What is at stake in our economic decisions today
is not some grand warfare of rival ideologies
which will sweep the country with passion, but
the practical management of a modern economy.
What we need is not labels and clichés but more
basic discussion of the sophisticated and technical
questions involved in keeping a great economic
machinery moving ahead.

President John F. Kennedy, June 11, 1962

Today, Europe's social capitalism relies on a delicate balance of free enterprise and government regulation that is constantly in the process of being recalibrated and fine tuned in reaction to ever-changing economic conditions. You can't really examine Europe's economy separate from the workfare support system, because the two are intricately linked, like two sides of the same coin. They function as a unit in what properly should be called a "steady state economy."

A steady state economy requires a refined tuning of the various economic levers and pulleys in order to foster vibrant commerce at a steady growth rate. At the same time, the goal is to provide sufficient jobs, adequate compensation, and workfare supports, but without stifling entrepreneurship and reasonable profit making or destroying the habitable ecology. A steady state economy grows not too fast but not too slowly; it steadily expands the economic pie without inciting inflation, and it also ensures that as many people as possible get a piece of the pie. Prior to the recent economic meltdown, when America's toxic financial products based on shaky mortgages damaged all major and developing economies around the world, Europe's steady state economy had reached a mature stage in which the growth curve was less steep than in previous decades but sufficiently upward nonetheless. Europe maintained its growth by having one of the consistently highest levels of productivity in the world, producing more goods and services per hour worked than just about any other economy. Researcher Klas Levinson, at the former National Institute for Working Life in Stockholm, Sweden, told me, "Europe doesn't need the growth rate of China or the United States because its productivity is high, and because it is so good at spreading the wealth around more evenly and efficiently than those two countries do." He estimates that economic growth of 2 percent is sufficient in a steady state economy.

In addition, the European workfare system creates vehicles to help individuals and families better prepare for more insecure times in their lives, whether those spring from economic downturn, old age, sickness, disability, or accidental tragedy. In fact, the system *forces* individuals to prepare, paycheck by paycheck, by deducting from workers and businesses the funds necessary to pay for the workfare infrastructure that secures their future. By comparison, the more deregulated U.S. system is known for allowing individuals to keep more of their paycheck—presidents from Ronald Reagan to George W. Bush were famous for declaring, "We let you keep your own money"—and leaves it up to Americans' discretion whether to prepare for the long run by saving money and handling the costs of health care, retirement, child care, and family security, or to spend it all in the short run. The U.S.-style "ownership society" should be called "on your own" society, because you are truly left on your own, for better or worse.

In theory, this should lead to Americans paying less in taxes and having greater discretionary income than Europeans, but this assumption has been mostly an illusion. As we will see in chapter 5, while Europeans pay higher income taxes than Americans, they generally don't pay as much in state, local, property, and social security taxes. Moreover, in return for their taxes, Europeans receive a whole host of benefits and services for which Americans must pay out of pocket with their supposedly discretionary income, via fees, premiums, deductibles, and tuition, *in addition to* their taxes. In an age of globalized capitalism and increasing economic insecurity, many of the things Europeans receive for their taxes are hardly discretionary; health care, child care, university education, job training, and adequate retirement, to name a few of their benefits, are necessary in order to enjoy a basic level of security and comfort. When you sum up the total balance sheet, including all the different types of taxes paid and benefits received, you discover that many Americans pay out just as much as Europeans, but we receive a lot less for our money. Furthermore, Europeans don't seem to have any less discretionary income, because they enjoy the same standard of living with access to the same material comforts and consumer goods (such as electronic gadgets and appliances) as Americans have.

What this points to is that in today's insecure age resulting from globalized capitalism, a middle-class standard of living is not only about income levels or economic growth rates but also about adequate support institutions for individuals and families. Europeans have established various vehicles to ensure their health, productivity, and quality of life, not only in the present, but also in the future. Properly understood, these workfare supports are a necessary part of infrastructure investment, just like the Obama administration's fiscal stimulus spending on physical infrastructure, such as bridges and roads, or spending on energy efficiency. But this "social infrastructure" invests in the most precious resource of all—people—even as it helps create jobs and stimulates consumer spending, which are two major components of a modern economy. While Europe and the United States both rely on a powerful capitalist engine as the core of their economies, the presence of a more robust social infrastructure is the reason that Europe has a higher level of economic security for its people than the United States has with its deregulated capitalism. This is Europe's way of ensuring one of America's chief principles, "life, liberty, and the pursuit of happiness," with results that are vastly different from America's "on your own" society.

In short, the European steady state economy acts like a blue chip stock instead of a venture capital startup. In normal economic times, it doesn't go up or down much in the short term, but in the longer term the trajectory is steadily upward. And because the European economies try to spread what is produced among more people, they use wealth more efficiently and more sustainably so that growth rates do not need to be as high as they are in the U.S. "trickle down" economy, which has a poor distribution system and fails to provide adequately for all Americans, even when the U.S. economy periodically performs better than Europe's. A steady state economy necessitates a whole new metric to gauge its utility and effectiveness. As we will see in chapters 2 through 5, economic growth rates, unemployment rates, tax rates, and other measurements have different implications in Europe's steady state economy than in America's trickle down economy, and reveal important distinctions that often are ignored by the media and political leaders.

This is the famous European consensus, an ingenious framework of social capitalism in which Europeans' economic system supports their workfare system, which supports their economic system, which supports their workfare system: a continuous feedback loop. Even conservative leaders in Europe today agree that this is the best way.

DEMILITARIZED SOCIAL CAPITALISTS

This discussion of basic differences between America's Wall Street capitalism and Europe's social capitalism would not be complete without recognition of the great gap in military expenditures on each side of the Atlantic, and the trade-offs of military spending vs. social spending. Following the fall of the Soviet bloc in the late 1980s, bipartisan policy in the United States still continued to fund huge military budgets that were three times larger than the combined budgets of all conceivable enemies.[6] The U.S. spends vast sums on outmoded weapons systems and military strategies that have little relevance to America's actual national defense needs, and maintains over 700 military bases around the world.[7] But the tragic events of September 11, 2001, followed by the Iraq and Afghanistan wars, took that American posture and pumped it full of steroids.[8] The U.S. spent at least $1.5 *trillion* on the theater of operations in those two wars.[9] Outside that spending, President Bush's 2008 budget froze discretionary spending on most domestic programs even as his more than $500 billion defense budget was the highest since World War II—until President Barack Obama proposed a defense budget for 2010 that was slightly higher than his predecessor's.

Currently U.S. military expenditures are eating up over 4 percent of the country's gross domestic product, compared to less than 2 percent of Europe's GDP spent on its military.[10] That works out to well over 20 percent of the U.S. federal government budget, more than either Social Security outlays or the costs of Medicare and Medicaid combined (and that does not include the huge expenditures on the Department of Homeland Security, the National Security Agency, the CIA, the Veterans Administration, or the parts of NASA and the Department of Energy that are engaged in military-related activities).[11] To put that into perspective, creating a European-like system of universal health care that includes the 47 million uninsured Americans would cost an additional $100 to $150 billion annually, only a fraction of one year's expenditures on the Iraq war. Creating European-like universal child care would cost $35 billion annually; the entire annual budget for the United Nations is only $16 billion.[12] The amount spent by the U.S. government on research and development for alternative energy in 2006 was only $4 billion, while the amount spent on R&D for new weapons was $76 billion.[13]

U.S. militarism has long been a core part of the American Way, doing triple duty as a formidable foreign policy tool, a powerful stimulus to the economy, and a usurper of tax dollars that could be spent on other budget priorities. "Our problems are those of a very rich country which has become accustomed over the years to defense budgets that are actually jobs programs and also a major source of pork for the use of politicians in their reelection campaigns," says Professor Chalmers Johnson, a prominent military critic.[14] Fifty years after Republican president Dwight Eisenhower warned against an insatiable military-industrial complex, the American system is still bedeviled by a classic guns vs. butter dilemma that the vastly less militarized European system has managed to avoid. This gargantuan difference in military spending is one of the greatest gaps between the American Way and the European Way, in some ways the elephant in the living room that overshadows most other aspects of the transatlantic relationship.

One of the underlying themes of this book is examining the appropriate role of the military in the twenty-first century. While Europe is no slouch militarily, it certainly has a much smaller stick than America. Yet, as we will see in chapters 11 and 12 on foreign policy, Europe's very success with its smart power and America's failures with its hard power raise a legitimate question over the best tactics in this post–Cold War, multipolar world. Perhaps the American Way of big-stick diplomacy, which has been practiced with varying degrees of success since the late nineteenth century, has overstretched its usefulness. Not only has it been marginally successful of late, it also is extremely expensive. The European Union's way of foreign policy, meanwhile, uses carrots instead of a big stick; it succeeds not because of coercion but because it is so attractive to other countries who wish to join the E.U. or trade with it and receive investment and foreign aid (Europe has become the world's largest bilateral aid donor, providing more than twice as much aid to poor countries as the United States).[15] The E.U.'s velvet diplomacy also costs a lot less money, allowing those resources to be steered instead into social spending and workfare supports that better support families and individuals.

Having rejected militarization decades ago, Europe's hyperefficient steady state economy is no longer geared to allow such a military orientation, and Europe shows little inclination to reconfigure its economy to allow this anytime soon. Critics of the Europeans' lack of military orientation claim that they are "free riders" on the backs of American military power, but that view is overly simplistic. Europeans have a different view, a different philosophy—born of their history of horrific wars—of the best way to enact peace and prosperity partnerships. And the European Union has had considerable success enacting foreign policy gains over the last two decades, while American foreign policy, leading with its military hand, has been bogged down in its share of quagmires.

A LANDSCAPE OF ENERGY EFFICIENCY AND CONSERVATION

Not only have Europeans crafted an economy infused with more fairness and equality and less dependence on military stimulus than that of the United States, but they have also embarked on a bold quest to do this in an ecologically sustainable way. I still recall my first time passing through Amsterdam's Schiphol Airport, when my eye was struck by the escalators turning on and off automatically. When no one is standing on the belt, they stop—an eminently sensible thing to do—until a traveler steps forward onto the lip; then a weight sensor detects his or her presence and the stair resumes operation. The logic of it is immediately admirable. The escalators are a model of energy efficiency and design, as are the low-flush, two- or three-button toilets and the motion-sensitive hallway lights in most European hotels, museums, and households, which sensibly click off when nobody is about and click back on when someone enters the room. The bulbs used are the new low-wattage kind that yields the same luminosity for a fifth of the power instead of the incendiary 100-watt fireballs still used in most American living rooms and offices. Seeing as how "Turn off the lights!" was drilled into my head from an early age, I am struck by how the Europeans have mastered this little kind of detail, practically raising energy conservation to the level of an art form.

During the past decade, as the oil chieftains in the Bush-Cheney White House resorted to increasingly desperate strategies to secure more oil, the European landscape was being slowly transformed by new renewable energy technologies that looked like something out of a futurist sci-fi movie—giant high-tech windmills, vast solar arrays, underwater seamills, and "sea snakes" bobbing off the coast, transforming wave motion into enough juice to power isolated coastal villages. Most European advances, though, have been more mundane—just better ways of boosting conservation through greater energy efficiency, better mass transportation, and the incorporation of "green" principles into everything from building design to urban planning. Europe has gone both high and low tech, joining Japan in leading the development of mass public transit, high-speed trains zipping from city to city, and fuel-efficient autos, but also creating thousands of kilometers of bicycle and pedestrian paths crisscrossing the continent.

And Europeans have discovered what a previous generation of American leaders once knew: investment in infrastructure pays dividends in multiple ways that pave the way for the future. While President George W. Bush and other leaders pitted the environment and energy innovation against the economy and loss of jobs, Europeans discovered that greater energy efficiency is actually good for their economy as well as their businesses. Not only have their renewable energy and conservation efforts led to the rise of new technologies and industries, but also those in turn have created tens of thousands of jobs. While businesses have had to make some initial investment in upgrading their facilities, that has resulted in their being more competitive and insulated from energy price spikes. Europe's greater energy productivity enables it to produce the same standard of living as the United States, even though Europeans consume a lot less energy and belch lower quantities of greenhouse gases.[16]

So to Europe's initial social capitalist model of harnessing a robust economic engine to provide broadly shared prosperity and workfare supports for individuals and their families, it now has attached a technological revolution in energy, conservation, and transportation. Those innovations not only decrease Europe's environmental impact, dependence on oil, and carbon emissions that contribute to global warming, but also further spur its economy and increase its productivity.

THE EUROPEAN WAY: A MODEL FOR DEVELOPMENT
IN THE TWENTY-FIRST CENTURY

Much of the drama of nations is told through a rehashing of historical events, with the actors of that drama being the leaders of each epoch. But in sifting through the European story over the last six decades, I found that an equally compelling way to understand it is through a more careful examination of *institutions* and the trajectory of their evolution. Institutions are the means for what President John F. Kennedy called "the practical management of a modern economy." By examining specific fulcrum institutions, we gain a better sense not only of each country's current status in the world but also of its future status. In this insecure age of globalized capitalism and global warming, having the right institutions will make a big difference in how each nation will fare.

Most Americans, including most academics, journalists, and political analysts, whether from the left, right, or center, are not well versed in fundamental European institutions and practices such as codetermination, works councils, supervisory boards, flexicurity, proportional representation, Children's Parliaments, universal voter registration, "shared responsibility" health care, sickness insurance funds, green architecture, cogeneration, cap and trade, civic literacy, and more.[17] Not intimately conversant with these institutions, we fail to grasp how America's and Europe's health care systems are premised on different goals, how our energy infrastructures have different objectives, and how our economic institutions and practices, even our media outlets, project different values. As we will see, Europe's and America's attitudes toward property, individual rights, corporations, the common welfare, the social contract, government, and democratic pluralism have diverged, linked to distinct histories and cultures, even different Christian traditions. And these attitudes have been injected into the institutions on each side of the

Atlantic. It is all these differences in key, basic, fulcrum institutions that, working together as an integrated whole, compose a European Way that is distinctly different from the American Way (or a Japanese, Russian, or Chinese Way).

I am calling these "fulcrum institutions" because they are the crucial ones on which everything else pivots. They play a key Archimedean role by affecting all other policies that shape people's lives. In particular, four fulcrum institutions form the foundation for the rest—the political, economic, media/communication, and workfare institutions. The economic institutions are the core of our daily lives, but in a democracy, ensuring that the political institutions rule the economic, not the other way around, is always a struggle. The workfare support institutions foster equality, fairness, and solidarity, essential features in an insecure age of globalized capitalism, while the media and communication institutions inform the other three, crucially so. Taken together, these four fulcrum institutions play a catalytic role in deciding ever-evolving policies that affect people's daily lives. They incorporate the unwritten rules and social contracts that guide our respective systems. They are as much the "infrastructure" of a nation as are the bridges, highways, energy grid, and telecommunications towers, injected with the values and ideology of each place.

In each of these four, Europe has departed significantly from the American model that dominated for most of the post–World War II era. As we will see, Europe's cleverly designed fulcrum institutions are the end product of decades-long advances in economic restructuring, health care, workfare, energy, transportation, democratic pluralism, consensus building, ecological sustainability, and quality of life. With both the Republicans and the Democrats today lacking in anything like the comprehensive vision that the Europeans have fashioned, the European Way is better suited to today's world.

Many insightful books that have proficiently analyzed Europe or explored the transatlantic relationship, such as Timothy Garton Ash's *Free World,* T.R. Reid's *The United States of Europe,* Chris Patten's *Cousins and Strangers,* and Jeremy Rifkin's *The European Dream,* nevertheless have been mostly silent on the impact of these various fulcrum institutions and practices. These and other books tend to hover at the macrolevel of key events, broad policy, political or historical trends, and the leaders who led the way, and neglect to examine the key institutions that define a particular nation and its political economy. But a certain amount of focus on specific institutions is the difference between viewing the subject matter from thirty thousand feet or coming in for a landing and having a look around. So one of this book's contributions is filling this gap in our knowledge by focusing the lens specifically on certain macro- and micro-institutions that are fundamental to the European Way. While the United States spent the post–World War II era focusing on the strategic global tussle of the Cold War, Europe patiently stitched together these institutions, and they have been quietly incubating for decades.

Ironically, "old Europe" is a political youngster with relatively new institutions and laws, whereas the United States is the country that is looking increasingly sclerotic with outdated institutions and laws, many of them rooted in the eighteenth and nineteenth centuries.

THE MEDIA GET IT WRONG—AGAIN

What has been ironic about the remarkable rise of this European Way is that you would never learn much about it by reading or watching the American media. While gazillions of newspaper reports, magazine cover stories, and television newscasts have been devoted to overawed coverage of China's rise—some with marvel and others showing "yellow peril" alarm—Europe's rise mostly has been ignored. At worst, Europe has been portrayed as being in perpetual crisis. To Americans, the words *Europe* and *crisis* go together like Holland and windmills or Great Britain and the queen. Media reports have used *Europe* and *crisis* in the same story so many times that if you type those words into Google's search engine, over fifty-eight million hits pop up.[18] Even before the economic crisis of 2008–9, the European economy (and especially the economies of Germany, France, and Italy) was regarded as in a state of continuous crisis, written off by most American analysts as a clumsy, sclerotic basket case, a "sick old man" condemned to long-term decline. Here's a small sample of the mid-decade brassy headlines that appeared in mainstream U.S. media outlets, trumpeting the imminent collapse of Europe:

> "The End of Europe"; "Europe Isn't Working"; "Will Europe Ever Work?";
> "What's Wrong with Europe"; "The Decline and Fall of Europe"; "Old
> Europe Unprepared for New Battles"; "Western Europe Is Cursed";
> "Reforms in Europe Needed"; "Is Europe Dying?"; "The Rise of the
> Fortress Continent"; "The Decline of France"; "Political Crisis Paralyzing
> Europe"; "Europe's Long Vacation Is Ending"; "Why America Outpaces
> Europe"; and "Europe Turns Back the Clock."[19]

Those sorts of gloom and doom headlines prevailed in the American media starting in 2003 and lasting until late in 2006, when—surprise, surprise—it was discovered that the European economy actually was surging and had equaled and then surpassed the U.S. economy. In fact, an article published in the *international* version of *Newsweek* on November 20, 2006, blared the headline "The Great Job Machine: Despite Its Laggard Reputation, Europe Continues to Grow Faster, and Create More Jobs, than America"—yet that story never appeared in the *domestic* version of *Newsweek*.[20] Another article in *BusinessWeek* reviewing health care systems in the United States, France, and the United Kingdom gave the nod to France as having the most efficient and affordable system. But it was never published in the U.S. print edition. To this day, the patriotic U.S. media continue to shield Americans from injections of reality that are badly needed to understand our country's relative decline in the world.[21]

The fourth estate, which according to democratic theory is supposed to act as a watchdog of government, too often acts as stenographers to those in power, deferring to official explanations and reinforcing stereotypes that misinform the public. This happens in all countries to some degree, including those in Europe: French president Nicolas Sarkozy's cozy relationships with powerful French businessmen who own media interests have raised concerns over his political interference in the news, and Italian prime minister Silvio Berlusconi is a media magnate himself, using his private media and entertainment empire to further his political career. But as we will see, Europe's much better funded and independent public broadcasting sector provides an important journalistic balance to the private corporate media, a balance that is mostly lacking in the United States.

In the minds of many Americans, even intellectuals and journalists who should know better, Europe is synonymous with France, so France's shortcomings become those of an entire continent. The riots of France's minority youth from the *banlieue* suburbs in November 2005 became the proof and pretext for condemnation of an entire continent, even though no other European country suffered such domestic unrest. After bombarding their audiences with "sick man Europe" stories for the first half of this decade, did American journalists note Europe's surge and shifting economic tide? Hardly at all. The U.S. media went noticeably silent on the subject, and Europe's economic rebound in 2006 through the first half of 2008 was mostly a nonevent in the United States.[22]

In fact, to hear the American media tell the story, Europe always has been in crisis. Gloom and doom news reports date back to the early 1990s, warning that the German economy, the largest in Europe, was "slumped at the razor's edge."[23] There were dire predictions of impending declines in personal income and shorter vacations, as well as forecasts of rising unemployment, crime, and taxes to "a level not seen since the Weimar Republic."[24] Yet by the late 1990s a prospering Germany had become the world's leading exporter and further reduced the length of its official workweek for the same amount of pay, adding to Germans' leisure time and further surpassing the United States in the level of workfare benefits and economic security enjoyed by its people. Not content with being wrong once, the media in 1999 warned that the "sluggish E.U. economies" would foil the introduction of the euro.[25] Yet within a short time the euro had surpassed the dollar in strength and by 2008 was trading over 50 percent higher than the dollar, as any American tourist discovered when you received so few euros in exchange for your 98-pound-weakling dollars.

The truth is, just as the American media misreported Iraq, weapons of mass destruction, the housing bubble, and an imminent economic meltdown, the crystal ball gazers in the U.S. media have a terrible track record when it comes to Europe.[26] To go back and read their gloomy predictions regarding Europe from the spring of 2006 and to see how far off the mark they were only a few months later is almost comical. As a result of this substitution of national myth for reality, news traveling across the Atlantic has failed to keep up with actual conditions on the ground. But this has only kept U.S. leaders and the public from understanding the world and America's place in it, and from recognizing that Europe has evolved a new set of fulcrum institutions and a new way of structuring one's society. We are witnessing a momentous shift that holds great promise, even as it fosters a new dividing line between the United States and Europe that cannot be swept easily under the carpet of either the Oval Office or the Palais Elysée.

In the next two chapters, we are going to take a closer look at the economic engine that powers Europe's social capitalism and delve into its specific institutions and practices (such as codetermination, supervisory boards, works councils, and flexicurity), as well as industrial strategies that have been deployed to harness European capitalism's tremendous wealth-creating capacity.

TWO

THE CAPITALIST ENGINE
THAT HUFFED AND PUFFED . . .

Imagine that you are flying in a spaceship high above the earth, surveilling an aerial view of the European continent. The geography below reveals a sprawling landmass stretching from the Atlantic Ocean all the way to Russia, with the Arctic zone to the north, the Mediterranean and North Africa to the south, and the vast lands of Anatolia and the Arabian Peninsula to the southeast. If you overlay most of that geography with a map of the twenty-seven nations of the European Union, you take in a half billion people, representing about 7.4 percent of the world's 6.7 billion tenants.

Yet with only about 7 percent of the population, the European Union produces 29 percent of the world's economy, making it a gargantuan commercial crossroads, with $16 trillion in gross domestic product (GDP)—the largest economy in the world. If we add in the non-E.U. but closely affiliated nations of Norway and Switzerland, that brings the "E.U. Plus" to $17 trillion in its gross domestic product, nearly a third of the world's economy.[1] Like the United States, the European Union now has the advantage of a huge and for the most part single common market. A business can reach a half billion consumers from the western shores of Portugal to the far eastern reaches of Romania and Bulgaria on the Black Sea, without worrying in most countries about borders, currency, or national approvals. European businesses and investors have their fingers in every corner of the globe, making Europe the largest foreign investor in the United States and by 2004 overtaking the U.S. as the largest trading partner with China.[2] In just a very short time since its "birthquake," by any estimation the European Union has become a global force.

By contrast, the United States has a smaller population—300 million people (4.5 percent of the world)—and a smaller economy, $14 trillion in gross domestic product, or 24.5 percent of the world's economy. Japan is smaller still, with 128 million people (2 percent of the world) and 8.7 percent of the world's economy. Despite all the hype, China, with 1.3 billion people (19 percent of the world's population), is still an economic dwarf compared to Europe and the U.S., producing $4.5 trillion in GDP, less than 8 percent of the world's economy. India is smaller still, with $1.2 trillion in GDP. Thus, Europe's economy is nearly as large as those of the United States and China *combined.* That we hear much more about China than about Europe as an economic powerhouse reflects a gross misunderstanding of the many ways that Europe's continental economy is much more than the sum of its individual nations. It has many of the characteristics of a single national economy, much more so than the U.S.-Canada-Mexico free trade relationship. We are not really sure how to analyze this supranational bloc, or to measure its impact, so many journalists just ignore it, continuing to examine the component parts (i.e., individual nations) and comparing them to other individual nations such as China and the U.S. But this misses the big picture and risks distorting economic reality.

While China gets the hype and the attention, Europe, along with America, is where the world still goes if you want to do business. Between 2000 and 2005, when U.S. analysts were calling Europe's economy sick and sclerotic, inflows of foreign direct investment to just the fifteen core nations of the European Union (known as the E.U.-15)* amounted to almost half of the global total. In fact, stock market returns in Europe outperformed those in the United States. "Old Europe is an investment magnet because it is the most lucrative market in the world in which to operate," Dan O'Brien, a senior economist with *The Economist,* said at the time, but few in the United States were listening.[3]

A historic moment occurred quietly on Thursday, March 29, 2007: for the first time since the end of World War I, the value of the European stock market surpassed that of the United States, a tiding that Khuram

---

*The E.U.-15 is composed of the first fifteen nations to join the European Union: Germany, France, the United Kingdom, Italy, the Netherlands, Belgium, Spain, Portugal, Denmark, Ireland, Austria, Finland, Greece, Sweden, and Luxembourg.

Chaudhry, a chief analyst at Merrill Lynch, called "an empire change."[4] Considering the U.S. view of Europe as an economic basket case, it is more than a bit ironic that Europe is corporate America's biggest target for foreign investment, with affiliates of U.S. companies in the E.U.-15 showing profits of $85 billion in 2005, far more than any other region and twenty-six times more than the $3.3 billion they made in China. The $19.2 billion invested by U.S. companies in the tiny Netherlands nearly equaled U.S. investment in all of Asia ($22.4 billion).[5] Observed O'Brien, if European conditions for business are so dire, why haven't foreign investors shunned the region? "The reality is that they flock to the Continent," he said.

With so much investment, both foreign and domestic, the results were predictable, if not widely reported. From 1998 to 2008 the European nations using the euro currency[6] saw per capita economic growth rates slightly higher than in the United States. From 2000 to 2005, Europe added jobs at a faster rate than did the United States, had a much lower budget deficit, and posted higher productivity gains and a $3 billion trade surplus. Meanwhile the U.S. economy struggled with stagnant incomes, a collapsing housing market, a plummeting dollar, declining productivity, a mountain of personal debt, staggering trade and budget deficits, and an expensive military quagmire in Iraq and Afghanistan.[7]

A myth has been oft-repeated in the echo chamber of the American media: that European economies are not competitive because of strangling amounts of bureaucratic red tape. Yet, according to the World Economic Forum's measure of national economic competitiveness for 2008–9, European nations took six out of the top ten spots for economic competitiveness and twelve out of the top twenty spots (with the United States ranked first).[8] That hardly sounds like an economy that is sclerotic, one of the frequent charges hurled by Euroskeptics. One also would think, on the basis of American claims regarding the "sick economies" of Europe, that most European companies must be clinging to life support. Yet a quick snapshot of some of the European workhorses shows their raw economic power and dominance.

Of the Global Fortune 500 rankings (published in July 2009), 179 of the top 500 companies were European and 140 were American, while 68 were Japanese and 37 Chinese; of the 60 largest companies in the world, 30 were European, 18 were American, 5 were Japanese, and only 3 were Chinese.[9] Fifteen of the top twenty commercial banks in the world were European, including the top five. The behemoth oil companies Royal Dutch Shell (Netherlands) and BP (British) were the first and fourth largest companies in the world. In food consumer products, two European giants, Nestlé and Unilever, ranked first and second in the world, and Air France/KLM and Lufthansa were the two largest airlines in the world. In the telecommunications industry, European companies held six of the top ten spots in the rankings, and in the chemical industry the German company BASF was the world's leader, with two other European companies ranked third and fourth. In the food and drug store retail trade, three European companies, Carrefour, Tesco, and Metro, were tops in the world. In motor vehicles, Toyota was on top, but Europeans owned eight of the top fourteen auto companies, with Volkswagen second.

In fact, European economic might is so prevalent that an exhaustive number of formerly American companies and products are now owned by European companies. European companies also have giant footholds in America's cultural fabric. Bertelsmann, a 167-year-old German company, is the world's fourth largest entertainment and media company and the largest book publisher in the world, owning the formerly American marquee name Random House. The French company Vivendi owns Universal Music Group, the largest family of record labels in the world, including Motown Records (which has produced Stevie Wonder, Michael Jackson, the Supremes, the Temptations, and others) and Geffen Records (which produces Tom Petty, Nirvana, B.B. King, Steely Dan, Mary J. Blige, Snoop Dogg, and Counting Crows), and produces other artists such as Lil Wayne, Kanye West, 50 Cent, Eminem, Mariah Carey, Janet Jackson, Aerosmith, and more. You cannot even rely on the word *America* in the brand name to determine if a product is American: the Radio Corporation of America name is owned by Thomson Consumer Electronics, a French company.

While American businesses have significant investments in Europe, it turns out this transatlantic investment is not a one-way street: European companies and investors are by far the top source of foreign direct investment in the United States. Contrary to the "Rising Sun" and "yellow peril" stereotypes of Japan and China buying up half the good ol' USA, in 2004 Europeans were responsible for nearly 75 percent of all foreign investment in the United States, being the top foreign investors in forty-five states with over $1.4 trillion in investments. With the value of the dollar plunging by almost 50 percent against the euro from 2002 to 2008, U.S. assets became relatively inexpensive buys for European investors. In states such as Dick Cheney's Wyoming, as well as Utah,

Oklahoma, New Mexico, Kansas, Idaho, Alabama, and Alaska, Europeans made over 65 percent of all foreign direct investments. In George Bush's Texas, Europeans invested over $50 billion, more than twice as much as U.S. investments in all of Asia.[10] In 2005, sixteen of the top twenty acquisitions of U.S. firms, worth a total of $46 billion, were made by European buyers,[11] and approximately two million U.S. workers were employed by German and British companies operating in the United States. With so much business and trade passing back and forth across the Atlantic, it is no surprise that 60 percent of all international air traffic occurs between the United States and Europe.[12]

By contrast, Chinese companies had invested a mere $3.6 billion outside China by 2005, and Japan had invested $31 billion in all of China—far less than Europe had invested in Texas. Much has been made of the fact that China and Japan are the two largest holders of trillions of dollars in U.S. debt, but as the dollar has continued its steady decline, their investment in U.S. Treasury bonds has turned out to be an unsound investment in depreciating paper. Meanwhile, the Europeans have snapped up real assets—companies, buildings, and other real estate—at bargain prices, thanks to the strength of the euro over the dollar.[13]

European acquisitions are not well known among the American public, even while various grandstanding U.S. politicians and media pundits get agitated over China's (and before that, in the early 1990s, Japan's) alleged buying of the U.S. economy. But what these numbers reveal is how deeply and intricately enmeshed the American and European economies are. That in turn made the Bush administration's tantruming over European rejection of the Iraq invasion look all the more ridiculous. Americans could no more walk away from "old Europe" than Europeans could walk away from the "cowboy Americans" without catastrophic economic results. We are joined at the hip and neck like conjoined twins, and any economic or foreign policy that does not recognize this is delusional.

So as Europe looks toward the future, trying to respond to the needs of its people in an age of globalized capitalism, as well as in the midst of a severe economic downturn, it starts from a place of advantage because it is powered by a dynamic economic engine, thriving businesses, and a commanding international presence. European-based global companies are matching and in many cases surpassing their American, Chinese, and Japanese counterparts, putting their indelible stamp on the world's stage. In some industries, European businesses are clearly the market leaders, while in others, U.S. or Japanese companies are the frontrunners. When it comes to the global economy, the world is multipolar now, and the post–World War II era of U.S. economic dominance is over.

EUROPE'S ECONOMIC AND INDUSTRIAL STRATEGIES

Europe's economy employs various strategies and unique institutions that have evolved over decades and make it highly productive and competitive in the global economy. These include a continent-wide geographic division of labor that combines high-end manufacturing in western Europe with assembly-line manufacture in central and eastern Europe; an export-driven sector that specializes in high-quality, value-added products churned out by a highly skilled workforce; an industrial strategy that benefits from close government-industry partnerships and taxpayer-supported "national champions" in key manufacturing, high-tech, financial, and industrial sectors; tremendous health care and pension efficiencies that allow businesses to plan their costs better, rely on a healthy workforce, and avoid bitter battles with their workers and unions over these necessary workfare supports; and "green" business practices that produce more conservation and energy productivity, which in turn reduce the costs of businesses and make them more competitive. Europe also has one of the most technologically advanced economies in the world, and after Japan it is the most wired to the Internet. Finally, Europe has a thriving small and medium-size business sector, larger than that of the United States. All of these strategies and practices combined give European economies and businesses a competitive edge that has contributed to a vibrant economy. Let's examine each of these in turn.

Health Care and Pension Efficiencies

Europeans' health care and retirement pensions are not work or company-based as they are for millions of Americans. Instead, they are individual-based and universal—everyone has health care and a pension, regardless of where you work. Instead of being solely responsible for their employees' health care and pensions, as are many U.S. businesses, European businesses instead pay a certain amount per worker—a fixed percentage of salary—into an insurance fund (either government-run or privately held but government-regulated, depending on the country) to provide these workfare benefits for their employees. The amounts are reasonable and usually much less than what U.S. employers pay for their employees' health care premiums.

For example, a study by the New America Foundation found that private employers in the United States spent on average about 11.3 percent of payroll on health insurance contributions in 2006, and 18.3 percent if you factor in only those workers who are actually enrolled in health care through their employers.[14] In comparison, employer health care costs for five U.S. trading partners all having universal health care—Germany, France, the United Kingdom, Canada, and Japan—averaged only 4.9 percent of payroll. The hourly cost of health benefits in the U.S. manufacturing industry was $2.38 compared with only $0.96 among the five trading partners.[15] U.S. automobile manufacturers estimate that employee health insurance costs add $1,500 to the price of every new car.[16] From a business perspective, what is nearly as important as the overall cost is the greater *predictability* of these costs in Europe from year to year, which enables business leaders to project their costs and plan accordingly. They are not saddled with the type of unpredictable and escalating health care costs and pension payouts that American businesses have to cope with. All these factors give European businesses a competitive and increasingly important advantage over those in the United States.

Moreover, Europe has the mechanisms in place not only to prevent rampant escalation in health care costs but also to provide quality universal coverage and keep its workers healthy. Says William Drozdiak, the president of the American Council on Germany, "In the United States, the fact that health care is largely provided by the employer is a risk for the worker as well as the company, which must pay an extra premium and incur costs not shared by their competitors in Europe and Japan."[17] All in all, Europe spends approximately half per capita what the United States spends on health care yet produces much better results and, generally speaking, has a healthier workforce. (Health care will be discussed in greater detail in chapter 8.)

"Green" Business

Many European businesses have become world leaders in creating and implementing environmentally friendly "green" business practices, especially for energy efficiency and conservation. In an age of escalating energy and transportation costs, green practices are good not only for the environment but also for the bottom line, as businesses are discovering.

European businesses are doing the obvious, simple, low-tech things such as replacing incandescent lightbulbs with energy-saving, low-wattage ones and installing "occupancy sensor" lights that click off when a room or building is empty. But increasingly more businesses are going high tech, incorporating green building concepts that use efficient building location and design, such as skylights and courtyards to maximize the amount of daylight, and photo sensors that dim the lights when natural daylight is sufficient. Internal transoms and vents in the roof send hot air upward and out to keep the air circulating and improving indoor air quality, which is good for employees' health. Toilets save water with a dual- or triple-button-flush option, light or heavy, depending on the amount of human waste.

One of Britain's leading chain retailers, Marks & Spencer, has powered some of its stores with windmills, dramatically lowering their greenhouse gas output by an expected 95 percent, and collecting rainwater to be used in flushing toilets, which helps lower water usage by 40 percent. It has reduced its packaging and built an eco-factory in Sri Lanka that incorporates the latest conservation strategies. After fine-tuning these technologies in a few stores, M&S rolled out some of them in its stores across the United Kingdom.[18]

Sweden's Ikea is perhaps the most emblematic of this pro-green business attitude. When you walk into one of its cavernous halls the size of airline hangars and stroll beneath its familiar blue and gold pennants, you are doing more than entering the world's emporium of bargain furniture. You are also stepping across the threshold of one of the world's great commercial experiments in using green practices, designed to help both the environment and Ikea's bottom line.

Ikea has installed solar panels on rooftops and reduced store electricity use by half. It has decreased greatly the use of packaging and vigorously recycles what it does use. In fact, the company's stores reclaim 67 percent of their store waste, and Ikea aims to increase that to 90 percent. The company has perfected the "flat pack," its signature packing technique for unassembled furniture that allows it to pack more units into one cargo shipment, thereby cutting energy and transportation costs. Not only do Ikea's green practices put every big American retailer to shame, but Ikea is also kind of the anti–Wal-Mart. Wal-Mart forces its suppliers into the worst labor and environmental practices in order to lower its prices to compete. But Ikea expects a high code of conduct from its suppliers concerning the environment and working conditions, so its green attitude ripples throughout the economy.[19]

But Ikea's most cutting-edge practice has been to install its own miniturbines as the core of a decentralized energy grid to power its facilities on-site. These turbines incorporate cogeneration—also known as CHP, or "combined heat and power"—that recycles the 65 percent of the fuel normally lost in the power generation process as wasted heat. Ikea uses this usually lost energy to warm things and even to generate air-conditioning. That achieves an efficiency of up to 90 percent and an energy savings of up to 40 percent when compared with conventional generation, a huge increase in energy productivity.[20] At one Ikea outlet in Carugate, Italy, estimates indicate that Ikea's cogeneration plant saves seventy tons of oil and two hundred tons of carbon dioxide annually.[21] Ikea's savings at warehouses and factories, which are much larger facilities than the retail outlets, are projected to be even greater. So Ikea's tough green standards not only are good for the environment but also result from good business practices that save money and give the company a competitive edge.

Ikea is not the only European business embracing such innovations. An increasing number of businesses, factories, and stores have installed their own miniturbines to power their facilities on-site. Small-scale cogeneration is becoming popular with businesses because its decentralized grid allows more efficient use of fuel and significantly reduces carbon emissions (a reduction that will increasingly add value to a business's bottom line as the European carbon trading system continues to kick in). It also decreases exposure to escalating energy prices and ensures a high-quality power supply. Europe is taking this kind of decentralized energy creation much more seriously than the United States has—it accounts for 25 percent of total power production in some European countries—but in the United States, only 4 percent of total power comes from decentralized energy creation.[22]

In their bid to find even more competitive edges, Europe's business and political leaders are leaving few stones unturned. And they accomplish this while keeping their economies growing and their workfare support system funded. (I will discuss Europe's changing energy and transportation landscape, including the large number of jobs that are being created in this burgeoning sector, in more detail in chapters 9 and 10.)

Like individual-based health care and retirement, all of these and other adaptations help contain business costs and provide competitive advantages. They are becoming so widespread in Europe that *BusinessWeek* has written that Europe "most likely would be the best buffered" against any high price increases in oil or the expected impacts of peak oil.[23]

West to East Manufacturing

A third European practice that has given Europe a competitive advantage is that its businesses have been relatively quick to retool the industrial sector in western Europe to take advantage of economic and growth opportunities in central and eastern Europe. The rise of China and India with their low wages, low level of regulations, and high pollution rates could have brought massive job losses to Europe. But with the incorporation of the relatively moderate-wage central and eastern European countries into the European Union (moderate compared with China and India), Europe has created an economic buffer and a vigorous dynamism between the eastern and western parts of its continent, where a rising tide truly has been floating more boats.

In central Europe, where under E.U. guidance formerly communist nations have been dissolving the last vestiges of the Soviet satellite system, companies from all over the world, including from western Europe, the United States, Japan, and China, are renovating old Cold War–era factories bought on the cheap. U.S.-based Alcoa invested $900 million in aluminum production facilities in Hungary, stuffing old brick buildings full of Japanese robots and German equipment. U.S. Steel invested $249 million in old plants in Slovakia and Serbia, generating $188 million in profits in one quarter, one-third of its total operating income.[24] Eastern Europe has become the world's newest car capital, dubbed "Detroit East" by *BusinessWeek*.[25] By 2007, Slovakia was producing more cars per capita than any other country in the world. Before the economic crash, annual car production in the Czech Republic reached the one million mark, Poland churned out more than 850,000 gear boxes a year, and one out of every twenty-five cars sold around the world contained an engine produced in Hungary.[26]

Usually globalization is expected to cause investors to flock to low-wage, low-regulation countries like China and India, which certainly tends to be true. But in a strange paradox Chinese manufacturers have plowed hundreds of millions of dollars into establishing factories in central and eastern Europe. Japanese manufacturers have been there for a decade.[27] What attracts these investor companies is not only the bargain prices paid for old factories but also the availability of a quality, educated, and adaptable workforce, as well as proximity to the huge and wealthy European consumer market. Their factories have benefited from hardworking native employees and also from an influx of several hundred thousand workers from E.U. neighbors Ukraine, Russia, Belarus, and Moldavia, who have sought employment in these boom economies in central and eastern Europe that (until the crash of 2008–9) were experiencing annual growth rates of between 4 and 9 percent, some on a par with those of India and China.[28]

While relocation of industrial plants and investment from western to eastern Europe has caused some job losses in western European factories—and understandable anxiety among those watching their jobs heading east—it has also spurred additional job growth and a retooling of the western industrial sector into a high-quality, value-added, knowledge-based platform that better positions it for the future.

"Western Europe clearly does not have a future as a producer of low value–added, mass manufactured goods," says Katinka Barysch, chief economist at the Centre for European Reform.[29] So business leaders have wisely responded by specializing in high-end manufacturing, industrial research, and technological design. Information and communications technology (known as ICT) and the automobile industry are good examples of how Europe's new geographic division of labor works. The big western European car companies have invested billions into car and auto parts factories in central Europe, while in their home countries they have concentrated on design and marketing as well as the production of the technically difficult parts, which they ship to eastern Europe for assembly.

To remain competitive, Ericsson (a Swedish company) and Nokia (Finnish) now produce their mobile phone handsets in Estonia and Hungary, while at home they do R&D, design, and some high-end manufacturing. Neither country saw a rise in unemployment when production moved east. Similarly, in the late 1990s Ireland assembled a third of all the PCs sold in the European Union. Since then, its assembly lines have moved to Hungary and elsewhere in eastern Europe, while Ireland's well-qualified engineers have moved on to high-value-added production and related services. "Enlargement, and the opportunities for outsourcing labor-intensive production, have left western Europe better prepared for globalization," says Barysch. "While foreign direct investment from west to east may have caused some job losses, it also has helped German, French or Dutch companies to stay competitive on a global scale and even to preserve jobs."[30]

Indeed, a 2004 survey found that 20 percent of German companies with investments in eastern Europe had shifted jobs eastward, but three times as many (60 percent) said their investments had helped to preserve or create jobs at home. In the first three months of 2004, Germany's exports to the ten new E.U. member-nations surged by more than 17 percent, even while its exports to the United States fell by 2.3 percent.[31] At the same time, central and eastern Europe saw huge increases in foreign investment, high economic growth rates, and a 66 percent increase in their gross domestic product (from 2003 through 2007).[32] And the pay gap between Europe's richest and poorest countries has narrowed significantly.[33]

In addition to the intra-Europe geographic division of labor, the European economies have positioned themselves to be dynamic exporters of high tech–driven products to the world's fast-growing emerging economies. In China, India, Brazil, Russia, the Gulf oil states, and elsewhere, there has been a sizable appetite for infrastructure equipment, a forte of European companies. Germany's Siemens has built large chunks of the Chinese telecommunications system while selling the nation equipment for dams, power plants, and railway projects. Swiss-Swedish engineering giant ABB Ltd. has supplied the Chinese steel and petrochemical industries, while French utility companies Suez and Veolia Environnement have won billions in contracts for water and waste-treatment systems. Volkswagen has become China's dominant auto maker, and Paris-based L'Oréal has three cosmetics factories in China.[34] Europe's growing foothold in new and emerging markets is revealed by the fact that about 20 percent of exports from E.U. countries head to Asia, and only 15 percent across the Atlantic.[35]

By early 2008, despite the beginnings of the U.S. economic downturn and a strong euro, German engineering companies were enjoying their biggest boom in forty years. Most of these companies were part of Germany's *Mittelstand*—family-owned small and medium-size outfits—which have repositioned themselves as global exporters, producing high-quality and energy-efficient products that are much in demand.[36] In Europe, the rising tide has lifted many more boats and has contributed greatly to the continental economy that now is leading the world, keeping pace with the United States and Japan and far outdistancing China, Russia, or India.

Small and Medium-Size Businesses

While Europe's robust corporations receive most of the headlines with their brand familiarity, the European economy has been boosted by a thriving small and medium-size business sector. In fact, that sector provides two-thirds of the total employment in the European Union, compared with only about half of the total employment in the United States.[37] While the American business community touts the idea that small businesses are the backbone of the U.S. economy, Europe has far more small and medium-size business enterprises than does America. France, despite its reputation of having a rigid bureaucracy with strangling red tape, created a record 322,000 companies in 2005 and set a similar pace for 2006.[38] Germany's *Mittelstand* has long been a main rail of its economic vitality. These small and midsize businesses have been able to keep pace with the profitability of large companies by being smart and efficient, light on their feet, and technologically advanced. They pool their resources and talents in larger networks, including industrial clusters and cooperatives, to gain the advantages of economies of scale without sacrificing the innovativeness and flexibility of smaller-scale operations.

AIRBUS AND THE EUROPEAN INDUSTRIAL STRATEGY OF PUBLIC-PRIVATE PARTNERSHIPS

Europe's technological prowess has been underestimated and compared unfavorably with that of the United States. Yet the World Economic Forum's "Global Information Technology Report 2008–2009," which ranks nations according to their degree of information and communications technology, ranked European nations in the top three spots and in seven of the top ten. The United States was ranked third.[39] Europe's capability is reflected in the high-tech preeminence of numerous European industries. In Sweden, the biotech industry of the "Medicon Valley" is thriving, thanks to abundant venture capital, top-tier academic institutions, close relationships with pharmaceutical giants, and laws that spur innovation by allowing scientists to own their research.[40] In aerospace, Airbus, an industrial consortium started decades ago by several European governments, has become a commercial aircraft powerhouse rivaling Boeing, which was the undisputed world leader in aircraft sales for more than thirty years until Airbus overtook it. Airbus sold more airplanes than Boeing from 2001 through 2005; then in 2006 Airbus struggled and Boeing surpassed it until 2008, when Airbus was first again. This kind of jockeying is likely to continue for some time in what has been called a "mature duopoly."[41]

The Airbus story is an important one, because it is emblematic of a key component of Europe's highly successful industrial strategy—close government-industry partnerships and taxpayer-supported "national champions" in key industrial sectors. This strategy goes back to the Jean Monnet–inspired European Coal and Steel Community, founded to pool the steel and coal resources of its six member states. The United States strongly supported this pact as part of its strategy for rebuilding postwar Europe, wisely seeing it as a way to bind former military enemies into an economic pact that might form the basis of political peace. The strategy worked beautifully. In 1967, Airbus was initiated as another collaboration among three of the earlier partners, the British, French, and German governments (the British eventually dropped out). Many Euroskeptics predicted that Airbus would fall flat on its face, just as they predicted—wrongly—about the introduction of the euro. But continental cooperation built Airbus into an aerospace giant that today has more than fifty-seven thousand employees scattered across sixteen sites in four different European countries (Germany, France, Britain, and Spain).

Free market purists in the United States, and in Europe too, condemn such government-industry partnerships. Indeed, Boeing executives complain loudly that Airbus is an E.U. welfare project, kept alive by massive government loans and subsidies. But to this charge the Europeans plead guilty, happily so, because government support for firms competing in global markets is part of the highly successful European industrial and technological strategy.[42] Today in the post–economic crash era, in which state regulation and state direction of economies have a newfound legitimacy, this American free market fundamentalism seems nostalgically quaint, especially since the government-owned sovereign wealth funds of China, Saudi Arabia, the Gulf states, and elsewhere manage about $3 trillion in assets and investments all over the world, and huge state-owned enterprises such as Russia's Gazprom, Saudi Arabia's Aramco, and China's SINOPEC rely on much greater government involvement than does Airbus.[43] The economic rules have shifted dramatically, but the United States, even under the Obama administration, still remains mired in an antiquated free market ideology. (Besides, Boeing has little room to complain—it has received billions of dollars in government handouts in the form of tax breaks and noncompetitive contracts from Washington DC. In fact, the Buy American Act requires the U.S. government to buy all its aircraft from a domestic source, i.e., Boeing, though Airbus cleverly circumvented that barrier in March 2008 when it joined with the U.S. firm Northrop to win a $35 billion Pentagon contract out from under Boeing's nose, an announcement that jolted the airline industry.)[44]

The success of Airbus and its government-industry partnership has prompted other such collaborations. The European Council for Nuclear Research, known by its French acronym CERN, houses the world's largest particle accelerator and physics laboratory just northwest of Geneva on the border between France and Switzerland. The convention establishing CERN was signed in September 1954 with twelve European governments as the original signatories, and since then membership has grown to twenty member states. Some sixty-five hundred scientists and engineers representing eighty nationalities—about half of the world's particle physics community—work on experiments conducted at CERN, producing some of the most groundbreaking research with wide technological applications. Also located in southeast France is the ITER project, an international consortium led by the European Union, with assistance from the United States, Japan, China, India, Russia, and South Korea, to develop the world's first fusion power reactor, which has the potential for producing nearly unlimited power with minimal radioactive waste or pollution. At $13 billion, the project is one of the most prestigious and expensive international scientific efforts ever launched.[45]

Connections between European governments and particular industries are often stronger than any such connections seen in the United States, and they have been a winning industrial strategy. European government involvement usually includes assistance from research universities, such as in Tampere, Finland, where the university's engineering labs are essentially an extension of Nokia's research and development arm. In addition to Tampere, other places in Europe also have become leading high-tech centers with government support, including the regions around Munich, Geneva, and Milan, where one can see vibrant biotech and software hubs. Southern France has an "arc of innovation" stretching from Airbus's massive airframe assembly plants just outside Toulouse to the microchip fabrication labs near Nice. There's so much technological production going forward that a stretch of Europe from southern Germany and Austria to the top of Italy and into southern France and Switzerland reports the highest per capita income in the world.[46]

The European Union also has funded the second largest space operation on earth, the European Space Agency (ESA), a counterpart—some say a competitor—to NASA. Headquartered in Paris, the ESA is composed of the national space organizations and other entities of seventeen different European countries. ESA has launched hundreds of satellites and space probes for various purposes, including a robot probe that landed on Mars, a solar orbiter, a weather-predicting satellite, and polar-orbiting satellites measuring environmental change, oil spills, and other pollution hazards. By 2030 it plans to send a team of European astronauts to become the first humans to land on Mars.[47] One ESA satellite project, however, is the most controversial; called Galileo, it is designed to go head to head with U.S. space supremacy in navigational and positioning satellites. Galileo will offer a more accurate and improved version of the U.S. Global Positioning System (GPS), which is used all over the world. Galileo's locational signal has been designed to offer resolution precise enough to find a bicycle, a school of fish, a traffic jam, or an oil well. E.U. leaders believe Galileo's greater capacity can spark a multi-billion-dollar industry that can find its way into many more markets for mobile phones, navigation, tracking, and safety-critical applications such as guided trains and buses. Many countries have indicated a desire to switch to Galileo, and despite tough American lobbying, China has agreed to invest heavily in the Galileo project, which has angered the Pentagon.[48]

Strategic government investment also has played a key role in Europe's catching up with and surpassing the United States in Internet access and high-speed broadband availability. As recently as 2001, the percentage of the German population with high-speed access was only half that in the United States, and in France less than a quarter. By the end of 2006, both countries had surpassed the United States, which was ranked twenty-first in digital opportunity, just behind formerly communist Estonia.[49] Across Europe, high-speed connections are less expensive and lightning fast compared with those in the United States, with French broadband connections more than thirty times faster for a fifth of the price.[50] Indeed, the city of Berlin is launching free wireless Internet access for the whole of central Berlin, using antennae mounted on traffic lights.

Consequently, the United States is lagging in new Internet applications that depend on ultrahigh speeds, such as high-definition teleconferencing and telemedicine, the latter of which allows urban doctors to diagnose diseases from a distance and allows pathologists using high-definition video and remote-controlled microscopes to conduct various procedures from afar. France is leading the world in the number of subscribers to Internet TV, while the United States isn't even in the top ten.[51] Michael Calabrese, director of the Wireless Future program at the New America Foundation, says, "Kids today in Japan, Singapore, Sweden, Netherlands and France will be the ones launching the future, hip, cool internet startups tomorrow, because they are playing around on the internet with connections that are many times faster than that available to American kids."[52]

Public-Private Funding of Infrastructure Projects

One of the most compelling stories of Europe's strategic use of public-private partnerships is the way it has utilized them for financing massive infrastructure projects, such as for trains and other forms of mass transit, ports, bridges, roads, and even broadband Internet availability. The rigid American way of thinking spurns government involvement in the private sector as well as private investment in public infrastructure, leaving it to the government to pay for and undertake most public infrastructure projects. This creates a major bottleneck when the government is running big deficits, resulting in the delay or outright canceling of crucial infrastructure investment. But European governments, not so hidebound by fundamentalist economic preaching, have played an active role in creating investment vehicles to attract hundreds of billions of dollars from private investors across the globe to finance local and national infrastructure development. They have created financing partnerships with foreign pension funds, sovereign wealth funds, financial institutions, insurance companies, and other entities.

"Participants in Europe's infrastructure market marvel at how European national and municipal governments, generally considered to be less market friendly and more suspicious of the private sector than American government, could be so far ahead of the United States in using creative partnerships with the private sector and innovative capital market tools to raise vast sums for infrastructure projects," says Heidi Crebo-Rediker, an investment banker.[53]

They have used vehicles such as "covered bonds" to create public-private partnership loans that are backed by the government and can be used to attract large pools of global capital for investment.[54] By doing this, a small amount of public money can be used to leverage huge amounts of private investment that usually is uninterested in the much smaller U.S. municipal bond market, which is the usual financial vehicle in the U.S. for infrastructure investment.[55] Roughly 16 percent of all infrastructure investment in the United Kingdom comes through such an investment vehicle, called the U.K. Treasury's Private Finance Initiative.[56] Ironically, the world's largest private investors—including U.S. banks—have provided large amounts of financing for infrastructure in Europe but not in the United States.[57] That's because the U.S. lacks public-private financial mechanisms like covered bonds that can attract large amounts of private global capital for infrastructure investment. While congressional legislation has proposed the creation of the National Infrastructure Development Corporation, its ambitious goals were accompanied by a pitiful amount of strictly government funding, only $3 billion annually for three years. By comparison, as of January 2007 the European Investment Bank had a capitalization of $255 billion. Meanwhile, the American Society of Civil Engineers estimates that the United States must spend $1.6 trillion over the next five years to maintain the nation's infrastructure.[58]

Says Crebo-Rediker, "It is ironic that while many of the former socialist countries of the 'old world' now look to the private sector and capital markets to invest in and upgrade their infrastructure, the world's greatest capitalist nation looks increasingly to the federal government." As Europe has discovered, public-private partnerships have a vital role to play, whether it's in supporting infrastructure development via creative financial vehicles backed by the government or in supporting entire industries in fulfilling strategic industrial goals and technological development. And now, since the crash of 2008–9 and the revival of a pro-Keynesian mind-set, government involvement in the private economy has a renewed sense of purpose and utility.

FLEXING EUROPEAN ECONOMIC MUSCLE

As Europe tries to grow its economy and uphold its comprehensive workfare system, it starts from a place of strong advantage. It has a capitalist engine with robust free markets, the latest technology and innovations, "green" design and productivity gains, health care and pension efficiencies, a thriving small and medium-size business sector, and a thriving corporate sector, which in strategic ways is supported by the national and E.U. governments. All of these together produce a robust locomotive of wealth creation.

In many ways Europe's global economic influence even surpasses that of the United States. Because Europe has the world's largest market, it also has become the de facto standard setter for regulation and technology. The E.U. regulators have cracked down on marquee U.S. companies like General Electric, Microsoft, and most recently Intel for antitrust violations when U.S. authorities sat on their hands. In May 2009 the E.U. competition regulators levied a record $1.5 billion fine against Intel, the world's largest computer chip maker, letting it be known that a dominant company's efforts to crush rivals by threatening customers or rigging prices will not be tolerated.[59] In 2006 the E.U. passed a law known as REACH, which covers the testing, production, and use of more than thirty thousand chemical substances used in industry and in homes. The 849-page law took seven years to pass, and it has been described as the most important legislation of its kind, the strictest law to date that regulates chemical substances and will impact industries throughout the world.[60]

These sorts of interventions are based on what Europe calls the "precautionary principle," which requires companies to demonstrate that a chemical is safe before it can be sold or used—the opposite of regulatory policies in the United States, where concern about a product's safety is not enough to justify regulation. Irrefutable evidence of harmful effects is required, which is an elusive scientific standard to meet. Consequently, the United States remains one of the few developed countries with, for example, no limits on chemicals such as phthalates in children's toys and teethers, despite scientific studies that have found them to be toxic. As Robert Donkers, who served as the European Union's environment counselor in Washington DC, has explained, "Unlike in the United States, we don't wait until we have 100 percent proof. Rather, if there's scientific suspicions that [a chemical] could cause irreversible damage in the future, we don't want to wait. By the time it's proven, it could be much too late."[61] Whether E.U. regulators are scrutinizing antitrust violations or household chemicals, in the cost-benefit analysis weighing the benefits to society against the costs to industry of making the change, Europe and the United States fall on different sides of that equation. But with Europe being the largest global market, even American companies are pushed to toe the line, despite U.S. laws lagging behind.

What makes Europe's economic success even more remarkable is that, unlike the United States, Europe has accomplished all this without relying on periodic military spending as a "booster shot" to its economy like the kind that has continually stimulated the U.S. economy over the last sixty-five years. Currently the United States has a defense budget of more than half a trillion dollars per year and spends more than twice as much of its GDP on the military as Europe. That's an annual economic stimulus that subsidizes millions of jobs, both domestically and abroad. Europe, however, has invested in other parts of its economy and in its people. Its steady state economy—growing not too slowly, but not too quickly either—has emerged as a major economic power. Europe is standing astride the world, remaking the globe in its own image. For those Americans used to seeing continual media accounts about the "sick man of Europe," this will come as a surprise. But the truth is, with the dramatic rise of economic inequality in the United States, millions of hard-working Americans have fallen behind their European counterparts.

In the tradition of saving the best for last, I have not yet mentioned two other pivotal economic strategies employed by Europe—the marvels of "codetermination" and "flexicurity." Codetermination makes the European economies the most democratic the modern world has ever seen, yet hardly anyone outside Europe has heard of it. And flexicurity provides a way to blend the appropriate amount of workfare support for workers and families with labor flexibility for business owners and managers. Together, they form a powerful combination of economic restructuring and revisioning that holds great potential to democratize the economy in this age of globalized capitalism and competition. I will explore Europe's innovations of codetermination and flexicurity in the next chapter, as well as examine the major challenges that Europe's economies face in the upcoming years.

THREE

EUROPE'S SECRET ADVANTAGE

Economic Democracy

THE GERMAN INFLUENCE

Six decades after Hitler's bunker suicide amid the wreckage of his twisted dream of a rule that would last a thousand years, another dream has emerged as one of Germany's greatest gifts to humanity. That is the dream of economic democracy.

In the aftermath of World War II, a group of German economists proposed what they called the "social market economy." Ludwig Erhard (minister of economics under Chancellor Konrad Adenauer after 1949 and later chancellor himself from 1963 to 1966), Walter Eucken, Alfred Müller-Armack, and others believed that a free market should also serve broader social goals, and looked for macroeconomic structures that might facilitate that. Interestingly, the victorious Allied powers were greatly encouraging of this line of thinking, since it manifested in economic structures that decentralized economic power, shifting it away from the German industrialists who had supported the Nazis. Unlike the Bush administration, which badly mangled matters in post-invasion Iraq, American planners in postwar Germany understood the pragmatic impact of institutions. They knew exactly what they were doing, and they "punished" the Germans with economic democracy as a way of handicapping concentrations of German wealth and power.[1]

One of the macrostructures that evolved out of this thinking was known as codetermination *(Mitbestimmung)*. It included a framework

of supervisory boards *(Aufsichtsrat)* where elected worker representatives sat side by side with stockholder representatives on corporate
boards of directors, and works councils *(Betriebsrat)* in every workplace, which gave workers a great deal of input at the shop floor level.
Interestingly, it was a conservative Christian Democratic government
that introduced codetermination in the early 1950s, not the more leftist
Social Democrats. Codetermination was extended and formally established as German federal law by the Codetermination Act of 1976,
launching the most democratic corporate governance structure the
world had ever seen.

CODETERMINATION:
HARNESSING THE CAPITALIST ENGINE

The magic of what is known as "codetermination," "supervisory boards,"
and "works councils" provides Europe's economy with a distinct advantage over America's that will become increasingly apparent over the next
several years, as the impacts of global capitalism deepen. These distinctly
European advances are perhaps the most important innovations in the
world economy since the invention of the modern corporation itself. And
yet hardly any American journalists, leaders, or activists, right, left, or
center, are aware of their existence.

Unquestionably, capitalism has proven itself to be the greatest wealth
generator ever, raising the living standards for hundreds of millions of
people around the world. What is at issue is our ability to harness
that wealth-generating capacity for the good of the many instead of
the enrichment of the few. That harnessing requires a balancing act,
an optimal mix of free enterprise and Schumpeterian creative tension,
combined with the right amount of government regulation that does not
unduly burden entrepreneurship and commerce. Codetermination—
specifically supervisory boards and works councils—is one of the keys
to that harnessing.

Klas Levinson, a researcher for the former National Institute for
Working Life in Sweden, is one of the world's experts on codetermination. I met with Professor Levinson at the institute's Stockholm headquarters, a sleek glass structure with the air of a university campus.

"Codetermination," he told me, "is Europe's little secret advantage."
He emphasized in particular the crucial role of supervisory boards with
employee representatives, broadly overseeing company managers who
are handling the day-to-day operations. "The idea that elected worker

directors should sit side by side as equal decision makers with stock-holder representatives, supervising management, is a little-known yet unprecedented extension of democratic principle into the corporate sphere." Half of the supervisory board members for the largest corpo-rations in Germany—Siemens, Bertelsmann, BMW, Daimler, and many more—are elected by workers; in Sweden, one-third of the directors of their corporations are worker elected.[2] Imagine Wal-Mart's board of directors having anywhere from a third to a half of its directors elected directly by its workers. It's hard to even conceive of such a notion from the American standpoint, yet most European nations employ some version of this as standard operating procedure. The impact has been immensely significant.

Professor Levinson's research shows that, contrary to fears that employee representation on corporate supervisory boards would create difficult tensions or render decision making too cumbersome and time consuming, it actually has fostered a healthy degree of communication and cooperation between management and workers. This in turn has benefited the businesses. Workers have input, even into important deci-sions, so the companies are less plagued by labor strife and internal schisms, which can easily paralyze a company. According to Levinson, one of his studies of Swedish businesses found that two-thirds of com-pany executives viewed codetermination as "very or rather positive" for their company, because it contributed to a "positive climate," "made board decisions more deeply rooted among employees," and "facili-tated implementation of tough decisions." Eight of ten chairmen were satisfied with the arrangement and felt it was not important to reduce worker representation on their supervisory boards.

Says Professor Levinson, "With supervisory boards, workers and management still have disagreements, and in some nations even strikes. But there is a more balanced institutional structure for working out contentious issues and charting consensus strategies." And for Europe, that has proven crucial to both its economic success and its broadly dis-tributed wealth. An E.U. directive establishing a continent-wide frame-work for board-level employee representation in European companies went into effect in October 2004, firmly rooting supervisory boards in Europe's economic landscape and culture.

The other twin pillar of codetermination, works councils, are just what their name implies—elected councils at individual companies through which workers gain significant input into their working condi-tions at the shop-floor level. Works councils are not the same as labor unions—though many workers are union members as well—nor are they some feel-good or symbolic exercise. Works councils have real clout. They enjoy veto power over certain management decisions pertaining to the company's treatment of individual employees, such as redeployment and dismissal. They also have "codecision rights" to meet with management to discuss the firm's finances, daily work schedules, scheduling of holidays, work organization, and other operating procedures. In addition, they benefit from "information and consultation rights" in regard to planning for the introduction of new technologies, mergers, and layoffs and obtaining information that is useful in contract negotiations, such as profit and wage data. In some individual nations—Germany, Sweden, and France, among others—works councils have acquired even more rights and greater influence.[3]

When I interviewed labor leader Witich Rossman, from Germany's largest trade union, IG Metall, he told me, "Because of the works councils, I have no problems getting into a factory. I only have to say I want to visit the works council, and nobody can hinder me. I can go with the works council members through the factories and discuss with the workers." As a result, says Rossman, "many workers don't feel like a trade union is something outside of the company; they feel it as a part of the company." Compare that with the United States, where unions mostly are banned from the workplace even while management has unlimited access to their employees, using that access to promote anti-union sentiment and even to harass pro-union employees. A nationwide study by the University of Illinois at Chicago found that 30 percent of U.S. employers fire pro-union workers, and 91 percent force employees to attend coercive, anti-union meetings with their supervisors.[4]

In France, after the food manufacturer Danone met with its works councils, it agreed to very specific rules related to job cuts, including the consideration of union proposals to avoid layoffs and the transfer of workers to other positions. The Polish union Solidarity has said that the inclusion of central and eastern European worker representatives in works councils is "the most effective and sometimes nearly the only way" for them to obtain information on multinational companies' operations.[5] German law stipulates that workers' assemblies of the whole factory must be held at least four times a year for a management representative to report about the situation of the plant and the business. The head of the works council also reports, and workers use these assemblies to promote their views and, if necessary, to criticize company decisions in front of management.[6]

Codetermination's "spirit of consultation" pervades other aspects of company relations that give European companies a competitive advantage. At Germany's BMW, just about everyone—from the factory floor to the design studios to the marketing department—is encouraged to speak up about product development and industrial design. New approaches and innovation are valued, creating what has been called a "fine-tuned learning system." In 2007, at a time when General Motors and Ford were suffering severe setbacks and layoffs, the Bavarian automaker was flying high, setting the benchmark for high-performance premium cars and customized production. BMW has benefited from an almost unparalleled labor harmony and in return offers job security and broad sharing of its company profits among all employees. It has been negotiating a winning combination for decades.[7]

Since 1994, when the European Union issued a pioneering directive on works councils, every multinational company with at least 1,000 workers within the E.U. or with at least 150 workers in two or more E.U. nations must negotiate agreements with works councils. Other nations have supplemented that directive by requiring works councils in every workplace. The members of the works councils are elected by workers using a proportional representation electoral system, thus guaranteeing broad representation, and while there is no stipulation that representatives must be union members, most of them are. Consequently, at the shop-floor level, unions and works councils mostly move in the same direction. Various academic studies have concluded that works councils contribute to efficiency by improving the flow of communication within companies, which in turn improves the quality of decisions. Works councils also facilitate the implementation of decisions by making them more legitimate in the eyes of the workers. These studies also suggest that works councils are associated with lower rates of absenteeism, more worker training, better handling of worker grievances, and smoother implementation of health and safety standards.[8]

"The practical effect of codetermination," says Professor Levinson, "is that corporate managers and executives must confer extensively with employees and unions about health and safety standards, wages, length of work week, pensions, bonuses, job training, the introduction of new technology, layoffs, even about the future direction of the company." Codetermination in European companies generally gives workers a say in their workplace and work conditions far beyond what any workers in the United States can even imagine. It acts as a barrier against CEOs playing god by having the unchecked prerogative to fire everyone, or to reduce wages, health care coverage, and pensions, at a moment's notice. Codetermination reflects European communitarian values and long-term strategic vision much the way grotesquely paid corporate executive salaries and a focus on quarterly profit sheets reflect the American culture of individualism. In an uncertain age dominated by globalized capitalism, when flows of capital and investment are international in scope but the movement of workers mostly is not, the interests of businesses and their employees often seem to collide. But codetermination facilitates a more harmonious route and gives Europe a distinct advantage over its competitors. In fact, Professor Levinson believes that eventually codetermination will be used throughout the world, since it's a better system in an age of globalized capitalism. "It's better for long-term planning, and it's better for making everyone feel like they have input into their economic destiny," he says.

Critics allege that codetermination hurts the competitiveness of businesses and the overall economy. When the American business media sneer about Europe's lack of "labor flexibility"—the ability of employers to fire employees if they deem it necessary—codetermination is one of the practices they are targeting. But the success of the European economy and of its many businesses, including having a lot more Fortune 500 companies than the U.S. (179 to 140), belies this criticism.

As a case in point, consider the fact that the World Economic Forum in 2008–9 ranked Denmark, Sweden, Finland, Germany, and the Netherlands in the top ten for having the most competitive economies in the world. All these countries also employ some degree of codetermination, which in turn contributes to their ranking at or near the top of most lists for their superb workfare and health care benefits for individuals and families, as well as their quality of life indicators. But while the United States with its maximum "labor flexibility" has been ranked first in competitiveness, it is near the bottom of the pack in workfare supports, health care, and quality of life indicators. Sweden, Germany, and the other European nations are proof that you *can* have it all— but only if you have the right institutions to facilitate both a powerful economic engine and the supportive institutions and benefits to harness that engine and keep employees and families healthy and productive.

In the decades following Germany's launch of social capitalism, some degree of codetermination spread throughout most of Europe, and it also is used to some degree in most of the new E.U. member states.[9] Some members of the European Union, most notably the United Kingdom, have dragged their feet on implementing the E.U. directives. But upon taking office, even Chancellor Angela Merkel, from Germany's conservative Christian Democratic Party, sounded like a labor union leader when she reasserted Germany's desire to "retain essential elements of . . . social protection" and "secure the future of the social market economy."[10] Sixty years after its Deutschland genesis, codetermination is now a core feature of the European economy, an integral part of the European consensus, and it forms one of the main economic pillars that distinguish the European Way from the American Way.

LABOR UNIONS AND MANAGEMENT: COEXISTENCE AND CREATIVE TENSION

Besides codetermination and works councils, traditional labor unions are a third vehicle for fostering an economy balanced between free enterprise, regulation, and workfare supports. While European labor unions function much like American unions, the overall context in which they operate is quite different. Labor laws are not as anti-union as they are in the United States, making it easier to organize a workplace and resulting in a much higher percentage of the workforce being unionized. In Sweden, 78 percent of the workforce is unionized, in Belgium 55 percent, and in Britain 29 percent, compared with the United States, which has dropped to an all-time low of 12 percent (and only 8 percent in the private sector). In most European nations, labor-management relations are viewed as more of a creative tension between symbiotic forces, all representing legitimate interests that must work together. There is a mutual recognition that workers without jobs are no better off than businesses without healthy, satisfied workers. It's a dance, and certainly sometimes workers and management step on each other's toes, resulting in periodic strikes and job actions. Yet often an atmosphere of partnership and consultation exists, though with notable exceptions, such as in France and Italy, whose labor relations tend to be more adversarial. Contrary to stereotype, however, France also is not highly unionized, with only 8 to 10 percent of its workers belonging to unions. But France also has works councils and other sites of codetermination, which together contribute to a high level of labor solidarity that seems to have all but evaporated in the United States.

In addition to its higher rates of unionization at the national level, Europe has the European Trade Union Confederation, which is an umbrella of eighty-one national trade union organizations with sixty million members from a total of thirty-six European countries (by comparison, the AFL-CIO, which is the largest federation of unions in the United States, is made up of 65 unions representing only 10 million workers). The ETUC serves as an official "social partner" with two employers' associations. Together those associations and the Confederation hammer out continent-wide agreements, including some that have led to E.U. directives such as ones on parental leave and part-time work. This and other dialogue bodies have helped build consensus for the European social model, even among business leaders. This kind of creative tension is possible only because of codetermination, which acts as the foundation for European-style social capitalism. It has worked in Europe for decades and will continue to provide an advantage to Europe's national economies as well as the continent-wide economy.

American critics of codetermination have been as vociferous as they have been poorly informed. Besides criticizing codetermination for its lack of labor flexibility, analysts have criticized it for discouraging bosses "from taking the tough measures needed to restructure" for the adoption of new technologies, as Barry Eichengreen wrote in his book *The European Economy since 1945*.[11] But Eichengreen, who was writing in early 2006 and was gulled by the perception that the European economy had stalled earlier in the decade, when in fact it was in the process of surpassing the U.S. economy, turned out to be flat wrong. Codetermination has not proven to be a barrier to restructuring or adopting new technologies. Workers, when directly consulted, are capable of acquiescing to appropriate decisions necessary for modernization precisely *because* of codetermination, since they were included in the decision making and know their labor rights have some protection. Codetermination is here to stay, and Eichengreen's book is just another of the many American prognostications declaring Europe dead that have turned out to be way off the mark because they fundamentally misunderstand the European economy.

FLEXICURITY = FLEXIBLE SECURITY

Besides codetermination, "flexicurity" is another great European invention that provides an economic advantage. Flexicurity permits relatively easy hiring and firing of workers in exchange for job training and retraining, apprenticeships for new workers, and generous financial and other workfare supports for those who lose their jobs. The goal is to have a dynamic economy in which nimble businesses can shed workers

during a downturn, but those workers are provided the support to maintain themselves during their displacement and to quickly retrain and get
plugged into new employment. Hence the name "flexicurity," which is
short for "flexible security."

Flexicurity finds its highest expression in Denmark and its signature mix of free enterprise, workfare support, and vocational training. Danish employers can easily hire and fire their workers, but the
government also invests huge amounts in retraining the jobless, placing
them in new jobs, and providing generous unemployment compensation and other workfare supports for those who are laid off. Every year,
over 4 percent of Danish gross domestic product is spent on supporting
and retraining the jobless, about the same percentage the United States
spends on its military budget while allotting a mere 0.7 percent to job
retraining and support.[12] About a fifth of Danish workers lose their job
in any given year, but most find a new job relatively quickly.[13] That's
because the Danes have job placement down to a quasi-science: experts
prepare what is known as a "bottleneck analysis," using pollsters to
survey employers on what jobs they will need in coming years. The
feedback is then used to identify the next labor shortages and to pick
the correct training courses for individuals. Kirsten Thomsen, one of
the analysts, says, "In our system, we can make supply and demand
match," an impressive boast but one that makes Denmark's intriguing hybrid possible. A proactive government can help a flexible labor
market to flow better, the Danes have discovered.[14]

As a result of these practices, Denmark's success has been striking:
about two-thirds of Danes who are laid off have a new job within a
year. And this flexicurity hybrid has helped Denmark slash its unemployment rate, from about 10 percent in the early 1990s to 2.6 percent
in June 2008, less than half the unemployment rate in the United States
at the time. In addition, Denmark also enjoyed a robust economic
growth rate of 3.4 percent in the middle of this decade, higher than
either the United States or the rest of the European Union. It has accomplished all this while providing affordable universal health care, free
child care, free university education, generously paid parental leave,
paid sick leave, six weeks of paid annual vacation, and a host of other
workfare benefits that make the United States look like a developing
nation by comparison.

With Denmark's impressive numbers, flexicurity has won plaudits
from both business leaders and labor unions alike. The director of
the Danish Federation of Employers, a businessman by the name of

Henrik Bach Mortensen, says that employers value the system both for its absence of industrial conflict and for its supply of good workers. The collaborative vocational training system, he notes, is essential for Danish competitiveness. This view was confirmed in an extensive survey of Danish employers conducted for a Boston University study. Companies were found to support the model because it brought them tangible benefits in the form of skilled and adaptive employees.[15]

The Danish system has attracted attention as a model that other nations can copy, and some have been experimenting with certain aspects. Austria has made progress by offering workers solid social benefits, training, and job-search assistance. In 2003, it introduced an innovative system of "portable" severance pay, involving employers paying a small sum into each worker's severance account, which provides cash in the case of dismissal or else gets added to a worker's pension. This measure encourages labor market flexibility while providing a sense of financial security for workers.[16]

Other European nations have impressive job-training programs that foster a highly trained workforce. In Germany, 65 to 70 percent of teenagers enter apprenticeship programs in which on-the-job training is combined with classroom time. Germany has job training for older workers as well, and Sweden, Austria, Switzerland, Finland, and other nations also have well-funded vocational and educational training for workers of all ages. These countries also provide generous unemployment benefits, health care, and other benefits on the theory that dislocated workers need support until they have been retrained for new employment. But in the United States, which spends a lower percentage of its gross domestic product on job retraining for the unemployed than any of the E.U.-15 nations, vocational training is fragmentary at best, unemployment compensation is stingy, and "health care" for many without employment is a hospital emergency room.[17]

Unique institutions like flexicurity, as well as codetermination, supervisory boards, and works councils, are resulting in various national hybrids that make Europe an exciting laboratory of economic experimentation. Supervisory boards and works councils are at work in most European nations to one degree or another. Some nations are further along than others in implementing these policies, with a fair amount of variety from nation to nation. There's no one size that fits all; it's as if all the various European nations are acting as a grand test lab for one another, each nation trying its own unique blend of methods. Each nation is learning from the others, even as the United States remains for the most part stuck in its orthodox free market fundamentalism, with its paltry workfare supports that are failing so many Americans. Even the Obama administration has made little progress in evolving America's antiquated ways and attitudes.

One of the criticisms levied against this part of the European model is that some countries lag in implementing the various E.U. directives. For example, not all businesses have established supervisory boards, and not all employees in the nineteen hundred or so European firms required to form works councils have requested one in their workplace. And some works councils allow a bare minimum of worker input and consultation (though that's still a lot more than most American workers have). But the overall trajectory is unmistakably clear, and the presence of codetermination or flexicurity or both in some businesses and countries has a ripple effect in other businesses and countries, just as the presence of a few anti-union "right to work" states reverberates across the United States. Generally speaking, these institutions are supported by all political sides in Europe, right, left, and center. In 2008, the European Union even extended its workplace protections and workfare supports to temporary workers (part-time workers already had been included). There are some eight million temps across the European Union, and they now enjoy the same employment rights as full-time and part-time permanent staff and the same guarantees in terms of pay, working hours, and maternity and annual leave from the day they join a company.[18] In fact, they have more rights and supports than many permanent full-time workers in the United States. This is what is known as the "European consensus," which is not always easy to identify or quantify until you compare it with the American consensus. Then the differences become crystal clear.

Essentially, what Europe's macroeconomic structures reflect is that, to ensure that the benefits of a capitalist economy are broadly shared and to provide the levels of individual security necessary in this globalized world without stifling entrepreneurship and wealth creation, it has been necessary to depart significantly from the U.S. model and in fact to redesign the modern corporation. Europe's new capitalism has injected two essential values into its economies: first, a degree of real economic democracy, from the boardrooms to the shop floor; and second, comprehensive worker training, skill development, and job placement. In incorporating these values, Europe has fashioned its trademark social capitalism, an invention with enormous consequences for the world.

Naturally, for those corporate magnates who view the world as their playground for squeezing every drop of profit out of their investments, codetermination and works councils are the devil incarnate. American companies like Wal-Mart, trying to penetrate the European market, have had great difficulty in adjusting to the new rules of the game. Just imagine the highly hierarchical—some would say dictatorial— Wal-Mart facing pesky worker representatives on its board of directors, demanding consultation, or being confronted by works councils when it came time to discuss health benefits, vacation, salaries, and part-time work, or being asked to pay into a retraining fund for its laid-off workers. When General Motors announced in 2000 that it was about to shut down a British plant in Luton, the works council for GM-Europe suddenly mobilized forty thousand workers in five countries to participate in rallies at multiple GM sites. GM later agreed to a moratorium on closures and to discuss all future moves with the works councils. GM didn't change Europe; Europe changed GM.[19]

Despite their fundamental importance as fulcrum institutions of the European Way, codetermination and flexicurity mostly have been overlooked by American observers—even though codetermination's origins were partly of American design in the post–World War II period. The conservative right, in its ideological fervor, ignore them and hope the forces of globalization will eventually undermine them, because they see these practices as leading down a slippery slope toward creeping socialism, which of course is ridiculous. Europe is staunchly capitalist, but as one European businessman said to his American counterpart, "I believe in capitalism, but you believe only in making money. There's a big difference."

The American left, while searching for effective responses to globalized capitalism and mostly coming up short, appears to be completely unaware of these intriguing European inventions. A much-heralded film, *The Corporation,* after regaling its viewers with the evils of corporations writ large, proposed the anemic interventions of revoking corporate charters of offending businesses (which would likely result in massive job losses), more "Battle in Seattle" protests, and a vain call for more CEOs with a conscience. It mentions nothing at all about codetermination, supervisory boards, works councils, or flexicurity, nor does it recognize that European corporations are fundamentally different animals from their U.S. counterparts. When I asked a leading globalization critic from the Economic Policy Institute his opinion regarding codetermination and works councils, he seemed unclear about what they were, and when I explained he replied dismissively, "Bah, those just lead to company unions."

So while the American left wallows in its ineffective solutions and outright ignorance, and the right brushes aside ways to renew capitalism and give it some real family values, and the American workforce loses out because of a lack of national leadership and vision on the issue, the European mainstream is busy carving out unique and innovative responses to the uncertainties of globalized capitalism. Europe's social capitalism has been decades in the making, and its arrival is none too soon, since it allows its businesses to be both competitive and socially responsible.

EUROPE'S ECONOMIC CHALLENGES

Europe has had its share of economic trials and tribulations, with new challenges just around the corner. As the crash of 2008–9 showed, no economy is immune to the fluctuations of the global system, whether due to the popping of economic bubbles, inadequate regulation, or the ups and downs of the economic cycle. Today's winners can become tomorrow's losers in a twinkling. But what Europe has done is to build into its economic system a degree of fairness, consultation, and democracy that has contributed greatly to ensuring that its prosperity is broadly shared. But there have been criticisms of European Way economics as well, and it is helpful to examine them.

One of the standard knocks against the European economies, in particular the major economies of Germany, France, and Italy, is that they lead to high unemployment; some have even pilloried Europe as the "land of double-digit unemployment." Another knock is that the United States has a higher per capita income, which indicates America must be a wealthier country. A third criticism is that Europeans are overtaxed, which decreases their level of personal consumption. Critics also say the European economies are likely to be held hostage to their dependence on Russia and the Middle East for most of their energy needs. A fifth is that in some European nations, such as Germany, Italy, and Spain, levels of female employment lag behind those of other nations. And Europe has been disparaged for supposedly underfunding its universities, making them less capable of being world-class research centers that can spur technological innovation and stimulate economic growth. Based on all these reasons and more, the frequent argument is that not only is Europe's economy not as dynamic as the U.S. economy but the emerging economies of China and India will one day match and even surpass the European economies, leading to Europe's eventual economic decline and irrelevance (even though China's and India's economies are mere dwarfs today and Europe's continent-wide economy is the largest in the world).

Many of these criticisms involve degrees of truth, but also a fair amount of stereotyping that gets exaggerated by the Europessimists. For example, the characterization of Europe as a land of double-digit unemployment had not been true for some time prior to the crash of 2008–9, yet the myth prevailed. According to the standardized figures of the Organisation for Economic Cooperation and Development, by July 2008 the European Union was enjoying its lowest unemployment rate in twenty-five years, 6.9 percent, as well as its highest employment rate during that time, 66 percent, with the United States having a 5.8 percent unemployment rate at that time. Many European nations have experienced effective full employment in recent years, and their unemployment rates have been the same as or lower than that in the United States.[20] Following the economic crash, European economies benefited from built-in automatic stabilizers that kick in during an economic downturn but which are lacking in the United States. As a result, by the spring of 2009, while the U.S. unemployment rate had increased by 3.5 percentage points from the previous year, the European unemployment rate had increased by only 1.3 percentage points, resulting in the U.S. and European unemployment rates reaching the same level of 8.5 percent. Indeed, a report was released in May 2009 by the Center for Economic and Policy Research with the headline "U.S. Unemployment Now as High as Europe," and a month later, U.S. unemployment had risen higher than Europe's. (The different responses of Europe and the United States to the economic crisis will be discussed in greater detail in chapter 6.)[21]

But in comparing unemployment rates between the United States and Europe, it is important to keep in mind a couple of crucial points. First, many of the jobs created in the United States in recent years not only were part-time, temporary, or low-paying, but they also included few if any workfare supports. And once people get laid off, they lose whatever measly benefits they had at their jobs. But in Europe, the jobless still have access to health care, generous replacement wages, job-retraining programs, housing subsidies, and other benefits. In the United States, by contrast, the unemployed can—and do—end up destitute and marginalized. Being unemployed in Europe is a much different experience than being unemployed in the United States.

Second, we also have to be clear about exactly what the unemployment rate measures. For example, during the French student protests in March 2006, the *Financial Times* chief statistician found that a wildly inflated and inaccurate youth unemployment rate was reported for France as a result of nothing more than the methodology that was used to determine it.[22] Another example is that unemployment rates typically don't include prisoner populations. Since the United States has the highest incarceration rate in the world—2.3 million people behind bars, 1 of every 100 adults, an astounding seven to ten times the incarceration rates in Europe—excluding prisoners from unemployment estimates artificially decreases the unemployment rate much more in the United States than elsewhere.[23] Including prisoners would have the effect of increasing the U.S. unemployment rate by about 1.4 percent and Europe's by only about 0.2 percent.[24]

If these increases had been added to the July 2008 unemployment rates of 5.8 percent in the United States and 6.9 percent in the European Union, that would have resulted in real unemployment rates that were virtually the same. If added to the post-crash unemployment rates, it would have resulted in a U.S. jobless rate that was substantially higher than Europe's. It is reasonable to include prisoners in the unemployment rate because if those individuals were not in prison, then jobs would have to be found for them. Moreover, people in prison tend to be individuals with the least amount of skills and education and are the most difficult to employ. So built into the way unemployment is measured is a distortion that ignores the fact that many of America's least employable people are in prison and therefore excluded from being counted as part of the labor force, artificially deflating the unemployment rate in the United States by about 1.2 percent compared to Europe.

The criticism based on America's higher per capita income strikes at the heart of how the European Way and the American Way conceive of a good economy. In a time of increasing economic insecurity, a middle-class standard of living is based not only on income levels but also on adequate workfare supports for individuals and families. If standard of living is assessed purely in terms of annual income, Americans are nearly 30 percent wealthier than Europeans. But if one includes in measures of the good life the workfare supports enjoyed and the amount of vacation, the average European is much better off. Americans' greater emphasis on work shows up in income figures, but Europeans' choice of universal workfare benefits and more leisure does not. Professor Robert Gordon, of Northwestern University, estimates that although western Europeans work only three-quarters as much as Americans, they acquire 90 percent of what Americans have, yet with far lower poverty rates and more equal income distribution.[25]

These built-in biases inherent in our methods of economic measurements do not allow them to account for quality-of-life considerations such as shorter work weeks and more vacation, even though such choices are fundamental economic decisions.[26] Europe's more modest income level mainly reflects a series of conscious policy choices that have tended to put a premium on leisure, economic security, and equality at the expense of greater individual wealth. Furthermore, Americans' longer working hours are not necessarily a matter of personal choice or different cultural values; most Americans complain about their inability to balance work with other aspects of their lives. Among the increasing number of Americans who say they would like to work less are men who express a desire to spend more time with their children.[27] Time reported that 71 percent of Americans would rather have a job that provides more workfare benefits such as health care and a defined pension benefit plan than a higher-paying job.[28] So it turns out that average income is only one measurement of wealth, and a pretty inadequate one at that.

In regard to Europe's reliance on Russia and the Middle East for its oil and natural gas, crystal-ball gazing on this front is risky. Europe's ongoing diversification of its gas supply has resulted in Russia's share of E.U. gas imports being cut in half, from 80 percent to 40 percent since 1980, and Russian gas represents only 6.5 percent of the overall E.U. primary energy supply. Russia's ongoing gas wars with Ukraine mostly affect a handful of the smaller eastern European nations that rely on Russia for most of their gas needs. The European Commission has called for the creation of a continent-wide power supergrid that would allow E.U. countries to share gas supplies anytime Russia turns off the taps, as well as linking North Sea wind farms and the electricity grids of the Baltic region in northern Europe with the countries bordering the Mediterranean.[29] In addition, as we have seen, Europe's businesses lead the world in using green technologies and designs to reduce their energy dependence. But these technologies will take time to implement more fully, and in the meantime Europe will continue to wrestle with the Russian energy bear. (I will explore Europe's changing energy landscape in greater detail in chapters 9 and 10, and relations with Russia and the Middle East in chapter 12.)

In regard to the charge that Europe has underfunded universities and a lack of world-class research centers, it's true that its universities, especially outside Britain, have not been able to keep up the pace of new inventions and innovation seen in the United States or to some extent in Japan or China. But this supposed disadvantage is way overblown. In a globalized world, it matters less where the inventions originate than what is done with them. Europe has excelled at taking new technologies, regardless of origin, and applying them on a massive scale. So has Japan. Companies like Finland's Nokia lead the world in cell phones, Airbus in aviation manufacturing, BMW and others in auto design. Many of the innovations in renewable energy technology have been invented by American companies, yet their use is becoming widespread in Europe, not the U.S. The Euroskeptics like to rant about Europe as being practically backward technologically, which is belied by on-the-ground reality, including the expansiveness of Europe's economic might. (I will touch upon other aspects of Europe's education system in chapters 4 and 5).

The reports of Europe's impending economic irrelevance as it is eclipsed by China, India, and other emerging economies can be likened to a quote by Mark Twain; while on a trip in Europe, he reportedly cabled the U.S. press, "The reports of my death are greatly exaggerated." Although China's development has been impressive and its influence is ascending, its economy is currently a mere fifth of Europe's. When I visited China in August and September of 2008, in the aftermath of the Olympics, the country that I saw, whether in Shanghai, Beijing, or the rural areas, was a long, long way from being a global leader in any meaningful sense. The Chinese economy's high growth rates mask the bottlenecks that will constrain its development at some point unless fundamental political and economic reforms prevail. China is beset by medieval levels of massive inequality, corruption, a population aging as fast as some European countries', and fouling of its air and water that has made Beijing, Shanghai, and other cities into toxic fishbowls. Helter-skelter deregulation has allowed shadowy businesses to poison the food and medicine supply, memorably leading to the poisoning deaths of pets around the world, followed by the injury of tens of thousands of children via poisoned milk formula. Seventy thousand protests, some of them intense and sometimes violent, occur every year in protest against the ongoing failures of the Chinese system, not to mention that the ruling Communist Party still does not allow even a modicum of democracy at the national level, which might let some of the steam out of this cauldron of brewing troubles (although a degree of local democracy now is widely practiced). Without profound reform in China, its internal backlash is inevitable.

In addition, a study by a Wall Street investment banking firm concluded that if the new E.U. member states in eastern and central Europe close the gap between their standard of living and that of the rest of the European Union in the same way that Spain, Portugal, and Ireland once did, this growth could lead to a scenario in which "Europe could actually see its weight in the world economy increase over the next 15 years. By 2020, the E.U. could have a lead over the U.S. of about 45%."[30] If the European Union adds even more member states, such as Turkey, Ukraine, or Morocco, that will result in an even larger economy and more growth.

No, the dire European outcome predicted by the Euroskeptics is by no means written in stone. Many of these all too typical American media stereotypes simply do not jibe with the more complex reality, yet they are powerful and regularly used by American boosters to bash alternatives to our system and discourage Americans from considering the European model. (The problems presented by a relative shortage of female labor will be discussed in chapter 18, and the stereotype of the overtaxed European will be discussed in chapter 5).

Like any economy, Europe's has had and will continue to have its rough patches and its ups and downs. Certainly the rapid economic decline that began in the fall of 2008 humbled many an expert, from Alan Greenspan and Warren Buffett to economists, bankers, and pundits on both sides of the Atlantic. But the downs in Europe have been exaggerated by the American media, and the ups—such as the one from 2006 to 2008—mostly have been ignored. That's partly because the patriotic American media side with the home team, but it's also because American observers simply don't understand how different the European economy is from the U.S. economy. Its goals are different, and its institutions and strategies are unique. Even though both economies are capitalist, Europe has evolved unique and unnoticed institutions and practices that, in their amalgam, provide the foundation for a fundamentally new type of capitalism. Europe's capitalist economy is powered by a dynamic, wealth-creating engine that measures up to that of any economy in the world; and that powerful engine is being harnessed by institutions such as codetermination and flexicurity, among others, to finance the most advanced social workfare system in the world, based on a universally broad distribution of benefits. Europe's brand of social capitalism is destined to lead the twenty-first century because it provides a workable mix of wealth-creating free enterprise, social securities for individuals and families, and an ecologically balanced economy, a mix that has eluded the United States.

In this chapter and the previous one, I have outlined the main components of the European economic engine and some of its unique and most important characteristics, including various macroinstitutions and strategies. In the next chapter I will outline Europe's workfare institutions that combine with the capitalist engine to create not a welfare state at all but rather a comprehensive system well designed to keep European workers and families healthy, working, and productive. This system can be more accurately described as a "workfare support state." This is family values—true family values—in operation. There too, as we will see, reality outstrips the stereotypes.

FOUR

FAMILY VALUES, EUROPEAN STYLE

One day when I was visiting my friend Meredith, who lives in the small rural town of Lautrec, France, about an hour's drive outside Toulouse, she was stung badly by a wasp, causing sizable and painful swelling on her hand. She called her doctor, and to my great surprise within fifteen minutes he had shown up at her door—the famous French doctor's house call. I couldn't get over it. "House calls in the U.S. went out when Eisenhower was president," I told her, shaking my head.

My father-in-law had a similar experience while vacationing in Switzerland. He awoke one morning with what turned out to be a painful urinary tract blockage. The doctor paid a house call with hardly any wait at all and inserted a cleverly designed catheter that had no drainage bag. My father-in-law paid approximately $100 out of pocket for this emergency service. Back home in Minneapolis when he had to go to the emergency room a couple of years later, he waited nearly nine hours to receive medical attention, even though he had health insurance.

When a friend in Germany gave birth to her daughter, she was given three and a half months off work—one and a half months before the birth and two months afterward—at 100 percent of her salary. She and her husband also began receiving approximately $200 per month from the government as a kiddie stipend, which will continue every month until their daughter's eighteenth birthday, to be used for buying clothes, diapers, food, and whatever else is needed. Yet this friend is not a low-income "welfare queen"; in fact, she and her husband are

All German parents receive a kiddie stipend and paid
g a birth.

quaintance from Denmark got bogged down one day in
le Internet debate with participants from several countries, including several obnoxious Americans crowing about U.S. economic superiority over the sick man Europe. So my Danish friend told
them about his thoroughly middle-class life in the land of crisis.

> I am a teacher, and so is my wife. We have together a yearly income of
> $120,000. We have raised four kids; one has finished his free college
> education, and the other three are on the way. Besides free education,
> they receive about $660 a month from the state. I was operated on my
> shoulder last week, free of course, while still receiving full salary during
> my absence from work. We live in a modern apartment, rent about $820
> per month including heat. Since our children don't live home anymore,
> we have sold our house to our oldest son, who is married and has three
> children. We have a cash fortune of about $100,000 and a summer cot-
> tage worth $200,000, car, and other consumer goods. We have also
> pension savings that will guarantee us a net income in our old age of
> about 75 percent of our present salary. In the last twelve months we
> have been two times on the Canary Islands (sun and beaches) and one
> time in Portugal (more sun and beaches) on vacation. We pay about 42
> percent of our overall income in direct taxes, and for that we get social
> security, free health care, free education, old age pension, and a lot of
> other services. All that with a thirty-seven-hour working week and six
> weeks' vacation, and a Danish unemployment rate of about 3 percent.
> Yes, it is surely hard to live in Europe!

The Internet armchair theorists had no response, of course, but their
ignorance is all too common. Most Americans are only vaguely aware
of the breadth and depth of the generous benefits and services received
by the Danes and other Europeans. What is it that Europeans have that
Americans do not have? Quite a lot, it turns out. Simply put, when it
comes to differences in the performance of our respective social systems, to paraphrase Robert Kagan's famous formulation regarding the
military prowess of Europe and the United States, Americans are from
Mars, and Europeans are from Venus.

The comprehensive level of social securities, supports, and benefits
enjoyed by European families and workers is truly impressive. Universal
health care, generous retirement, paid parental leave, paid sick leave,
affordable child care, monthly kiddie stipends, free or inexpensive
university education, generous vacations, decent unemployment benefits, job training, elder care, affordable housing, heating subsidies in
the winter—the list is seemingly endless. It's all the more impressive

since these services are nearly entirely missing from the quality of life enjoyed by most Americans—unless you are a member of Congress or the president, who generously provide European-level support for themselves and their families.

As we saw in chapter 1, America, geared to be the world's RoboCop with huge military budgets, spends over 4 percent of its gross domestic product on defense, more than $500 billion in 2009 (and even larger amounts if you include the $1 trillion to $3 trillion for military operations in the Iraq and Afghanistan wars, and hundreds of billions of dollars for agencies doing military-related activities, such as the CIA, Veterans Administration, and Departments of Homeland Security and Energy). Europe, on the other hand, spends less than 2 percent of its gross domestic product on defense and so has vastly more resources to plow into workfare supports for its people.[1] According to the Organisation for Economic Cooperation and Development (OECD), the United States devotes 16 percent of its $14 trillion economy (or $2.2 trillion, about $7,300 per person) to workfare supports. But European countries contribute 27 percent of their $17 trillion economy to workfare supports, a whopping $4.6 trillion, about $9,200 per person, which amounts to 25 percent more "social dollars" spent per capita (and that's probably an underestimate).[2] That's a huge difference in social spending, showing once again how the oversized gap in military vs. social spending between the American Way and the European Way is one of defining magnitude. Not surprisingly, by any objective measurements Europe has surpassed the U.S. in most quality-of-life categories. Even many of the new democracies in eastern and central Europe, with average incomes barely half that of the U.S., surpass us in many ways.

Despite the ups and downs of the economic cycle that periodically have resulted in some cutbacks, Europeans still enjoy cradle-to-grave support in a range of areas. And the benefits are "universal," meaning everyone in the society receives them, even immigrants—no exceptions, no excuses.

The Swedish Social Insurance Agency publishes a brochure that precisely captures the prevailing philosophy: "Social insurance is founded on the idea of people helping each other through a kind of social safety net, which is in place from birth to retirement."[3] Dutch Labor Party leader Wouter Bos has argued that Europe's social state is based on "enlightened self-interest" since "We all run the same risks, so we might as well collectively insure ourselves against those risks."[4] As one British political analyst told me, "Europe doesn't so much have a 'welfare soci-

tem designed to produce healthy workers and families." This philosophy
is backed by broad agreement across the political spectrum, including
from conservatives and the so-called far right, forming the basis for the
oft-touted "European consensus."

The resulting workfare support system is a core part of the European
Way, centered around a distinctly European conception of "life, liberty,
and the pursuit of happiness." As we will see, the comprehensive level
of workfare enjoyed by all European workers and families is a marvel
of solidarity and design and is nearly entirely missing from the lives of
most Americans.

MORE THAN TALK: FAMILY VALUES THAT MATTER

Perhaps the best way to compare Europe's workfare approach to America's is by examining which system better supports families. American
conservatives and leaders of the Republican Party have boasted that
their philosophy and policies are based on "family values," and Democrats have followed along so as to not be outflanked politically. But what
does that term mean in actual practice? According to the OECD Social
Expenditure database, Europe spends *three* times more per capita on
families than does the U.S. In today's world, access to health care, sick
leave, parental leave (following childbirth or to care for a sick child),
affordable child care, quality and affordable nursing home and senior
care, access to education and training, a reasonable mix of work and
leisure with one's family, a sufficient retirement pension, and affordable
housing are increasingly necessary if we truly want to support families. Using those categories, let's compare the family-values policies of
Europe with those of the United States, starting with birth and ending
with old age.

Parental Leave

In Europe, paid parental leave from work for both mothers and fathers
is the norm, whether following childbirth or to care for a sick child.
But the U.S. is one of only 5 countries out of 173 that do not guarantee
some form of paid maternity leave (the others being the impoverished

African nations of Lesotho, Liberia, and Swaziland, along with Papua New Guinea). Fathers are granted paid leave in sixty-five countries, including thirty-one that offer at least fourteen weeks of paid leave, but the United States guarantees fathers, as well as mothers, nothing.[5] A majority of Americans are not even eligible at their jobs for *unpaid* parental leave,[6] and the proportion of U.S. companies offering paid maternity leave fell from 27 percent in 1998 to 16 percent in 2008.[7]

The Scandinavian countries set the gold standard. In Sweden, mothers get an incredible 1.3 years (69 weeks) off and receive about two-thirds of their usual wages during the leave. In Norway, mothers get up to a year off at 80 percent of their usual wages. In both countries after the leave is over, the mother returns to her job, and the employer is legally required to take her back in the same position. Then it's the father's turn to stay home and care for their child's second year of life, receiving about 50 percent of salary. In other countries paid parental leave is not as generous as in Sweden and Norway but is still substantial, with parents receiving at or near 100 percent of salary for three months or longer. Even formerly war-torn Croatia, with a per capita income less than a third of that in the United States, has paid leave for parents following a birth.[8]

Europe's family values recognize that raising a child is real work, and doing it well is valuable for the entire society. Breast-fed children, for example, have lower rates of infections, childhood diabetes, eczema, obesity, and asthma, and maternity leave better facilitates such breast feeding. Companies benefit from parental leave because by allowing mothers and fathers to return to work when their children are a little older, employers escape the additional costs of having to replace them and losing all that work experience. So new parents are paid to leave their jobs temporarily and stay home. This is funded either through government payments or by requiring employers to continue paying part of a parent's salary while the employee is on leave. In October 2008 the European Commission unveiled plans to extend minimum maternity leave in Europe by a month, from fourteen to eighteen weeks.[9]

But that's not all. Many European countries provide free afterbirth care immediately following the birth. In the Netherlands, for example, that begins with seven days of five-hours-per-day home assistance in which someone comes and does your laundry, vacuums, and teaches you how to care for a newborn. That's followed by a regimen of regular checkups for the baby at the public health clinic.[10]

Europe puts real money behind its "family values" rhetoric, but in the United States the only parents paid by the government to raise and

In most European countries, after both parents have finished caring for their newborn during the first year or two and returned to work, the infant then goes to a professional state-run or state-certified day care provider. Especially in the last ten to fifteen years, as more women have entered the workforce, a shift has occurred from mothers and grandmothers to professional services as the main providers of child care and early education. In the European Union, the proportion of four-year-old children in preprimary education averaged about 86 percent in 2004, with a number of countries reporting participation rates close or equal to 100 percent, compared with only about 62 percent in the United States.[11]

Sweden and Denmark are considered to be the child care leaders in Europe, offering universal, high-quality, and publicly funded child care. In Denmark, child care is free, and in Sweden, working parents pay a low percentage of their income to the government for each child at a state-subsidized nursery. The cost for one child is about sixty dollars per month, which includes breakfast and lunch, with the monthly fee reduced for each extra child. Compensation for teachers and staff is high, with Sweden's public child care accounting for over 2 percent of its gross domestic product.[12] In addition to child care for working parents, many Swedish communities also offer free "open day cares" for nonworking parents (including those taking parental leave) and for parents of newborn children. Parents can take their children there to play and to meet other parents and children, and the day care staff runs activities and gives help and advice to first-time parents. One Brit working in Sweden observed, "[In Sweden] childcare is seen as a basic service. It is as much a part of the infrastructure of going out to work as decent transport."[13]

France, Belgium, and other countries also have quality, affordable child care. From the age of three, children are entitled to a place in free public preschools, and nearly all children attend. For children of age two, preschool programs are available for which families pay on a sliding scale, typically about $130 monthly, which includes lunch.[14] Britain, Italy, and Germany have been the European slackers when it comes to child care, but with the necessity of helping more women to enter the workforce, Britain and Germany have been taking important steps. German chancellor Angela Merkel pushed for $16 billion to triple the number of day care placements for children under three and increase preschool for four- and five-year-olds.[15] Compared to Europe, child care in the United States is hard to find, of mediocre quality, and prohibitively expensive. Child care in the U.S. costs about $12,000 per year for a family with two children, $500 per month per child.

Kiddie Stipends

To assist with their children's needs and early development, parents in most European nations receive a monthly benefit check from the government for the first eighteen years of each child's life, with which they can buy food, clothes, diapers, toys, or whatever is needed. The German and Dutch governments pay one of Europe's most generous cash allowances, the equivalent of two hundred dollars per child per month.[16] Sweden pays approximately a hundred dollars per month, and France pays extra for second and third children as an incentive for having larger families. Some U.S. analysts have equated these monthly stipends with the Earned Income Tax Credit (EITC); however, the EITC is not a cash payment but merely a refundable tax credit for poor families earning less than about $1,000 per month. American middle-class families get nothing from EITC; it is more an anti-poverty measure and has been derided as "welfare." But in Europe, the kiddie stipends are for everybody, regardless of income, since universal coverage is the norm.

Compare that degree of comprehensive support for mothers and families with the support offered in the United States, where state funds for child care assistance fell for six years in a row.[17] Working families in America have been left to their own devices to juggle it all, with little family-friendly infrastructure or policy. After spending five years in France, author Judith Warner returned to the United States as a new mother and was appalled by the differences in support for French mothers compared with their stressed-out American counterparts. Warner wrote a best-selling book, *Perfect Madness: Motherhood in the Age of Anxiety,* describing American mothers as "tired and harried," saying:

> We can learn [from the French] that families need, in a very concrete way, to be supported . . . through measures that make life more affordable and less scary. We mothers need to feel that we are not essentially on our

agree that Europe's way is the best way. Valgard Haugland, conservative leader of Norway's Christian Democratic Party, has commented, "Americans like to talk about family values, but we have decided to do more than talk."[19] It is difficult for the United States to put our money where our rhetoric is when doing so is derided as "welfare" or "creeping socialism," instead of being seen as support for working families and family values. Too often in the United States, ideology trumps common sense.

Balancing Work and Leisure

Europeans have decided that family values means having enough leisure time to actually spend time with your family. And they have structured the balance of work and leisure time accordingly. While Americans work an average of 1,976 hours per year, German and French workers average some 400 fewer hours, the equivalent of fifty extra full-time days off (about seven weeks), for the same standard of living. France officially has a thirty-five-hour workweek, and in practice French workers labor on average thirty-seven to thirty-eight hours per week compared with Americans' average of forty-two to forty-four hours per week. Even British workers, who put in more time on the job than anybody else in Europe, work two hundred fewer hours (twenty-five days) per year than their overworked American counterparts. In fact, about 134 nations worldwide have laws establishing the maximum length of the workweek, but the United States does not have such a limit, nor does it have a limit on mandatory overtime per week.[20]

Europeans' greater number of days off is a combination of more vacation, more holidays, and a shorter workweek. They receive anywhere from four to six weeks of paid vacation per year compared with about two weeks for Americans, prompting Europeans to call the United States the "no-vacation nation." With the United States being the only advanced economy in the world that does not guarantee at least some paid vacation, about a quarter of U.S. workers in the private sector get no paid vacation time at all; they practically live the lives of working serfs.[21] In addition to paid vacation, Europeans enjoy a cornucopia of paid holidays celebrating various saints' days and holy days, at least twenty-three days in Britain, twenty-five days in France, and thirty days in Sweden; in contrast, the overworked American has to get by with a meager four to ten mandatory holidays, depending on the state, since there is no national law guaranteeing any paid holidays.[22] When you add it all up—the number of hours in the workweek, weeks of paid vacation, plus paid holidays off—U.S. workers work a half day or in some cases nearly a full day longer *per week,* and the equivalent of nearly two months longer per year, than European workers.

Family-friendly Europe is far ahead of the United States, not only in advancing a shorter workweek, but also in allowing the flexible work hours necessary for juggling work and family. Belgium, for example, has introduced "time credits," which allow a more accommodating balance between one's work and home lives. One of my Brussels friends, who is a busy director of an international policy institute and the mother of two energetic children, told me what a difference this makes. "Belgian law provides employees some degree of flexibility around their work schedules to accommodate the needs of families," she told me. Besides a more flexible weekly schedule, workers are allowed to take a paid sabbatical of one year over their career or reduce their hours to half-time without loss of benefits or their career. During their time off they receive a government allowance of $500 to $700 per month. Workers can also request paid leave to take care of an ailing family member, such as a sick child, or to provide medical assistance to a parent or other relative. In Sweden, parents can take off up to sixty paid work days per year per sick child. American employers would be aghast at providing such flexible career breaks and generous time credits. They would complain about losing their competitive edge, yet European companies are just as competitive, and the workforce in most European countries is just as productive as the U.S. workforce.[23]

Sick Leave

European countries also have mandatory paid sick leave. In fact more than 160 nations around the world provide paid sick days, with 127 providing a week or more annually.[24] Unfortunately the United States is not one of them. We are still one of only a handful of nations that have no national law guaranteeing paid sick leave, leaving some sixty million workers—43 percent of the private industry labor force—without

to report to work and infect your coworkers and customers; if your child is sick, we force you to choose between being a good parent or being the breadwinner. During the swine flu outbreak in the spring of 2009, at one point President Barack Obama urged workers with flu symptoms to "stay home." But for far too many American workers, especially for many service sector and low-income employees, that was more easily said than done. There's a good chance that any employees handling food in a restaurant or handing out change in a grocery store can't afford to stay home when they are sick. Care for some swine flu served with your French fries, anyone?

To prevent abuses of sick leave, each European country has different rules, but generally a worker's use of sick leave is carefully monitored by his or her employer and then, after a certain number of sick days, by a doctor or the state bureaucracy (though abuse of sick leave has been a problem in some countries, leading to some reforms). Also, if you are injured and your capacity for work is permanently reduced, you are eligible for "activity compensation," which ensures you will not suffer loss of income. With all these supports in place, sickness is not generally an obstacle that can ruin your life. Instead, you can heal, go back to work, and get on with your life.

Health Care

I will explore the impressive health care systems of various European nations in more depth in chapter 8, but for now what is important to know is that Europeans have affordable, quality health care for all—including universal dental care at least until age nineteen and free prescriptions for children up to a certain age—despite spending only about half per person of what the United States spends nationally on health care. Russell Shorto, an American writer living in Amsterdam, reports that while he lived in the U.S. with his family of four, he paid about $1,400 a month for a policy that didn't include dental care and was rife with co-pays, deductibles, and exemptions of coverage. A similar Dutch policy, by contrast, has cost him about $390 per month with no co-pays and included dental coverage; about 90 percent of the cost of his daughter's dental braces was covered.[26]

The World Health Organization rates various European nations' health care systems as top-ranked in the world, but the American system is ranked only thirty-seventh. In the United States, our patchwork system has left forty-seven million people without health insurance— over 15 percent of the population, including an estimated eight million children—and more than one-third of Americans go without health insurance for long periods of time.[27] Various surveys reveal that many Americans without insurance are middle class and employed, yet President George W. Bush tried to deflect criticism by callously saying that those without insurance could "just go to an emergency room."[28] He apparently was unaware that numerous studies have shown that people without health insurance tend to postpone treatment until a minor illness becomes worse, and they ultimately die sooner, imposing greater costs on society.[29]

Not only do Europeans have better formal health care systems, but they also have an informal sector that better facilitates exercise and fitness as forms of preventative care. This sector includes a vast network of bicycle and walking paths for daily transportation and exercise and year-round spas, swimming pools, saunas, and exercise and training rooms, with classes for group exercise and aerobics open to the public. The cost to use the facilities is government-subsidized and very reasonable. The governments believe that it is less expensive in the long run to have healthy, active citizens than to have couch potatoes who can't afford a health club membership. In numerous ways, the European culture is one that prioritizes health and *la dolce vita* (this aspect of personal health will be explored in chapter 7).

Retirement and Pensions

Retirement pensions in Europe are far more generous than those in the United States, underscoring the belief that families and workers perform best when knowing that their future is to some extent secure. In the late nineteenth century, Germany's Otto von Bismarck first pioneered the idea of old-age government pensions, and they have since become a European staple. As in the United States, retirement pensions are funded by payroll deductions from both workers and employers, generally about 8 percent of salary paid by each. But Europeans can expect to receive a retirement pension in the amount of 70 to 80 percent of their working salary, compared with most American workers,

payments in the United States are so paltry, most experts believe it will take at least $200,000 to $300,000 in addition to those payments
for the average American to have a secure retirement, yet most older Americans have saved only a small fraction of that amount.[32] In fact, many Americans have a negative savings rate, portending problems for the future. These working Americans really will have to scramble to supplement their meager Social Security with private savings.

Elderly Care

According to the OECD, Europe spends nearly 25 percent more per capita of public money on old age care than the U.S. spends. Care for the elderly in Europe relies on the traditional venues of nursing homes and assisted-living facilities, and the care tends to be of excellent quality with professional, trained staff. But increasingly, elder care advocates are looking for ways to help seniors stay at home longer, living independently and remaining outside costly state-backed institutions. In the 1990s, a number of countries began providing a cash payment to elderly recipients, who could then use those funds to pay informal caregivers, including relatives and neighbors. In Norway, Denmark, and Finland those caregivers even become municipal employees, complete with regular pension benefits. In the Netherlands, which gives dependent seniors the option of receiving a "care budget" to pay for their own services in lieu of an institutional bed, the maximum yearly allotment is about $75,000, which is generous but actually only two-thirds of what the state would pay for expensive nursing home care. In 2006, eighty-five thousand people opted for the personal budget, saving the Dutch government at least $500 million, so it's both cost effective and allows the elderly to remain in their homes and around friends and family, which is better for their well-being. In many countries, 80 to 90 percent of older persons using services are those who rely on this kind of home care.

In some countries, such as Denmark, the latest innovation is the do-it-yourself retirement community. In these shared accommodations, friends or other groups of like-minded people develop their own village or apartment collective. They each have their own home but share dining areas, gardens, craft workshops, and the like. Collectively they hire care services when needed. In Spain, such groups are creating planned retirement communities that offer everything from on-site physical therapy to pottery classes and sightseeing trips. Across Europe, new assisted-living technologies are being developed, including a barrage of gadgets such as fall-detecting sensors and even robot nurses that follow you around.[33] The European Commission has outlined plans for a $1.5 billion research program to find innovative ways to use technology to improve the lives of older people and prolong their independent living, including helping seniors to take advantage of accessible online services that can support their needs.[34]

Education

In most parts of Europe, university tuition remains free or nearly free. Even in Britain, which tends to lag behind the rest of Europe in its more American-like qualities, the Tony Blair government introduced a sliding tuition fee based on family income, with a maximum tuition of $4,000 per year.[35] In Germany, some of the state universities recently have begun charging up to $630 per year in tuition.[36] But in the United States the average annual tuition for a four-year university in 2007–8 was $23,712 for private college and $6,185 for a public college.[37] As a result of soaring costs, U.S. college students graduate on average with $20,000 in debt, a figure that has more than doubled since 1995;[38] graduate students are saddled with nearly $46,000 of debt. Nearly one in three college students reported using credit cards to help pay their tuition, up from one in four in 2004, many of them using cards with high interest rates.[39] Rising tuition costs and cuts in college aid have made it increasingly difficult for many young Americans even to complete their university program, causing the United States to rank fifteenth among twenty-nine nations in the proportion of college students who complete university degrees or certificate programs, falling behind most European nations.[40]

Unlike American college graduates, European students do not have to mortgage their futures by going into exorbitant debt to pay for a university education. That allows them to begin building their careers more quickly than U.S. students can. Still, the issue of how to pay for education is a growing problem for countries around the world. All face a tradeoff between keeping tuition low and having enough funding to ensure that universities provide a quality education and

sion between access and quality is complex, and I will address it in more detail in the next chapter. For now, the take-home point is that European students still enjoy affordable higher education, which is an increasingly difficult challenge for millions of young Americans, and the quality of the European education system consistently fosters a highly educated populace.

Affordable Housing

In the European worldview, affordable housing also is part of the "family values" package. Europeans view adequate affordable housing—sometimes called "social housing"—practically as a right. Consequently, European countries have a more proactive approach, making housing policy a top public priority, with local and national governments having a well-articulated strategy and higher levels of funding. Some of the affordable housing stock is owned by the government, but much of it is owned by private, nonprofit housing associations. The nonprofit associations develop and manage affordable housing as a social-oriented business. In the Netherlands and the United Kingdom, several large nonprofit housing entities own from fifty thousand to seventy thousand dwellings apiece. It is common for a private nonprofit to control more than twenty thousand units, substantially more than most comparable entities in the United States.[41] In London, developers of new housing are required to have 25 to 35 percent of the new units built as "affordable." In Finland, the Helsinki city council decided that 40 percent of the apartments in new areas had to be "social housing."[42]

This European consensus in favor of social housing has not been easily arrived at. It is the result of hard-fought battles by housing activists and anarchists in the 1970s and '80s, involving building takeovers (known as "squatting") and pitched street battles. According to estimates, as many as twenty thousand squatters lived in Amsterdam in the early 1980s. Eventually this resulted in the passage of various housing laws, including laws against absentee landlordism. Today in the Netherlands, any building, office, or house that has not been occupied by the owners for a year or more is subject to legal squatting and move-ins. The squatters typically fix up the building, making neglected repairs, switching on the electricity, and turning it into their home. It can take years to evict them legally, and the owners may have to pay relocation costs. This ensures a low rate of owner absenteeism, preserves the quality of the housing stock, and acts as a drag against attempts to manipulate the housing market by keeping properties off the market.[43]

Another key difference between European and U.S. strategies to provide housing is that typically Europe mixes the affordable units with market-rate housing, so they are not segregated or stigmatized. No "government housing" exists as it does in the United States, where it has created segregated poverty zones. Instead one finds a mixture of renters, low- and moderate-income homeowners, and market-rate homeowners. (The one European exception is France, which created American-style segregated ghettos of high-rise public housing in its suburbs, like the U.S. housing built in inner cities in the 1960s, with similar disastrous results.) While the terms *public housing* and *government housing* have been stigmatized in the United States, in Europe they are so common that this type of housing can't be hidden away. Government-owned or nonprofit-owned homes and apartment buildings are found in every neighborhood of every city and town, and their inhabitants include not just the poor but many from the middle class. The presence of so much social housing acts in a competitive market as a check against escalating rents and mortgages and against speculation in the private housing sector.

In addition to those living in government or nonprofit housing, families with children and young people eighteen to twenty-eight years old are eligible for housing subsidies, with the amount dependent on income, size of household, and housing costs. Seniors living on a pension also are entitled to a means-tested housing subsidy. Marginal people, who in the United States end up homeless, are provided basic housing, food, clothing, medical care, and, if they need it, psychological counseling.

Compare Europe's concept of "social housing" to the worldview in the United States, where housing mostly is left to the free market and private real estate developers who focus on the more profitable homeownership market. The recent speculative housing bubble and subsequent collapse were just the latest example of the shortcomings of the American approach. They also reflected the manic overemphasis on homeownership that results in too little new rental housing being built (which is the primary housing for most of America's low- and

between housing needs and what the free market supplies, in 2005, 17 million American households paid more than 30 percent of their monthly income for housing, and there was a glut of vacant condos even while many families were doubling up and grown kids were moving back in with their parents due to the lack of rental housing. And that was *before* the housing market collapsed in 2008–9.[44] As Americans have seen too often, such as during the aftermath of Hurricane Katrina, the absence of a plan is an absence of leadership; today, America suffers from a complete lack of a national housing policy.

But in Europe, the presence of so much social housing acts as a check against the excesses and speculation of the private housing industry (though Spain, Ireland, and Britain were hurt by the housing crash). Europe mostly does not have the kinds of abject slums you see in the U.S. Nor does it have the armies of beggars and homeless who populate the inner core of most U.S. cities today. One London acquaintance told me, "I would love to take you or any American to see what is our worst neighborhood in London. It makes the slums of the American South seem like Brazil's *favelas*."

Poor Families and the Unemployed

Europe particularly stands out when it comes to helping poor families. As we have seen, Europe's workfare support state begins at birth, with government payments for each newborn child and generous support for parents. This is hugely beneficial to its poorest citizens. Poor and low-income working families also benefit from access to universal health care, as well as from a much higher minimum wage than is paid in the United States. In the European Union the minimum wage has been 53 percent of the national average wage but in the United States only 31 percent of the average wage. (In 1956, it was 56 percent of the average wage in the States.)[45] Not surprisingly, the United States has many more low-wage workers than Europe has, with nearly a quarter of American workers classified as low-wage compared with only 6 percent in Sweden and fewer than 16 percent in Germany (though, curiously, Germany has not had a minimum wage).[46]

According to a study by Germany's Institute for Employment Research of the Federal Employment Services, the United States spends a far lower percentage of its economy on monthly compensation for the unemployed than any of the E.U.-15 nations, about half the amount spent in the United Kingdom and only a seventh of that spent in the Netherlands.[47] The unemployed in Europe are given various supports and a measure of dignity and respect that are lacking for their American counterparts. Unemployed European workers not only receive continued health care and a monthly payment of 70 to 90 percent of their last salary for a year or two (up to four years in Denmark, though some countries have a maximum monthly salary cap), they also receive a helpful level of subsidies for housing, utilities, food, and child care, as well as job retraining and counseling.[48]

But in the United States, the unemployed receive a paltry unemployment check, usually no more than 50 percent of the last salary for a period of six months, depending on the state—practically poverty wages if you are supporting a family. That's if they receive a check at all; according to the U.S. Department of Labor only 37 percent of unemployed Americans received benefits in 2007, down from 55 percent in 1958 and 44 percent in 2001. Astoundingly, six in ten workers who became unemployed during the economic crash of 2008 did not receive any unemployment benefits because they either did not qualify for various bureaucratic reasons, never applied, or had exhausted their benefits.[49] Those who don't qualify include an increasing number of part-time workers, since the New Deal–era system hasn't been updated enough to reflect an age of more frequent job changes, more part-time work, or people who have multiple jobs.[50] If your income is low enough, you can also receive some help in buying food (with the stigmatized Food Stamps program) and paying utility bills. If you are unemployed long enough, you may also receive government-supplied health care through Medicaid. Otherwise you receive health care from a hospital emergency room. You can end up truly hard up and vulnerable, especially if you have a family to provide for in the face of soaring costs for housing, health care, fuel, and more. The stress can be very debilitating.

Case study: An acquaintance in Switzerland, who had been an accountant for twenty-five years, suddenly found himself unemployed and encountering more difficulty than usual in finding a new job. He was collecting unemployment, 70 percent of his last salary, when he was beset by an unfortunate and untimely injury: he fell and broke his kneecap in multiple places, requiring extensive surgery and an eleven-

he found a well-paying job and resumed his career. Reflecting on his experience, he told me, "I would not even try to think about what would happen in the U.S. if this case happened to anyone."

In fact it did happen, and to a friend of mine. Doug, at the age of forty-nine, discovered he had a congenital heart defect requiring a valve transplant. He had insurance that paid for most of the surgery but still left him with thousands of dollars in bills. Plus there was a complication necessitating his being out of work longer than planned. His meager savings dwindled, though he received a paltry disability check for a time which provided barely enough to live on but not enough to make his car payments. His car was repossessed, so that when he finally was well enough to go back to work he didn't have transportation. These kinds of gotchas and Catch-22s are all too common in America. Having no job and inadequate health care is not a place you want to end up in the good ol' USA.

The different treatment of the unemployed in the United States and Europe reflects different cultural attitudes. The experience of the unemployed in the U.S. is punitive, as if it is *your* fault the economy has taken a downturn. But in Europe, unemployment is seen in part as the result of the inevitable ups and downs of a cyclical economy. Individuals are not blamed and consequently are allowed to retain their dignity—as well as sufficient income, health care, child care, housing subsidies, skills retraining, job counseling, and more—supported by a comprehensive system designed to assist them in getting back on their feet. Europe's unemployed have access to what is truly a safety net, while the unemployed in the United States live a meager, marginal existence unless they have their own accumulated savings (which is not very likely).

The lack of health insurance for the unemployed in the United States is perhaps the best illustration of the backwardness of the U.S. approach. In America, where health insurance mostly is employer-based, the unemployed are subject to a rather cruel irony: they are dropped from the ranks of the insured at the moment when they are most vulnerable and can least afford to get sick. The experience of the Swiss accountant could have resulted in prolonged misfortune if it had occurred to an American, and in fact many unemployed Americans, like my friend Doug, have been struck by such medical misfortune with little safety net to catch them from a really long fall. This social approach strikes Europeans as being particularly backward. A junior minister in Sweden's Health Ministry told *Washington Post* reporter T. R. Reid, "It seems to me that your country takes away the insurance when people most need it."[51] That logic has evaded most policymakers in the United States, at least until recently. The Obama administration's stimulus package passed in February 2009 subsidized 65 percent of the health insurance premiums for individuals laid off during the economic crisis.[52] That was a good start but it provided coverage for only nine months, and for many of the unemployed even paying 35 percent of sky-high premiums has been more than they can afford.

These are the major categories in which the European workfare support state shines, but there are others, including subsidies for heating homes during long winters, transportation subsidies for those with disabilities and others that qualify, even bereavement benefits to assist with burial after a death in the family. The Netherlands gives parents about $400 per child each year to help pay for their school materials. Austria, Germany, and Switzerland offer a few extra days of vacation for young workers; Norway offers an additional week of vacation to workers over sixty. In the ultimate "vacation nations" of Austria, the Netherlands, and Sweden, they even pay workers about to go on vacation an additional bonus above their standard paid vacation days to help with vacation-related expenses![53] A comprehensive catalog of the full range of workfare supports would take too long to list. They are the sea in which Europeans swim, suffused throughout a system in which health care, pensions, vacations, and the like are not called "benefits" but instead are considered to be basic universal rights. Susan Neiman, the director of the Einstein Forum in Germany, says these rights are based "on fundamentally different assumptions about humanity than the system Americans have."[54]

In short, Europe's pro-family policies put America's to shame. They have put some meat on the bones of their family values, with institutions and practices that are well integrated and have an internal logic: If a worker gets sick, European nations have the health care system to nurse her or him back to health, and mandatory paid sick leave to ensure she or he stays home instead of reporting to work and infecting coworkers and customers. If a mother wants to work, they have the child care infrastructure to ensure that she doesn't have to choose between a family and a career. If a worker loses her or his job, they have time to spend together. Parents enjoy paid leave after their child's birth to assist with that important life transition, or when they need to stay home to care for a sick child. And workers know that if they play their role in this well-designed system, a decent salary, a good living, and a comfortable retirement await them.

While the U.S. still fumbles the ball in coming up with universal anything, even health care, the clever Europeans have come up with that and much, much more. Even part-time and temp workers in Europe enjoy workfare supports that many full-time workers in the United States don't receive. A 2007 study by Harvard and McGill university researchers found that the United States lags far behind virtually all countries with regard to family-oriented workplace policies, such as maternity leave, paid sick days, and length of workweek, among others. Workplace policies for families in the United States are weaker than those of all other high-income countries and even many middle- and low-income countries. "More countries are providing the workplace protections that millions of Americans can only dream of," said the study's lead author, Jody Heymann, founder of the Harvard-based Project on Global Working Families and director of McGill's Institute for Health and Social Policy. "If you look at the most competitive economies in the world, all the others except the U.S. have these policies in place."[55]

Europeans are not necessarily aware of how far ahead of the United States they are, just as Americans aren't aware of how far behind they have fallen. Europeans take much of their approach for granted, viewing their vaunted workfare system as their birthright. And in recent years, as a result of the pressures to keep their economies competitive, many countries have undertaken steps to trim their workfare benefits. It remains to be seen how much the economic crash of 2008 will affect availability and quality of services, but even with recent cutbacks, Europe's workfare remains far more generous than anything comparable in the United States. One acquaintance from Romania who came with his family to the Oakland, California, area to work as a mental health professional was incredulous over the American shortfalls. Each week he would discover a new omission from the American workfare system. "What, no state-run day care to drop off my children?" he said with exasperation one week. "Pay for my own health care? No maternity leave?" he said another week. Another week he exclaimed, "Only two weeks' vacation? In Romania we had five weeks!" That's in Romania, one of the newest members of the European Union but still a poor country, which not that long ago was ruled by the ruthless communist dictator Ceauşescu.

Welcome to the land of stingy Uncle Sam, where many benefits that European families routinely enjoy are not even on the radar screen of the American public or its politicians. When was the last time any major politician in the United States talked about providing mandatory paid parental leave after the birth of a child or inexpensive day care, kiddie stipends, paid sick leave, free university education, a decent retirement pension, affordable housing, or cash payments for home caregivers of the elderly, all of which have been enjoyed in Europe for years? Even in the 2008 presidential campaign, when health care was a major issue of contention between the two leading Democratic candidates, Hillary Clinton and Barack Obama, neither of them proposed a health care plan that came anywhere close to European-level care, with its checks on for-profit insurance companies and built-in cost controls. And Republican candidates hid their heads in the sand over the issue, as usual. What kind of family values are those?

THE MYTH OF THE OVERTAXED EUROPEAN
AND OTHER MODERN FABLES

The typical American retort to the generous and comprehensive nature of the European workfare support system is that Europeans pay much higher taxes. Surely "no taxation without representation" Americans would never go along with that. That's just one of the many myths and fables that bounce around the American landscape about the European "welfare" state. Another myth says that Americans are wealthier and better off than everyone else in the world, including Europeans, so why mess with success? Both of these claims oversimplify and distort reality.

Let's look more closely at the tax details of Europeans and Americans. The business magazine *Forbes* has been at the forefront of this anti-tax mantra, publishing an annual Tax Misery Index, which shows European nations as the most "miserable" and the low-tax United States as happy as a clam—right next to Indonesia, Malaysia, and the Philippines.[1] But upon closer inspection, this charge turns out to be a caricature, just like the myth of Europe having chronic double-digit unemployment (as we saw in chapter 3). When we add up the total local, state, and federal tax burden that Americans pay, a different story emerges. Constanze Woelfle, an American accountant based in the Netherlands, says that people coming from the U.S. to the Netherlands focus on the top tax bracket, which at 52 percent can sound daunting compared to the top bracket of 35 percent in the U.S. "But consider that the Dutch rate includes social security, which in the U.S. is an additional 6.2 percent. Then in the U.S. you have state and local taxes, and much higher real estate taxes. If you were to add all those up, you would get close to the 52 percent."[2]

But that's not all. In addition to what Americans pay in taxes, you would have to pile onto that the tuition, insurance premiums, co-payments, hidden fees, and other charges that most Americans pay beyond their taxes to receive various services and benefits. A thorough analysis would need to create a ledger in which all the workfare supports and services Europeans receive are listed on one side, and the amount of taxes and any additional fees they pay are listed on the other; and then it would do a similar analysis for Americans, listing on one side of the ledger the same level of benefits and services as those received by Europeans, and on the other side what Americans must pay in the form of taxes as well as out-of-pocket expenses for those same services. This would clarify that for Americans to acquire health care, university education, parental leave, child care, elder care, retirement pensions, and so on—the things that Europeans receive for their taxes—we have to pay additional fees, premiums, deductibles, and out-of-pocket charges beyond our taxes.

For example, my siblings and some of my friends are saving about $100,000 for each of their children's college education, even as European children attend universities free of charge or close to it. In the United states, *public* spending on old age care is nearly 25 percent less per capita than in Europe, but *private* spending on old age care is nearly three times higher per capita, because Americans mostly self-finance their own senior care. Many Americans are scraping to save the hundreds of thousands of dollars experts say they will need for retirement beyond their Social Security, trying to stuff as much as possible into their IRAs and 401(k)s because the Social Security pension is so paltry and American businesses are walking away from providing guaranteed pay-out pensions. But the European state retirement systems are more generous and better funded, providing individuals a greater share of their retirement income.[3] Also, many Americans are paying extra for child care, self-financing their own sick leave or parental leave after a birth, and more. But Europeans receive all of these and more—in return for paying their taxes.

Beyond paying their taxes, many Americans pay out of pocket for escalating health insurance premiums, deductibles, and co-pays. I met one taxi driver in San Francisco who self-financed minor surgery for his mother so that her monthly premium wouldn't increase. Other taxi drivers I have met of South Asian descent have traveled back to India

National Institutes of Health Clinical Center, has found that the average family of four in the United States is coughing up $29,000 a year
for health care due to out-of-pocket medical expenses, taxes, and lost
wages resulting from employers paying higher insurance premiums and
lower salaries.[5] It may not be in the form of taxes, but Americans are
paying significant amounts for services that Europeans receive for free
or nearly so in exchange for their taxes.

Europeans of course pay the notoriously sky-high VAT, which is
short for "value added tax" and, like our sales tax, is a consumption
tax charged for most purchases. The VAT can range anywhere from
16 percent in Spain to 25 percent in Sweden, compared with approximately 6 to 8 percent sales tax in the United States, depending on the
state. But what is missing from this "tax misery" calculation is that, in
addition to sales taxes, Americans pay a bewildering number of "nickel
and dime" taxes and hidden fees that for the most part Europeans
don't pay. The assorted taxes, surcharges, and fees charged on bills
for telephone, cell phone, cable TV, and gas and electric utilities often
come to well over 20 percent of the total bill—as much as the VAT in
most European countries.

Tax code analysis by political scientist Jacob Hacker reveals yet
another way that the tax situation in the United States has been falsely
portrayed. It turns out Americans are paying higher taxes for their sub-
standard health care than they realize, because these costs have never
been presented to the American public in the form of a bill. Instead
they're hidden in the form of huge tax deductions given by the U.S. government to private employers for the health care coverage they provide
to their employees. In 2005 alone, the government gave more than $300
billion in tax breaks to businesses for their employee health benefits,
$1,000 for every man, woman, and child in the United States—forty-
seven million of whom have no health insurance at all. That amount is
easily sufficient to finance a real universal health care system covering
every American. Says Hacker, "If America's tax code and private benefits are taken into account, U.S. social spending is slightly higher than
average compared with other rich countries—higher, in fact, than the
spending of Denmark."[6] In other words, the U.S. government is spend-

ing our tax dollars like "socialist" Europe, but they're poorly spent and have done little to bring our health care system or workfare supports up to European standards.

These sorts of complexities are not calculated into *Forbes's* Tax Misery Index or other attempts to compare transatlantic tax burdens. When all of these different fees, premiums, tuitions, deductibles, and hidden taxes are added up, it turns out that many Americans actually are paying out as much as Europeans—we just receive a lot less for our money. It really depends on which American you are and whether you need to purchase any "extra" services to keep your family healthy and prospering. The American attitude seems to regard things like quality child care, higher education, sick leave, vacations, parental leave, efficient mass transportation, and even health care as luxuries. But increasingly these supports are necessary to enjoy a decent quality of life in today's insecure world. Europe regards these as essential features of its workfare system, helping to create personal security for all.

Without access to a system that makes these workfare supports easily obtainable, many Americans simply choose to do without them. They live a riskier and less insured lifestyle, either because they can't afford these premium services or because they would rather take their chances and keep their money in their pockets. But too many Americans who accept these risks pay a price in the long run, through either poorer health or a poorer quality of life. When their risk goes awry, for instance, when someone without health insurance winds up in the hospital, then all taxpayers assume the cost of that risk. One way or the other, someone has to pay. In a sense then, the European system is more honest about the shared societal costs and the individual benefits and services needed for a decent quality of life.

Interestingly, while Europeans supposedly are taxed to death and have a lower per capita income than Americans, almost by magic they have managed to maintain a much higher savings rate than Americans. The French and Germans have a savings rate of around 12 to 14 percent of their income, compared with a lower or even a negative savings rate among "lightly taxed" Americans. Americans can't save in part because they are spending so much of their disposable income on purchasing these other necessary workfare benefits and services out of pocket. Unfortunately, most Americans are only vaguely aware of these complexities and nuances, having been barraged with the stereotype of the "poor overtaxed Europeans."

Even American leaders at the highest levels of government and busi-

John Breaux from Louisiana and his wife. Breaux, a conservative, anti-tax Democrat, asked my acquaintance about Sweden and swag-geringly commented about "all those taxes the Swedes pay," to which this American replied, "The problem with Americans and their taxes is that we get nothing for them." He then went on to tell Breaux about the comprehensive level of services and benefits that Swedes receive in return for their taxes. "If Americans knew what Swedes receive for their taxes, we would probably riot," he told the senator. The rest of the ride to the theater district was unsurprisingly quiet.

So the "overtaxed European" is another stereotype, like the myths of double-digit unemployment and the sick, sclerotic European economy, which are used to scare Americans away from the European model. It cannot be emphasized enough that this is not "welfare," as many American pundits and leaders derogatorily refer to it. Instead, the European economy and the workfare system are two halves of a well-designed system that work in conjunction, as a single unit, to keep workers and families healthy, happy, and productive. And Europeans are willing to pay for these workfare supports because they know the supports are an integral part of their success story. Europeans' taxes allow the creation of institutions and support structures that help individuals and families to be better prepared for the insecure times that are inevitable in everyone's life. In today's world, a middle-class standard of living is not only about income levels and economic growth rates but also about adequate support for workaday people. The Europeans have established the right set of institutions and workfare securities to create a more symbiotic balance between workers and their employers, between corporations and communities, and between the steady state economy and the social system. This is social capitalism in action, and this in turn imparts yet another advantage to Europe over its competitors.

MEANWHILE BACK IN THE USA . . .

Many Americans, when they are asked at all, profess a belief in the United States as the wealthiest and best country in the world. They believe this steadfastly even though the world has become riskier today for most American families and workers, and even though their lives are filled with anxiety about the future. For decades, the "corporate benefits" system was Americans' guarantee of the good life, but now American employers say they no longer can afford to provide those benefits because it hurts their global competitiveness (which is certainly true, since businesses in Europe, Japan, and elsewhere do not have to shoulder as much of these responsibilities). Thus, old-style, employer-based, guaranteed pay-out pensions and health care plans are on the chopping block. The ties of the social contract that have bound us all together are weakening; the post–World War II pact among employer, employee, and government is fraying.

This downward trajectory of America's corporate benefits system has been going on for some time. In 1979, nearly 70 percent of American workers received health insurance coverage from their employers. Twenty years later, the proportion had dropped to just over 50 percent, and it continues to fall. Among workers earning roughly $8.50 an hour, the drop has been even steeper, from 46 percent coverage to only 26 percent today.[7] The percentage of moderate-income Americans (earning between $20,000 and $40,000 annually) who were without insurance for at least part of the year jumped sharply over four years, from 28 percent in 2001 to 41 percent in 2005.[8] Companies that have retained coverage have made workers pay a larger share of the costs, shifting much of the risk from their own balance sheets to employees' check-books, resulting in health care payments for family coverage increasing by 102 percent in recent years.[9] Political scientist Jacob Hacker says, "We are seeing the death throes of a corporate insurance system. . . . With this system's slow but steady demise comes a massive shift of risk from employers onto workers and their families."[10]

Even though the United States has been the dominant power in the post–World War II era, we suffer from more economic inequality than any other nation in the advanced democratic world. In the 1970s the top-earning 1 percent of Americans took home 8 percent of the nation's total income, but by 2007 they took home over 22 percent, even as the total federal income tax rates they paid dropped from 50 percent three decades ago to 35 percent in 2008.[11] Based on such research, Harvard researchers Claudia Goldin and Larry Katz concluded that since the mid-1970s America has experienced "exploding inequality," with the gap in income as great today as it was in the Gilded Age.[12] The poverty rate has increased in recent years to include thirty-seven million people in the United States, 12.7 percent of the population compared with 6 percent in France, 8 percent in Britain, and 5 percent or

western world with the exceptions of Russia and Mexico." The United
States ranks twenty-ninth in the world in infant mortality, tied with
Poland and Slovakia (in 1960 the U.S. was ranked twelfth), and twenty-
ninth in life expectancy.[15] Clearly the United States is going backward.

According to a Federal Reserve study, the wealthiest 10 percent of
people in the United States now owns 70 percent of the wealth, and the
wealthiest 1 percent owns more than the bottom 95 percent, compared
with Germany, where the top 10 percent owns 44 percent.[16] The ratio
of CEO pay to average manufacturing employee pay is 475:1 in the
United States, compared with 24:1 in Britain, 15:1 in France, and 13:1
in Sweden; even in nonmanufacturing sectors in the United States, the
average CEO earns more in one day than the average worker earns all
year.[17] But that's not because U.S. workers haven't been plenty productive. In fact U.S. productivity levels have been among the highest in the
world. But because the American political democracy is so antiquated
and broken, the gains have been siphoned into increased corporate
profits, CEO pay, and golden parachutes, as well as increased health
insurance premiums. Little of the substantial corporate profits has
trickled down to American workers in the form of bigger paychecks
or more workfare supports. Whether Democrats or Republicans have
been in control, politics has been trumped by economics.

So while CEOs made out like bandits in the Bush years, average
American workers fell behind. The *Financial Times* reported that median
household income declined by $1,700 from 2000 to 2004, the first
time on record that household incomes had failed to increase for five
straight years.[18] Lacking sufficient income, more American workers
went deeper into debt, with the average household's credit card debt
over $8,500 (up almost 15 percent from 2000) and with the average
college debt more than doubling since 1995 (to $20,000). The nation's
savings rate, which had exceeded 8 percent of disposable income in
1968, stood at 0.4 percent in 2008 and by some estimates was slightly
negative.[19] Even before the crash of 2008–9, roughly one-third of the
nation—thirty-four million households—had borrowed against their
existing homes, many of them to cope with the rising costs of housing,
health care, and education, resulting in a savings rate for this group of
negative 13 percent (which later improved to negative 7 percent in late
2007, when tightened standards made loans harder to get).[20] According

to the U.S. Bureau of Economic Analysis, Americans' total spending in 2005 exceeded their earnings by a whopping $41.6 billion, the first year since 1933 that spending had outstripped earnings.[21]

In what was a major wake-up call, the *Wall Street Journal* reported that the United States, which is supposed to be the land of opportunity, has had less economic mobility than "old Europe," completely turning convention on its head.[22] A United Nations survey of 120 major cities in the world found that Atlanta, New Orleans, Washington DC, and Miami had inequality levels similar to those of Nairobi, Kenya, and Abidjan, Ivory Coast.[23] These and other findings are what prompted Ted Halstead, founder of the New America Foundation, to declare, "U.S. performance on many social indicators is so poor that an outsider looking at these numbers alone might conclude that we were a developing nation." It's been a race to the bottom that American leaders seem determined to pursue, dragging down American workers and families to the point that low-wage, high-pollution countries like China and India may end up setting the pace.

And that was *before* the economic meltdown of 2008–9. Once the world emerges on the other side of that calamity, it's possible that these trends will have been greatly exacerbated. We *have* to come up with a better way.

BETTER MEASURING STICKS
FOR THE TWENTY-FIRST CENTURY

One essential component of figuring out this better way is to refine the methods for how we measure "progress." The extreme limitations of the current ways we keep score have become increasingly obvious to more and more experts. Economists and social scientists have created new indexes and statistics to determine quality of life beyond the overused gross domestic product, unemployment rates, economic growth rates, and the like.[24] These indexes have names such as the Index of Economic Well-Being, Weighted Index of Social Development, United Nations' Human Poverty Index, Genuine Progress Indicator, the Ecological Footprint, and Mothers Index (ranking the best and worst places to be a mother and child). *The Economist* magazine, the World Economic Forum, and the European Commission also have developed their own quality-of-life indexes. These various indexes include a number of human values that are ignored in purely economic calculations, such as income inequality, access to health care, life expectancy, pov-

Meanwhile, European countries always occupy the top ratings. Such side-by-side comparisons reveal Europe's greater success and undermine the credibility of American claims of superiority or leadership. Europe easily surpasses the United States because its brand of social capitalism has produced results that make a difference in people's lives. The U.S. government has not even begun to try to measure quality of life in a more sophisticated, comprehensive fashion beyond gross domestic product, average income, tax rates, and unemployment. Instead, American leaders continue to rely on cherry-picking data and citing misleading economic measurements, which allow the United States to maintain the fiction that it is the world's leader.

But increasingly Americans are paying a high price for our misreadings of reality. Professors Richard Wilkinson, Robert Putnam, Henry Milner, and others have traced the deteriorating social relations found in unequal societies, showing that such societies tend to have more violence, lower levels of trust, less involvement in community life, lower voter turnout, and more discrimination against women and minorities. Wilkinson references more than fifty studies showing that rates of violent crime and homicide are higher where income inequalities are greater.[25] As the developed world's most "unequal society," America is suffering the slow, corrosive deterioration of having the wrong values, misplaced priorities, and inadequate fulcrum institutions that are producing this unequal society.

Not surprisingly, many Europeans are alarmed by America's inequality and rightly question the "growth at any cost" zealotry that has pervaded their transatlantic cousin. Many have concluded that even if Europe were to lag behind in economic growth, so what? As Joaquín Almunia, the European commissioner for economic and monetary affairs (comparable to a U.S. presidential cabinet position), put it, "For Europeans, economic growth is a tool, not an end in itself. We are not in a race with the U.S. Our goal is not to grow as fast as the U.S. or anybody else but to do what we need to protect our economic and social model . . . and to keep the moral principles underlying it alive."[26] With a fair and comprehensive workfare system that better distributes society's wealth and without a bloated military budget siphoning off trillions of tax dollars, Europe's steady state economy has not needed to grow as fast as America's trickle down economy to produce better results.

So much for family values. While Americans stand by and watch corporations renege on their part of the social contract and watch their government plow their hard-earned taxes into huge military budgets, Europeans live wrapped in an economic security blanket that provides decently for the health, security, and prosperity of their families and the workforce. The blanket has frayed some in recent years, and adjustments and rollbacks have occurred. But Europeans for the most part do not live in fear of being financially wiped out by illness, economic decline, or stock market crashes (far fewer Europeans own stock than Americans, interestingly).[27] Nor do they worry that if they lose their jobs or become injured, their children will live a life of severe privation or that in their elder years they won't be provided for. Yet for too many Americans these are real fears that dog us most of our working life. These fears are part of the Made in USA background noise, part of the static of everyday living, so it's hard to notice them or realize that life doesn't have to be this way.

In these uncertain times, no doubt the debate over how to measure wealth, the health of the economy, quality of life, and general welfare has only just begun. Such debate surely will intensify as we move further into the twenty-first century with its looming challenges.

CHALLENGES AND THREATS
TO THE EUROPEAN WORKFARE SYSTEM

In recent years, various European governments have found it necessary to trim the most generous—some say excessive—parts of their workfare system. Some of the reasons for this are related to the dips and bumps of the economy; each country is usually in some phase of reallocating, trimming, or fine-tuning its level of benefits to react to economic fluctuations. Trying to maintain these supports for a half billion people is a complex task, to say the least. Other reasons are related to bringing more efficiency to the system's generosity. Not surprisingly, the European benevolence sometimes has been taken advantage of by a handful of ne'er-do-wells trying to milk the system. For example, in some nations the pensions have been ridiculously generous; in Italy, so-called baby pensioners can begin collecting a lifetime pension at age thirty-six, after only eighteen years of work.[28] And concerns have

Some of these abuses, along with the ups and downs of the economy, have led to some cutbacks and attempts to crack down. But most of the cutbacks have been extremely mild by U.S. standards, even falling into the category of "no-brainers." In Germany, for instance, a ridiculously generous degree of government benefits earlier in the decade reportedly had been funding Viagra pills (taxpayer-funded sex, as one pundit called it), breast implants, cooking courses, and taxi fares.[29] That kind of budget fat is easy to trim. But assistance for more essential things like eyeglasses and dentures also was reduced. Among the eliminated benefits were payouts from the state—thousands of dollars—to families when a loved one died to help with burial expenses; for years Germany paid not only when you came into the world (via parental leave and kiddie stipends) but when you left it as well. Now the latter assistance is gone.

And you can always hear stories in various countries about the social system failing to meet demand or to perform adequately. Within countries, some regions inevitably are better served than others and sometimes temporary shortfalls occur, especially during a sudden rise in demand. One friend in Stockholm told me about a shortage of child care that created waiting lists in the central city due to a baby boom. He complained that sometimes when the children played outside, inattentive staff seemed to spend more time talking to one another than supervising the children. And who can forget the thousands of elderly in France who died over the course of an unexpectedly blistering heat wave during August 2003, when too many doctors and hospital staff, as well as the victims' relatives, were away on vacation during the traditional summer holiday period?

In Germany, the effects of trying to absorb formerly communist East Germany still show signs of struggle, nearly twenty years later. The integration was affected by the abrupt way in which it took place, leaving no room for East Germany to retain the best features of its previous system. Today, in eastern Berlin and other parts of eastern Germany, pockets of child poverty approach U.S. levels.[30] In eastern and central Europe, the formerly communist states are still in the process of catching up with western Europe. An American friend of mine who lives in Prague, Czech Republic, writes, "I have been in situations where I had to call an ambulance for someone, and the drivers basically extorted cash from us before they would take him to the hospital. In general, doctors treat patients with disdain here."

The education system also has been criticized, especially the university system, drawing complaints of underfunding and poor quality. Europe believes in a mandate for free or inexpensive higher education, but this involves a tradeoff between keeping tuition low and having enough funding to provide a quality education with adequate facilities. Outside British universities like Oxford, most European universities are not ranked very high on the global lists measuring the quality of universities. But these rankings typically are based on the influence of universities as research facilities, or the number of alumni that have been named as Nobel Prize winners, or the number of articles published by alumni; when a different criterion is used, such as the number of alumni holding CEO positions in one of the five hundred leading worldwide companies, many European universities do much better. Controversy has swirled around these rankings and the specific criteria used.[31]

Still, some of Europe's public universities have overcrowded classrooms and are lacking in the most modern facilities; academic pay has not always kept pace with that of other professions, resulting in a "brain drain" of some of the best academics and Ph.D. students to private elite universities abroad, including Harvard, Yale, and Stanford in the United States. Certainly America's private universities have become a magnet for elite students and faculty around the world.

Yet it's not clear how this edge helps most American students, since most don't qualify academically or can't afford to attend those elite universities. In fact, while the number of students enrolled in America's best science and engineering graduate programs increased by 25 percent from 1994 to 2001, the number of U.S. citizens enrolled in those programs declined by 10 percent.[32] Foreign students, over a half million of them, increasingly have been the ones filling the classroom seats in America's elite universities, with only a brief drop following the September 11 attacks.[33] Allowing a high percentage of foreign students into America's elite universities offers some domestic benefits, such as fostering international goodwill (which an isolated America badly needs) and forging relationships with some of the foreign leaders of tomorrow. Yet these admissions involve tradeoffs, since over a half million American students could benefit by filling those slots. And some of those foreign students will return to their countries to start businesses and invent technologies that one day will compete with their U.S. counterparts.

In addition, if America truly has the best higher education system

At the pre-college level the U.S. education system also ranks poorly compared to those of other developed nations. American fifteen-year-
olds rank twenty-fourth out of twenty-nine developed nations in math literacy and problem solving.[34] The National Geographic–Roper Geographic Literacy Study showed that Americans don't know much about the world; almost two-thirds of Americans of ages sixteen to twenty-four can't find Iraq on a map of the Middle East.[35] About 30 percent of all public high school students drop out, and this proportion increases to fully half of the students in the nation's largest cities; Detroit has a graduation rate of only 25 percent, and Indianapolis, 30 percent.[36]

But in the European Union, only 15 percent of all students drop out.[37] In Germany, only a tenth of all students and a sixth of students with immigrant backgrounds drop out.[38] Europeans are the most educated and informed people in the world about both their own domestic politics and international affairs, while Americans are some of the least informed. So it's not clear what benefits America is deriving from its better equipped but exorbitantly expensive universities. The tensions between access and quality, as well as the issue of how to pay for higher education, will continue to daunt educational institutions around the world. But in the meantime European students still enjoy affordable higher education and are among the most educated in the world.

In short, even with cutbacks and shortfalls, and even after the 2008 crash, the pro-family European democracies still provide a level of security and comfort that far outshines anything available in the United States. Yet the American media seem to be either unaware of this or unsure how to report it. For example, *USA Today* reported, "Economic pressures are cutting into leisure time," stating that Italians were trimming back their traditional August vacations from an average of 14.5 days to 12 days, apparent proof of an Italian crisis. But the article failed to mention that Italians still have as many vacation days in the single month of August as most Americans have in an entire year, with Italians taking another three to four weeks of vacation during the rest of the year.[39] Germany's Social Democratic government under Chancellor Gerhard Schroeder cut back the duration of unemployment benefits in 2003 from a maximum of thirty-two months to only twelve months, quite a drastic cutback—yet that is still twice as long as the duration of unemployment benefits in the United States.

Cutbacks of course never feel good to those on the receiving end. Nobel laureate and psychologist Daniel Kahneman and his colleague Amos Tversky have shown that people dislike losing things they already have much more than they like gaining things they don't have—a phenomenon known as "loss aversion."[40] Certainly Europeans will continue to experience some degree of loss in the future, depending on where they are in the ups and downs of their economic cycle. But from an American's standpoint, the cutbacks have been pretty mild. Certain benefits and services that Americans have *never* enjoyed have been reduced—not even eliminated, just trimmed. But Europeans have become used to the best, and so even these modest cutbacks are perceived as the equivalent of Maggie Thatcher and Ronald Reagan together wielding a huge fiscal axe on their budgets. My German and French friends have told me with horror about the cutbacks they have experienced, and while sympathetic, at a certain point I have found myself reacting with a shrug: "If you think those are bad, try living in the USA."

QUESTIONS TO PONDER

How is it that the European economy, which is portrayed by American leaders and media pundits as being a ninety-eight-pound weakling, a rickety old man on a cane, can afford all this? Or perhaps better questions are: How is it that the world's lone remaining superpower cannot afford at least as much? And how is it that Americans don't know how far they have fallen behind their European counterparts?

What is so jarring is not simply that Europe and America perform differently on the big-picture scorecard, but the extent to which the United States is behind in nearly every socioeconomic category that can be measured. And yet Americans don't know this. While Europe and the United States are both powered by a mighty capitalist engine as the workhorse of their economies, Europe's robust workfare support system has provided a higher level of economic security for its middle classes and its poor. This is how Europe ensures the principle of life, liberty, and the pursuit of happiness, and Europeans aren't afraid to pay for it. They put their money where their family values are. One can't help but wonder at what point it will dawn on Americans that patriotism and massive military armaments are a pale substitute for real improvements in their quality of life.

THE ECONOMIC CRASH OF 2008–9

Wall Street Capitalism vs. Social Capitalism

> The engine of that growth, the American economy, has gone off the rails and threatens to drag the rest of the world down with it. Worse, the culprit is the American model itself: under the mantra of less government, Washington failed to adequately regulate the financial sector and allowed it to do tremendous harm to the rest of the society.
>
> **Francis Fukuyama,**
> **author, *The End of History and the Last Man***

The economic crash that began in the fall of 2008 stunned the world with its velocity and scope. Like a tsunami that arose seemingly without warning—though actually there had been ample alarm bells, but few had listened—it flooded everything in its path. Countries whose prospects had been bright less than a year before suddenly were deluged with bank failures, financial collapse, and ruin. The speedy economic contraction resulted in millions of jobs lost, factories closed, businesses shuttered, exports sitting on the docks, and homes repossessed. It saw the vanishing of more than a trillion dollars in stock market wealth in a single day, with more losses to follow. Worldwide economic activity slowed and seized to a degree that none of the experts had thought possible. The economic pandemic spread from the United States to Europe, China, Japan, Brazil, India, Russia, Korea, Australia, Saudi Arabia, Iran, Pakistan—none were immune from its ravages. Besides the obvious human suffering and government hand-wringing, economic theory itself lay in tatters. The crisis demanded the rewriting of the economics textbooks, because nearly all the experts had been so wrong.

What was especially revealing about the crisis was the different ways that the United States and Europe, by far the world's two leading economies, coped with it. Singular interventions were tried on each side of the Atlantic that, not surprisingly, mirrored the qualities of social capitalism vs. Wall Street's casino capitalism. When a crisis strikes, paradoxically that can create either a tendency to freeze in place or an opportunity for new interventions and ideas. No less an authority than Milton Friedman, one of the architects of what has been called "disaster capitalism," once said, "Only a crisis—actual or perceived—produces real change. When that crisis occurs, the actions that are taken depend on the ideas that are lying around."[1] So this economic crisis gave us a chance to see what ideas were lying around in Europe and in the United States, and who was ready to lead the way toward reform of the collapsed economic system. In a by now familiar pattern, Europe looked for ways to spur reform while the United States, under the new Obama administration, turned away from the obstructionist policies of the Bush administration but still dragged its feet over real reform. While proclaiming that America's leadership had returned, the Obama administration failed to follow up the rhetoric with bold action.

THE PHYSIOLOGY OF AN ECONOMIC CRISIS

The economic crash was widely blamed on a hyper-deregulated U.S. financial system that allowed a contagion of toxic financial products known as derivatives, fed by shaky mortgages and historically low interest rates that produced a housing bubble, to spread throughout the U.S. and global economies. Numerous banks, mutual funds, and investment portfolios, trusting in the AAA rating given to these risky investments that had the backing of such reputed Wall Street stalwarts as insurer AIG, overinvested in the "easy money" derivatives and over-leveraged their balance sheets. Lax regulation allowed banks, hedge funds, insurance companies, and other financial institutions to increase their debt-to-net-capital ratios to dangerous levels, sometimes to as high as forty to one in the United States. When the housing bubble finally popped the dominoes fell, not only in the United States but all over the world, sending the world's economy into a tailspin.

As Angel Gurría, secretary-general of the Organisation for Eco-

the willingness of financial agents at all levels—from Federal Reserve chairman Alan Greenspan to the local loan officer—to suspend belief in sound economic principles. This breakdown in prudence and common sense allowed derivatives of bundled mortgages to become what billionaire investor and financial guru Warren Buffett has called "financial weapons of mass destruction," seeded throughout the global system.[3]

But blame did not lie just with the United States. Said European Commission president José Manuel Barroso, "Mistakes were made on both sides of the Atlantic. It's true, the crisis originated in the U.S. But it's also true that European financial markets had major exposure. I don't want to get into a blame game."[4] Indeed, some European banks, having trusted the U.S. ratings system that graded the financial health of investments, became more overleveraged than American banks, with Germany's top commercial banks particularly vulnerable due to massive loans to eastern and central Europe.

Both the U.S. and Europe were slow to recognize the impending crisis. But once its magnitude became apparent, both cautiously launched into a host of remedial efforts. They pinned the world's hopes on interventions designed to unfreeze the financial and credit markets and to initiate a Keynesian-type stimulus based on government spending to spur the economy, create jobs, and maintain consumer spending. During times of crisis, Europe sometimes is criticized for its lack of unity, but sometimes that multiheaded hydra affords certain advantages. Having so many powerful nation-states allows each nation to act as a laboratory for the others, all learning from one another's successes and shortcomings.

For example, when the massive financial meltdown first struck in the fall of 2008, causing the markets to reel, and U.S. secretary of the treasury Hank Paulson announced a $700 billion bailout plan for U.S. financial institutions, Europe was harshly criticized for its initial failure to craft its own continent-wide bailout. Euroskeptics saw it as another example of disunity and weakness. But that was a rush to judgment. Each country initially tried its own bailout formula, and less than two weeks later the strategy employed under British prime minister Gordon Brown, which provided a government guarantee for banks' solvency and interbank loans as a way of shoring up confidence in the banking system and restarting bank lending, proved to be the most workable.

So the rest of Europe followed the British lead, as did the U.S. after Paulson's plan proved ineffectual.

The European plans also included tight controls over the bailout money, including a reduction in dividends paid out to stockholders as well as concessions from the bankers in terms of salaries and bonuses, all of which were lacking in the U.S. bailout. Many of the European governments also seized equity in the rescued banks, partly nationalizing them; Germany, for example, took more than a 25 percent stake in Commerzbank in return for an additional $13 billion capital injection into the bank.[5] Britain nationalized several of its banks, including the Royal Bank of Scotland.[6] These interventions were modeled after one that succeeded in Sweden in the early 1990s. When the Swedish banking sector hit the skids, the government mounted a program of nationalizing some of the banks, then cleaning up the balance sheets and finally auctioning them off. Not only did the banks eventually return to private ownership, the taxpayers got back some of the money that had been used for the bailout. But the United States kept throwing good money after bad into institutions such as Citigroup, Bank of America, and AIG, even though these companies essentially were broke, with a net value lower than the amount of public funds they had received.

"Europe showed the capacity to respond to a crisis more quickly than the U.S.," says Leon Brittan, who served as home secretary under Britain's conservative prime minister Margaret Thatcher. "It shows that the American conception of Europe as an economic basket case is outmoded and wrong."[7]

Then, when it came to enacting a fiscal stimulus plan to spur job creation and consumer spending, Europe adopted a plan, worth hundreds of billions of dollars at the continental and national levels, months earlier than the United States, which had to await action from the new Obama administration. Despite a strained and at times bitter east-west divide resulting from over a century of antagonistic history, the continent's leaders also created a special bailout fund of billions of dollars to assist those eastern and central European nations that were especially hard hit (though not all were, with Poland, the Czech Republic, and others mostly weathering the storm). With a lame-duck Bush administration followed by an untested Obama administration, Europe had no choice but to lead, and for the most part it did just that. In typical fashion, the process for figuring out a common policy for twenty-seven sovereign nations was at times noisy and cantankerous, but at the end of the day Europe found its way.

"Tomorrow's Europe: Not Necessarily Influential"; "Spirit of Divided
Europe Back on Scene in Spite of EU"; "Subprime Europe"; "A Continent
Adrift"; "Divided Europe Holds Financial Crisis Summit"; "Economic
Malaise Threatens to Undermine European Unity"; "Tremors of European
Financial Collapse Will Be Felt Worldwide"; "East-West Divide Plagues
Europe"; "Growing Economic Crisis Threatens the Idea of One Europe."[8]

While the U.S. bailout plans were crafted by U.S. secretaries of the
treasury Hank Paulson and Timothy Geithner behind closed doors,
practically in secret and with hardly any oversight, Europe conducted
its policy making in full view of the public. Every disagreement or per-
sonality clash between Britain and France, or between Germany and
France or Britain, or between western and eastern Europe, got played
out on the front pages and the evening news. Americans can't seem to
get used to the fact that European policy making is typically accompanied by a lot of background noise, like static on a radio, even as the
program eventually comes through, loudly and clearly.

As the contagion spread into 2009, European leaders once again
took the lead in formulating fixes to the system. German chancellor
Angela Merkel and French president Nicolas Sarkozy proposed sweeping regulatory changes, including a U.N.-level international financial
regulator and a redesign of the international architecture of financial
institutions. Using the subtle, coded language of diplomacy, they warned
the new Obama administration not to block attempts to build this architecture; indeed, they urged President Obama to join with them.

While the Obama administration was still dipping its toe into the
water during its first months in office, Europe rolled up its sleeves and
got to work. It led two crucial efforts, one by the High Level Group
on Financial Supervision in the E.U., under the direction of Jacques de
Larosière, a former head of the International Monetary Fund, and a second by the Financial Services Working Group of the "Group of 30," an
informal group of leading economists from Europe, the United States,
and a few developing countries, including former U.S. Federal Reserve
chairman Paul Volcker. Both groups issued reports with specific recom-
mendations for global financial reforms. The G-30 report proposed a
significant overhaul of the global financial system, including a dramatic
expansion of government control over banking and investment activi-

ties, arguing for increased oversight of the overall financial system, strict limitations on the size of banks, regulation of hedge funds, and greater scrutiny of rating agencies.[9] The G-30 report recognized that there are lessons to be learned from the E.U. experience of coordinating such policies among twenty-seven different countries, and it provided an intellectual foundation to the policy debate that had been largely lacking in Washington during the presidential transition from the Bush to the Obama administration.

Those European efforts in early 2009 then became the basis for many of the oversight provisions agreed to during the Group of 20 meeting in early April 2009, a meeting charged with the crucial task of refocusing economic recovery efforts for both developed and developing nations. In his first appearance as president at an important international conference, President Barack Obama smartly made an unexpected concession to Europe by agreeing to a regulatory role for a Swiss-based body, called the Financial Stability Board, or FSB, that was charged with creating standards for financial institutions around the world. The board consists of central bankers and financial regulators from major economies, including the United States, as well as the World Bank and the International Monetary Fund. It establishes standards to govern hedge funds, tax havens, executive compensation, and capital requirements in financial institutions, among other areas. The standards are only voluntary, and the board itself does not possess policing powers (the United States in particular objected to outside policing). But if the FSB finds that a country's regulations aren't up to its standards, then other countries can block access by the rogue country and its financial institutions to their financial markets. European regulators had already threatened to do that to U.S. investment banks earlier in this decade, prompting marginally stronger oversight by the Securities and Exchange Commission.[10]

In a note to clients following the G-20 agreements, Federal Financial Analytics, a Washington DC–based financial consulting firm, called the Obama administration's agreement to the FSB "a major concession" to the European Union and suggested that it could bring swift change to global finance. While a lot of the regulation will be done by each individual country, "the FSB will provide an overall umbrella to make sure this is happening," said Uri Dadush, the World Bank's former director of international trade.[11] Others were not so optimistic. Simon Johnson, a professor at M.I.T. and former chief economist at the International Monetary Fund, said the agreements were "sensible

exist," as Johnson wrote. With the Obama administration unwilling to cede any policing powers to a regulatory body, bold initiatives were pushed to the sidelines.

THE "AUTOMATIC STABILIZERS" OF SOCIAL CAPITALISM

Besides financial regulation, Europe's other major component of economic recovery was the use of a fiscal stimulus in the form of targeted government spending as a way of jump-starting its national economies, creating jobs, and maintaining levels of consumption to prevent a downwardly spiraling depressive cycle. Europe's well-designed workfare system allowed it to take a different approach to fiscal stimulus than in the United States; Europe's tack was misunderstood, and therefore controversial. President Obama and other American leaders pressed hard on the Europeans to spend more on fiscal stimulus and match the nearly $800 billion that America was spending. But the Europeans agreed to spend only about half that amount. They argued that their existing workfare supports already were more generous, and that during economic down times these supports automatically kicked in with additional stimulus that was better targeted and more efficient, and therefore did not require as much money. For example, the workfare support system automatically provided increased levels of generous unemployment benefits and other government supports, including universal health care, which served to soften the blow of rising economic distress. The reflexive nature of these mechanisms has led them to be called "automatic stabilizers."

With its stronger workfare support system and automatic stabilizers, Europe was spared some of the urgency felt in the United States. Since new legislation was not needed to produce a countercyclical boost, the response in Europe was nearly immediate, while the still-new Obama administration was forced to push legislation through a hesitant Congress and fine-tune the stimulus on an ad hoc basis. For this reason the public mood in many European countries did not become as bleak as in the U.S., and there was less demand that politicians do more.[13] Nobel Prize–winning economist Paul Krugman wrote that one thing working in Europe's favor during the economic crisis was "the very thing for which it takes the most criticism—the size and generosity" of its workfare supports, "which are cushioning the impact of the economic slump." Europe's automatic stabilizers ensured that there wasn't "as much sheer human suffering in Europe as there is in America. And these programs will also help sustain spending in the slump."[14]

In Germany, for example, instead of laying off some employees, many businesses began cutting back the hours of *all* their employees so that the pain was spread around to more workers. Then the German government made up roughly two-thirds of lost wages out of a special fund filled in good times through payroll deductions and company contributions, a program known as *Kurzarbeit,* which translates as "short work."[15] *Washington Post* columnist Harold Meyerson compared it to Joseph's advice to Pharaoh to set aside resources in the seven fat years to get Egypt through the seven lean ones, an effective countercyclical program.[16] Over a million workers, including nearly seventy thousand employees of the automaker Daimler, were placed on short-hour status. While that meant a lot of people with slightly lower incomes, on the positive side it meant these employees still had jobs and money in their pockets that would help maintain consumer spending at a sufficient pace. It also meant that the workforce would mostly remain intact, and employers would not lose their skilled workers whom they had spent so much to train.

But in the United States, instead of cutting back all workers' hours a bit and maintaining the workforce, businesses began laying off millions of employees. For many months in a row over six hundred thousand workers lost their jobs, at one point resulting in the biggest three-month drop since immediately after the end of World War II, when the defense industry was shutting down for conversion to civilian production. Over three million jobs were lost in 2008 alone, with millions more workers getting their pink slips in 2009. According to OECD figures, the U.S. unemployment rate for June 2009 was 9.5 percent, more than double the 2007 rate, while in Europe the unemployment rate was 8.9 percent, having increased only 1.3 percentage points since 2007. Indeed, the U.S. unemployment rate suddenly was higher than that of France, which American economists and pundits used to love to lecture about its "rigid labor markets" and high unemployment (and as pointed out in chapter 3, if people in prison had been counted, the U.S. unemployment rate was much higher than those of both France and Europe due to the U.S. incarcerating seven to ten times the number of people as did Europe).

Europe's *Kurzarbeit* policy and other practices reflected its core

as conventional wisdom got turned on its head—suddenly "the land of high unemployment," Europe, was losing fewer jobs than the United States.

Germany and other European nations also deployed other precisely targeted efforts toward fiscal stimulus and maintaining jobs. For example, during prosperous times many companies wisely had given workers the flexibility to save their overtime pay so they could carry it over for a rainy day, and many workers began drawing on these savings during the downturn. Then, to spur the automotive industry, which is a core part of the continental economy that employs millions of workers directly and acts as the hub of a vast network of smaller businesses, early in 2009 various European nations enacted a "Cash for Clunkers" program in which government subsidies were provided to drivers who junked their old jalopies and traded up to new models. The amount of the discount on the sticker price varied from $1,300 to $3,000, depending on the country, and often rewarded the purchase of smaller, more fuel-efficient vehicles. In Italy, drivers could receive a $6,500 discount if they traded in a car that was at least ten years old and bought a vehicle powered by electricity, natural gas, or hydrogen.[17]

The program greatly exceeded expectations, with car sales in Europe quickly jumping nearly 20 percent, resulting in millions more cars being sold. The program was open to all auto manufacturers in Europe, including U.S. automakers such as Ford and GM. Sales of GM's Opel Corsa tripled in Germany, resulting in workers in Germany and Spain returning to full production schedules. After running on a reduced schedule from October to February, the Fiat plant in Melfi, Italy, began running at full capacity again. In France, 30 to 40 percent of new car sales resulted from this subsidy. Auto plants in Poland, Romania, and the Czech Republic also saw sudden bursts of production. Along with helping the industry and keeping autoworkers employed, the plan removed hundreds of thousands of pollution-spewing clunkers from the road, while lifting safety standards overall. After hearing about the effectiveness of the program, President Obama proposed, and Congress passed, a similar "Cash for Clunkers" program.

German chancellor Angela Merkel summarized a key transatlantic difference when she said, during a widely watched interview on a

German television talk show, "In contrast to America, our social systems are not on the decline right now. Pensions are not cut, unemployment insurance is not reduced. On the contrary, we can register stable and, in some sectors, also rising expenditures, and this makes me hope that our social market economy will enable us to cope with this complicated situation."[18]

Critics of European systems of workfare support have always said that they undermine entrepreneurial spirit and perpetuate inefficient companies that should be allowed to perish so that free market forces can be allowed to purge the weak through "creative destruction." But, says William Drozdiak, president of the American Council on Germany, "Germans argue that their system tames the worst abuses of raw capitalism and acts in a more humane way that alleviates the suffering of employees during a downturn, if only by keeping them gainfully employed so they can continue to spend money as consumers."[19] To American criticisms that Europe should spend more money on further fiscal stimulus, Europeans responded that their workfare supports and safety nets, derided by free market disciples as crippling impediments to growth, automatically provided much of the spending boost that the U.S. Congress had to legislate.

GROPING TOWARD A NEW CAPITALISM

The different reactions and policy proposals of Europe and the United States in response to the economic downturn show their distinctive visions for capitalism and economic development playing out. In Europe, the solutions depended greatly on existing social capitalism and workfare supports, operating like two sides of the same coin, which during down times automatically kick in with additional stimulus. And that stimulus was precisely targeted to keep as many people as possible working and with money in their pockets, based on a core value of social solidarity. In addition, Europe looked to enact stronger financial regulation to ensure that the economic bubbles that have fostered a boom and bust cycle over the last two decades would be tamed. But in the United States, the stimulus had to be enacted as a separate step by Congress amid much controversy and partisan bickering, and as a result kicked in much later and was not as precisely targeted. Financial regulation largely was an afterthought for the United States, tepidly agreed to by the Obama administration mostly because the Germans and the French insisted upon it.

mostly on overleveraged paper wealth. A dangerously high level of "nonperforming assets" had not been based on anything physical or concrete manufactured in a factory or on an assembly line somewhere, but instead had arisen from speculation, deal making, and leveraging—in effect, vapor money. Since World War II, the financial sector in the United States has tripled in size as a percentage of the overall economy and of corporate profits. That increase accelerated during the eight years of the Bush administration,[20] even as the United States lost 5.5 million manufacturing jobs.[21]

Additionally troubling were changes in the intricate workings of the financial sector. In 1958, 75 percent of financial sector debt was with traditional financial institutions—banks, savings and loans, and finance companies—but today that proportion has shrunk to 18 percent. The rest of the debt today is invested in a dizzying array of financial products and institutions that were created over the last half century to borrow money, speculate, and forge financial deals. Taking the economic concept of the "multiplier effect" to a steroidal level, in recent years "one loan to a consumer could create a myriad of debts as it was bundled into a pool that issued securities to buyers that, in turn, borrowed money to finance their purchases," writes *New York Times* reporter Floyd Norris. "That created a mound of debts that enhanced profits in good times, but left financial institutions vulnerable if the value of their assets began to fall."[22] And fall they did, starting in 2008, with the decline accelerating at the end of that year and into 2009, its menace spreading like a metastasizing disease.

Europe's financial sector also got caught in this trap, to worrying levels. However, led by Germany, most of Europe also has continued to emphasize manufacturing and industrial policy. German chancellor Angela Merkel once was asked by then British prime minister Tony Blair what the secret was of her country's economic success, which includes being the world's largest exporter and running substantial trade surpluses in recent years. She famously replied, "Mr Blair, we still *make* things."[23] Harold Meyerson, *Washington Post* columnist, explains further. "In Germany, manufacturing still dominates finance. . . . German capitalism didn't succumb to the financialization that swept the United States and Britain in the 1980s, in part because its companies raise their capital, as [America's] used to, from retained earnings and banks rather than the markets."[24] Werner Abelshauser, an economic historian at the University of Bielefeld in Germany, says the European way of running the economy "is fundamentally about a banking system based on patient capital and firms that emphasize high-quality products and long-term relationships between suppliers and customers."[25] Company managers set long-term policies, while market pressures for short-term profits are held in check. Gunter Verheugen, vice president of the European Commission, echoes the virtues of Europe's strong, competitive industrial base, succinctly stating Europe's recipe for success: "Don't try to be cheaper. Try to be better."[26]

This focus on quality and long-term performance over short-term gain is precisely what is reinforced by Germany's codetermination, with worker representatives sitting on boards of directors, high levels of unionization, more equitable income distribution, and more comprehensive workfare supports. By giving workers a sizable stake in the health of companies, their products, and the economy in general, a symbiotic relationship lumps everyone into the same boat. A rising or ebbing tide affects everyone together.

Says the *Post*'s Meyerson, "It would be a positive development if [the United States] had a capitalism that once again focused on making *things* rather than *deals*." One of the challenges for the United States, then, is to transform itself back to an economy in which we actually manufacture products again, and don't have such a high percentage of our gross domestic product contingent on financial wealth that contributes to speculative bubbles. The Reagan-Thatcher revolution's economic philosophy, which favored finance over manufacturing, has led to the decline of U.S. manufacturing and not only to a negative balance of trade but also to a business community less and less concerned with America's productive capacities. U.S. ratios of manufacturing to consumption and wealth creation to debt creation "have gotten dangerously out of whack," says Meyerson.[27] The U.S. financial sector must be scaled back and regulated, and corporations should be made legally answerable not just to shareholders but also to stakeholders—their employees and communities—via codetermination and other instruments. As the economic success of Europe shows, these changes can be realized without reducing the dynamism of the economy, says Meyerson, "particularly since Wall Street often mistook deal making for dynamism."

So beyond economic revival, what the Europeans see at stake in the recovery from the crisis is the overall vision for how a national economy

on those same dead end principles and policies, including launching huge levels of overleveraged fiscal stimulus, which the United States has done. They believe that a manufacturing economy with strong stakeholder influence is the best hope for getting away from a Wall Street capitalism that has led to such catastrophic bubbles. There is a trust issue here; perhaps it's an oversimplification, but Europe does not trust the United States, and who can blame them after the disastrous eight years of the Bush administration? "Ten years ago, America's capitalist evangelists thought they could save the rest of the world from its economic sins. Now, the big struggle is to save the rest of the world from America's own failings," wrote the *Financial Times*'s Chrystia Freeland.[28] Added Dominique Strauss-Kahn, managing director of the International Monetary Fund, "The crisis originated in the US . . . and a lot of people in emerging markets are saying to the US, 'You should be more humble. If this crisis had happened in another part of the world you would be lecturing us.'"[29] Frank-Walter Steinmeier, Germany's foreign minister, expressed the widespread opinion, "You are hugely mistaken if you think that this is just a storm and that we'll be back to the same old rules after a few difficult months."[30]

Yet in the spring of 2009, complaints began to grow in the U.S. Congress, in the media, and in capitals around the world that President Obama's appointed regulators were industry insiders who were not going to reform things. They had gotten rich by being players in the very casino game that had spun out of control. Wall Street executives, after first being cowed over their incompetence and having to accept government handouts, began rediscovering their bravado and digging in against fundamental changes. The Obama administration and other key authorities, such as the New York Federal Reserve, began standing back while Wall Street tried to resurrect much of the ultracomplex trading system, including the failed agencies, that had led to such a spectacular global collapse. Derivative trading and the giant, too-big-to-fail firms like Goldman Sachs that profited from them began positioning themselves to dominate the financial landscape once again. And that meant they began fighting European-type regulations of the industry.

Timothy Geithner, secretary of the treasury, was prepared to require more transparency and a bit more oversight via privately run clearinghouses, but not much else. His statements in the weeks prior to the April 2009 G-20 meeting indicated his desire for more regulation, saying, "Our hope is that we can work with Europe on a global framework, a global infrastructure which has appropriate global oversight, so we don't have a Balkanized system at the global level, like we had at the national level."[31] But his actions said something else, and it seemed increasingly clear by late spring that the Obama administration was not going to use the collapse to reorganize American banking along healthier lines. Geithner resisted anything bold, such as substantially revamping the rating agencies like Europe did, or requiring all trading, especially hedge fund trading, to occur on publicly recognized exchanges. Exchange trading gives the government authority over fraud and manipulation, and it creates the kind of public transparency that isn't possible in Geithner's privately run clearinghouses. *Newsweek*'s Michael Hirsh wrote, "It's unlikely [Geithner's] proposed changes will do much to change Wall Street." "The old culture is reasserting itself with a vengeance," said Hirsh. "Even as we are still picking up the debris, we seem to be ready to embrace that world once again."[32]

The significance of this was not missed in Europe. Jacques Attali, an economics expert who has advised both conservative and socialist governments, said that U.S. bankers "are going to accept a minimum of regulation. Not more. We see this clearly with the Geithner plan, which reinforces the mechanisms that led to the crisis." According to Attali, there will be no fundamental change in U.S. behavior on fundamental questions such as leverage, securitization, and debt because "the Anglo-Saxon world lives off that."[33]

As a result, some Europeans have pushed for the continent to go it alone when enacting financial and economic regulation. An article in the German weekly *Die Zeit* by Uwe Jean Hauser was headlined "If Necessary, Without Obama" and said, "The good news is that the Europeans can regulate a lot by themselves." The E.U. should stop waiting for the United States and simply start requiring regulatory approval "of every new financial instrument." Europe can get away with this, wrote Hauser, because its economic size and might means that "foreign investors won't be able to avoid our continent."[34]

While the economic crisis—and the interventions tried by governments—remained a work in progress throughout 2009, some analysts began sounding a more upbeat note, musing that perhaps this economic crisis may further spur a more robust convergence of economic models between the United States and Europe. During the previous

Andrew Moravcsik, a professor of politics and international affairs at Princeton, suggested that Europe's example could cause some badly needed rethinking in the United States.

"Americans, especially conservatives, have a particular view of Europe as over-regulated, therefore suffering from weak growth and Eurosclerosis," he said. "This [crisis] could change that view, and create more respect for the European view of regulation more generally."[35]

Mario Monti, the former European commissioner in charge of tax policy and competition, seconded this view. "The crisis is leading countries embracing the Anglo-Saxon model, such as the U.S., the U.K. and Ireland, to reconsider some of its features," he wrote. "Perhaps they relied too much on market mechanisms and too little on regulation; overextended their financial industry while neglecting manufacturing; and did not care enough about inequalities and welfare systems. They now look with greater respect, as does China, at countries in Europe that have long followed social market economy models." Just as Europe moved in the last decade in the direction of less regulation and increased competitiveness, the Anglo nations should not feel embarrassed by their partial conversion, says Monti. "This convergence on the middle in domestic models gives the international community an unexpected political opportunity."[36]

Other observers also have glimpsed a potential for profound change spurred by crisis. "The progressive exhaustion of natural resources, climate change, public indebtedness: it's more likely that we are witnessing the rupture with a specific development model and mode of reasoning," wrote French philosopher Pierre Calame.[37] "We're going to have to enter a great transition to a sustainable society. The present crisis is structural and it calls for structural responses. The transition will take time because it involves a profound renewal of concepts, institutional agency and regulatory methods. If we undertake that today, we will make the crisis an opportunity." But this has been how Europe usually has evolved, in reaction to and out of the depths of crisis. The Jacques Delors Commission (1985–95) was able to achieve a dramatic extension of E.U. powers that helped to forge greater continental unity only after the last major phase of "euro-paralysis." Some analysts believe that as the European Union emerges from this latest crisis, the precedent set by coordinated treatment of the financial sector, along with arguments that the union needs more tools to do more in the fiscal sphere, may create the grounds for strengthening E.U. institutions.[38] "Progress in Europe is usually the result of a crisis," says Sylvester Eijffinger, a monetary expert advising the European Parliament during the economic meltdown. "This could be one of those rare moments in E.U. history."[39]

While this has been a time of deep economic crisis, Europe has shown its mettle, despite arguments to the contrary by the Euroskeptics. And during more normal times, the European continent has been economically vibrant with a marked ability to produce the most human-centered system in the world, just as its founders planned it in the aftermath of World War II. Europe is a remarkable testament to the power of well-designed institutions and their ability to channel human activity into peace and prosperity partnerships. For those Americans used to seeing media accounts with their continual yarn about the "sick man of Europe," this will come as a surprise.

One other crisis that also is in full swing and looms ever larger on the American horizon is that of health care. Health care costs in the United States are spiraling out of control and threaten the financial solvency of future generations, even as forty-seven million Americans remain without any health care other than a hospital emergency room. Europe has devised ways of health and health care that keep its populations fit and productive even while spending a lot less money for universal coverage than Americans spend for patchwork care. We turn now to an investigation of health and health care in Europe, to see what lessons America might learn.

HEALTHY EUROPE

THE EUROPEAN WAY OF HEALTH

When I think about health and health care in Europe, I don't think immediately about hospitals, doctors, and insurance premiums. Instead, I picture bike paths and walking trails crisscrossing the cities and countryside, and Europeans of all ages, including seniors, pedaling from town to home with their daily bread in their handlebar baskets. I picture health spas where people of all ages soak their limbs in the warm healing waters and steam baths. And I picture fields of organic grains and grasses tossing in the breeze and European gourmands with their "slow food" philosophy. I picture cheese, bread, and wine makers using the same time-tested formulas for their savory products that have been developed over centuries, and I picture Europeans strolling leisurely and lingering for hours over food and drink in outdoor cafés, hobnobbing at an unhurried pace. For many Europeans, health and *la dolce vita* are a passion, and those values are reflected in many aspects of their lives, including their formal health care systems.

One of the ironies of Europe is that, while it is leading the world in high-tech transportation innovations, such as high-speed bullet trains and fuel-efficient autos, it also specializes in low-tech options. Whether in Amsterdam, Prague, Berlin, Vienna, Paris, Stockholm, Oslo, Barcelona, or any of the thousands of small towns that dot the countryside, bicyclists and pedestrians are on the go.

Once when I was visiting Germany's Mosel Valley and its meandering landscape of vineyards, verdant riverfronts, and towering castles,

I was struck by the number of senior citizens pedaling along the bike paths on the side of the road. Their handlebar baskets held a few groceries. They were not out for a leisurely jaunt; this was their transportation for errands. When I was in Umeå, Sweden, a smallish city several hundred miles northeast of Stockholm, I saw the same thing: people of all ages, noticeably the elderly, pedaling their bikes around town and along the riverbank. Amsterdam has so many bicyclists that you have to be just as wary of bikes as of automobiles when you cross the street, particularly because bicyclists aren't as loud. In Rothenburg ob der Tauber, Germany, where I stayed once for several weeks, I went walking every afternoon along the numerous *Wanderwegs*—walking paths—that crisscrossed the brilliant yellow fields and blossoming hills. And I had plenty of company: it seemed that for many Germans, walking and bicycling are more than hobbies, they are a way of life.

Europeans seem to be literally biking and walking their way to health, and research bears this out. One study found that whereas walking and cycling account for less than a tenth of all urban trips in American cities, they account for a third of all such trips in Germany and an incredible half in the Netherlands. The average was 36 percent of all trips across eight different European countries, compared with 7 percent for the United States. Perhaps most striking are the large differences in transportation behavior among the older populations of various countries. Walking actually increases with age in both the Netherlands and Germany. The Dutch and Germans who are seventy-five and older make roughly half their trips by foot or bike, compared to only 6 percent of trips for Americans age sixty-five and older. Cycling is almost nonexistent among the American elderly, but it accounts for a fourth of all trips made by the Dutch elderly. This activity not only provides the Dutch and German elderly with valuable physical exercise, but it also assures them a level of mobility and independence that greatly enhances their quality of life.[1]

It also contributes to longer life expectancy. The European countries with the highest levels of walking and cycling have much lower rates of diabetes, hypertension, and obesity than the United States. The Netherlands, Denmark, and Sweden, for example, have obesity rates only a third of the U.S. rate, and Germany's rate is only half as high. Also, the average life expectancies in those four European countries are 2.5 to 4.4 years longer than the U.S. life expectancy, even though their per capita health expenditures are about half those of the United States.

public policy choices have made walking and cycling inconvenient, unpleasant, and, above all, unsafe. But in Europe, the most obvious symbol of better policy is the massive and ever-expanding network of bike paths, which provide separate rights-of-way for cyclists. From 1978 to 1996, the Dutch more than doubled the extent of their already extensive network of bike paths and lanes, and the Germans almost tripled theirs; Amsterdam alone has more than three hundred miles of bike lanes. One Dutch city has five bicycle parking garages, one of which can hold five thousand bikes. Just as important, the bike paths and lanes in the Netherlands and Germany form a truly integrated, coordinated network, covering both rural and urban areas. Unlike the fragmented cycling routes in the United States, Dutch and German bikeway systems serve practical destinations for everyday travel, not just recreational attractions for young cycling enthusiasts.

Other nations besides Germany and the Netherlands have embraced bicycling, both for its health benefits and to lower reliance on autos for transportation, especially in cities. In 2007, Paris followed the lead of Amsterdam and other cities and introduced a highly successful program that put over twenty thousand bicycles on the streets, rented from a thousand unmanned kiosks located around the city. The rental cost is about a dollar, plus a $200 deposit paid for with a credit card to ensure the bicycle's safe return. You rent the bicycle from one spot, ride it to work, and drop it at another kiosk nearby (and then your deposit is credited back). Commuters have taken to the program with enthusiasm, prompting one journalist to write that Paris, the land of the Tour de France, has gone "cycling mad."[2] These bike-sharing programs now can be found across the European continent, from Vienna to Barcelona, from Rome to Oslo.

Pedestrian-only zones have become so widespread that they can now be found in virtually every European city. In large cities, such zones often encompass much of the city center and the expansive public squares, providing sizable areas where pedestrians have their own right-of-way. Of utmost importance in a densely populated settlement, the square preserves a sense of openness and light in the living environment. Many of the main streets and cozy alleyways terminate at or crisscross the plaza, so the urban design literally channels the feng shui energy of the city into a focal point or hub, like a magnifying glass focuses sunlight. This gives a particular sense of space, an energy flow, to the living environment. The concept of a square is ancient, and for hundreds of years every European village had its own square or commons, and most still do. These ancient spaces still linger, even as they have been nearly decimated in the United States by the car culture and shopping malls.[3] Most American towns don't have a center anymore, and few American cities have a grand central plaza, though many have nice parks scattered here and there. But the disappearance of the central square is an unquantifiable loss, for this sense of the ancient harkens back to our deepest human longing for community and contact, of shared, womblike physical space as opposed to atomized and individualized space.

Besides the overall urban design, other features sensitive to the needs of pedestrians and bicyclists help create an environment friendly to them. These include extensive use of traffic-calming techniques in residential neighborhoods (speed bumps and narrow traffic lanes, for example),[4] rigorous traffic education of motorists, and strict enforcement of regulations protecting pedestrians and bicyclists. Dedicated pathways and route systems help insulate cyclists and pedestrians from motor vehicles, which are involved in most bicyclist and pedestrian deaths or injuries. Denis Baupin, the transportation chief of Paris responsible for the City of Light's hugely successful bicycle-sharing program, also has reduced auto speed limits to just nineteen miles an hour on a thousand streets and closed many to cars altogether. Baupin has changed the face of mobility in Paris, making it easier for pedestrians, bikers, and users of public transportation, and less accessible to car drivers.[5] All of these efforts are guided by a philosophy that recognizes that efficient and affordable low-tech transportation methods are crucial to the democratization of mobility.

But in the car-dominant United States, authorities have made only a few halfhearted attempts to improve pedestrian and cyclist safety, with most measures falling far short of the need if they cost much money or would inconvenience automobile drivers. Thus, a lack of political will and vision has prevented Americans from enjoying the health, transportation, and quality-of-life benefits that result from more walking and cycling and less car travel.

SLOW FOOD AND SLOW DOWN

When I think of health in Europe, I also think of a remarkable woman by the name of Renate Künast, who was the German minister of food,

food scares over mad cow disease and genetically modified foods. Künast mounted the bully pulpit to crack down on unsafe food production practices such as "animal cannibalism," which involves feeding slaughterhouse waste and guts such as blood, meat, fat, and bone meal to other livestock, a precarious practice still permitted in the United States.[6] She also promoted rigorous consumer protections, such as more comprehensive pesticide regulations and the use of mandatory food labeling, especially of genetically modified foods. Because of the efforts of leaders like Künast, when it comes to food safety the European Union operates according to the "precautionary principle." That means if there is a scientific suspicion that something *could* cause harm, Europeans don't wait until they have 100 percent proof before taking preventative action. In weighing the benefits to society against the costs to industry, Europe and the United States set dramatically different priorities. While Europe's agricultural sector has its own special interests and lobbyists to contend with, the situation is nothing like that in the United States, where a revolving door has existed between government agencies such as the Food and Drug Administration and the Environmental Protection Agency and corporations such as Monsanto.[7]

More broadly, Künast and others within the European Union have promoted a new philosophy of food and health, with a special emphasis on organic agriculture. I saw Künast speak at a conference in Berlin and afterward had the opportunity to chat with her. Her philosophy was simple and rather Nader-like: consumers, not the agro industry, should be the key decision makers when it comes to mixing technology with the food supply. "We need to change our attitude to food and understand the close links between food and landscape, food and nature, and food and health," she told me. "Putting consumers first is the key to reshaping globalization." Künast, a leader in Germany's Green Party, made this attitude one of the pillars of Germany's agricultural policy and, by extension, that of Europe.

Out of Italy comes a complementary movement called Slow Food, dedicated to preserving and supporting traditional ways of growing, producing, and even preparing food. As its name implies, this movement is meant to be the antithesis of the fast food industry, emphasizing slow preparation of food from freshly picked ingredients—otherwise known as "cooking," an increasingly infrequent activity in the fast food–dominated United States. The preparation and quality of food and drink are revered like a quasi-religion, and the movement has adopted the snail as its official symbol. As a result of these food movements, which embody the famous maxim "We are what we eat," European consumers have become more knowledgeable, discriminating, and health and environmentally conscious. Food movements that strongly advocate the labeling of food and oppose genetically modified foods have spread across Europe and acquired a degree of political power and popularity.

In particular, food movements have led to a much stronger emphasis on organic food production, making it one of the pillars of the European Union's agricultural policy. Organic farming means an end to the use of artificial fertilizers, pesticides, and other toxic chemicals on crops and in the food supply. Instead, organic farming uses natural fertilizers and various farming techniques to deal with pest control. Since the beginning of the 1990s, organic farming has grown rapidly in almost all European countries. As of 2007, 6.7 million hectares in Europe were managed organically by over 189,000 farms, 3.5 percent of Europe's agricultural area. The United States, by contrast, has only 0.2 percent of its agricultural land area under organic production.[8] In Austria, more than 14 percent of agricultural land is organic, 11 percent in Switzerland, 8 percent in Italy, 6 percent in the Czech Republic, and 5 percent in Germany.[9] In Germany, all the major supermarket chains offer organic foodstuffs, and in many European nations baby food is produced almost exclusively from organic ingredients, since infants are more vulnerable to pesticides and toxins in food. Much of this recent development has been driven by official E.U. policy promoting organic agriculture, specifically the 2004 launch of the European Action Plan for Organic Food and Farming. Most European nations have ambitious goals to expand organic agricultural production, including Sweden's and Austria's goals of reaching 20 percent and 30 percent, respectively, by 2012.[10]

Complementary to slow food, an agrarian outlook is still very much a signature part of the European identity. The European countryside, with its sun-washed hills and ancient hilltop villages, is achingly beautiful, and a glance out the train window on approach to many European cities reveals how deeply embedded this agrarian mentality is. Encircling the urban zone in a kind of pastoral ring, the casual traveler sees a patchwork of community and individual garden plots, known in German as *Schrebergarten*. A multitude of neatly ordered and colorful

cal. A clutter of rakes, hoes, and stacks of flower pots lean against trellises and the sides of gardening huts. A cross-section of Europeans—all walks and ages—till their gardens, unhurriedly plunging their fingers into the dark, rich soil.

These urban ring gardens rose in importance during World Wars I and II as sources of otherwise hard-to-get fresh fruit and vegetables. After the Second World War, a lack of housing resulted in families erecting small structures on the plots for shelter. Today, those small structures look like miniature houses amidst a patchwork of garden colonies, where a family might spend the afternoon on a sunny day to escape the city. Sometimes when the weather is warm, you can see entire families gathered at their pea patches, gardening, barbecuing, and enjoying the sunshine. This is a deeply cherished part of Europe's ecological heritage and partly explains why Europeans still cling to heavy government subsidies for agriculture and rural communities, an attitude that greatly complicates international negotiations over the Common Agricultural Policy (CAP). It is a part of who they are.

Slow food goes hand in hand with a philosophy of "slow pace." Many Americans I met who are living in Europe talk about how the pace of living differs between Americans and Europeans. The Europeans are fond of saying, "To Americans, one hundred years is a long time; to Europeans, one hundred miles is a long way." Those differences in attitude play out in interesting ways. In Europe people still enjoy unhurried pleasures, whether food, drink, art, architecture, saunas, or strolling or bicycling along their meandering pathways. While Europe is fully modern, sometimes it feels as if it is caught in a nineteenth-century time warp, or like a land of Tolkien's hobbits, purposefully so. Living environments are more humane and well planned, with their magnificent public plazas that create such a sublime sense of openness.

When I was driving with my friend Meredith through Castres, a town east of Toulouse, in southwestern France, I noticed that the city center was quiet, with stores shuttered and hardly any foot traffic even though it was about 1:30 P.M. on a workday. Meredith said that was because a lot of workers and students go home for lunch; having lunch at home, not at the workplace or school, is part of the French sense of family and pacing. "That's why you see three commute times a day here instead of two," she said. "One in the morning, one at midday, and one in the evening. About 1:50 P.M. you can see all the cars and bicycles coming back into town to return to work or school by 2 P.M. Talk about family values. The French timetable is soooo different from the U.S." One can say the same about the Spanish, with their midday siestas, or the Germans, whose shops close in the middle of the day; many still close on Sundays as well.

Says Carlo Petrini, Italian founder of the Slow Food movement and one of the high priests of the canon, "The art of living is about learning how to give time to each and every thing. But if I have sacrificed my life to speed, then that is impossible. . . . Ultimately, 'slow' means to take the time to reflect. It means to take the time to think. It is useless to force the rhythms of life."[11] Slow food, slow pace, afternoon siestas, long, languid dinners, they're all quintessentially European—and part of a refined conception of sanity and health.

But then, it makes sense that a society that values its people enough to give everyone quality health care, sick leave, a decent retirement, parental leave, child care, adequate vacation and leisure time, and other family-centered supports also would value having a slower pace of life and nutritious home-cooked meals and would create an infrastructure, like bike and pedestrian paths and time schedules, to support that way of life. In so many ways the European Way reflects a philosophy that values health, family, and quality of life.

A CULTURE OF HEALTH

When I think of health in Europe, I also think of *bads*. No, not "bad," as in the opposite of "good," but *bads* (pronounced like "bods")—the German name for what Americans call health spas. Spas in the United States tend to be for affluent people and are mostly located in exclusive hotels, but in Europe they are for everybody and are located in large public facilities. They are very family-oriented environments, with not only hot tubs and saunas but also swimming pools and water slides, where the children as well as adults cavort. Upstairs are the saunas, where the adults don't wear clothes of any kind, even bathing suits, a bit of a shock to most Americans, who are not used to seeing so many naked bodies of all ages, shapes, and sizes. But in the saunas it feels perfectly normal. The cost to use the facilities is government subsidized and very reasonable. In the Czech Republic, which has a per capita income less than half that of the United States, health insurance covers visits to spas that help arthritis, joint injuries, or respiratory problems. Compare that with the United States, where even in a progressive com-to soothe their aching joints and maintain their limb flexibility. Penny wise and pound foolish, as they say.[12]

Health spas have been common in Europe for two thousand years, dating back to the Romans. Today, all across Germany you can see dozens of towns with names like Bad Mergentheim, Bad Reichenhall, Wiesbaden, and Baden-Baden; in France, instead of *bad* they use the term *bain*, and you can see dozens of towns with related names: Aix-les-Bains, Évian-les-Bains, and Digne-les-Bains. These towns are more than simply spa facilities; they are places where the entire town, historically, has been visited for health reasons to "take the waters." People from all around come to soak in the hydrothermal springs that leak from the earth in those parts and are claimed to have health and healing properties. Saunas have been important in Scandinavian cultures also, and most European countries are dotted by numerous spa towns. Europeans are serious about their spas; they are a defining part of who they are.

This kind of dedication to health and bodies is obvious across the continent, although it manifests in different ways from place to place. In Norway, this somatic aesthetic has been elevated to the high canon of an art form—literally. Oslo is a land of sculpture, and every park, many street corners, even private dwellings, seem to be studded with sculptures, old and new, traditional and modern, with a fair number of them showing naked figures, reflecting the Norwegian sensibility that reveling in the flesh is a sign of health, not license. This refreshing esteem for human bodies shorn of pretense and artifice is expressed in surprising ways.

One day in Oslo I saw the front page of a daily newspaper with a huge color photo showing ten bust-baring, smiling women. But this was not a Hugh Hefner product or a Rupert Murdoch, page-three cheese-cake photo, like those that marinate many British dailies. No, most of these women were at least sixty years old, many of them older, and wizened. A new form of erotica for the elderly, I wondered? Hardly. Each of the women was missing one of her breasts. All of them were breast-cancer survivors, it turned out, who were unabashedly sharing their stories during a week of breast-cancer awareness. And their topless group photo was right there on the front page of a major daily newspaper, surgical scars and all. These modern-day Amazons smiled into the camera unashamedly, fearlessly, because health and naked bodies are Norwegian values that are inextricably entwined.[13] There is something about it that smacks one as being very balanced, sane, and, well, healthy.

The apotheosis of these cultural representations of health and the human body are the astonishing Vigeland sculptures located in Oslo's Frogner Park. My first encounter with the Vigeland sculptures was near to a religious experience, basking in the presence of genius. The park contains 192 separate sculptures with more than 600 human figures, all life-size or larger, by the brilliant sculptor Gustav Vigeland. Vigeland expertly rendered his human figures, casting them into bronze or carving them in granite, over a period of nearly four decades, between 1907 and 1942. The outstanding signature of his monumental body of work is the way the hundreds of sculpted men, women, and children are portrayed in various stages of life—male and female adults, young adults, adolescents, toddlers and infants, even a fetus, and finally the elderly and a decomposing skeleton of death. The entire cycle of life is represented, from birth through adolescence through maturation to demise, in all its multiple joys, sadness, and eternalness. All of the sculptures are naked, not a stitch of clothing on any of them, yet the display is all modest and appropriately engaging, not lurid in the least. The females are sturdy and solid, the males robust but tender. Male and female genitalia are in abundance. The figures are frequently clustered together in allegorical groups, showing adolescents playing leapfrog, or a mother and father with their child, or a mother with her son or a father with his daughter; or two bodies linked in a sort of yin-yang apposition, or two lovers in a state of bliss, foreheads touching tenderly, and another two lovers in a state of conflict. Some of the figures are arrayed around a large, grand fountain portraying the cycles of our lives, others line up evenly on either side of a bridge. Still others are scaling a giant granite obelisk jutting into the sky, and they are writhing but not in despair, like those in Rodin's *Gates of Hell*. Instead there is a sense of togetherness, of carefully supporting one another, on their way toward some kind of resurrection or salvation at the summit, which is covered by sculptures of small children.

I walked among these nearly two hundred sculptures as if through a forest of human bodies, overwhelmed and awed. Vigeland's artistic achievement is on the scale and magnitude of Michelangelo's Sistine Chapel, Gaudí's La Sagrada Família, and Monet's Water Lilies series. While his sculptures have not received the recognition of those famous works, they are nothing less than an artistic giant's monument to

tiple forms. The Vigeland sculptures are unmistakably ideological in that they represent a celebration of our bodies, female and male, and a celebration of the cult of life as opposed to the cult of death which ravages so much of our oversexed, overly violent media and world. Something about the Vigeland Sculpture Park struck me as distinctly Scandinavian, and European as well, in the sense that it was about health and vitality, a particular idiom of *la dolce vita*, infused with the mentality of slow food, organic agriculture, urban gardens, and bike paths, but in this case manifesting as these magnificent concrete expressions in granite and bronze. And it was about not only bodies but bodies that are au naturel, lacking embarrassment or modesty, yet not salacious, their nakedness just a normal part of life—like something you would see in a sauna or *bad*, come to think of it.

The Vigeland sculptures are a source of great pride for Norwegians. This was apparent when I mentioned the subject to one stoic taxi driver, a typical older Norwegian who had white-streaked hair and a chiseled chin, wore square aviator eyeglasses, and gave one-word or one-line responses and an occasional smile. But his face lit up when I praised the Vigeland sculptures. "Thank you," he smiled more widely, bowing slightly but in a prideful way that meant he thanked me on behalf of his country.

These were just a few of the many manifestations of the attitudes and policies toward health that I found in Europe. Sometimes the Europeans really do remind me of hobbits, with a love of leisure, nature, relaxation, good food, a stimulating glass of wine or dark, earthy beer, and steeped in the values of health, family, and quality of life. It is these values and this outlook that they bring to their workfare system and their social capitalism, instilled into them in both intent and design. It's also the values they inject into their formal health care system, which we now turn to in the next chapter.

EIGHT

LA SANTÉ D'ABORD

The Formal Health Care System

It's not surprising that nations that have produced such amazing cultural artifacts and testaments to the importance of health and bodies have also produced a pretty darn good system of formal health care. Especially when compared with the costly and fractured U.S. health care system.

The multipolar world of the twenty-first century is going to be more economically and geopolitically competitive than the post–World War II world that the United States dominated, and in which most of today's adult Americans formed their self-identity. A price will be paid for inefficiency and wastefulness in all parts of the economy. A health care system that leaves forty-seven million people—over 15 percent of the population—without coverage and more than one-third of Americans without health insurance for long periods of time will undermine American competitiveness. Not only does this system result in a workforce that is less healthy, it also hurts the businesses that provide health care for their employees and are facing escalating costs and rising tensions with their employees over who bears responsibility for health care.[1]

Our health care system also is immoral, given our nation's great wealth. Even the moderately poor and formerly communist countries in eastern and central Europe have universal health care. In the Czech Republic, the government was nearly toppled when it wanted to introduce a co-payment of less than two dollars per office visit, because

showing America's poor performance when it comes to infant mortality, life expectancy, the number of physicians, hospital beds, medical errors, high out-of-pocket expenses, and much more,[3] it is hardly surprising that the World Health Organization (WHO) has ranked the United States 72nd of 191 countries for "level of health" and 37th for "overall health system performance," just behind Costa Rica and Dominica and just ahead of Slovenia and Cuba, countries with a fraction of our wealth.[4] France and Italy, which have universal health care coverage for all their residents, even recent immigrants, were ranked first and second in the WHO listing. Many other European nations also were ranked near the top.

Yet, despite this difference in performance between the U.S. and European systems, somehow Europe manages to spend only a fraction of what we in the United States spend on health care. According to WHO, the U.S. spends 16.5 percent of our economy on health care, about $6,100 per person, compared with an average 8.6 percent in European countries. France spends far less, just $3,500 per person, or 10.7 percent of its economy.[5] The difference—6 to 8 percent of economic output—suggests that the waste in the U.S. system comes to nearly a trillion dollars per year. Says Dr. Christopher Murray, director of WHO's Global Program on Evidence for Health Policy, "Basically, you die earlier and spend more time disabled if you're an American rather than a member of most other advanced countries."[6] That's the state of health care for the world's lone remaining superpower.

How do the French, Italians, and other European countries manage so well? How do they provide better health care to their people than most Americans receive and for about half the per capita cost? While certain details differ from nation to nation, we can also find some broad generalities to point to. These give us a pretty good snapshot that should be instructive to the United States as we grapple with our own inefficiencies that continue to hurt American workers and businesses and increasingly will hurt our competitiveness in the global economy.

HEALTH CARE FOR PEOPLE, NOT PROFITS

The first overriding difference between the American and European health care systems is one of philosophy. The various European health care systems put people and their health before profits—*la santé d'abord*, "health comes first," as the French are fond of saying. In Europe, health care is run mostly as a nonprofit venture with the goal of keeping people healthy and working, compared with the U.S. approach of running health care as a for-profit commercial enterprise. It's no coincidence that as America tries to grapple with soaring health care costs and lack of universal coverage, UnitedHealth Group CEO William McGuire received an obscene $124.8 million in compensation in 2005.[7] He's just one of many grossly overcompensated kingpins of the U.S. health care industry. The health care industry's profits were up 34 percent in 2006 from the previous year, led by UnitedHealth Group's $4 billion in profits, which was a 26 percent increase.[8] Even allegedly "nonprofit" insurers like Kaiser and Blue Cross Blue Shield rake in huge profits and pay out multimillion dollar CEO salaries.[9] Health care corporations will spout platitudes about wanting to provide good service for their customers, but there's no escaping the bottom-line reality that the CEOs of giant health corporations ultimately are accountable to one small group—their stockholders.

One subtle but revealing example of how this difference in philosophy and goals manifests itself is how medical information is used. In Europe, patients provide as much personal medical history as they can to assist their doctor in making an accurate diagnosis leading to the best treatment. But in the United States, your personal medical history can be used against you by the insurance companies in a game of "gotcha" to deny treatment—the famous "preexisting condition clause." So the patient has incentive to withhold information from the doctor or to manipulate it to the point of lying in order to fool the insurance bureaucracy and receive service, which can contribute to a misdiagnosis and medical error. The fact is, the highly profitable corporate insurance companies that dominate the American system, such as UnitedHealth Group, have a motive to provide as little care as possible, because providing care cuts into their profits; at the same time, they charge as much as possible to increase profits. If a society's goal is to achieve personal and public health, the incentives and values in the American profit-motivated system reveal themselves over and over to be illogical and perverse. The extravagant executive pay and profits of private insurance and drug companies are revealed to be contrary to any concept of "public health." Providing quality health care and maximizing profits pull in opposite directions, like two yoked oxen.

Once a health care system with the proper values is in place, the rest becomes relatively straightforward and leads to impressive results.

often picked as the top places. In those countries, health care is affordable and comprehensive, with short wait times for services, including
surgery, even shorter waits than in the United States. Patients are free
to choose their doctors, most of whom are in private practice, and
they have no limits on the number of services covered.[10] I met many,
many people who each told his or her own version of the following
scenarios.

One American friend told about having arrived in Paris with his
family to begin teaching constitutional law in a French university.
Within a few days, his daughter developed a severe earache, and they
knew practically no one. He was instructed to call a particular phone
number for medical help, although he had no idea what to expect.
What happened next still leaves him marveling.

"A doctor arrived at my door in thirty minutes, diagnosed the problem in ten minutes, and wrote a prescription to be filled at the local
drugstore. The earache was gone within a couple of days." The whole
affair, including having the prescription filled, cost him about sixty
dollars, out of pocket. "And that's for perfect strangers in Paris, with
no membership in their health organization. Can you imagine? A house
call?" He also received ready help when he had trouble with his wisdom teeth and no French dental insurance. The charge? Around $100
for the service.

An American expatriate living in Belgium told me that both he and
his sister in Minneapolis had a procedure called a catheter ablation
of the heart, to eliminate an irregular heartbeat. She, with full medical coverage from her employer, spent $2,400 out of pocket for the
procedure, which was performed with a mild sedative in an outpatient
facility. For the same procedure in Belgium, he paid just under $100
and received the full royal treatment, including two nights in the hospital for observation and post-op recovery. The medicine he now needs
to take costs him about four dollars for a three-week supply, but in
the United States that same medicine costs his sister nineteen dollars,
nearly five times as much.

THE FRENCH TAKE THE GOLD

France's health care system, rated by the United Nation's World Health
Organization as the best in the world, is a good one to study more

closely, to see how the French produce affordable, comprehensive, and quality health care for their sixty-two million people. Whatever other difficulties France may suffer, including a restless population of young minorities and immigrants, all of the French have access to good health care. Yet France spends far less than the United States to achieve that.[11]

Contrary to stereotypes portrayed in the American media, France and many other European nations do not use what is commonly known as "socialized medicine" or "single payer" health care. Under single payer, the principal source of funding is general taxation and the centralized system is mostly owned and operated by the national or local governments, which establish price levels and cost controls. In most cases the doctors, nurses, and medical bureaucracy work for the government, and hospitals usually are government run. Britain uses a single payer system, as do Sweden, Denmark, Finland, Norway, Spain, and Canada (except that in Canada most doctors and nurses work for private health organizations). But France, as well as Belgium, Germany, Austria, Switzerland, the Netherlands, and many other European nations, does not use single payer.

Instead, France and these other nations have health care systems based on the principle of "shared responsibility" among workers, employers, and the government, all of which contribute their fair share to guarantee universal coverage, reasonable costs, and quality care. Participation for individuals is mandatory, not optional, just as a driver's license is mandatory for driving an auto. Also, the backbone of the French system is private insurance companies, as in the United States, and most French doctors and nurses work in private practices or for private health organizations, not for the government. There's no "in-network" or "pre-authorization"; you can pick any doctor or hospital and be covered by your health insurance. Doctors are required to post their prices on the wall of the waiting room, so the unaccountability of American-style medical billing is removed.

But here's the real critical difference: unlike the insurance companies in the United States, which are huge, profit-seeking corporations, the French insurance companies are *nonprofits*. There are three of them, called Sickness Insurance Funds, or SIFs, with national headquarters and regional networks. These funds are financed by compulsory payroll deductions that amount to 13 percent of employees' wages, with employers paying 70 percent of this amount and employees the other 30 percent (much like Americans have wages deducted for Social Security). However, French employers contribute a smaller amount toward their health care.[12]

An average worker making $35,000 per year will pay approximately $114 per month to have full access to the excellent French health care system, and the employer will pay $265. For those who cannot afford to pay their share, the government makes up their amount, allowing the poor to have full access to doctors, hospitals, and clinics, free of charge if necessary. An underlying principle of France's system is that those who earn less also pay less, whereas high-income earners pay more.

The second key difference between the French and U.S. health care systems is cost controls. As in the U.S. system of Medicare, charges for services in France are negotiated among representatives of the health care professions (doctors, nurses, etc.), the government, patient consumer representatives, and the three principal SIFs. Together they establish a national agreement for treatment procedures, fee structures, and rate ceilings that prevent health care costs from spiraling out of control.[13] For some services patients may pay a small out-of-pocket fee, and the average charge for an office visit, whether to a general practitioner or to a specialist, is around twenty dollars. These kinds of government-regulated price controls keep cost levels well below those in the United States. That's not only good for health care consumers, it's also good for French businesses, since they are paying less money for their employees' health care and can forecast with greater assurance their health care costs. In fact, because America has nothing like these sorts of price controls (outside Medicare), some of Europe's drug companies make one-third of their profits in the U.S. market, where they can sell their prescription drugs for a lot more money than they can in their own countries. Sometimes the same tablet made in the same factory costs a dollar in the U.S. and twenty cents in Europe.[14]

Those are the key elements of the French "shared responsibility" health care system, including nonprofit insurance companies and negotiated price controls, which is ranked first in the world in "overall health system performance" and fourth in "level of health."[15] Yet France spends only a fraction per capita of what the United States spends. One Paris taxi driver told me he pays about $725 per month for himself, his wife, and his three children to have health care, and then he pays a small co-payment for some services. Compare that with what a U.S. family pays in health insurance premiums, which reached an average of $14,545 in 2006, about $1,212 per month, more than doubling the

2001 average. The taxi driver, an Algerian-descended Muslim, said that the French health care service was excellent. Generally speaking you don't hear too many of the French complaining about their health care (though they will give you an earful on other subjects regarding the shortcomings of their government). Their first-class health care system is a great source of pride for the French, as are the systems of Belgium, Austria, Switzerland, and others for their people. Health care is viewed by most people as a vital part of the internal glue that makes their societies stick together, an essential element of solidarity and fairness to all.

In various European nations, individuals who can afford it increasingly are purchasing supplemental private insurance for extra services. One Austrian colleague told me that in addition to the monthly amount deducted from his paycheck for health care, he pays about seventeen dollars per month for extra hospital insurance, so that if he ends up in the hospital he is in a room by himself or with no more than one other patient, instead of in a large room with the general patient population. If he has not used this hospitalization insurance after twelve months of paying this monthly premium, he receives a rebate of three months of the premium. Most countries are adapting to new challenges and rising costs by making themselves flexibly modular in that way, so that those who wish can purchase more services, but everyone enjoys a high level of guaranteed services.

When one's health care system isn't so obsessed with raking in high profits for the usual corporate-type CEOs and operatives, delivery of services is liberated to develop in other commonsense ways. One American living in Albi, near Toulouse, France, talks about how gynecology in France is the best in the world. His French wife was a gynecologist, and he says French gynecologists will treat the same family for generations. He says his wife had four generations of one family as patients—the grandmother, mother, daughter, and granddaughter. "This is not uncommon," he adds.

Germany's health care system, like France's, also is not a single payer system but is a "shared responsibility" type of system in which Germans pay into nonprofit, government-regulated sickness insurance funds. The risk and cost are shared by all—universally—with those who earn less paying less, those who earn more paying more. "The principle is that the rich pay for the poor, the young for the old, the healthy for the sick," says Ulla Schmidt, Germany's federal minister of health. "Our funding is based on the concept of solidarity. This means

receive benefits that correspond to their needs."[16]

Despite spending only about 55 percent per capita of what the U.S. spends on health care, Germany still gets much better results for the eighty-two million Germans who use it. Germans contribute 6–7 percent of their salary for health care, and the employer also contributes 6–7 percent of the worker's salary, which, as in France, is a much smaller share than is paid by U.S. employers.[17] So a worker making $35,000 per year pays about $190 per month, which is also what the employer pays. Unlike France, which only has three SIFs, Germany has over two hundred of them, and the SIFs cover 92 percent of the German population, with a small number of the population covered by private, for-profit insurance.[18] Like French physicians, most German physicians are not salaried employees of the government but rather are in private practice and paid on a fee-for-service basis. Representatives of the SIFs negotiate with the regional associations of physicians, nurses, and other health care professionals—along with patient representatives who are given a seat at the table—to determine treatment procedures, prices, and rate ceilings, preventing costs from spiraling. As in France, this system is better not only for individuals and families but also for German businesses, since it makes their costs lower than in the U.S. and allows them to better forecast and plan their health care costs.

Interestingly, a move has been afoot in the United States to try a watered-down version of the German and French health care systems based on shared responsibility. Presidential candidate Hillary Clinton proposed such a plan, as did Governor Arnold Schwarzenegger in California. In 2007 Massachusetts actually passed a variant of this system, becoming the first state to create an "individual mandate" requiring its citizens to purchase health insurance. But the Clinton, California, and Massachusetts plans all have several major defects compared with those used by France, Germany, and other European nations. They all allowed their insurance companies to remain for-profit instead of nonprofit, and also they did not include a mechanism for negotiating fees or any other form of cost controls. They are depending on an unproven theory that bringing younger and healthier people into the overall health care pool by making health insurance mandatory will help pull down health care costs. But it hasn't worked. Economist Paul Krugman has written that the Massachusetts plan "has done little to address the fundamental problem of a fragmented system, and as a result has done little to control rising health care costs."[19] It will remain impossible to bring down skyrocketing costs as long as the profit-seeking insurance companies have an incentive to increase premiums and deny treatment. And those individuals in Massachusetts now mandated to purchase health care are stuck footing the bill for escalating insurance premiums, an expense that many cannot afford. Consequently, two years after passage of the Massachusetts law, roughly half of the uninsured remained without coverage, despite the individual mandate and major state spending.[20]

Another defect in the Massachusetts plan is that while it is mandatory for individuals to purchase health care, unlike in France and Germany it is not mandatory for businesses to contribute their fair share. Massachusetts businesses only need to pay a small token amount per employee into a government fund. Some health care experts are predicting that rising health care premiums eventually will force more and more Massachusetts employers to drop coverage of their employees, opting instead to pay the government's token amount. That will leave the state picking up the tab for more and more individuals, which in turn will increase the likelihood that state coffers will be drained by continuing cost increases that put taxpayers' money into insurance company coffers, making the program unsustainable.[21]

As many experts have pointed out, cost containment is the real linchpin of any successful health care reform. But Massachusetts and California swept that contentious issue under the rug because dealing with costs meant taking on the insurance companies. As we saw above, in the French and German systems insurance companies are nonprofit and government-regulated, with prices and fees negotiated between all the stakeholders. But in the American system even the so-called nonprofits are huge corporations that make obscene profits and pay outrageously high salaries to their executives because of the unregulated, for-profit environment.

The lesson here is, if you are going to copy the French or German system, you can't do it part way. While universal coverage is a major goal, cost containment must be part of any attempt to fix health care in the United States. Otherwise you just lock in place a system that has the United States paying twice as much per capita for health care as most other nations. And real cost containment means reining in the profit-hungry insurance companies. If nothing else, the U.S. health care system provides a salutary lesson illustrating that corporate profits and universal health care are not a viable mix.

Germany has incorporated an innovation into its health care system that has great potential for cost savings and boosting the quality of care. This innovation, which the Obama administration has pledged to emulate, involves using electronic medical records and laptop computers with specially designed software that allows for much better tracking of medical care and diagnosis. This in turn leads to a marked decrease in the types of medical errors and misdiagnoses that a study in 2000 found had resulted in up to ninety-eight thousand hospital deaths each year in the United States, a scandalous 4 percent of all annual deaths. So this is an area where the United States has much to learn.

German doctors enter their orders and prescriptions into a computer that immediately checks them against the patient's records. If the various doctors working with a patient have prescribed an inappropriate combination of medicines, the computer sends up a red flag. When hospital pharmacists fill the prescription, the computer system generates a bar code that goes on the bottle and registers what the medicine is, who its recipient is, when it should be administered, and in what dose. Each patient also has an ID bracelet with its own bar code, and so does each nurse. Before administering any drug, a nurse must first scan the patient's ID bracelet, then her or his own, and then the bar code on the medicine. If the nurse has the wrong patient or the wrong medicine, the computer will sound an alert. The computer will also generate a report if the nurse is late in administering a dose and can track an end-to-end trail of service.

With everything computerized, in an instant doctors or nurses can see not only all of the patient's latest data but also a complete medical record going back years, including records of care performed in any other hospital or clinic, anywhere in Germany. Also, patients can access their own complete medical records from their home computers or give permission for others to do so, allowing adult children to help their aging parents in a way never before possible.

Ironically, Germany learned much of this innovation from the unlikeliest of sources—the U.S. Veterans Health Administration. In the 1990s, VHA hospitals were known as dangerous, dirty, and scandal ridden, but according to several studies today they are producing the highest-quality care in the United States.[22] The VHA developed its "laptop medicine" using state-of-the-art software that allows for the best tracking and medical diagnosis in the entire health care industry. The software plays a key role in preventing medical errors and medication mistakes that can lead to tragedy. The VHA was able to identify within minutes which of its patients were on Vioxx when that popular arthritis medication was recalled. In the midst of a nationwide shortage of flu vaccine, the system allowed the VHA to identify which patients were in greatest need and to prioritize those patients.

Germany, as well as public health care systems in Finland, France, and elsewhere, tried out the VHA system, with the software made available free of charge. Germany was so impressed with its trial of electronic records that it took a giant step—it created a nationwide electronic health system that links all eighty-two million Germans, more than a hundred thousand office-based physicians, twenty-two thousand pharmacies, twenty-two hundred hospitals, and roughly three hundred private and statutory health insurers. Says health minister Schmidt, "Every physician—anywhere in Germany—will have easy access to the health details of their patients and be able to avoid treatment errors. By providing better information while reducing paperwork, it will serve to avoid errors and generate major savings." This will also contribute greatly to better coordination of treatment. (Security precautions to protect the privacy of individual medical records have been built into the system.)[23] Similarly in France, every person now has a green plastic card, the *carte d'assurance maladie*, that has completely replaced paper billing and medical records, contributing to low administrative costs of 3 percent, compared to 25 percent in the U.S.[24]

Dr. David Brailer, national coordinator for health care information technology under President George W. Bush, estimated that if the U.S. health care system as a whole would adopt electronic medical records and computerized prescription orders it would save as much as 2 percent of gross domestic product and also dramatically improve the quality of care. Despite the obvious benefits, America's corporate health care system has proven incapable of implementing these innovations, with only about 17 percent of the nation's physicians using computerized patient records.[25] President Obama has made this a priority of his administration, and his February 2009 fiscal stimulus package included billions of dollars for improved health information technology, yet the challenges are daunting. Why? As Lawrence Casalino, a professor of public health at the University of Chicago, puts it, "The U.S. medical market as presently constituted simply does not provide a strong business case for quality."[26] Translated, that means that in America's very decentral-

care corporations don't easily share records, the VHA model has been impossible to copy. But in Germany and France, where the philosophy is "health care for people, not for profits," the VHA-invented system could be adopted on a nationwide basis.

HEALTH CARE, PAST, PRESENT, AND FUTURE

Organized health care systems that benefited the greater population barely existed a century ago. In the 1880s Germany's chancellor Otto von Bismarck began fashioning what was to become the world's first rudimentary workfare support system in which the government assumed a degree of responsibility for the social and economic welfare of its people. Bismarck's reasoning was not all that altruistic: he was trying to let some of the air out of the balloon that was giving a lift to labor unions and revolutionary socialist forces. So Germany enacted a law requiring employers to make contributions to health coverage for low-wage workers in certain occupations, adding other classes of workers in subsequent years. This was the first example of a state-mandated health insurance model.

Today's health systems are modeled to varying degrees on one or more of a few basic designs that emerged in the nineteenth and twentieth centuries and have been refined since then. There are three basic models of health care in the developed world today. The two just discussed are the single payer, or socialized, system, in which health care services and facilities mostly are government owned and operated, and the shared-responsibility system, in which services are provided by private, nonprofit insurance companies and funded by mandatory payroll deductions from employers and employees. Both have cost controls built in, and both are universal; that is, they give every individual access to all health care services.

The third model, represented by the United States, is mostly a privatized system. Instead of taxes or revenue pooling, shared by all, private funding accounts for a much bigger share of total health care spending. Most workers and their families have been insured privately through their employer or their own individual plan, with the elderly and the extremely poor receiving publicly funded health care (from Medicare and Medicaid). But the number of employers providing health care coverage to their employees has been dwindling, while health care contributions by individuals and families have escalated. Employers who still provide coverage have pushed more of their costs onto their employees through either higher premium deductions or lower wages. Consequently, huge gaps in coverage exist in this patchwork, privatized system. Since 2000, workers' health care contributions for family coverage have increased by 102 percent.[27] Everyone is feeling squeezed, with the only winners being the profit-soaked insurance companies and to some extent U.S. doctors, who are generally highly paid compared to their European counterparts.[28] The U.S. health care industry rakes in billions of dollars in profits each year, and with profit margins like those, it's not hard to figure out why costs are escalating and why it is so hard to enact substantive reforms.

Some defenders of American health care rebut criticisms by saying that most white upper- and middle-class Americans have good health care, that the problem is really among poor people and minorities—a rebuttal that seems to dismiss the poor and minorities as undeserving of quality health care. However, studies comparing the United States with other countries show how *all* Americans, even white and affluent Americans, are lagging behind their international counterparts. For example, while infant mortality among poor Americans is double the rate among the wealthy, astoundingly the rate for the *wealthiest* quintile of the U.S. population is higher than the rate for Canadians in the *lowest* quintile of wealth.[29] And a large international study led by the Rand Corporation, using samples limited to whites and excluding recent immigrants in order to control for racial and ethnic factors, found that middle-age people in Britain are "much healthier" than their U.S. counterparts, even though the United States spends twice as much money per capita as the United Kingdom on health care.[30]

One commonsense yardstick for measuring the relative merits of different nations' health care systems has been called "the heart attack question": If I have a heart attack, are my chances of survival better in the United States than in other countries? The answer is a decided "no." The best place to have a heart attack is Japan if you are a man, France if you are a woman. The United States ranks only twenty-second for men and twenty-third for women among industrialized nations, according to the American Heart Association.[31]

Some Americans reading such a negative profile of U.S. health care won't recognize their own situations in it. That's because the quality of health care in the United States's patchwork system depends greatly on your income level and job situation. If you are the president of the United States or a member of Congress—whose European-level benefits

Apple, Chevron, or some other profitable corporation, you have some of the best health care in human history, with access to extremely sophisticated medical technology. But the American middle class meanwhile is stuck in a casino of medical care, as increasingly many businesses scale back their commitment to their workers' health, and as insurance companies devise ever more clever ways to deny services and increase premiums. And of course if you are an American who is poor, a member of a minority, or from the most rural areas, you have health care worse than that of Croatia or Cuba.

Even many of those who are fortunate enough to have health insurance lack basics found in other nations, such as annual physicals, prescription drug benefits, dental care, eye care, and an absence of "pre-existing condition" clauses. My aging parents, like most Americans their age, receive their primary insurance through Medicare, and I was shocked to find that Medicare doesn't provide an annual physical for the elderly. If it's true that an ounce of prevention is worth a pound of cure, then it makes absolutely no sense that the primary insurance for most seniors in the United States does not pay for an annual physical, since early detection of age-related ailments is crucial to preventing them from turning into life-threatening and costly situations. Health policy expert Kenneth Thorpe says, "Our health care system focuses on providing high-tech services for complicated cases. We do this very well. What we do not do is provide basic primary and preventive health care services. We do not pay for these services, and do not have a delivery system that is designed to provide either primary prevention, or adequately treat patients with chronic diseases."[33]

Something is very wrong with this picture. America's critics of excessive government spending for social programs, whether on education, poverty programs, human services, or national parks, frequently complain that you can't fix the problem by simply throwing more money at it—and when it comes to health care, these critics actually are correct. The United States already spends nearly twice as much money per capita as our European counterparts for worse results. The problems are more fundamental than the amount of spending, stemming from the perverse mixing of the pursuit of profits with people's health. America has entrusted the nation's health to huge corporate bureaucracies that have great incentive to see each patient as something akin to an ATM from which to withdraw maximum fees in return for minimum service. Fixing this mess will require an overhaul of the entire system. We've hit rock bottom, and Europe has a lot to teach us about how to climb out of the hole we have dug for ourselves.

SINGLE PAYER VS. SHARED RESPONSIBILITY

If America's privatized system is a dead end, which of the other two systems is best: the single payer type used in Britain, Canada, and Sweden, or the shared responsibility system of France, Belgium, Germany, and Japan?

Either of them would be vastly better for most Americans than what we have now. But in talking to different people in many European countries, including doctors, nurses, and consumers, I came to the tentative conclusion that the shared responsibility systems seem to offer a few advantages over single payer, including more choice and shorter waiting periods for surgery and other procedures. I heard much praise for the French, Belgian, and Swiss systems, including from many people who had lived in several countries and could compare their experiences in different health care systems. I interviewed two personal assistants to a Swedish member of the European Parliament who were living and working in Brussels, so they were in a good position to compare Sweden's single payer system with Belgium's shared responsibility system. Jeanette said the Swedish health care system had declined somewhat in recent years, that her grandmother had had to wait three years for hip replacement surgery. There were other waits too, though the wait times had declined a bit in recent years as a result of government responsiveness to consumer complaints. But overall it was her opinion that the Belgian health care system seemed to deliver more efficiently and more quickly than Sweden's. Other people I spoke with had similar observations.

I found it interesting that Sweden had experienced longer wait times, like other single payer nations, such as Canada and Britain. But shared responsibility nations were noted for having shorter wait times than either single payer nations or the United States. Generally speaking, their health care systems had a better reputation among the people who used them, I found. In fact, it is not uncommon for those who live in single payer Britain to travel across the English Channel to the shared responsibility countries of France or Belgium to avail themselves of certain health care services and surgeries, because the lines are shorter and the care better. (Individuals from E.U. member nations have reciprocity to use one another's medical services.) I'm certainly no expert in health care policy, but this trend seems noteworthy and worth further investigation. Instead of relying on the assumption that universal health care is synonymous with single payer, U.S. proponents of quality, affordable health care should examine the shared responsibility systems of France, Belgium, Germany, Switzerland, and other countries.

CHALLENGES TO EUROPEAN HEALTH AND HEALTH CARE SYSTEMS

Certainly the European health care systems have their share of problems too. Providing health care for half a billion people is a huge undertaking and bound to result in shortfalls, complaints, and occasional failures. Something went tragically wrong in the summer of 2003 when thousands of Europeans, most of them elderly, died in the middle of a torrid heat wave.[34] Europeans do love their summer vacations, when entire towns empty out and head to the coasts for weeks at a time—including most of the health and social service workers in France, Italy, Spain, and elsewhere. So when the mercury hit over 100 degrees Fahrenheit for a period of several weeks in what turned out to be the hottest European summer since the nineteenth century, no one was available to check in on the elderly, especially those who were the most isolated and vulnerable. The cumulative result of such poor planning was one of the great health care tragedies in modern European history. But the Europeans learned from that episode and have not seen a repeat on that scale (even though they continue to have periods of soaring summer temperatures, especially in the Mediterranean countries).

Other contradictions abound, despite the Europeans' emphasis on health. How about the Germans, who are so extraordinarily health conscious with their saunas and myriad bike and pedestrian paths yet smoke cigarettes like chimneys and eat a fat-drenched diet abounding with sausage and red meat? Amazingly, as the German magazine *Spiegel* has puzzled over, many Germans who munch their organic whole wheat bread and insist that their organic eggs come from free-range chickens still smoke pack after pack of cigarettes. Germans remain some of the most enthusiastic smokers in all of western Europe.[35] The United States has done a much better job than most nations in reducing smoking, and the European Union has finally targeted a reduction in smoking as a major health policy initiative. All across Europe, packs of cigarettes now include dire warnings in huge block letters on the front and back of each pack, covering half the viewable area, with scary alerts like

SMOKING KILLS, SMOKING CAUSES AGING OF THE SKIN (obviously directed at youthful vanity), and, one of my favorites, SMOKING CAN CAUSE A SLOW AND PAINFUL DEATH. Yikes! That's enough to grab you by the collar.

These sorts of public awareness initiatives, along with outright bans on tobacco advertising in all media and a ban on smoking in public places (including bars and restaurants) in many E.U. countries, appear to be working. One study found that smoking among men has fallen in twenty-two of the twenty-five E.U. countries studied, with some dramatic drop-offs observed. The prevalence of smoking among women also has fallen in most E.U. nations.[36]

Within a particular country, differences in the quality of health care are not uncommon from one region to another, in part because their regional or local governments have a hand in deciding how much of local resources will be allocated to health care. Just as some states in the U.S. put more resources into certain services and end up with differing quality levels, so too does this occur in the European health care systems. Also, sometimes hard choices have to be made about where to focus health care resources, what services to provide free of charge, and what ones to charge at least a co-payment for, which can result in shortcomings for certain health care services. For example, some studies have found that Europe lags behind the United States in detecting and treating certain forms of cancer. A 2001 study found that European women who develop breast cancer are more likely to be diagnosed when the tumor has spread and less likely to survive than American women. This was mostly a result of less emphasis in Europe on early diagnosis, especially through medical screenings to detect breast cancer and breast self-examination. Germany did not even initiate an official screening program until 2003. And for leukemia, the American survival rate is almost 50 percent, but the European rate is only 35 percent.[37] Spurred by these sorts of statistics, most countries have taken remedial measures.

Beyond that, the biggest problems facing the European health care systems are quite the opposite of those of the stingy American health system. Like other parts of Europe's comprehensive workfare services, health care sometimes has been too generous, necessitating some cutbacks in certain services for nonessential things, such as Viagra pills and breast implants.[38] But other cutbacks have been more deeply felt, such as for eyeglasses, dentures, and certain medications. People also now must dig deeper into their own pockets for things like expensive fertility-related treatments, artificial insemination, and sterilization procedures.

Cutbacks also have meant the introduction of a gatekeeper into the German health care system, meaning patients now must see a general practitioner before they can go to specialists, much like how HMOs operate in the United States. Of course, this is something that has been required by insurance companies in the U.S., as well as by Britain and other countries for many years, yet it was resisted mightily in Germany. Also resisted was the idea of a co-payment, typically a twelve dollar co-payment per doctor visit every three months and about eighteen dollars if a patient insists on visiting a specialist without an initial referral from her or his family doctor.[39] Cutbacks never feel good to those on the receiving end, but from an American's standpoint those cutbacks are minor.

For Americans, there are many lessons to learn. No question, the world today is riskier for U.S. workers, with the steady demise of employer-based health care and pension systems in the United States putting the squeeze on individuals and their families. If tens of millions of Americans can no longer rely on the post–World War II social contract that provided various workfare supports via their employer, what is to take the place of that system? Might European systems of health care, particularly the shared responsibility types, offer a solution to this dilemma?

There are some real ironies here. American conservatives share an ideological belief that smaller government is better and that social spending should be kept to a minimum. Yet even with the government in the hands of the Republican Party for much of the past decade, many times more money has been spent on health care for Americans than in any other nation—over 16 percent of the nation's economy. Yet we Americans are not getting our money's worth. It is only our patriotic and ideological blinders that prevent us from learning from the French—or the Swiss, the Germans, or the Belgians—when it comes to health care. And it is only our entrenched beliefs that prevent us from distinguishing between different types of health care methods, such as shared responsibility and single payer, and induce us just to blindly lump them all together as "socialized medicine." I know it's hard for certain Americans to believe that the solution to some very real problems can be found, ironically, in that part of the world that many American demagogues love to ridicule—old Europe—but it's true.

Americans love to be number one and to win the gold, whether in Olympic skiing, the World Series, the Super Bowl, or the Tour de France. But I'm still waiting for the day when Americans decide they want to be number one in health care. Wouldn't it be grand to beat the French for a change at something that really matters?

PART THREE

SUSTAINABLE EUROPE

NINE

WINDMILLS, TIDES, AND SOLAR BESIDES

The European Way of Energy

Picture windmills, tidal turbines, and solar panels on rooftops, dotting the picturesque European landscape. Imagine large cylindrical "sea snakes" bobbing in the ocean, generating enough electricity from ocean waves to power isolated coastal villages. Or undersea "windmills" ceaselessly churning in the currents, harnessing the allure of seemingly limitless energy from the ocean. And vast solar arrays with tens of thousands of panels that have tracking technology to follow the sun, and "smart" energy-efficient buildings that monitor the temperature and sunlight to open and close the blinds and window panels automatically. Imagine cement that cleans the air by "eating" smog,[1] or how about harnessing the body warmth of 250,000 daily commuters to produce heat for a nearby office block? Or car-free city centers populated with throngs of bicyclists and pedestrians, and city buses running on hydrogen fuel cells, with high-speed trains circling it all, linking major cities, whisking passengers in comfort and carbon-friendly efficiency?

While these may sound like science fiction, all of these inventions and more are becoming reality in Europe. Perhaps no single horizon better illustrates Europe's technological advances, combined with political will and future-thinking, than its leadership in launching the world into a new era of renewable energy, conservation, and low greenhouse gas economies. Just as Europe's social capitalism has been leading the world in figuring out the best way to harness prosperity into broadly shared workfare supports for families and workers, so too have Europe's

energy innovations been leading in devising ways for modern economies to strive for ecological sustainability. With the world facing energy
shortages, unstable prices, geopolitical struggles over energy supply,
and dramatic climate changes that demand less fossil fuel consumption
and reduced carbon emissions, Europeans have embarked on changes
in their energy regime that over the course of the next half century will
have as profound an effect on society as coal and steam power did in the
nineteenth century.

While the Bush White House oil chieftains continued to engage in
increasingly desperate searches for oil, Europe stepped quietly into the
role of global trailblazer. In March 2007, the heads of all twenty-seven
European Union nations met and, led by German chancellor Angela
Merkel, who has emerged as a world leader of the first magnitude, agreed
to cut carbon emissions by 20 percent and to make renewable energy
sources 20 percent of the E.U.'s energy mix by 2020 (up from a 6.5
percent share, which was already twice that of the United States).[2]
Displaying an important principle that will be crucial to any global
climate agreement, the richest European nations agreed to contribute a
greater share toward combating greenhouse gases and climate change
than the less well off. Considering that the E.U. has the largest economy
in the world, this climate protection agreement—known as the 20–20–
20 Plan—was nothing less than epochal in its impact.

Meanwhile, the United States has become not only the largest per
capita polluter in the world, but under the Bush administration a rogue
nation that refused to rein in its extravagant ways. With less than 5
percent of the world's population, we lead in consuming 25 percent of
the world's oil and in belching nearly 50 percent of greenhouse gases
emitted by automobiles.[3] Each American generates about forty-five
thousand pounds of carbon dioxide a year, twice as much as the average European or Japanese and many times more than someone living
in China, India, or any other developing country.[4] Our large, hulking
automobiles are champion gas guzzlers, with engines about twice as
large as those of cars in any other nation.[5] Our inefficient toilets flush
away more cubic inches of water, and our old-style incandescent lightbulbs, still in widespread use, burn up more kilowatts.

Not only does our environmental greed hurt the world, it also impacts
Americans negatively. A study by researchers at Columbia and Yale Universities, in collaboration with the World Economic Forum, ranked the
United States 97th out of 133 nations in air quality (behind nearly all
of Europe, including Poland, Bulgaria, and even Russia), 96th in water

quality (behind all of Europe except Romania, and just ahead of Cuba), and 80th in sustainable energy (right behind Turkey and just ahead of Panama).[6] Our ecological "footprint," the measure of the earth's capacity consumed by a population, is twice that of Europe even though we have the same standard of living.[7] While carbon dioxide emissions in 2007 decreased in Denmark (by 8 percent), Britain and Germany (both by 3 percent), and France (by 2 percent), they increased in the United States by 2 percent.[8] As one European acquaintance observed, "You don't have to be a mathematical genius to realize that the world cannot afford too many countries that consume so many times their fair share."

The settled scientific and political consensus now is that the twenty-first century will be a make-or-break one for the human stewardship of planet Earth. President Barack Obama has pledged to turn the page on the sorry years of failed leadership by both Republican and Democratic parties,[9] but his early policy announcements, while making up for years of neglect under the Bush administration, have not come close to matching European or Japanese standards. As just one example, when President Obama announced in May 2009 new nationwide rules for mileage standards, he set a goal that the U.S. motor vehicle fleet should reach an average of 35.5 miles per gallon by 2016. But Europe and Japan already have long surpassed this standard and even China has pledged to reach it by around 2010.[10] The fuel standard of European vehicles is set to rise to fifty miles per gallon by 2012, with Japan already averaging forty-five miles per gallon.[11]

At this point the United States is so far behind the other advanced democracies that it will take a concerted effort, maintained over time, to close the gap. Because the United States is the world's greatest per capita polluter, the whole world is hoping that Obama succeeds. If ever global leadership was needed, that time is now. And that leadership is being provided by "old Europe," not the United States.

THE LANDSCAPE OF AN ENERGY (R)EVOLUTION

We are currently facing a third economic revolution, a revolution which, after the industrial and technological revolutions, will consist of the transition from an economy dependant on carbon to an economy based on renewable energy.

José Luis Rodríguez Zapatero, president of Spain

On the European continent, a revolutionary evolution in energy efficiency, conservation, and transportation has been quietly occurring. For centuries, the land of the Enlightenment has produced brilliant inventors, scientists, writers, artists, musicians, composers, entrepreneurs, and political leaders. In his book *The Discoveries: Great Breakthroughs in 20th Century Science*, Alan Lightman lists what he considers to be the twenty-two greatest scientific breakthroughs of the twentieth century: eight of them were made exclusively by German scientists, two more had Austrian and German collaborators, and five others were made by British and Dutch scientists. This tradition of inventiveness and ingenuity is in evidence all across the European continent today in small and grand ways, particularly in matters of energy efficiency and conservation.

I'm never less than impressed by the two- and three-button flush toilets, with one button a low flush that uses little water, and the other buttons for larger flushes if needed. (No, these are not the old European toilets with the little shelf that gives you a bird's-eye view of your last meal; this is a new generation of toilets that allow you to use only precisely as much water as you need to complete your business.) In an Italian seacoast village, my shower had a small, nearly soundless ventilating fan driven not by electricity but by sea breezes, easily turned on or off by a simple string-pulley system. And I'm always delighted by Germany's ingeniously designed, energy-efficient windows that, simply by turning the latch a different direction, you can either swing wide open horizontally like a French door, or tilt back vertically on the bottom hinge, allowing you to adjust precisely for cool air or precipitation.

Many public buildings have escalators tripped by motion sensors, saving energy when no one is in the stairwell. Likewise, in Brussels's Gare-Midi train station, a huge glass turnstile is powered by motion sensors, revolving when someone enters it but otherwise switched off, saving electricity. Many of the hotels, buildings, and homes are illuminated by low-wattage CFL bulbs, which also are tripped on and off by motion sensors. When I visited the natural history museum in Umeå, Sweden, I noticed that the lights were tripped by motion sensors so that when no one was in a particular room of the museum, the light was very dim (though not completely dark). When someone walked into that room, the overhead lights snapped on. Very efficient. (This efficiency, however, is not without its occasional downsides. Once, after getting stranded in an old grand hotel in the Swiss Alps because the snowy mountain roads had been closed, I used its public bathroom with motion-activated lights. After I had been sitting in the toilet stall for a bit, suddenly the lights blinked off and I was sitting in the pitch dark!)

Those are the little things. Then you start noticing some of the bigger things, new or improved technologies that produce renewable energy or greater energy conservation with minimal carbon emissions and impact on the environment. These are the ones that really stand out, and they are starting to make a difference.

Take wind power: Europe leads the world in the production of wind power, and Germany leads Europe. All across rural Germany giant windmills line the landscape, rows of them standing massively tall like a new-fangled crop, blades turning with a slow, steady patience. In the northern German state of Schleswig-Holstein, its twenty-six hundred wind turbines are capable of filling one-third of its electricity needs by utilizing just 1 percent of its land mass.[12] Across Germany more than twenty thousand windmills generate 8 percent of the country's electricity, some twenty-one thousand megawatts (MW) of power—45 percent of Europe's total wind power—enough to power ten million homes and save an estimated forty-two million tons of carbon dioxide.[13] Germany has plans to build an additional thirty offshore wind farms, with some two thousand windmills in the North and Baltic seas providing eleven thousand more megawatts of electricity.[14]

But that's just the beginning. In Britain, a joint venture of several European power companies is constructing the world's largest wind farm twelve miles off the coast, near where the Thames River flows into the North Sea. The numbers are staggering: the ambitious $2.7 billion project will consist of 341 turbines occupying an area of ninety square miles and will add one thousand megawatts of capacity. Combined with the output from a second wind farm being built off the coast nearby, the 440 turbines all told will produce enough to power a third of London's three million households. And it's all renewable energy, no belching carbon dioxide or toxic emissions, resulting in a decrease of over two million tons of carbon dioxide emissions every year.[15]

The world's fastest-growing producer of wind power is Spain, which boosted its capacity by 38 percent in 2004, to eighty-five hundred megawatts, equal to 6 percent of its overall power supply. On a windy weekend in March 2008, wind power in Spain produced an average of 28 percent of all electricity consumed nationwide and over 40 percent during peak moments.[16] Portugal is building $1.3 billion worth of wind turbines around the country, enough to power 750,000 homes.[17]

The Swedish power company Vattenhall is building northern Europe's biggest wind turbine park in the Baltic Sea, between Sweden and Germany.[18] Denmark already gets about 20 percent of its total power from wind energy, led by the existing largest wind installation in the world at Nysted, where seventy-two turbines generate enough power for 110,000 households.[19]

These are starting to add up to serious numbers in terms of the amount of power produced. Wind power has taken off in recent years in all corners of Europe and is becoming a major business with enough megawatts installed in Europe during 2006 to power nearly four million homes, a 23 percent increase over production in 2005. Three-fifths of the world's seventy-four thousand megawatts of wind power are generated within the borders of the European continent. Meanwhile, the United States has been lagging with only a third of Europe's wind power capacity.[20] Moreover, the U.S. is afflicted by an antiquated power grid designed a hundred years ago that makes it difficult to move large amounts of power over long distances, such as from the windy, lightly populated plains states to the heavily populated coasts. Fortunately President Obama has pledged to build a "smart" energy grid with greater capacity, an important step toward increasing wind power in the U.S. and bringing it up to European levels.[21]

Another renewable energy technology enjoying a surge is solar power. Once again, Europe is leading the world, and Germany is leading Europe. In the heart of conservative Bavaria, a thirty-acre solar facility went online in 2004, becoming the largest solar energy park in the world at the time. This park, combined with two other nearby solar parks, which together are composed of an array of 57,600 silicon and aluminum panels, generates enough electricity to power over nine thousand German homes.[22] Attesting to the seriousness with which Germany's government regards this technology, the country became the world leader in solar installations in 2005, surpassing the former leader, Japan. In that year, Germany had 57 percent of the global market (compared with the United States's 7 percent, Japan's 20 percent, and all of Europe's 60 percent). Continued double-digit growth is expected in Germany's solar industry, and at the current rate of expansion Germany will produce twelve thousand megawatts by 2012, enough to power approximately six million homes, the same capacity as Britain's entire nuclear power industry.[23]

But Germany is not the only European country soaking up the sun. Most countries have ambitious solar projects under way, and photovoltaic capacity in the European Union has been growing at a stunning annual rate of 70 percent.[24] Portugal, which is blessed with a lot of sun, has built the world's largest solar photovoltaic power plant, an eleven-megawatt station composed of fifty-two thousand photovoltaic modules. It produces enough electricity to light and heat eight thousand homes and saves more than thirty thousand tons a year of carbon dioxide emissions.[25] Solar water heating, a modern version of an old technology, is enjoying a resurgence, using passive solar panels not to generate electricity but to heat pipes of circulating water for hot showers, dishwashing, and laundry, reducing water heating bills by 75 percent. In Europe, 13 percent of hot water generation is produced by solar thermal, compared with just 2 percent in the United States. Austria installed forty times more systems in 2005 than California did, although it has a quarter of California's population and a lot less sun.[26] The solar plant in Portugal also is bringing jobs and development to the traditionally poor Alentejo region, 125 miles southeast of the capital, Lisbon. Ironically, Portugal's partners are American companies, PowerLight Corporation and GE Energy Financial Services, which transact more business in Europe than in the United States.

Solar power and wind power have proliferated as a result of several factors, the most important of which are technological advances and visionary government support. First, technological advances have made modern windmills far superior to the picturesque old Dutch wooden windmills on postcards, or even to the more premodern kind that dot California's Altamont Pass. The quaint windmills of old have been replaced by turbines that stand as high as twenty-story buildings. These more powerful turbines can generate up to seven times more energy than the first modern models produced, helped by features such as longer blades and pivoting rotors that, at the direction of a computer chip, tilt and turn the blades to harness the wind optimally.[27] Even when the wind is relatively weak, they are able to harness enough to generate power, and that helps to lower the cost per kilowatt hour.

Solar power today utilizes tracking technology that enables the panels to follow the sun, resulting in significantly more electricity production than is possible with fixed ground-mount systems. And the advent of "nanosolar," which instead of using costly solar cells made of silicon uses "thin-film" solar cells made by printing special-purpose ink on sheets of light-weight foil, is creating great excitement because it will lead to a drastic reduction in cost. Estimates are that thin-film solar cells will cost as little as 10 percent of what current silicon cells cost and can be manufactured five to ten times more efficiently. German companies are some of the biggest investors in this promising technology.[28]

Second, conscious, clear-eyed government policies have boosted the proliferation of wind and solar power technologies by offering financial incentives. In Germany wind power has benefited from a 2001 law that requires energy companies to pay wind power producers a price three times greater than the amount paid for power produced from conventional sources. That incentive was so successful that Germany also enacted legislation in 2004 guaranteeing producers of solar electricity a price that is four times the market rate for conventionally generated power. Guaranteeing operators a premium fixed price for every kilowatt produced has created a fertile business climate for renewable technologies to take off. As the industry has reached economies of scale, the cost per energy unit has declined, so these technologies have become closer to competitive with other fuel sources. The German government also has provided research grants and spurred demand by establishing a "100,000 rooftops program," which provided low-interest credits for home buyers of solar systems. Other countries, such as Britain, Denmark, Portugal, and Spain, have followed suit. Not surprisingly, wind and solar are two of the fastest growing markets in Europe. By 2010, solar power investments in Germany alone are expected to reach $20 billion, which on a per capita basis would be comparable to $75 billion in the United States, a huge sum.[29]

In addition to the impressive energy benefits, the wind and solar industries also are creating thousands of jobs, most of them in rural areas, where job creation can be difficult. Germany's economy and exports have received a huge boost as a result of massive investment in the renewable energy sector. Thousands of people in the German state of Schleswig-Holstein, and over eighty-four thousand nationwide, have found employment within the wind industry. Germany's entire renewable industry, including wind, solar, and biomass power, shot up to 249,300 new jobs in 2007, a 50 percent jump over 2004.[30] On a per capita basis, that is comparable to the creation of a million jobs in the United States. These industries have expanded Germany's exports, with German wind turbine manufacturers producing over half of the turbines and components manufactured worldwide in 2004, which has built the wind business into a $6 billion industry.[31] A study by the German government predicts that by 2020 four hundred thousand domestic jobs will exist in the renewable energy sector.

In Spain, renewable energy provides jobs for nearly two hundred thousand people, and in the last four years the production of renewable energy has increased by 50 percent.[32] Other European nations are enjoying similar surges in economic activity, as the business of wind, solar, and other renewables becomes deeply rooted in the fertile European soil.

CAPTAIN NEMO'S DREAM: POWER FROM THE SEA

While wind and solar power are the biggest of the renewables, other energy forms gradually are being utilized and show impressive potential. One of these is power derived from the sea. Harnessing the sea has long been the stuff of science fiction, the allure of seemingly limitless and continuous energy (unlike solar or wind, since the sun doesn't always shine or the wind blow). Science fiction is becoming reality in Britain, Portugal, Spain, and elsewhere. With the services of a Scottish company, Portugal is the first to pioneer an eye-popping new technology known as a "sea snake" or "energy eel." Sea snakes are long, floating cylinders that bob semisubmerged in the waves and convert wave motion to electricity. Each sea snake is about 400 feet (120 meters) long and 11 feet in diameter, composed of three or four segments linked together, end to end. The ocean's constant wave motion causes them to undulate in the sea like a giant snake, up and down and side to side, the motion pumping fluid through pistons that drive generators, both of which are housed inside the cylinders. The power produced is then fed into underwater cables and brought to land, the entire array composing a wave farm that provides energy that is inexhaustible and more predictable than wind or solar power.

Portugal's first sea snake had three segments, producing over two megawatts of power, which met the electricity needs of an entire coastal village, some fifteen hundred homes. Now Portugal is planning to expand that to thirty segments capable of producing twenty megawatts of power, sufficient for fifteen thousand households, saving some thirty million tons of carbon emissions. Scotland also has purchased four of the sea snake segments to produce three megawatts of power off the coast near the Orkneys, with talk of expanding to a thirty-megawatt wave farm that would occupy a half square mile of ocean and provide sufficient electricity for twenty thousand homes. Twenty of these farms could power a city the size of Edinburgh, the capital of Scotland.[33]

Europe has long led the world in marshaling power from the sea. The world's first tidal station was the Rance Estuary dam, built in

Brittany, France, in 1966, which harnesses an exceptional tide differential with a range of twenty-seven feet to produce 240 megawatts of power for a hundred thousand homes. But modern technology is allowing the futuristic promise of tidal energy to step up to a new level. Britain is pushing forward with a new tidal machine that has created a stir of excitement. Imagine taking a windmill, turning it on its side, and sinking it into the ocean—that, in effect, is what engineers have done in the Bristol Channel, south of Wales, about a mile off the British coast. Sixty feet beneath the sea surface, thirty-five-foot-long turbines turn seventeen and a half times a minute, generating renewable energy from the water's current. Above the surface, only a white and red-striped tower is visible. Just as dozens of windmills can be deployed in a field to create a wind farm, these underwater "seamills" create the possibility of grids of undersea turbines producing hundreds of megawatts of carbon-free power—an energy sea farm.[34]

Europe is employing a whole array of these energy technologies and more. Italy, Iceland, Switzerland, Germany, and Portugal are developing geothermal energy, which makes use of the earth's interior heat to produce steam that rotates turbines. Italy has 95 percent of the European Union's installed capacity, and volcanic Iceland produces over 50 percent of its electricity from geothermal sources. Finland, Britain, and Sweden are developing biomass energy, which generates electricity from the combustion of forestry and agricultural by-products; the Welsh region of the United Kingdom is constructing the largest biomass power plant in the world, which will power half of the homes in Wales.[35] Slovenia and Poland are developing small-scale hydro. Denmark already generates more than 25 percent of its energy from sustainable sources and, by combining those with extensive conservation methods, has reached a point that it produces 55 percent more power than it needs, making it an exporter of energy.[36] Some have even tried to repopularize nuclear energy, particularly France, which obtains 77 percent of its electricity from nuclear power and claims this source is "clean" in that it doesn't produce carbon emissions, though its millennium-lasting radioactive waste continues to make it a controversial option and one opposed by other European countries.

The European Union overall is nearly on track for reaching its 2010 target of generating 21 percent of its electricity needs (excluding transportation) from renewable energy sources.[37] In 2007 Germany generated 14 percent of its electricity consumption from renewable energy, preventing 114 million tons of carbon dioxide emissions. Meanwhile the United States generates a paltry 6 percent of electricity from renewables.[38]

In this age of oil uncertainty and unstable energy prices, and with the urgency of Europe's governments to meet their goals for sustainable energy and greenhouse gas reductions, Europeans are experimenting with all sorts of renewable energy and transportation options that previously had limited appeal. Each country is deploying different technologies and acting as a laboratory for the others, plotting a meandering course toward the future. But unlike in previous episodes of experimentation, this time there is a surge of momentum and resoluteness at the highest official levels. Motivated by the increasingly urgent crisis of global climate change, previously futuristic ideas now are seen to be within reach scientifically as well as economically. Some countries have set ambitious goals, such as Sweden's goal of generating 60 percent of its electricity from renewables by 2010 (it already generated 40 percent of its energy needs from renewables in 2005),[39] Austria's goal of 78 percent, Portugal's of 45 percent, Finland's of 31 percent, and Spain's and Denmark's of 29 percent.[40] Prime Minister Gordon Brown has boldly called for Britain to generate nearly 100 percent of its electricity from clean, non-carbon-emitting energy sources by 2020.[41]

Of course, such pronouncements and proclamations would be hot air without the funding to back them up. But substantial capital investments are being made, not only by governments but also by venture capitalists, major banks, financial institutions, and blue chip technology companies. At a national energy summit convened by Chancellor Angela Merkel, Germany's energy industry pledged to invest $50 billion in new renewable energy infrastructure by 2012, $20 billion in the solar industry alone.[42] On a per capita basis, that would be equivalent to the United States investing $180 billion, nearly $30 billion per year, in renewable energy, an unprecedented sum. Portugal is investing $10 billion over the next five years in developing wind, solar, and wave power,[43] which on a per capita basis is equivalent to the United States investing $300 billion, $60 billion per year, an astronomical amount. Instead, under the Bush administration, U.S. development and research showed a heavy tilt toward nuclear energy, coal, and other fossil fuels, with the Department of Energy spending two times as much on nuclear research and development and three times as much on coal as it spent on solar research and development. The Obama administration has done much to change these priorities, with pledges that amount to $150 billion over ten years—$15 billion per year—to be spent on renewables. Not quite European levels, but a big step in the right direction.[44]

The outline of a low carbon economy is emerging, with Europe at the forefront. "Renewable energy is the source of energy for the future," says Manuel Pinho, Portugal's economics minister. "We think this can create an industrial revolution and a lot of opportunities for jobs and research, and we want to be ahead of the curve."[45]

That's how Europe is viewing this—as a new industrial revolution. And it is at the lead of this revolution.

ENERGY CONSERVATION AND PRODUCTIVITY: "THE GREATEST RENEWABLE OF ALL"

With all the talk of energy eels, wave dragons, solar arrays, undersea windmills, and even a newly developed $13,000 compact car that allegedly gets 157 miles per gallon,[46] Europe starts sounding like a renewable energy Disney World. But the fact is, while the amount of power provided by all these impressive new technologies is growing exponentially, it's still a small proportion of the overall power supply. And it is likely to remain so for another decade or two. So in both the short and medium terms, ways must be found to deal with an economy that will continue to be based primarily on the use of fossil fuels that belch significant amounts of greenhouse gases and cause global warming and its ominous side effects.

On this point, virtually all the experts agree: in the short term, the cheapest, easiest, and fastest way to reduce carbon emissions and tackle many of the world's energy shortages is through energy conservation. But this conservation requires more than just using less energy; it requires a more efficient use of energy and getting greater results from the same quantity of energy used—what is called "energy productivity." Increasing energy productivity makes it possible to reduce the amount of energy used and put less carbon dioxide into the atmosphere without compromising our standard of living. That's why energy experts like Lisa Margonelli, author of *Oil on the Brain,* say energy productivity is the biggest "renewable" of all. Even the oil insiders know this. Sadad al-Husseini, who oversaw one-quarter of the world's oil reserves as a former executive at the world's largest oil producer, Saudi Aramco, says, "The best alternative energy is energy efficiency. There is too much wastage. There are too many cars that are far bigger than what they need to be. . . . in the home often heating and air conditioners are on unnecessarily."[47] And the United States knows this too, having once been a champion of conservation and energy productivity. According to Margonelli, since 1970 the United States has met 75 percent of its new energy needs through greater efficiency rather than new energy supplies.[48] So that knowledge is locked within our national DNA, trying to get out.

And yet Europe is the one leading the charge into a new era of energy productivity and conservation. Helpful in understanding Europe's approach is a review of the findings of an important study by the U.S.-based McKinsey Global Institute, the economic research arm of global business consultants McKinsey & Company. The McKinsey study found that it would be relatively easy for industrialized nations—and the United States in particular—to greatly reduce energy demand as well as greenhouse gas emissions without reducing our standard of living. To achieve this we wouldn't need huge investments, costly research, or high-tech solutions—just more widespread use of existing technology. In other words, this is low-hanging fruit, with realistic and cost-effective potential.[49]

The McKinsey report's analysis is grounded in the reality that residential and commercial buildings and road transportation will drive 57 percent of energy growth between now and 2020. And 75 percent of global energy use occurs in urban areas, where geographic compactness can aid in designing and disseminating more efficient systems.[50] McKinsey identifies five sectors—residential, commercial, transportation, industrial, and power generation—where significant reductions in energy use and carbon emissions can be achieved without great sacrifice by targeting efforts to implement currently available technology to these sectors.

Residential Sector

The residential sector is the largest single consumer of energy worldwide, responsible for 25 percent of global energy demand, and also has the largest potential for improving energy efficiency. In the size of our dwellings, Americans are world gluttons. The typical new U.S. home is 40 percent larger than that of twenty-five years ago, even though the average household today has fewer people; and the United Nations says homes in the United States take up a third more space than those in western Europe, twice as much as in eastern Europe, four times as much as in Syria, and six times as much as in Pakistan.[51] Not only do

Europeans have smaller homes, but also they have methodically implemented available technologies that harvest some of the low-hanging fruit, such as high-efficiency building shells (including the highest-grade insulation and windows), energy-saving lightbulbs, more efficient "standby power" requirements for household appliances, and solar water heaters that substantially cut energy use.

"Europe and Japan already do many of the things necessary and have a much smaller ecological impact as a result," says Diana Farrell, lead author of the McKinsey report.* "Yet they still have a high standard of living and strong economies—proof that energy productivity and efficiency do not have to hurt the economy."

She cites as one example the difference between common household appliances in the United States and Europe. "The standby power consumption in the United States of televisions and other appliances can account for up to ten percent of residential power consumption. Yet the technology is already available and being used elsewhere to reduce that standby power from up to sixty watts to one watt. This is an area that is ripe for a government efficiency standard," meaning a government regulation mandating that TVs, stereos, and kitchen and other appliances purchased in the United States must include technology to reduce standby power.

Other simple changes include motion sensors to switch off lights when no one is occupying a room and replacing traditional incandescent lightbulbs with eco-friendly, low-wattage CFLs, which use a fifth of the power of incandescents. Lighting alone accounts for 10 to 15 percent of domestic and 25 to 30 percent of commercial power use, making motion sensors and CFLs important tools in the battle to reduce energy use. A total switch to CFLs would cut worldwide electricity demand by 18 percent.[52] Ireland already has banned incandescent lightbulbs, and the E.U. has approved the phasing out of incandescents by 2012, giving ample time for European governments to vigorously promote CFLs. Estimates say that getting rid of incandescent bulbs would reduce the European Union's carbon emissions by 25 million tons a year.[53] In the United States this changeover mostly has been left to random consumer discretion. And motion sensors for lights are hardly in use, as evidenced by any downtown area at night, where office buildings can be seen blazing at full wattage even though all the workers have gone home.

---

*In early 2009, Farrell was appointed by President Barack Obama to be his deputy director of the National Economic Council.

Widespread implementation of other existing technologies offers the promise of large gains in energy efficiency in heating buildings. For example, in conventional electricity generation, only about 35 percent of the fuel is converted into electricity while 65 percent is lost as wasted heat that is belched up the smokestack. But Europe has been pioneering the use of what is known as "cogeneration," or "combined heat and power" (CHP) systems, which recapture the heat and recycle it, putting it to use not only to warm things but even to generate air-conditioning. Cogeneration can achieve an efficiency of up to 90 percent, producing energy savings of up to 40 percent compared to conventional generation.[54]

Denmark is leading the world in warming buildings with cogeneration methods. Hundreds of thousands of Danish homes and other buildings are warmed by surplus heat from power plants. Homes used to be heated entirely with oil, often by inefficient individual boilers in their basements, just as in the United States. But in the 1980s the Danish government embarked on a massive overhaul of the country's approach to heating. It developed a combined heat-and-power system in which surplus heat, produced as a by-product at power plants, is transported in insulated pipes to heat homes and offices. This cogeneration, or "district heating," technology wasn't new but had been confined to compact quarters, such as university campuses. Building the district-heating system for a large community, such as a city or town, was a pharaonic undertaking that took a decade. Streets had to be torn up for the installation of massive underground pipes so that the heat could be transported from hundreds of small power plants near cities.[55]

The result? About 61 percent of household heat is produced from surplus heat from power plants. Denmark's energy consumption has remained stable for more than thirty years, even as the country's economy has doubled, with cogeneration accounting for about half of Denmark's energy savings. During the same period, energy consumption in the United States rose 40 percent. The average American now uses 13,300 kilowatt hours of electricity a year, compared with the average Dane's use of 6,600. Recycled energy from cogeneration amounts to over 50 percent of all energy used in Denmark today; it makes up nearly 40 percent of all energy used in the Netherlands and Finland, and 20 percent in Germany, Poland, and Portugal, but only 8 percent in the United States.[56]

Another technology showing real potential for the residential sector is called "passive housing," and it has been introduced in Germany and

Scandinavia. A passive house uses ultra-thick insulation and complex doors and windows to encase its living space inside an airtight, hermetically sealed shell that barely allows any heat to escape or any cold to seep in. It then uses an ingenious central ventilation system where the warm air going out passes side by side with clean, cold air coming in, exchanging heat with 90 percent efficiency. That means a passive house can be warmed not only by the sun, but also by the heat from appliances and even from occupants' bodies. Even on the coldest nights in central Germany, the passive houses there get all the heat and hot water they need from the amount of energy that would be needed to run a hair dryer.

These houses are part of a revolution in building design. In Germany, passive houses cost only about 5 to 7 percent more to build than conventional houses, yet they use about one-twentieth the heating energy. There are now an estimated fifteen thousand passive houses, and the industry is starting to thrive. School buildings in Frankfurt are being constructed with this technique, and the European Commission is promoting passive-house building, while the European Parliament has proposed that all new buildings meet passive-house standards by 2011. But in the United States, passive housing doesn't exist; in fact, the advanced windows and heat-exchange ventilation systems needed to make passive houses work properly are not even commercially available.[57]

Equally impressive is another residential housing technology that has been introduced in Great Britain—the first hydrogen-powered home. Inside one such home, which looks no different from any of the others in the middle-class cul-de-sac where it is located, a refrigerator-size fuel cell unit produces 65 percent of the power and 75 percent of total energy demand for both electricity and heat for the occupants of the house. Natural gas first is pumped into the house via a steam reformer that breaks it down and generates the hydrogen, which is then combined with oxygen in a fuel cell unit that produces electricity and heat without producing carbon dioxide. Overall the use of the hydrogen fuel cell, which costs about $3,000 to purchase, cuts household emissions by 40 percent compared with a house running on natural gas alone. If the hydrogen could be produced by using renewable energy sources, such as solar panels on the roof, then household emissions would be close to zero. This technology is being closely monitored for the possibility of widespread implementation.[58]

Commercial Sector

Similarly, in the commercial sector—businesses, municipalities, universities, schools, and hospitals—more low-hanging fruit can be plucked, according to the McKinsey report. Buildings (both commercial and residential) are estimated to account for 50 percent of total energy use in newer cities and more than 70 percent in older urban areas.[59] In the United States, buildings account for 65 percent of electricity consumption and 30 percent of greenhouse gas emissions.[60] Better building codes and office equipment standards, including incentives for "green" building construction that maximizes the energy productivity of buildings, and better auditing to ensure implementation of these codes and standards, would greatly decrease energy consumption.

Europe has become a leader in using green building design and construction practices, including for large commercial buildings as well as residential. Since the mid-1990s, all new construction in Europe has had to meet basic requirements for design efficiency, making green architecture an everyday reality. Europe has pioneered the use of natural lighting, cogeneration, solar power, fuel cells, advanced ventilation, motion sensors to switch off lights and control fans, special glass that allows daylight in but keeps heat and ultraviolet rays out and minimizes heat loss in winter, and much more. A new generation of architects has expanded the definition of green design so that it is now common practice.

These architects are breaking barriers with eye-popping, award-winning designs. One of the best examples is a building known as Energon, a five-story office building for 420 employees in Ulm, Germany, which makes use of the earth's natural temperature for its heating and cooling. Like the previously mentioned passive residential designs, Energon's passive, hermetically-sealed interior has done away with conventional mechanical heating and cooling systems. Besides employing common green design features, such as optimal positioning to the sun, ultra-efficient insulation, solar panels on the rooftop, and a central, large glass-roofed atrium, the building uses a bold innovation to regulate its temperature. It sucks air into the building from underground canals extending three hundred feet into the ground. At that depth the surface temperature no longer influences the air temperature since the earth's natural temperature remains nearly the same, no matter the season. Then, with the help of forty vertical probes, the air can be further cooled or heated, adjusted by a heat exchanging device before it is sucked into the building. The air then circulates through the atrium and through canals leading throughout the five stories of the building. Despite the building's sci-fi design, its construction costs were comparable to those of a standard office building of the same size, yet its ongoing operating costs are far cheaper. Energon's ability to deal with the frigid German winters has surpassed expectations, maintaining optimum temperature even as the building uses less energy and produces 175 fewer tons of carbon dioxide than a normal office building does.[61]

Other innovative designs are found throughout Europe. In London, the city's classic British skyline close to the Thames has been interrupted by the oddball appearance of a forty-one-story building that looks like an enormous glass American football standing on end and jutting into the sky. Dubbed the Gherkin (apparently some think it looks like a pickle), what is as remarkable as its striking glass exterior shape is its energy-efficient interior, which consumes up to 50 percent less energy than a conventional office building. The building's curved shape maximizes the use of natural daylight, reducing the need for artificial lighting. The Gherkin also uses a system of advanced ventilation and computer-controlled blinds, as well as weather sensors on its outside surface to monitor the temperature, wind speed, and sunlight so that the blinds close and window panels open automatically, as necessary.[62]

Another pioneering design is Stockholm's central transit station, which harnesses the body warmth of 250,000 daily commuters to warm up water, which in turn is pumped through pipes to a new office block to heat its interior.[63] In Växjö, Sweden, the town utilizes a rather ghoulish source of cogeneration—it channels leftover heat from the local crematorium into homes. The Mercedes-Benz Museum in Stuttgart is an architectural tour de force, with a sophisticated ventilation system that, rather than recycling used air, as is typical for buildings that depend on old air-conditioning systems, stores hot and cool air in the museum's thick concrete walls. That air then is drawn into a towering central atrium and distributed throughout the building.[64]

On average, the lower running costs of green design features typically pay for the slight increase in their construction costs within a couple of years. At the same time, they dramatically reduce energy usage and carbon emissions. Despite all these obvious advantages, the United States has no federal regulations that require a minimal level of energy productivity achieved through building construction. It has some voluntary guidelines, the so-called LEED guidelines, which were drafted by the nonprofit U.S. Green Building Council. But being voluntary, they are followed by only a handful of architects and builders, less than 1 percent of the potential market, according to one estimate.[65] As green construction costs have declined, interest in using LEED guidelines has increased, but by European standards the LEED guidelines are less than adequate and lead to a narrow view of what sustainability means. One European architect working in the United States said that in Europe "energy consumption, the organization of the workplace, urbanism . . . are all seen as interlinked," but in the United States, green design has been narrowly tailored to LEED's checklist of dos and don'ts, so there is little attempt at whole system design. Commenting on a building he designed in San Francisco, he said, "We didn't even bother to go after the LEED ranking because it doesn't necessarily lead to the most efficient building."[66]

Not surprisingly, American buildings lag far behind their European counterparts in energy productivity. One study measuring heat efficiency in walls and windows and on rooftops showed the United States trailing Germany, Denmark, and Stockholm, Sweden, often by significant margins.[67] With the United States lacking enforceable standards and regulations, the average building here uses roughly a third more energy than its German counterpart.[68] Improving energy efficiency in buildings would translate to a 25 percent reduction in their carbon emissions. And various studies have shown that, beyond the environmental impacts, green design techniques also reduce operating costs, boost property values, create a more pleasant work environment, and improve employees' health and productivity. One study found that worker productivity in green buildings typically rises by about 6 to 16 percent as a result of the use of natural lighting, more windows, better air quality, and other features.[69] So the United States is missing out on all these benefits.

Rounding out the McKinsey report's results are those related to transportation (which I will explore in the next chapter) and the industrial sector. The industrial sector actually comprises several sectors that, combined, have the largest energy demand of all, 47 percent of the global total. This sector ranges from highly energy intensive industries such as steel, chemicals, and aluminum to a broad array of less energy intensive industries such as food processing, textiles, and electronics. Widespread use of current technologies should result in large gains in energy efficiency in this sector as well, possibly as high as 16 to 22 percent, according to the McKinsey report.

CAP 'N' TRADE:
FREE MARKET INCENTIVES FOR CARBON REDUCTION

Europe also is pioneering a new and significant innovation for greatly reducing carbon dioxide emissions into the atmosphere, what *Business Week* has called Europe's main tool in its fight against global warming—carbon trading, or "cap and trade," as it is popularly known. Established in 2005, Europe's is the world's first functioning trading scheme that caps the overall amount of carbon dioxide that is allowed into the atmosphere by industries, companies, and other entities. Each business is assigned an allowable amount of carbon emissions, and if one business figures out how to reduce its emissions below that allowable amount it can sell its surplus allowance to another business that is over its limit. Factories that pollute too much are required to buy credits; those that become more efficient can sell credits they no longer need. This provides great incentives to businesses to reduce their carbon emissions as a way of generating revenue while capping the overall amount of carbon dioxide emitted into the atmosphere by the entire sector.

Terry Tamminen, who was Governor Arnold Schwarzenegger's environmental chief responsible for designing California's own groundbreaking (though not yet implemented) cap and trade system, is effusive in his praise of this European achievement. "Fifteen thousand businesses and organizations in Europe are participating in the system, which is fantastic," says Tamminen. By early 2008 the European carbon trading market was worth an estimated $60 billion, and a prominent research company, New Carbon Finance, estimated that European carbon emissions in 2008 dropped by roughly 3 percent, with the cap and trade system being responsible for 40 percent of that drop because it had encouraged greater use of gas in power generation rather than dirtier fuels like coal.[70] Some believe this is the next financial market bonanza that could mushroom to $1 trillion within a decade.[71] The initial rollout of Europe's cap and trade system was bumpy, with the issue of some overly generous credits that failed to properly penalize some carbon polluting businesses. But after adjustments were made, *BusinessWeek* reported that it is now hailed by environmental economists as "by far the most significant accomplishment in climate policy to date" that will be "central to future global climate negotiations."[72]

Because Europe has the largest economy in the world, the impact of its carbon trading system has been global, even affecting the foot-dragging United States. While the U.S. has yet to pass a national energy plan for limiting greenhouse gases, Europe's already functioning cap and trade system has acted as a major catalyst to convince U.S. businesses that global rules aimed at slowing climate warming are inevitable. Wall Street is mobilizing, with attention to climate change at banks and investment banks, as well as at insurance firms and in hedge funds. Fund managers have raised billions of dollars to invest in projects that are combating climate change. The utility AES has partnered with General Electric to invest in U.S. projects that will eliminate ten million metric tons of greenhouse gases per year. The prospect of costly greenhouse gas regulation was a major factor in a decision by the private equity firms that bought Texas utility TXU to shelve eight of the company's eleven proposed coal-fired power plants.[73] These companies are seeing "green," not only environmental green but also the green of money, specifically in the opportunity to make a lot of it by selling carbon credits, or at least not lose a lot of it by having to purchase carbon credits for their coal-powered plants.

Most observers, whether scientists, the public, or increasingly even business leaders, recognize that the low carbon economy is fast approaching. Many have feared that the economic crisis would halt all plans for ecological sustainability, but the European Union has not allowed it to thwart its drive. E.U. Commission President José Manuel Barroso told the BBC, "The financial crisis is not an excuse. On the contrary, we can make it a win-win situation. We can create more green jobs; we can promote more investment in the low-carbon economy of the future." Europe is leading by example. In a friendly challenge to then President-elect Obama, Barroso said, "Our message to our global partners is: Yes, you can . . . especially to our American partners."[74]

Certainly those Americans looking for their country to become more of a partner in these efforts should be cheered by the fact that, as the McKinsey report makes clear, it will be relatively easy for the United States to reduce energy demand and greenhouse gas emissions greatly without reducing our quality of life, just by achieving a more widespread use of existing conservation methods and technologies. That's the low-hanging fruit. And it's also good news that, while many American leaders have rejected carbon limits by claiming that they would hurt American businesses and cost American jobs, Europe has shown the baselessness of that fear. Europe already has enacted far-reaching conservation measures and reduced its carbon footprint, even as its economy caught up to and surpassed the U.S. economy in 2007–8. In fact, as we have seen, many of the new technologies and emerging energy industries have *contributed* to job creation and stimulated Europe's economy.

On the other hand, a nation must have the political will to enact the right energy standards and offer the right incentives. Under the Bush administration that will was woefully lacking. Now it is up to the Obama administration to follow Europe's lead. Fortunately, there is strong evidence that Obama and his team understand what is at stake. He has appointed recognized scientists and experts to key cabinet positions and has pledged to promote renewable energy (like solar and wind) and alternative transport (like electric cars, ethanol, and high speed trains). The Obama administration has said it will chart a course that will result in 10 percent of U.S. electricity coming from renewable sources by 2012, and 25 percent by 2025, and the creation of four to five million "green" jobs. Obama also is supporting the introduction of a nationwide European-like cap-and-trade program to help reduce greenhouse gas emissions, and he has called on Congress to require U.S. utilities to generate 15 to 20 percent of their electricity supplies from renewable energy sources. To finance all this, President Obama's February 2009 fiscal stimulus included tens of billions of dollars in tax breaks and other financial incentives to boost the use of renewable energy and to produce a nationwide smart power grid. He has pledged to spend $150 billion over ten years on renewables. While that's not a lot of money by European standards, it still would be a good down payment on a new direction.

Only time will tell if this new direction produces the desired results and demonstrates that the United States truly has joined Europe in accepting global responsibility to reduce energy consumption and carbon emissions, and increase energy productivity.

TEN

REVOLUTION ON WHEELS

The European Way of Transportation

Each historical epoch has produced its own modes of transportation, arising from a nexus of the existing technology, energy sources, commercial needs, and geographic layout of that time and place. Whatever the modes, whether ox-drawn wagon, steam locomotive, or A380 jumbo jet, they are charged with the crucial task of moving quantities of things—people, products, raw materials—around the chessboard.

In today's mass industrial society, transportation is the circulatory system of daily life. The world's connection to Middle East turmoil is largely predicated on our need to slurp up large quantities of oil for transportation purposes, resulting in a global transportation sector that is responsible for over half of the worldwide petroleum use and nearly a fifth of the total energy use. Oil is the very blood coursing through the veins of our transportation networks. The use of such massive quantities of hydrocarbon fuel and its many derivates is greatly responsible for the global climate change crisis. So we have a lot at stake in finding new means of transportation beyond those that rely on oil, as well as in making current modes more efficient so that they use less fuel. We are engaged in a search of epochal proportions.

In the transportation sector we see a pattern that is familiar by now—Europe leading, the United States lagging. For several decades Europe has been implementing transportation innovations that leave it much better positioned than the United States in this era of unstable energy prices and greenhouse gas warnings. Its cars and trucks use much less gasoline per mile, it has developed efficient mass transportation based on a vast network of trains and subways, it is pioneering the use of non–petroleum powered vehicles, and it has done much to encourage low-tech forms of transportation, especially bicycling and walking. Consequently, while the United States has seen a 21 percent rise in oil consumption since 1980, most European countries have seen significant drops, with Denmark and Sweden's oil consumption dropping by a third, Germany's by 20 percent, France's by 14 percent, and Italy's by 13 percent.[1] Other nations, especially Japan, also have done much to make their societies more fuel efficient. If the world has any hope of making the leap to an energy efficient, low-carbon transportation paradigm, the United States as the world's largest per capita polluter has a lot of learning and catching up to do. And it matters to the fate of the ecosystem that we rein in our gluttonous ways, so the rest of the world is watching and waiting.

TRAINS AND SUBWAYS

The jewel in the European transportation system is its trains, whether between cities or within them. Famous for their efficiency, speed, and relatively low carbon emissions, Europe's trains and subways run on time, and they're comfortable, affordable, and usually convenient. Comparing Europe's trains with the United States's is like comparing a professional major league team with one in the minors. Europe has built a latticework of routes for high-speed trains that crisscross the continent, allowing travelers to connect between major cities in remarkably little time. France recently launched the fastest rail train in the world, which can reach a top speed of 357 miles per hour and regularly cruises along at an average of 140 to 180 miles per hour.[2] These high-speed trains use the latest railway technologies, from devices that tilt them on curves to underfloor traction systems that enhance their propulsion.[3]

Europe has shown that high-speed trains can compete with air travel not only in terms of travel time but also in terms of the impact on the environment. Trains emit an estimated 67 pounds of carbon dioxide per passenger compared with 187 pounds per passenger for air travel, a difference of over six tons per hundred passengers.[4] And because train travel embarks from city centers, you don't have to endure the hassle of traveling to the airport on the outskirts of the city or suffer the indignities of passing through post-9/11 airport security. You just show up at the station fifteen minutes before departure, board the train, and off you go. A trip from London to Paris or Brussels is as fast on the train as on an airplane when you add in time spent waiting in the airport and traveling to and from the airport.

Once I took the Eurostar train through the Chunnel, from Brussels to London. The Chunnel is one of the great engineering marvels of our times; just think of burrowing beneath the English Channel, the body of water separating the British Isles from the European continent, the one that saved Britain from the Nazis in World War II and from the Spanish Armada in 1588. As I boarded a comfortable car, I was eager with excitement and anticipation. My train entered the Chunnel at 2 P.M., and in my head I heard the sounds of heralds and trumpets marking the momentous occasion. I settled in for the ride, a bit anxious about the tons of salty water that surrounded us, literally swallowing the train tube through which I was hurtling. By the time we emerged into the English countryside a mere twenty-seven minutes later, I realized what was remarkable about the journey was how unremarkable it was. It felt like any other train ride in Europe. The ordinariness itself was a testament to the extraordinary achievement of this human invention that has bridged chasms of history and geography, part of the new glue of Europe.

Yes, the United States has a high-speed train line—at least in theory. Amtrak's Acela Express, which runs from Boston to Washington DC, uses the same high-speed French engine technology. But because of track limitations it rarely approaches anything like French speeds. For a grand total of 18 miles out of 450, the train maxes out at 150 miles per hour, but for the rest of the trip the Acela averages only 68 miles per hour, hardly high speed, and for a premium price.[5] Unfortunately America's railway system is chronically underfunded, underdeveloped, and consequently underutilized. Across the Atlantic, the European Union has earmarked $27.5 billion to finance trans-European networks, much of the funding going to five priority transcontinental rail links, which are due to be completed by 2015. Spain has become a leader in high-speed trains, with three lines now in operation, four more in construction, and several others planned for the near future. But in the United States, funding for the federal rail system has been a constant political football, seen by some political leaders as a government boondoggle to be axed from the budget.

Within European cities, the urban train and subway system also is impressive. Not only are the trains punctual, they also are cleverly designed. In Barcelona, the subway trains come every four to six minutes, and onboard a kind of electronic scoreboard above the door tells you what station you just left and which one you are approaching. (Recently I've noticed a few New York City subway cars also incorporating this technology.) As a result of a well-planned and well-funded transportation infrastructure, nearly six of ten Europeans spend less than twenty minutes each way commuting to work.[6]

One time in Stockholm, a friend and I were planning to catch the subway train at his Vastertorp stop to take me to where I was giving a lecture. My friend informed me, "The train will arrive at 11:05 A.M.," and so I said to him, "Perhaps we should get to the platform five minutes early or so to make sure we don't miss it." I was thinking in terms of the way mass transportation works in San Francisco, where I live—they don't even bother printing a bus schedule because they know they'll never keep to it; instead you wait on the curb, anxiously glancing at your wristwatch, often a nerve-wracking experience.

Brad, my American friend, just looked at me quizzically, not understanding, and then finally grinned. "This isn't the U.S.," he said. "When I say it will be here at 11:05, I mean *exactly* at 11:05." I just nodded my head and shrugged. But I still didn't believe him; I kept unconsciously rushing us to get there a bit early. We arrived on the platform at 11:04, and exactly one minute later the train arrived. I was inwardly giddy, even ecstatic, in a way I did not think possible over a train schedule. After experiencing the gross inefficiency of San Francisco's public transit system, as well as that of most other American cities, I was amazed at this triumph of engineering and public expenditure. It was like viewing the genius of a Monet painting or a LeBron James slam dunk.

In a new and significant turn, President Barack Obama's fiscal stimulus package in February 2009 allocated $8 billion for mass transit construction, including high-speed rail. It will take years for this money to be delivered and for any projects on the design boards to come to fruition, but this is a badly needed shot in the arm. It may be a sign that, finally, America the extravagant is ready to change.

THE "HORSELESS CARRIAGE" GETS A MAKEOVER

Europe also is blazing a new path in designing new fuels and energy-efficient technologies for motor vehicles. There's no better example of how the United States, the world's biggest per capita polluter, has refused to modernize its ways than the gross inefficiency of our automobiles. American vehicles have engines that dwarf those of other nations, double the average size of engines in France and Italy and nearly double the average in Germany and Britain.[7] That's hardly surprising, since for decades America's bipartisan policy lagged far behind Europe's and Japan's policies, letting Detroit cruise along at the wasteful standard of only 27.5 miles per gallon for cars and 22 miles per gallon for SUVs and trucks. "To travel one mile in the United States requires 37 percent more fuel than to travel one mile in Europe or Japan," says Diana Farrell, deputy director of the National Economic Council.

If the United States were to match the fuel economy standards of Europe and Japan, U.S. demand for oil would be cut by 4 million barrels per day, or 1.5 billion barrels of oil per year, according to various estimates. Given that the United States consumes about 8 billion barrels of oil per year—about a quarter of the world's total—oil dependence would be reduced by nearly 20 percent, a huge amount. A shift in standards also would accelerate the introduction of fuel-saving technologies, which in turn would spur the U.S. economy.

These gains would be more low-hanging fruit if the U.S. had the right laws and policies. But instead of demonstrating leadership, for years Democrats and Republicans alike enabled a plodding auto industry's refusal to get with the times. Washington even created outrageous loopholes that allowed buyers of extra large SUVs to take extra large tax deductions. Until recently, Congress hadn't changed the nationwide fuel standard from twenty-seven miles per gallon since the 1970s. While the Bush administration clearly was negligent in showing leadership, Democratic Party leaders also share the blame. During a crucial 2007 Senate debate over an energy bill, Michigan's two Democratic senators, Carl Levin and Debbie Stabenow, acted as shills for their home state's auto industry, watering down the proposed higher fuel standards. In the House, the powerful Democratic chairman of the House Energy and Commerce Committee, Michigan's John Dingell, for decades was the auto industry's stoutest defender. Could it have been related to the fact that Dingell's wife was a senior executive at General Motors and a member of the family who founded the company?[8]

So while European and Japanese automakers have had to innovate in order to meet their nations' high fuel standards at or near forty-five miles per gallon, creating vehicles such as the ever-popular hybrids and modified diesel engines, the Big Three could lumber along with their gas-guzzling cruisers until they were caught flat-footed when the price of gasoline escalated. At that point, they didn't have any car or truck models that could compete with the high-mileage Japanese or

European vehicles. That debacle led to the closing of plants and thousands of layoffs starting in 2006. By late in 2008, when the economy tanked and consumers quit spending, the auto companies were clinging to life support and had to be bailed out by Washington. General Motors, long the "general" of auto companies the world over, fell to its knees begging and eventually declared bankruptcy.

Europe also is spearheading other transportation innovations. As a way of dealing with traffic jams and too many cars on the roads, the cities of London, Rome, and Stockholm have pioneered the creation of "congestion zones" within their city centers, where motorists are required to pay to enter. Every week in cities across Europe and the United States, vehicles idling on congested roads waste fuel, cost billions of dollars, and contribute to significant health-related costs from breathing in exhaust-choked air. So London began charging eight dollars per day for any vehicle driving in the eight-square-mile city core, then plowed the revenue raised back into the public transit system. Initially there was an outcry, including the usual overhyped prophecies of commercial doom and despair. But now Londoners have been convinced by the remarkable changes: traffic in the zone has declined over 20 percent, and normally clogged streets have opened up. About a hundred thousand people pay the toll each day via cell phone, the Internet, or at retail shops across the city, and an array of seven hundred video cameras that read license plate numbers catches about three thousand scofflaws per day, who are fined $128 apiece. The fares and fines raise approximately $200 million per year, most of it for public transport, which has improved and is making more people willing to ride it to travel into the city center.

Stockholm enacted a similar plan and saw a 22 percent decline in traffic, and Rome saw a 20 percent decline. The mayor of Paris has unveiled plans to make a three-square-mile zone nearly car free by 2012. While American cities also are choked by traffic, and commuters as well as experts demand intervention, no mayors have had the political will or courage to implement congestion zones. When Mayor Michael Bloomberg, of New York City, showed interest, he ran into predictable opposition in the form of powerful special interests, as well as New Yorkers' apparent infatuation with their automobiles, even while they complain about congestion, smog, and all the related illnesses.[9]

Europe also has taken a different route than the United States in developing ways to run motor vehicles on non-petroleum substances. A lot of attention has been given to the development of plug-in electric cars and to converting bioproducts into fuel known as ethanol. Denmark plans to have in place an electric car charging network, including automated battery-swapping stations where drivers can swap in fresh batteries, by 2011. Once the network has been established, Danish utility Dong Energy will use its excess wind power capacity for charging the electric cars. Denmark currently gets 20 percent of its electricity from wind turbines, but a portion of that electricity is exported because it can't be stored economically. With the introduction of the electric car, Denmark can use that wind-generated electricity locally to charge car batteries.

Many other European countries and their automakers are in the advanced stages of electric car development. German automakers BMW and Mercedes are developing all-electric cars, with BMW unveiling its Electric Mini in 2008. Interestingly, while Denmark and other European countries are working closely with American companies to develop this technology, those same companies have had difficulty finding partners in the United States. Europe has been a much more fertile landscape than the U.S. for developing this technology, with supportive government policies (for example, the Danish government included incentives to help overcome the higher cost of battery-powered vehicles in the form of no sales tax on the purchase of electric cars). So American companies have been going where the business is. A California company, Better Place, worked with the Danish government and Dong Energy to line up almost $103 million in financing to go toward constructing their electric car network. Bob Kanode, CEO of American vehicle battery maker Valence Technology, says Europe is much further along than the U.S. in the race to deliver plug-in electric cars. "In Europe, the determination is absolute," he says. "They want to decrease their reliance on foreign oil . . . and they are absolutely committed to improving their carbon footprint, both the public and the governments. . . . [In the U.S.], the companies aren't here, the determination isn't here, and the markets aren't here. . . . It's absolutely no comparison."[10]

President Barack Obama and other U.S. leaders have pledged to develop this technology. On the campaign trail, candidate Obama pledged to put one million electric plug-in hybrid cars that can get up to 150 miles per charge on the road by 2015. His February 2009 fiscal stimulus included a sizable amount of money for development of advanced battery technology. As the U.S. prepares to move forward with these efforts, it will benefit from Europe's pioneering breakthroughs, and hopefully the commitment will be long-lasting.

Europe also has been leading in developing the promising alchemy of converting bioproducts into ethanol fuel. To its credit, the Bush administration ramped up production of ethanol—but from food crops like corn and soybeans, despite warnings from experts that those are the wrong bioproducts to use for raw material, because they compete with the food supply. Sure enough, in the spring of 2008 we saw a dramatic rise in food prices around the world. Also, experts at the Earth Policy Institute, based in Washington DC, have said that growing, transporting, and distilling corn to make ethanol uses almost as much energy as is contained in the ethanol itself. For all those reasons Europe has taken a different route, producing ethanol from less expensive and more abundant cellulose fibers, such as grass, straw, sawdust, and wood cuttings from fast-growing trees. Europe also goes after the agricultural leftovers such as corn and rice stalks and wheat straw, which can't be eaten and often are left in the fields or burned. Estimates say that collecting just a small portion of these leftovers could yield nearly fifteen billion gallons of ethanol, four times the current output, with no additional land demands and without competing with the food supply. President Obama is a big supporter of ethanol fuel, as are many of his top cabinet members and advisors. Energy Secretary Steven Chu has criticized corn-based ethanol while supporting cellulosic ethanol, and Obama seems to share those concerns. Ethanol seems certain to be a part of America's and Europe's energy mixes in the decades to come, but challenges remain to ensure that the ethanol is produced in such a way as to ensure the energy output is net positive.[11]

Air transport is a relatively small component of the transportation sector, consuming only 2 percent of global energy, compared to road transport, which consumes 16 percent. So not much effort has focused so far on air transport energy efficiency. But air transport is the fastest growing part of this sector, so at some point the focus will have to change.[12] On the whole, because of Europe's more robust and highly developed transportation sector, including its more fuel-efficient autos and its rapid mass transit providing excellent transport both between and within cities, *BusinessWeek* has written that Europe is likely "the best buffered from [oil] price increases."[13] The roller coaster ride of global energy geopolitics is not going to level off anytime soon, and Europe's transportation sector is much better positioned to navigate the ups and downs than America's gas-guzzling system, which is more exclusively reliant on the automobile.

EUROPEAN APOTHEOSIS: THE HYDROGEN ECONOMY

Once while I was standing on a street corner in Amsterdam near Centraal Station, the main transport hub, a public bus drove by with a slogan on its side announcing to the world, POWERED BY HYDROGEN FUEL CELLS.

Europe has been a leader in the development of hydrogen as a zero-carbon-emission source of fuel for vehicles and buildings, with various pilot projects launched. Hydrogen fuel is produced from water by using electrolysis to split off the hydrogen atoms and store them at high pressure. The process essentially is pollution free, giving off only water vapor and no carbon emissions. Its potential sounds almost too good to be true, but in recent years substantial progress has been made toward its development.

Europe's bid to push forward with hydrogen technology and create what is known as the "hydrogen economy" is a quintessential example of European leadership. Several nations are making advances on this front, but Iceland is the first to commit to becoming the world's first hydrogen-based economy. Iceland's government and industry have worked together to produce dozens of prototype hydrogen-fueled cars, as well as fueling stations (both roadside stations and ones that can reside in your home or office). The fueling stations use geothermal power to produce the hydrogen, which is ready for pumping into a car's fuel tank as if it were gasoline. A company called Icelandic Hydrogen has produced a prototype refueling station that can easily fit in a garage, where it will produce a couple of kilograms of pressurized hydrogen in a day, enough for nearly a full tank of fuel. Icelandic Hydrogen thinks hydrogen fuel is coming fast, predicting a substantial market for it by 2015, and not just in Iceland.[14]

The hydrogen fuel itself must be generated from renewable energy sources, because the use of fossil fuels to generate the hydrogen may actually *increase* carbon dioxide in the atmosphere. A pilot project demonstrating a renewables-based hydrogen economy is operational in Norway; it combines wind, solar, and hydrogen power. In periods when there is surplus wind and solar energy, the excess power is used for generating hydrogen, which then is stored for power generation in periods when there is little wind or sun. (Ocean power or other renewables also could be used to generate hydrogen fuel.) So these technologies are extremely complementary, fitting together like pieces of a jigsaw puzzle.

European leaders have pledged billions of dollars to this research and development, declaring that the European Union's scientific effort toward forging a hydrogen economy is as important for Europe as the space program was for the United States in the 1960s and 1970s. Commercial hydrogen fuel cells already have been introduced into the market for industrial, office, and home use. Large stationary fuel cells are being purchased by manufacturing and other companies to provide backup power during peak periods of electricity use or during rolling brownouts or blackouts. A hydrogen fuel cell power plant has been installed at the Munich Airport. Hydrogen-powered buses and auto-mobiles have been test driven on roads across Europe. (Some hydrogen buses have even begun appearing in various U.S. cities as well.) Iceland has even produced a whale-watching boat that uses hydrogen to run its auxiliary power system, the first time hydrogen has been used to fuel a water vessel. Former skeptics are no longer thinking *if* but *when,* with the first mass-produced automobiles expected to be in showrooms by 2015.[15]

Europe's vision of a hydrogen economy is a bold one, in some ways the apotheosis of the European trajectory, combining its many different innovative elements into the energy and transportation infrastructure of the future. Picture wind farms, solar arrays, tidal and wave farms, and other renewables producing energy, some of it directly powering homes and businesses but also used for the production of hydrogen fuel for vehicles. Imagine homes and businesses all across the land with rooftop solar cells, using some of this renewable energy to produce hydrogen fuel in situ, which can then be stored in a specialized closet in your garage or office and used for power generation on a cloudy day. Some of the hydrogen fuel could be stored in the trunk of your car, not only to power the vehicle but also to turn the car itself into a mobile "power station on wheels" that pumps unused energy either back into your home or into a national energy grid. Estimates say that if just 25 percent of drivers use their vehicles as power plants while their cars are parked at home or at the office to sell energy back to the grid, all of the massive plants powered by hydrocarbon or nuclear fuels could be eliminated. Today's centralized, top-down flow of energy, controlled by global oil companies and utilities and held hostage to Middle East politics, would become obsolete.[16]

Critics claim this vision is far-fetched science fiction, yet that's what critics said about the attempt to reach the moon. It's a vision for moving forward, and the journey to arrive at the goal will undoubtedly produce many technological advances along the way. That is the bet that Europe has made. Compare that with U.S. leadership under the Bush administration, which was deaf to the looming realities of global climate change and the entreaties of the world that we change our greedy ways. President Bush also proposed his own billion-dollar research initiative for hydrogen-based autos, but mostly his administration never followed through with money on the barrelhead. The Bush administration had a history of making dramatic but ultimately unfunded proposals in front of the TV cameras, and the hydrogen promise was no exception. It quietly faded and then was replaced by corn-based ethanol as the energy sound bite du jour. Toyota spent more on hydrogen research than the entire U.S. government under the Bush White House.[17] The Obama administration has shown some direly needed new attention to these energy and transportation issues, but it's hard to do an about-face very quickly with a hulking ship that has been so misguided and misdirected for so long.

REDIRECTING BEHAVIOR VIA A CARBON TAX

In the previous chapter we looked at Europe's launching of the world's first successful cap and trade system, which is attempting to cap the overall amount of carbon in the environment by creating market-based incentives for companies to swap carbon credits and reduce their carbon emissions. Another tactic deployed in Europe is a carbon tax designed to discourage certain activities and products that are harmful to the environment and to encourage other behaviors that are benign or even beneficial. You do that by charging a tax on activities that release carbon dioxide and other gases that are fueling destructive climate change. The carbon tax rewards green living and changes people's behavior; products and activities that are less harmful to the environment become less expensive, and harmful choices cost more. This tax also spurs technological innovation and green solutions as people and businesses look for ways to save money. Those who don't want to pay more taxes can control how the tax affects them through the choices they make. You can keep driving that SUV, but you will pay a premium for the privilege. You can even make the levying of a carbon tax revenue neutral, so that it is not perceived as just another way for government to pry money out of people's pockets, by simultaneously reducing other taxes, such as payroll taxes. "Tax what we burn, not what we earn" has become the motto of many proponents of a carbon tax.

Sweden introduced a transportation carbon tax in 1991. Swedes today pay an extra $1.50 per gallon when they fill their tank (although many key industries are exempted partly or wholly). "It was the one major reason that steered society towards climate-friendly solutions," says Emma Lindberg, an energy expert at the Swedish Society for Nature Conservation. "It made polluting more expensive and focused people on finding energy-efficient solutions." The Swedish minister for the environment, Andreas Carlgren, from the conservative Centre Party, adds, "Our carbon emissions would have been 20% higher without the carbon tax."[18] Finland, the Netherlands, Italy, and Norway also introduced carbon taxes in the 1990s, and more European countries likely will be adopting this approach in the near future. French president Nicolas Sarkozy has raised the idea of levying a carbon tax on imports from other nations that are not doing their fair share of reducing their carbon emissions. During the Bush administration Sarkozy singled out the United States as the worst violator that was refusing to do its fair share. Sarkozy proposed that monetary incentives like a carbon tax would force a change in Americans' behavior. But that idea was dropped with the election of Barack Obama, whom Europeans view as more willing to take the necessary steps to push the United States in the right direction.

EUROPE'S ENERGY CHALLENGES

The fragility of the oil-based global economy, the rise of wealthy and influential petro-nations, and the threat of climate change create trials for all nations. Securing a stable energy supply is fraught with geopolitical challenges and, no doubt, future surprises. The quest to create a "sustainable Europe" based on renewable energy sources and greater energy productivity has no certain outcome. Even eco-conscious Europe occasionally backslides, as shown by the decision of several European countries in 2008 to authorize fifty carbon-spewing coal-fired power plants to begin operating over the next decade.[19] In an economically competitive world, being green is a difficult challenge and the struggle to do so strikes at the heart of our modern, energy-intensive societies. Besides the obvious technological and economic hurdles to overcome, at least three other obstacles confront Europe.

First, the decentralized nature of the European Union has been both a strength and a weakness when it comes to energy and security challenges. On the one hand, the various nations have been deploying different policy options and technologies to achieve their goals—France, Spain, and Germany with their high-speed trains, Sweden and Denmark with their cogeneration plants, Germany, Spain, and Britain with wind power, Italy and Iceland with geothermal power, Portugal and Germany with major solar plants, and Portugal with its wave farm of sea snakes. Each country gains from the successes and insights of the others, creating a learning network that has made great strides in reducing Europe's ecological footprint to half that of the United States. But if Europe is to take its efforts to the next level and reach its ambitious low-carbon goals by 2020, this decentralized approach will present an obstacle, since it will prevent economies of scale and the degree of continental coordination necessary for cross-border transmission of electricity. And it contributes to puzzling contradictions, such as energy leader Germany, which, under the influence of its powerful auto lobby and Germans' love of fast cars, has rejected sensible speed limits that would cut carbon emissions and force carmakers to stop producing powerful cars for the high-speed autobahns.[20] And then there's France, one of the most nuclear-power-dependent nations in the world, despite the alarming and unresolved issues of long-term waste storage.

Related to this is the second obstacle: major power companies are treated by various countries as "national champions" and thereby shielded from competition and even, to some degree, regulation. There's a happy medium between the deregulated energy market chaos in the United States, which led to the Enron meltdown and the California gouging debacle, and the status quo in Europe, in which energy-generating companies do not have much competition or, as a result, great incentive to innovate and employ newer technologies and renewable energy sources on a scale massive enough to take Europe to a higher level of energy productivity. Europe needs to strive harder to find this happy medium between secure energy supply and competition.

The third obstacle is the global puzzle of energy geopolitics, which, in the European case, mostly has been dramatized by Middle East instability and Russian saber rattling. The blowback from the American-driven Middle East policy washes up on the European doorstep on a regular basis, resulting in an influx of refugees that fosters tensions within Europe's own domestic populations. And Russia, teetering on the edge of its autocratic past, supplies approximately 40 percent of the natural gas to Europe. Its unpredictable behavior has shown Russia's willingness to manipulate the energy lifeline in a contest for geopolitical leverage. But while Russia's brinksmanship has generated headlines, its impact is not as severe as it has been portrayed. Russia is the largest external gas supplier to the E.U., but it is far from a monopoly provider. Europe's ongoing diversification of its gas supply has resulted in Russia's share of E.U. gas imports being cut in half, from 80 percent to 40 percent, since 1980. Currently, Russian gas represents just 6.5 percent of the overall E.U. primary energy supply. Moreover, two-thirds of the E.U.'s imports of Russian gas go to western Europe, where supply is sufficiently diversified from other sources, such as Azerbaijan and North Africa, so that Russia's games are not a credible threat. But a few eastern European nations (especially Lithuania, Latvia, Hungary, and Slovakia), which together amount to a tiny share of Russia's overall exports to Europe, rely heavily on Russian gas for their energy use, and therein lies the predicament.

"The problem is divisiveness, not dependence," says Pierre Noël, a senior policy fellow at the European Council on Foreign Relations, specializing in energy security and E.U. energy policy.[21] While Europe's overall exposure to Russia's energy games is a limited one, the disproportionate impact on eastern Europe revives old east-west rivalries. The most effective way, says Noël, for the E.U. to counter Russian attempts to divide European nations would be to restructure its internal gas market so that it is not segmented along national lines. Currently, there is little cross-border trading of gas within the E.U., and when supply disruptions occur—as they did in January 2006 and 2009 due to a dispute between Ukraine and Russia—there is very little reallocation of supply between national markets. A single competitive and integrated European gas market would allow greater flexibility when supply is threatened.

To address this situation, the European Commission announced in November 2008 its E.U. Energy Security Plan, calling for the creation of a continent-wide power grid with a Community Gas Ring that would allow E.U. countries to share gas supplies if Russia shuts down the supply. The supergrid also would link North Sea wind farms and the electricity grids of the Baltic region in northern Europe with the countries bordering the Mediterranean.[22] But while this seems like an obvious and straightforward response, the European Commission has proposed this before and not followed through due to the reservations of some member states, especially Germany and France, that are wary of risking their own domestic supply. This issue taps into existing east-west tensions, and most experts agree that such a plan will take time to implement. In the meantime, disputes between Russia and Ukraine are becoming annual events, along with the disruption in supply for several of the smaller countries of eastern Europe.

The years ahead promise many potential pitfalls and challenges, especially in light of the impacts resulting from a major global economic downturn. Over the next couple of decades, no one power source is likely to dominate as hydrocarbons dominated the Age of Oil. Different nations and different regions will have their own unique mixes of energy supplies and technologies that will respond best to local needs. One of my favorite examples of local adaptation is that of Linköping, Sweden's fifth largest city, which runs its fleet of buses, garbage trucks, a train line, and some private taxis on biogas from methane harvested from—the guts of slaughtered cows![23] But while exotic examples like this one always attract headlines, the truth is conservation, efficiency, and increased energy productivity always will be the best energy supply of all.

EUROPE'S INDUSTRIAL (R)EVOLUTION

The looming threat of global climate change will be with us for years to come. It is the greatest challenge of our time. Much is at stake in the epic endeavor of halting the effects of carbon pollution. Hollywood storytellers already are spinning vivid tales of impending apocalypse, with films such as *The Day after Tomorrow, Blade Runner, Children of Men,* and Steven Spielberg's *A.I.* portraying the dire consequences if we fail. Given the stakes, Europe has emerged as "the indispensable nation," while the United States, the largest per capita polluter in the world, has been fiddling as the earth literally burns. The United States is woefully lagging behind Europe and Japan in reaching for the low-hanging fruit and implementing the existing technologies that could make a difference.

Fortunately there are signs of an awakening in the United States. The Obama administration has displayed a significant shift in perspective and policy compared to the Bush administration, having pledged billions of dollars to fund the development and deployment of more renewable energy, a smart energy grid, and more. Some of the state governments have stepped up to the plate, led by governors like Republican Arnold Schwarzenegger, of California, and Democrat Bill Richardson, of New Mexico. A relative boom in wind power has taken place, resulting in installed capacity in the United States growing by 45 percent in 2007 (though it started from a small base, so overall capacity is still small).[24]

National energy mobilization in the United States could do for the economy what the Internet boom did in the 1990s or what the GI Bill did in the 1950s for the housing construction industry. Yet ironically much of this boom in the United States is being constructed by *European* companies from Spain, Germany, and Portugal, since they have expertise and experience in developing large-scale wind projects. Foreign companies own two-thirds of the wind projects under construction in Texas, as American companies mostly have been missing in action.[25]

If the United States continues to refuse to change its energy ways, there is little incentive for China, India, and other emerging nations to do so, particularly since China's and India's per capita consumption is far below that of the much wealthier United States. As one Indian official said, "First you [the developed world] do virtually nothing to cut your emissions, and then you threaten us [the developing world] with drowning from global warming sea level rise if we don't cut ours. It won't wash."[26]

Fortunately, Europe is pointing the way toward a new industrial (r)evolution in energy. Led by pragmatic yet far-sighted leaders like Germany's Angela Merkel and others, who oversee the largest economy in the world with the power to drive global markets, European governments and companies are responding in a way that demonstrates that action on global climate change can bring tremendous environmental, economic, and social benefits. Europe has been able to lead the world in energy policy even as its social capitalist economy has grown to become the largest in the world, and even as it continues to provide a generous workfare support system to families and workers. Europe shows unequivocally that these goals are not incompatible; in fact they can complement each other quite well. It's a matter of having the correct vision, the right institutions, and able leadership that will spend money on the right priorities. Europe appears to have plenty of each, and the whole world is hoping that the Obama administration will follow in Europe's footsteps. It's a make-or-break century, with the fate of the inhabitable planet hanging in the balance.

PART FOUR

GLOBAL EUROPE

ELEVEN

THE RELUCTANT SUPERPOWER

Transatlantic Rupture and the Post-9/11 World

September 11 and the Iraq and Afghanistan wars proved to be defining events in the post–Cold War era. While the United States was bogged down in modern Mesopotamia and the Hindu Kush, portentous changes were occurring elsewhere in the international system. In three strategic regions of the globe—East Asia, the former Soviet Union, and the Middle East—leading nations decided that it had become necessary to band together in order to play defense to the American superpower offense. To do that, several of these key nations created the most important upstart organization that most Americans have never heard of: the Shanghai Cooperation Organization (SCO), a regional group linking China, Russia, and the resources-rich 'Stans of Central Asia.[1] At a key meeting of the SCO in 2006, Iranian president Mahmoud Ahmadinejad was invited to address the proceedings and meet with the bloc's leaders. Touting Moscow, Tehran, and Beijing's "identical" views on world issues, Ahmadinejad proposed making "the SCO into a strong and influential economic, political, and trade institution [to] thwart the threat of domineering powers." It was clear to all which domineering power he had in mind.[2]

Meanwhile, in a different part of the world, another vehement U.S. critic, Hugo Chávez, of Venezuela, also had been cultivating closer ties with China and Russia. The vaguest outlines of a new global alliance was taking shape: major oil exporter nations from around the world, who had trillions of dollars dumped into their state coffers as the price of oil has soared, have aligned with China, the world's second-largest oil consumer, which provides a ready market for their oil as an alternative to the United States and Europe. These petro-states now can consider reducing deliveries to the West. Venezuela's Chávez already has threatened to cut off all oil shipments to the United States, and Russia has used its resources to punish neighboring nations that lean toward the West, such as Georgia and Ukraine.

Forget President George W. Bush's "Axis of Evil"; this "Axis of Oil," as it has been called, has the potential to reshape global politics. Troublesome countries and factions such as North Korea, Syria, Libya, and even Al Qaeda and the Taliban, which have mounted deadly attacks but cannot greatly harm developed economies, are bantamweights compared with the members of this emerging alliance, whose potential threat has grown with the tremendous global influence they have gained over the past five years. The threads connecting these far-flung regions of the world are increasingly enmeshed, and the Cold War tactic of using military threats has less potency today. While the United States is still a great power, its foreign policy now is less dominant than it has been at any point since World War II. A number of analysts have warned that this alliance of oil-marinated regimes may pose the most serious threat to the United States and the rest of the West since the collapse of the Soviet empire.

Beyond the rise of this Axis of Oil, other festering tensions daunt the international system, including the Iraq and Afghan wars, the ongoing Israeli-Palestinian conflict, the fragility of nuclear power Pakistan, the hardships of Africa, global climate change, and more. It is into this global context that Europe must try to project its foreign policy. Europe has evolved a particular brand of "smart power" that has been animated by the same inclusive spirit as its domestic policy, namely, its signature combination of humane values, international law, multilateralism, and its own Marshall Plan–like incentives for development. Rather than launching U.S.-style military interventions, its power is based on more of a carrot than a stick approach by forging ever wider regional networks of nations into economic and political unions via a spreading web of trade, foreign aid, and investment. The basic premise is that countries that become mutually interdependent through trade don't make war against one another.

Indeed, the European Way of foreign policy has been a continual reworking of the chessboard strategy initiated by French leaders Jean Monnet and Robert Schuman after World War II, when they led the launch of the European Coal and Steel Community in 1951, which bound the former combatants Germany and France into a regional network that rendered war between them nearly impossible. Monnet's vision of using a series of small-scale, concrete proposals with practical outcomes as a gradualist vehicle for forging "peace and prosperity" partnerships has been surprisingly successful on a number of fronts over the past six decades. It has inspired some to think that it may be a harbinger of a more quietly potent type of foreign policy, better suited than American bellicosity for dealing with the Axis of Oil and other challenges.

Europe's power, which has been referred to as "soft" power (as a contrast to U.S. "hard" power) but which is better understood as "smart" power because of the way it seeks to build consensus among multiple players and interests, often has been unappreciated by Americans. So in this chapter I will first describe how the European Way of foreign policy works, and in the next chapter I will describe how it is being applied to hot spots around the world. In many ways, European smart power has been more effective than American hard power because it is more pragmatic and reality-based.

SMART POWER VS. HARD POWER: THE EUROPEAN WAY OF FOREIGN POLICY

One of the foremost proponents of the European Way of foreign policy is Mark Leonard, director of the European Council on Foreign Relations. He is the author of a slim but influential book, *Why Europe Will Run the 21st Century,* which in 2005 made its way up various bestseller charts in Europe. Mark Leonard's vision runs contrary to those who see the transatlantic world in terms of the lone remaining superpower hobbled by a "ninety-eight-pound weakling" in the form of the fragmented, bickering "old Europe," as Bush administration secretary of defense Donald Rumsfeld called it. Leonard's thesis is compelling, but you won't read about it in any American newspapers or periodicals, and you won't see him on *The Lehrer Report,* Fox News, or CNN.

I spoke with Mark Leonard on a bench overlooking the Thames River near his office on a lovely September day in 2006. We both enjoyed the spell of splendid fall weather, with a golden sunlight passing translucently through the leaves of oak trees that line the banks of the Thames. A stone's throw away stood the inspiring towers and spires of Westminster, where the British Parliament convenes, a historical treasure chest filled with old stories and relics of our common Anglo-American heritage. Leonard's manner and expression were affable and patient, but his gaze was steady and confident as he explained his thesis to me.

"The world that is emerging in the twenty-first century will not be centered on the United States, but will comprise a community of regional political-economic clubs following the model of the European Union," he explained. "The E.U. has what I call 'transformative power'—the power to change countries from within. Europe doesn't change countries by threatening to invade them. Its biggest threat is having nothing to do with them."

That was an intriguing statement, and I asked Mr. Leonard to elaborate. He smiled patiently and continued. "Europe is a sort of decentralized club, with the biggest single economic market in the world. It can offer poorer countries membership in that club—including trade and generous development aid and all the carrots that major powers have been able to dangle in the past—or it can withhold that membership and have nothing to do with them."

But the membership in the European Union is not just economic, and it does not come free. Oh no. It's more than a two-way street; it's a multiway street. To be admitted entry into the club, you have to agree to a whole host of laws and regulations—eighty thousand pages worth—regarding human rights, democracy, and free markets. "And that sort of legal power allows you to transform not just the regimes in other countries, but the whole of their societies," says Leonard.

This is not just some ivory tower theory. For many years Europe has been applying this smart power approach with extraordinary success. For starters, the European Union has made a dramatic difference on the European continent itself, home to a half billion people. It is easy to forget among the allures of Europe's wealth and charm as a tourist mecca that not that long ago it was a place ravaged by two horrific world wars, followed by a geopolitical struggle with Soviet-led communism, and most recently disrupted by savage ethnic conflicts in its southeast region of Kosovo, Serbia, Bosnia, and elsewhere. But in just fifty years, Europeans have made war unthinkable among the same European powers that fought numerous conflicts against one another for centuries. They have accomplished this by patiently stitching together the foundation for their union via a series of treaties—first, in 1951 the sharing of control of the coal and steel industries, then in 1957 the lowering of trade barriers and the creation of a common market, followed by other tangible projects for partnership. This model—composed of small, concrete, and verifiable steps for cooperation and collaboration—has been the key to developing a track record of trust and integration, paving the way toward "union." Patiently over a period of decades, the European Way has brought successive waves of European nations out of dictatorship and poverty and into democracy, prosperity, free markets, and respect for human rights.

José Manuel Barroso, the president of the European Commission (currently the closest position to a "president of Europe"), points to his own country of Portugal as proof of what Mark Leonard is saying. Until its 1974 "Carnation Revolution," Portugal was governed by the Salazar military dictatorship.

"Today, Portugal is a stable democracy, fully integrated into the European Union," says President Barroso, "but it was not always so." The establishment of a democratic system in Portugal and the raising of the social and economic conditions of citizens to levels similar to those in other European countries, as well as in the United States and Japan, "are clearly the most important achievements." The political shakeup and economic aid received as a result of E.U. membership helped Portugal's economy grow from 53 percent of the E.U. average in 1985 to 75 percent of this average today.[3]

Spain is an even more dramatic example of miraculous transformation. Thirty years ago Spain also was run by a dictator, the notorious General Francisco Franco, until 1975. Twenty years ago, the Spanish gross domestic product per capita was 71 percent of the E.U. average; today it is approaching 100 percent. In 1985, Spain's impoverished infrastructure showed barely twelve hundred miles of high-capacity roads; in 2004, it had over seventy-two hundred miles of roadway. And in 1992 Spain became the third country in the world to employ high-speed trains, with a number of lines now in operation and more in the works.[4]

Until the global economic crash of 2008, many experts were calling the European Union "a steroid for economic growth." Other nations touched by the wings of the E.U. phoenix include Ireland, which not that long ago was an economic backwater. For most of this decade the Celtic Tiger had one of the fastest growing economies and one of the highest per capita incomes in the world. A Belgian friend who lived briefly in Dublin twenty years ago returned there a few years ago observing, "What a miracle, like a person who was sick and withering and now is hearty and bursting with life." Under the incentives of E.U. nudging, in April 2008 Cyprus finally tore down the physical barrier that for decades had divided the island into Greek and Turkish sections. Poland also has benefited from admission into the club, as have other former communist nations in central and east European countries, where huge increases in foreign investment have resulted in high economic growth rates for the region (a 66 percent increase in their gross domestic product from 2003 through 2007).[5] In the Czech Republic, the unemployment rate plummeted from 8 percent in 2005 to 4.6 percent in early 2008.

My colleague Phil Longman, a senior fellow at the New America Foundation, visited Poland in 2007. "I was amazed to see in Warsaw and Krakow new, larger homes, the kind you see in the U.S. and western Europe, clear signs of an emerging middle class," he reported. Indeed, in a real-life version of the popular German film *Good Bye Lenin!*, a Polish railway worker who fell into a coma in 1988—a year before the fall of communism—awoke nineteen years later to a world of mobile phones, colorful streets, and abundant choices. He expressed his utter amazement.

"When I went into a coma there was only tea and vinegar in the shops, meat was rationed and huge petrol queues were everywhere. Now there are so many goods in the shops it makes my head spin."[6]

And when Poles do emigrate, instead of flocking to the United States and its centers of Polish immigration, such as Chicago, they are increasingly choosing E.U. cities such as Dublin, Glasgow, and London. Their earnings there are similar to U.S. wages, but a flight home is cheaper and shorter, and no visa or work permit is required.[7]

Robert Cooper, who was top foreign policy advisor to Prime Minister Tony Blair and has become one of the European Union's most senior foreign policy officials, says that Europe's "magnetic allure" compels countries to rewrite their laws and constitutions to meet E.U. standards.[8] Some have described the way Europe's "union" works as more like a corporate merger than a political conquest. Truly like an "invisible hand," Europe's focus on legal frameworks and economic development, using incentives rather than threats as the attraction for entering the club, can *transform* the countries it comes into contact with instead of just skimming the surface.

Mark Leonard amplified this point. "The U.S. might have changed the regime that rules Afghanistan or Iraq, but Europe is changing all of Czech and Hungarian society, from their economic policies and property laws to their treatment of minorities and what gets served on the nation's tables." The lonely superpower can bribe, bully, or impose its will almost anywhere in the world, but when its back is turned, its potency wanes. The strength of the European Union, conversely, is broad and deep. "Once sucked into the E.U.'s sphere of influence, countries are changed forever," he says.

Mr. Leonard then led me on a brief historical tour of recent efforts of the United States, and then Europe, to enact regime change. "The U.S. has sent troops into neighboring countries more than fifteen times over the past fifty years," he said, "but many of them—from Haiti to Colombia—have barely changed. They limp from crisis to crisis, with an overemphasis on military solutions that often end up sucking U.S. troops back in, or at least military aid."

Compare that with the real progress being made today in Bulgaria, Romania, and the Balkans (Croatia, Bosnia, Serbia, Macedonia, Montenegro, and Kosovo), which are spurred on by the allure of membership in the European Union. Less than twenty years ago and into the early 1990s, these places were Dante's infernos, communist police states followed by hellish war zones of intense ethnic violence and even genocide, as detailed in books like Robert Kaplan's *Balkan Ghosts*. Yet by 2007, this region was for the most part at peace. Under the umbrella of both European and American intervention, its people had emerged from the bunkers of war and cesspools of ethnic hatred to enjoy the fruits of a steady peace and slowly growing prosperity. Its economies had realized sizable increases in foreign investment and economic growth rates and a narrowing gap between the pay of its own poor countries and that of Europe's richest countries.[9] In response to a question I posed to Croatian president Stjepan Mesić about what he would tell young Croatians their southeastern European country might look like in ten to twenty years, President Mesić said optimistically that he envisioned Croatia as a nation distinguished by the rule of law, political stability, and integration into the developed world of Europe. In other words his Croatia would follow the path set by Spain, Portugal, and Ireland, advancing from national hardship and violent dictatorship to freedom, democracy, and increased prosperity as a member state of the European Union.

Even more dramatic, compare Europe's success in Turkey with the U.S. quagmires in Afghanistan and Iraq. Not that long ago Turkey was ruled by a military junta with a human rights record on a par with Saddam's Iraq. Plagued by military coups, the memory of the

Armenian genocide, and the 1974 invasion of neighboring Cyprus, it was regularly listed by Amnesty International and other organizations as one of the worst violators of human rights, particularly the rights of the minority Kurds and, as a Muslim country, the rights of women as well as press freedoms.

But with the incentives of joining the European Union, Turkey has been substantially transformed. Under its Western-oriented Muslim prime minister, Recep Tayyip Erdoğan, Turkey has abolished the death penalty, prison torture, the army domination of security courts, and most curbs on free speech (though it still backslides as it struggles with its Kurdish separatists). In recent years foreign investment in Turkey zoomed from $1 billion to $18 billion, exports nearly tripled to $86 billion (half of them to Europe), and the economy has grown at an annual average of 7 percent.[10] A single state-owned TV station has blossomed into three hundred TV stations and eleven hundred radio channels, including the broadcasting of programs in Kurdish and other minority languages.[11] In the 2007 election, Erdoğan's Justice and Development Party was peacefully reelected, as were two dozen Kurdish representatives, a display of political pluralism that would have been unthinkable previously.

The European Union has spent perhaps a tenth of the money in Turkey that the United States has spent on the invasion and occupation of Iraq, yet look at the difference in results: Iraq remains a tinder box of sectarian violence, ethnic cleansing, and destruction, but Turkey has slowly become a functioning democracy with a prospering economy. Turkey continues to have its shaky moments, and by no means has it fully arrived as a social capitalist democracy, but its progress is undeniable. "Unquestionably, Turkey has been greatly transformed by the incentives of joining the European Union," says Rouzbeh Pirouz, an entrepreneur I met who travels throughout the region. Adds Andrew Moravcsik, director of the European Union Program and a professor at Princeton University, "Surely [the European Union] ranks as the single most cost-effective Western instrument for expanding global peace and security since the end of the Cold War."[12]

"That's the difference between American foreign policy and E.U. foreign policy," says Mark Leonard. "One is patient and, compared to America's knee-jerk military solutions, fairly gentle. Yet it is incredibly effective. It possesses an extraordinary transformative power by drawing these nations into the E.U. orbit, embedding them in its legal and economic framework, and changing them from the inside out. Next to this transformative power, the United States's military might is fleeting and can change regimes but not societies."

Bernd Westphal, consul general of Germany, further pounded home this point when I met him, comparing the regional integration of western, eastern, central, and southeastern Europe with the dismal failure of U.S. policy toward Mexico. In Europe, the philosophy that a rising tide floats all boats has been taking hold as E.U. enlargement intricately links the fate of wealthy western Europe with the rest of the continent. Meanwhile the decennial American episode of saber rattling over illegal immigration has led to yet another impasse along the U.S.-Mexican border, even as Mexico continues to sink into a morass of corruption, narcotics traffickers, sabotage of oil pipelines, and assassinations of journalists, top law enforcement officials, even celebrities, a level of malfunction nearly on a par with Colombia's, another troubled U.S. client state.[13] Western Europe has implemented a plan to help its neighbors, utilizing its own version of a Marshall Plan, while the most politically viable American solution for Mexico is to build a more secure border wall, further shutting off the two nations from each other. Notice the irony: in Europe walls are coming down, but between the United States and its neighbor, walls are still going up. Said Consul Westphal, "The new member countries are receiving billions from the E.U.; even Turkey is receiving tens of millions. Compared to Europe's efforts, U.S. efforts with Mexico look rather timid."

The regional impact of Europe's foreign policy has been enormous, the transformation unparalleled, and why E.U. expansion has been called "the most successful foreign policy ever" by Chris Patten, former British Conservative Party leader and the last British governor of Hong Kong, who has been a great admirer of the United States's leadership role in the post–World War II era. Ironically, Europe thought it had learned much of its methods from Uncle Sam. The Europeans view foreign aid as another form of national defense; they don't see it as handouts or charity but as investments in the future, just as a post–World War II generation of American leaders once did, with the Marshall Plan originally called the European Recovery Plan. Americans forget the scope and generosity of the Marshall Plan. Historian Niall Ferguson has estimated that the total amount disbursed under the Marshall Plan was equivalent to roughly 5.4 percent of U.S. gross national product, or $740 billion in today's currency. That's a staggering sum (about the same amount as the Wall Street bailout in 2008 and President Obama's fiscal stimulus in 2009), especially when compared with actual foreign aid under the Bush administration between 2001 and 2006 which totaled less than $150 billion, an average of less than 0.2 percent of gross domestic product.[14]

While European development aid today doesn't approach Marshall Plan levels, it is still the world's largest bilateral aid donor, providing three times as much aid to poor countries as the United States.[15] The European Way understands that a successful foreign policy today is more dependent than ever before on economic and political development in struggling nations. A lot is at stake, and foreign policy is an area in which Europe excels, while American foreign policy has remained trapped in a Vietnam-era mentality of using military muscle and even invading nations as a way of dealing with unsavory elements.

But it is not just Europe proper that has benefited from the European approach to foreign policy. Around the core of the European Union and its twenty-seven nations and 500 million citizens is another zone of nations with approximately 385 million people—including some Arab countries—that share sea or land borders with the E.U. and have become networked ever more closely to the European core. Surrounding that zone is another 900 million or so people from nations whose biggest trade partner and source of foreign investment, credit, and aid is the European Union. All told some 80 nations, from North Africa to Anatolia to the regions of the former Soviet Union, are being networked via concentric circles of European trade, aid, and investment. Some, like Turkey, Ukraine, and Georgia, seek actual membership in the European Union. Other nations, while not aspiring to E.U. membership, nevertheless benefit from various types of multilateral arrangements and development aid and investment.

"These two billion people," says Mark Leonard, "fully one-third of the world's population, live in this 'Eurosphere' and are gradually being transformed by adopting European ways of doing things."

A couple of recent examples illustrate how the European Union has been extending its reach to its southern and far eastern perimeters through various regional pacts. In July 2008, French president Nicolas Sarkozy led an effort to launch the Union for the Mediterranean. This new transnational body brought together the twenty-seven countries of the European Union along with nations from North Africa, the Balkans, various Arab countries, and Israel—encompassing some eight hundred million people—to foster cooperation in one of the world's most volatile and troubled regions. It was the first time that Israeli prime minister Ehud Olmert and Syria's president Bashar Assad had sat at the same table together. For this Mediterranean Union, leaders agreed on six modest but tangible projects: cleaning up pollution in the Mediterranean Sea, improving shipping routes, developing solar energy, cooperating on natural and human-made disasters, instituting a Euro-Mediterranean student exchange program, and setting up a Mediterranean business initiative to help small and medium-size companies. By copying Jean Monnet's strategy for the E.U., the region's leaders hoped to establish a track record of small but concrete steps that would gradually build trust, cooperation, and regional partnership.[16]

Having extended its reach to the south, a year later the E.U. extended further east with the launch in May 2009 of its Eastern Partnership plan with the six former Soviet states of Ukraine, Georgia, Moldova, Armenia, Belarus, and Azerbaijan. This time led by Germany's Angela Merkel, the announced goal was to "accelerate political association and further economic integration" in the region. The E.U. encouraged the former Soviet states to bury their differences and cooperate in order to enjoy the benefits of the E.U.'s partnership initiative, which aimed to stabilize the region by encouraging countries to work together and adopt democratic and free market reforms.[17]

Leonard's eyes twinkled amiably as he further elaborated his vision for this "Europeanized" world. "Europe's success already has set off a regional domino effect that could change the nature of power beyond its borders. In every corner of the world, countries are drawing inspiration from the European model and nurturing their own neighborhood clubs," and as examples he pointed to ASEAN (the Association of South East Asian Nations), APEC (Asia-Pacific Economic Cooperation), Mercosur (the South American common market), UNASUR (the South American Union of Nations), the African Union, and the Arab League.[18] Indeed, the African Union directly borrows from E.U. structures, including modeling its most influential bureaucracy, the A.U. Commission, on the European Commission. ASEAN, with ten member countries (China is not a member), is perhaps the most advanced regional grouping after the European Union, having produced a road map for transforming the group into a single market by 2015.[19] "When ASEAN was thinking where it wants to be in 20 years time, they came here to Brussels," says the European Union's Robert Cooper. "And the Latin American dream is to have something like the EU."[20]

China aspires to be the center of an E.U.-like political economic regional club in East Asia. This European influence was apparent when China and Japan signed a historically significant agreement on joint development of gas fields located in the East China Sea between Japan and China. Sakurada Jun, associate professor at Toyo Gakuen University in Japan, compared this pact to the Jean Monnet plan forming the European Coal and Steel Community. "Taking the European experience into consideration," wrote Professor Sakurada Jun, "the joint development of gas fields can become a chance for both Japan and China to promote self-control in the sense that neither country will act selfishly or allow the other to do so."[21] And bitter Sino-rivals China and Taiwan tore a page from the Jean Monnet playbook in late 2008 in a bid to extend an olive branch across the Straits of Taiwan. They negotiated an agreement based on small-scale, incremental steps designed to foster engagement and trust, including the start of direct mail service, expanding charter flights and maritime shipping, and cooperation on food safety issues.[22]

Author Parag Khanna, whose book *The Second World* has grippingly outlined a global competition between the three most important powers today, the United States, Europe, and China, for influence in the second world of aspiring nations, has noted that many of these second world countries have keenly observed the way the European Union has given small or undeveloped countries an ability to shape their destiny on the world stage beyond their actual wealth, military might, and population size. Khanna told me that, in this global competition, the European model of "union" is proving to be an inspiration.

"In various capitals, they're looking to Europe for guidance, not the United States," says Khanna. "They are greatly attracted to the European notion that regional political-economic clubs can advance democracy, lessen historical rivalries between member states, help assimilate countries into the global economy, and foster common solutions to cross-border problems." E.U. policies, he writes in *The Second World,* "consistently pull ever more countries towards the European way."[23]

But this idea of pooling sovereignty—that is, the idea of giving up a bit of one's national sovereignty in order to gain a greater regional sovereignty and security—is not new. No less than Winston Churchill first proposed the notion in a speech to the Congress of Europe in 1948. Churchill was one of the original architects of the European Union, stating that closer political union "involves some sacrifice or merger of national sovereignty," but that this sacrifice should be viewed as "the gradual assumption by all the nations concerned of that larger sovereignty which can alone protect their diverse and distinctive customs and characteristics of their national traditions."[24]

Today, if you look at a map of the world you can see a zone of European influence spreading, from the west coast of Ireland through the eastern Mediterranean and into Russia and Central Asia, from the Arctic Circle to North Africa, from the Strait of Gibraltar to the Strait of Hormuz. "If the E.U. adds Turkey, countries like Iran and Iraq suddenly are European neighbors, with contiguous borders. Russia already is. It's just a matter of time," says Mark Leonard.

There was something about his vision for the future that I found compelling. He was right, Europe's type of smart power is so easy to miss amid all the headlines about military invasions, old and new tensions, and regime change. We Americans tend to think that removing a dictator, even ones that we helped install, can be accomplished as easily as plucking out a rotten tooth. After all, we have been doing it for nearly a century, though not always with success but at considerable human and financial cost. Even after the debacle of Iraq, the American media and public mostly still do not seem to question the use of this kind of hard power—even when torture, extraordinary renditions, and kidnappings are involved—and are rather dismissive of Europe's brand of smart power. It seems likely that if the Bush administration's Iraq misadventure had gone more successfully, as it did in the days leading up to Bush's ill-fated "Mission Accomplished" photo-op on an aircraft carrier, the American public would have remained supportive of their president's policies. President Barack Obama has expanded Bush-Cheney's aggressive policies in Afghanistan, a poor, ravaged country with an economy smaller than that of tiny Rhode Island and little strategic value other than having the unfortunate position of being the host country for the never-ending Osama bin Laden chase. Obama also expanded operations in Pakistan. It's not clear what lessons Americans or their imperial-minded political leaders have learned, other than they don't like to lose.

Mark Leonard concluded his historical survey by observing that Europeans and their political and economic union are reinventing, quite audaciously, the nation-state itself and its place in the world. As globalization intensifies, smaller countries in particular are being faced with stark choices: develop your own regional club based on an interconnectedness regarding one another's affairs, or face the world alone.

"The world that emerges will be a community of interdependent regional clubs, and even great powers like the United States and Japan, as well as emerging powers like China, India, Iran, Venezuela, Russia, and Brazil, will be sucked into the process," says Leonard. His is a hopeful and attractive vision, though the process is not without its missteps. But on the whole the shape of a global blueprint is coming into sharper focus. It has the potential to integrate the far-flung regions of the world, nudging them away from the path of adversaries conducting turf wars over finite resources, to one of regional political-economic clubs pursuing peace and prosperity partnerships, modeled on the European Union.

THE PERILS—AND PLUSES—OF DISUNITY

Despite Europe's success stories in its neighborhood, Americans have tended to sneer at Europe's smart power ways. Americans see European foreign policy as weak and ineffectual at best, and as bordering on ungratefulness or a Neville Chamberlain–like appeasement of axes of evil at worst.[25] Europe's decision-making process often appears to Americans as no better than a debating society among fractious national interests. Even some Europeans regularly sound warnings about the consequences of continental disunity, with Germany's former foreign minister Joschka Fischer famously complaining that it causes Europe to "punch below its weight." Europe's power has been denigrated as being too soft, especially when it comes to its military capability. American neoconservative analyst Robert Kagan has characterized the large gap in military capability between the United States and the European Union as the signature driving force behind our different outlooks and approach to geopolitics—"America is from Mars and Europe is from Venus," as he pithily stated.

While undoubtedly this view holds some truth, I find it to be overly simplistic. Contrary to American complaints, the European nations are no slouches militarily. As we've seen, in 2007 Europe as a bloc spent $319 billion, second only to the U.S. military's expenditure and nearly three to five times the estimated military spending of China. Europe's total armies number more active troops than the U.S. military has in uniform, including a rapid deployment force. In addition to the nuclear capabilities of both France and Britain, many E.U. nations have ample conventional ground weaponry, such as tanks and fighter jets, and Europe is producing its own global satellite navigation system, Galileo, with potential military applications. In recent years the European Union has had twenty-one missions in conflict zones and fragile postconflict countries, sending tens of thousands of troops and bringing vital military support and civilian expertise to a range of troubled areas, including Afghanistan, Lebanon, Kosovo, Bosnia, the Congo, Northern Ireland,

Macedonia, and other hot spots. Some nations, such as Britain, Poland, and others, also contributed thousands of boots on the ground in Iraq.

But certainly it's true that this considerable military capability has not been forged into a cohesive, continent-wide fighting force, which contributes even more to the complaint that Europe punches below its weight. Other shards of disunity, especially historical ones, also nag at the edges of continental consensus. The rift over the American desire to place antimissile defenses in Poland and the Czech Republic tapped into considerable historical baggage among western, central, and eastern Europe, as did the Russian bear's slapdown of Georgia president Mikheil Saakashvili's reckless invasion of the disputed province of South Ossetia in August 2008. Poland and the area now known as the Czech Republic have been invaded multiple times over the centuries by Germany, France, and other past European governments from the west, as well as by Russia from the east. These smaller countries often have been caught in the middle between warring major powers, and their bitter histories and old national rivalries have created hurdles to the creation of an even stronger continental union. The current boundaries of the European map have not been fixed all that long, prompting British political analyst Anatol Lieven to write, "History does not end when countries join the European Union."[26]

Henry Kissinger once famously asked, "Who do I call if I want to call Europe?" and Europe is still trying to definitively answer that question. A proposed European constitution contained provisions to foster a single, unitary voice for foreign policy and other policy areas, but that was defeated by French and Dutch voters in 2005. Even a scaled-back version was rejected by Irish voters in 2008. But European unity always has proceeded haltingly, two steps forward and one step back, trying to figure out a shape to its "union" that all of its member nations can live with. On a regular basis, the twenty-seven nations of the European Union face a degree of continental disunity and fear of centralized power that is reminiscent of America's early years in the 1780s and 1790s.[27] Indeed, even a figure as universally revered as President George Washington had to discreetly exert the influence of his office, since centralized power still lived under a monarchical cloud of suspicion, causing Washington to avoid political battles that threatened to push centralized authority further and faster than public opinion was ready to handle.[28] We can see echoes of this caution today in some of the tensions over Europe's unity.

But this lack of a unified European voice isn't always a disadvantage. It can permit a good cop–bad cop routine that can be effective, such as when German chancellor Angela Merkel and other European heads of state pulled out of attending the opening ceremonies of the Olympics in China to show displeasure with China's heavy-handed crackdown in Tibet and other abuses, but French president Nicolas Sarkozy and British prime minister Gordon Brown chose to attend. That kind of push-pull jujitsu keeps the pressure on without isolating the Chinese leadership. And when it's time to cast votes in multilateral organizations such as the United Nations, the World Trade Organization, International Monetary Fund, the Group of 20, and other global institutions, Europe has multiple votes to cast on behalf of the European position, like a swarm of insects, compared to a single vote each for the United States, China, Japan, or any other country. Europe sometimes acts like a single nation—with its vast continent-wide market of five hundred million people and the European Parliament and a powerful executive branch called the European Council—and other times like a union of individual nations. That duplexity can allow Europe to have it both ways.

But this kind of swarming behavior can be difficult to interpret for those Americans who like bold, clear stands. So despite Europe's considerable foreign policy achievements, it still suffers an entrenched reputation problem in the United States and even to some extent in the broader world. But military intervention is a last resort for Europe, not simply because the continent is too disunited, or because it doesn't possess significant military capability compared with its potential enemies, or even because it is always opposed to military force. (Europe followed the American lead to intervene with great force in the Balkans to put an end to Serbian aggression against its neighbors, with support from even the formerly pacifist German Green Party for this intervention.) No, Europe's smart power is based more on principle than on impotence: a continent of nations that spent centuries warring among themselves has learned a thing or two about the severe limitations of state violence, as well as the benefits of a regional prosperity that derives from steady economic growth among neighbors that is not interrupted by destructive wars.

This is a new horizon, a watershed in human history, that a great power on the order of the European Union should base its foreign policy so substantially on the principles of nonviolence and fostering peace and prosperity partnerships. Europe's success in fostering regional economic and political zones and, more broadly, the rise of an economic power of the magnitude of the European Union that does not combine it with an imperial use of military power—indeed, seems to have little desire to do so and to some degree *defines* itself by this lack of desire—may be a historical first. Certainly Russia's crushing of Georgia's rash invasion of South Ossetia showed some of the real challenges to Europe's approach in its periphery regions, not to mention in the world's flashpoints. Nevertheless, the advent of peaceful social capitalists who spread prosperity and security in concentric rings of connectivity that touch two billion lives is a momentous shift, unprecedented in its tone and scope.

It is difficult for most Americans, fed by media stereotypes and stuck along with their political leaders in the warring quagmires of Iraq, Afghanistan, and increasingly Pakistan, to grasp the magnitude of what European foreign policy has accomplished. While Europe certainly has a smaller military stick than does America, its very success with its smart power and America's failures with its hard power raise a legitimate question about the best tactics in this post–Cold War, multipolar world. For all the talk of the United States as the world's lone remaining superpower, the past decade of foreign policy stumbles have demonstrated the limits of that power, quite to the rude awakening of many in the United States, indeed of many around the world.

Given the deep and historical roots of its foreign policy, Europe is extremely unlikely either to spend more of its economic wealth on increasing its military power or to take a more aggressive military posture toward Russia, Iran, or the Middle East, despite pressures to do so by American political leaders and critics. President Barack Obama, like other American leaders, has stated that he wants Europe to step up and shoulder more of the responsibility for the world's security, but that receives a head scratch from most Europeans. They believe they already are doing their fair share, and Europe is wary of joining the United States in its military misadventures, and will remain so even with a new U.S. president. President Obama promised a new multilateralism and more consultation with allies, yet in early 2009, barely months in office, he chose to escalate the war in Afghanistan by sending in more troops and to widen missile strikes inside Pakistan beyond even Bush administration targets, all without consultation. Then he was disappointed when Europe rejected his request for more troops in Afghanistan. Like President Bush, Obama apparently does not understand Europe's strategic assessment of these matters. Nor does he grasp that, in the absence of a more direct and imminent threat, Europe is reluctant to spend more on its military and less on its domestic needs, lest it risk underfunding its people, its infrastructure, and its future—becoming more like the United States, in other words.

It's not that Europe doesn't understand what is at stake in Afghanistan and the war on terror, as some American critics have charged. In 2002, Germany's defense minister Peter Struck said, "The defense of Germany begins in the Hindu Kush," which is the mountain range that stretches from eastern and central Afghanistan to northwestern Pakistan. But Europe is looking for a partner across the Atlantic that is willing to be a power among peers instead of a messianic hero that regards itself as the "indispensable nation," as Bill Clinton's secretary of state Madeleine Albright once called the United States.[29] Europe has its own way of doing things, and the European approach to foreign policy has been extremely successful in the regions in which it has been applied. While it's true that Europe's smart power does not always achieve its desired result, at least not in the short term, neither does America's hard power. Indeed, a September 2008 intelligence forecast written by Thomas Fingar, the top analyst in the U.S. intelligence community, concluded that superior U.S. military power will "be the least significant" asset in an increasingly competitive world that is being reshaped by globalization, climate change, and shortages of food, water, and energy.[30] Secretary of Defense Robert Gates seconded this view when he said that the Bush administration's foreign policy risked "creeping militarization" by focusing too many resources on the Pentagon and not enough on U.S. diplomacy and international aid.[31]

"The EU is now a global superpower in every respect except high intensity military force: trade, aid, multilateral membership, peacekeeping and policing, and ideological legitimacy," says Princeton's Andrew Moravcsik.[32] But to take the Bush-Cheney worldview for a moment, given the nature of the various military and geopolitical threats that trouble the world, is it reasonable to think the European way of smart power might be effective at dealing with some of the world's flash points, such as Russia, the Middle East, and China? That's the overriding question going forward—can the European way of foreign policy, which has worked so well to foster zones of peace and prosperity in the greater European region and among its periphery neighbors, work in some of the more intractable tension spots of the world? We will explore that question in the next chapter.

TWELVE

THE EUROPEAN WAY OF FOREIGN POLICY, PUT TO THE TEST

With its successful track record in transforming former military dictatorships in Spain, Portugal, Turkey, and former communist countries, and economically backward places such as Ireland, Poland, and the Czech Republic, Europe has taken its principles of engagement and integration and begun applying them to the rest of the world. Contrary to the Bush-Cheney doctrine of unilateralism and aggressive bluster, Europe has practiced a patient multilateralism in trying to embed countries and regions such as Russia, China, Central Asia, and the Middle East into a web of incentives and disincentives, of trade, foreign aid, and investment, designed to nudge them slowly toward economic integration as a foundation for human rights and democracy.

Unsurprisingly, given the massive geographic size, history, and culture of Russia, China, the Middle East, and these other places, Europe's track record in these hotspots has been more mixed compared to its successes on the European continent and in its near-abroad. But Europe recognizes that this is a long-term project. The European Way is patient and steady, like a river that constantly applies gentle force to the riverbank, slowly changing its course over time.

President Barack Obama has said he is interested in breaking with the belligerent unilateralism of the Bush administration in favor of more negotiations with adversaries, including direct talks with Iran, and more consultation with allies. Time will tell what tenor and tone this new posture will take, but the current course of international affairs was

215

established in the post-9/11 era, when the world's lone remaining super-power decided to ride the upwelling of emotion from that horrible event to throw its weight around. Much can be learned about Europe's "smart power" approach by comparing it to the Bush administration's displays of "hard power" during the 2001–8 period. Contrary to the assertions of its critics, who see Europe as impotent and disunited, Europe's foreign policy has displayed a pragmatism and patience that, while having its setbacks and frustrations in the short term, turned out to be the wiser course.

DANCING WITH THE RUSSIAN BEAR

Dealing with the autocratic behavior of former Russian president and current prime minister Vladimir Putin certainly has tested Europe's resolve and vision. Putin has been willing to use Russia's vast energy resources as a foreign policy wedge, and he has taken over national television, emasculated the country's governors, turned the national parliament into a rubber stamp, jailed the main financier of the political opposition, intimidated political opponents, and handpicked his successor. In a sordid James Bond–like episode that seemed emblematic of the Putin regime, a Russian dissident, Alexander Litvinenko, was assassinated by covert poisoning in a London bar in 2006, and then Russia refused to honor the British government's request to extradite the chief suspect for trial.[1] Even after handing off the presidency in May 2008 to his successor, Dmitri Medvedev, Putin stepped sideways into the role of prime minister and has remained the power behind the throne, overseeing Russia's heavy-handed military operation in Georgia in August 2008.

When Americans look at Europe's response to Putin, they see yet another example of European helplessness and appeasement in its failure to confront Russia. But Russia's reactions were, in part, a response to Bush-Cheney's unilateralism and belligerence in regard to specific regional grievances that exacerbated old resentments and suspicions. These in turn have fostered Russian nationalism and pushed the government to look for economic and political relationships that do not involve Washington. While President Bush claimed to have looked into the soul of President Putin and declared him a good man, Vice President Cheney needlessly provoked the Russian bear over issues that were not essential to America's core strategic interests. These included attempts to bring Ukraine and Georgia into NATO (akin to Russia bringing

Mexico or Canada into a Russian-led alliance), supporting Georgia in its conflict with Russian-backed breakaway provinces, and trying to extend U.S. antimissile defenses of questionable military value to eastern Europe. This caused Russian defense minister Sergei Ivanov to complain that "the U.S. has created a circle around Russia" from which Russia has sought to find a release.[2] This was not a terribly smart thing to do, given Russia's regional military clout and stockpile of weaponry and, once the price of oil skyrocketed, its replenished national treasury.

Making matters worse, the Bush administration exhibited an all too familiar double standard when Vice President Cheney blasted President Putin for the latter's anti-democratic tendencies but immediately followed that by getting on an airplane to Kazakhstan, where he warmly embraced a notorious dictator, President Nursultan Nazarbayev. That was followed by Secretary of State Condoleezza Rice's praise of another dictator, President Ilham Aliyev of Azerbaijan. Certainly the despots of the world, not to mention U.S. allies, must have been confused by this erratic American behavior and rhetoric. Noted by everyone, of course, was that both of those Central Asian countries were ones where the United States was seeking to site military bases, as well as to gain access to significant lodes of oil and other energy resources. With all of this coming on the heels of the Abu Ghraib torture, Guantánamo detentions, and more, any criticism of Putin and Russia from such a notorious defender of human rights as Dick Cheney rang exceedingly hollow in Moscow, as well as in most of the world's capitals.[3] Cheney's bombast, which saw everything as a nail to pound down with the hammer of U.S. foreign policy, fostered its own blowback time and time again. His was the hubris of a superpower that turned out to be not so super.

In fact, Russian expert Anatol Lieven argues that Cheney's aggressive posture toward Russia actually was impractical and dangerous. Take, for example, the Bush administration's clumsy attempts to drive a wedge between Russia and some of the Caucasus states, such as Georgia and Ukraine. "The Russians," says Lieven, "have lost far more men fighting in Ukraine in various wars than have died in all America's wars put together, and the Russian flag was flying over Ukraine's naval port of Sevastopol before the United States was even created."[4] Former Soviet dictator Josef Stalin was a Georgian and is still greatly admired by many Georgians.

Leaving aside the deep historical and cultural ties among much of Ukraine, Georgia, and Russia, Ukrainians and Georgians also are economically dependent on Russia. Until it was reduced at the start of 2006, Russia's *annual* gas subsidy to Ukraine ($3 billion to $5 billion) was worth more than four times as much as the whole of U.S. aid to Ukraine in the five years after 2000 (less than $800 million). Millions of Ukrainians and Georgians work in Russia and send remittances back to their families, which make an immense contribution to their countries' economies. By contrast, only a handful of Ukrainians and Georgians receive work visas for the United States and the European Union. The West has done little in the past to help Georgia or Ukraine, nor is it likely to do so anytime soon. Georgia and Ukraine are stuck in Russia's Caucasus neighborhood.

Tensions there came to a head in August 2008, when Russia slammed Georgia hard after the latter's reckless president, Mikheil Saakashvili, invaded the disputed province of South Ossetia. Saakashvili, who had been criticized for his own anti-democratic tendencies,[5] tried to portray the one-sided fight as his country's small, fledgling, Western-oriented democracy being picked on by the Russian bear's authoritarianism. However much that depiction rang with a degree of truth for some in the West, it failed to recognize a grittier big picture that can never be ignored. If this tension with Russia were to spiral, it could lead to far more damaging tidings than a Georgian occupation. Russia could arm Iran against the United States and join global energy cartels—think Axis of Oil—to oppose the West more than Russia has. It also has the potential to inflict even more disastrous geopolitical humiliation on Washington if the United States were ever to agree, as Saakashvili wanted, to defend Georgia (or Ukraine) as part of NATO and then prove incapable of doing so, a near-certain outcome. The fact is, like the Iraq and Afghan wars, the crisis over Georgia served as a reminder, wrote *Washington Post* reporter Michael Dobbs, "that our ideological ambitions have greatly exceeded our military reach."[6]

So while the Bush administration's more belligerent tendencies showed little patience for Europe's smart power, its own sorry record undermined its credibility and stature. Said German Social Democrat lawmaker Gert Weisskirchen during the middle of the Russia-Georgia crisis, the Bush administration forgets "that Russia is our next-door neighbor. We can't afford and don't want to address Russia in terms that risk reviving Cold War sentiments."[7]

Better than the United States, Europe understands that it simply is not dominant enough—even with U.S. backing—to dictate to Russia. But that doesn't mean that Europe is impotent, not by a long stretch.

Europe does have "weapons" at its disposal. Trade between Russia and the European Union jumped 23 percent in 2007, to $284 billion; the European Union accounted for just over half of Russia's foreign trade in 2007 and 80 percent of foreign investment, making it Russia's biggest trading partner, far bigger than the United States.[8] Russia's entire economy is only the size of France's, and the Europeans have made clear to Russia that it is not wealthy enough to develop its economy without massive European investment, nor is it strong enough to push back against the West on every issue. As political analyst Parag Khanna points out, with Europe as Russia's largest investor, the much wealthier Europe is going to have great influence since in the long term Europe is staging a buyout of Russia, not the other way around.[9]

As was discussed in chapter 10, when it comes to energy dependence on Russia, Europe has been steadily diversifying its gas supply to the point where Russian gas represents just 6.5 percent of the overall E.U. primary energy supply. Russia's manipulation of its gas supplies mostly has affected a few small eastern European nations that rely heavily on Russian gas, not the core of Europe. The European Commission is exploring ways that would allow E.U. countries to share gas supplies if Russia turns off the tap, but this plan will take time to implement.

That doesn't mean that Europe doesn't assert its prerogatives from time to time—when the European Union launched its Eastern Partnership plan in May 2009 with the six former Soviet states (including Ukraine and Georgia), the Russian bear growled its predictable displeasure. Yet the E.U. pushed forward anyway, knowing that these sorts of steps must be taken delicately, as well as incrementally. So where American analysts see Europe's dependence on Russia, Europeans themselves see interdependence. Where Americans see appeasement, the Europeans see pragmatic engagement. They see Russia as an integral part of their future, of their near-abroad, and so Europe's posture toward Russia is based on a sensible policy of mutually shared interests and needs, including energy supply, human rights, democracy, and regional politics. Says Germany's former foreign minister Joschka Fischer, "The West needs Russia's cooperation on almost every important international issue of the day, be it North Korea, Iran, Iraq, the Middle East, South Caucasus, Central Asia, Kosovo, Darfur, climate change, energy security, or nuclear non-proliferation."[10] Echoing Fischer, Flynt Leverett, a former National Security Council senior director and CIA senior analyst, says, "The United States and its allies can have a mutually beneficial relationship with Russia. Russia does not want to exercise financial leverage over America or withhold energy supplies to Europe. Quite the opposite—Russia wants to expand its energy and financial ties to the West, but it will use the tools it has to defend its interests."[11]

That means that the best route—indeed the *only* route—to a democratic and secure Ukraine and Georgia is through the patient fostering of a more engaged and democratic Russia. If Russia remains a paranoid power invoking czarist nostalgia for regional dominance, the West's options for responding will remain extremely limited.

In short, better than the Bush administration and perhaps the Obama administration as well, Europe understands the realities of living in a multipolar world. It means you are locked in an embrace, in a long-term dance, in which the dance partners are bound to step on each other's toes. That's a given. But Europe's smart-power approach toward Russia, based on long-term engagement over mutually shared interests, is more grounded in the pragmatic realities of the world as it exists, while American bluster has been based on the same dangerous brew of imperial fantasies and fanaticism that led to the quagmire in the Middle East.

FINDING THE "MIDDLE" IN THE MIDDLE EAST

In the Middle East, again we see Europe's more pragmatic, smart-power approach compared with America's radicalism and resulting failed policies. Americans routinely fail to grasp that the Middle East is Europe's backyard. Europe's neighbor Turkey, which aspires to become an E.U. member, borders Iraq, Iran, and Syria, with Israel, Lebanon, Jordan, and Saudi Arabia only a short distance away. American disasters in the Middle East produce casualties that show up at Europe's borders. Europe takes a more delicate approach out of sheer pragmatism, since that approach creates less collateral damage to mop up. France's foreign minister (and later prime minister) Dominique de Villepin gave a speech at the United Nations in early 2003, just before the United States invaded Iraq, warning that "the use of force would be so fraught with risks . . . for the region and for international stability" that intervention would "exacerbate the divisions . . . that nurture terrorism." Said Villepin, "Having won the war, one has to build peace," a prediction that turned out to be prescient. But that was just one example of many in which the Bush administration behaved, as one British diplomat put it with characteristic English wit, "like a bull that carries around its own china shop."

In the Israeli-Palestinian conflict, Europe's smart-power instinct has been to engage more with all sides, providing more humanitarian funding than the United States has to all the players in the conflict, while the United States, with its hammer instinct, has armed Israel with billions in military aid and ignored and even isolated the Palestinian leadership, especially Hamas. Even within the Democratic Party, the leading candidates for president in 2008, including Barack Obama, all genuflected at the altar of Israel, not out of conviction or principle but because of the huge number of Jewish voters in the state of Florida, one of two key battleground states that decided the 2000 and 2004 presidential elections. With such a pro-Israel bipartisan policy, the United States has lost all credibility in the region as a broker of peace. Europe hasn't always been united or spoken with one voice on the Israeli-Palestinian conflict—France has been seen by the United States and Israel as pro-Arab and pro-Palestinian, while Germany's support for Israel has been strong, ranking it as Israel's second largest trading partner, with long-standing defense, scientific, and cultural cooperation.[12] But on the whole Europe's approach has been balanced, with Europe being the earliest proponent of the two-state solution, which even the Bush administration eventually realized was the only viable outcome.

In Iran, while the Bush-Cheney White House engaged in more saber-rattling, Europe's smart-power pragmatism led to a proposal for a "grand bargain," including development aid, technical expertise, and security guarantees in exchange for Iran's cooperation on nuclear and regional security matters. Europe's long-term strategy recognizes that Iran is a poor country badly in need of economic development. Despite all the oil, Iran's economy is smaller than New Jersey's, and it has a burgeoning population of young people who were born after the Islamic revolution and want a more secular and middle-class existence than the ruling religious clerics can deliver. Change is in the air, but it needs the right sort of push that doesn't produce an equal and opposite hostile reaction. European governments long resisted Bush administration demands that they isolate Iran by curtailing exports, blocking transactions, and freezing the assets of some Iranian companies. For that matter, U.S. ally India also rejected White House pressure to isolate Iran or to squash its own plans for an Iran-Pakistan-India gas pipeline, even when Washington linked this pressure to a highly favorable nuclear pact with India—yet another sign of how much U.S. influence has waned, even among allies.[13]

Europe already has come to grips with the impossibility of preventing Iran's nuclear capability without a massive military operation larger than the troubled one in Iraq—particularly since Russia, China, and the Shanghai Cooperation Organization seem quite willing to assist Iran as a vehicle for undermining U.S. hegemony in the region. Europe also believes that if Iran were to gain nuclear arms, the West could deter it from using them through carrot-and-stick diplomacy, just as it did with the Soviet Union during the Cold War. Rather than appeasement, this is a realpolitik conclusion that various American analysts have reached as well, including General John Abizaid, President George W. Bush's former U.S. commander for Iraq and the Middle East region. Said General Abizaid in a major address to the Center for Strategic and International Studies, "There are ways to live with a nuclear Iran. Iran is not a suicide nation. I doubt that the Iranians intend to attack us with a nuclear weapon" because of the risk of a catastrophic retaliatory strike.[14]

The European approach toward Iran, as toward Russia, turns on the belief that long-term engagement around mutually shared interests is the way forward. The Europeans are under no illusions that such a path will be a smooth one. But the Bush administration, in its refusal to sit down with Iran and negotiate, relying instead on threats and bullying displays of muscle such as aircraft carriers in the Strait of Hormuz, showed itself to be mostly toothless. Iran made a proposal for such broad discussions in 2002–3 that was rejected by the Bush administration. The proposal laid out a comprehensive agenda for U.S.-Iranian rapprochement, containing considerable detail about how to approach issues of central interest to the United States, including Iran's acceptance of Israel's right to exist, an end to its support for anti-Israeli militants, and action against terrorist groups harbored on Iranian soil. Flynt Leverett, a senior director at the National Security Council at the time, called Iran's proposal "a serious proposal, a serious effort," likening its importance to that of China's opening its doors to the United States in 1972. But Leverett says Secretary of State Colin Powell told him he "couldn't sell it at the White House," since the Bush-Cheney neocons were hell-bent on confrontation and aggression.[15] In the simplistic, black-and-white neocon worldview, talking with the enemy is more European-like appeasement.

Yet entreaties to negotiate originated not only from the "appeasing" Europeans but also from the U.S. bipartisan Iraq Study Group and the U.S. Congress, in addition to America's long-standing allies in the Middle East. So it was the Bush-Cheney administration's hammer approach that was the clear outlier, incapable of dealing with the Middle East as anything but a nail to pound down, despite the ineffectiveness of that policy. The limits of the American posture were recognized by nearly all but those bunkered inside the Oval Office. Ray Takeyh, Iran specialist at the conservative Council on Foreign Relations, stated, "The coercive track is undermining and negating the diplomatic track and preventing any sort of meaningful discussions."[16] Mohamed El Baradei, the director general of the U.N.'s International Atomic Energy Agency, was even more blunt in describing the Bush administration's belligerence. "It was a ridiculous approach," he insisted. "They thought that if you threatened enough and pounded the table and sent Cheney off to act like Darth Vader the Iranians would just stop. If the goal was to make sure that Iran would not have the knowledge and the capability to manufacture nuclear fuel, we had a policy that was a total failure."[17]

Finally, in May and July 2007, ambassadorial-level meetings were held between the United States and Iran. While mostly the meetings were to discuss a narrow agenda focused on the security situation in Iraq, nevertheless they were a small breakthrough because they marked the first time in twenty-eight years, since the Ayatollah Khomeini–led Islamic forces overthrew the corrupt U.S.-backed dictator Mohammed Reza Pahlavi (a.k.a. the Shah of Iran), that the U.S. and Iranian governments had sat down face to face at the discussion table. This was a meeting that was long overdue. Unfortunately, very little of substance was negotiated or achieved, mostly because the Bush administration still insisted on limiting the scope of discussions.

But today it is now clear that the U.S.-led removal of Saddam Hussein in favor of a Shiite-led Iraq has had the unintended consequence of tipping the delicate Mideast power balance in favor of Iran. In one of the biggest foreign policy blunders in American history, the Bush administration delivered the Iraqi government into the hands of Shiites with long-standing ties to Iran. Thanks to this Bush-Cheney-Rumsfeld folly, Iran has emerged out of decades of Western isolation into a new leadership role in the Saddam-less Middle East. Treated as a pariah state by the United States, Iran now feels no urgency to engage constructively. It is forming its own alliances, looking east not west, toward organizations such as the Shanghai Cooperation Organization. Unquestionably a new Middle East power center has arrived, and the immediate challenge is how to work with its leaders to nudge them—over time—toward a respect for regional peace, human rights, women's rights, democracy, free markets, and international law.

One indispensable way to accomplish this is to embody the behavior that you hope to spread, with as little hypocrisy and expediency as possible. Only Europe's practice of long-term engagement, building upon substantive points of mutual interest, seems to have the depth and breadth, the nuance and the flexibility, to succeed in this project. America unfortunately was led astray by an isolated Bush-Cheney White House entangled inside a congenital illogic, one that became increasingly divorced from reality. The Obama administration has expressed interest in a new beginning for Iran-U.S. relations, which is direly needed. It can start by observing more carefully Europe's smart-power approach of small but constructive steps of engagement over mutually shared interests.

CHINA: A WORK IN PROGRESS

Europe's policy toward China, and East Asia in general, has similarly shown the hallmarks of its unique approach. Its policy of engagement with the Far East, especially via trade and investment, traces all the way back to the times of Marco Polo, who was one of the first Westerners to travel the Silk Road to China, around 1274. Today, Europe combines this commercial approach with a patient (and some say all too quiet) nudging of China toward respect for human rights and democracy. These efforts are both aided and complicated by the intricate and increasing linkage of the two economies. The European Union is China's largest trading partner, having taken over that role from the United States and Japan in 2004. And China is the European Union's second largest trading partner after the United States. The E.U. imports more from China than even the U.S. does, with trade volumes with China doubling since 2003.[18] The E.U. is China's most important source of foreign investment capital and its biggest source of technology imports.[19] In the face of a plummeting dollar, China has increased the euro share of its massive foreign exchange reserves, and it now sends far more diplomats and experts, and twice as many students, to the European Union as to the United States.[20]

Yet when China cracked down on Tibetan protestors in March 2008, the European nations could nudge it in the right direction with their mix of responses: Germany's principled criticism, with Angela Merkel's refusal to attend the Beijing Olympics opening ceremony, and Britain and France's partial engagement, with Nicolas Sarkozy and Gordon Brown attending. Despite Chinese threats, the leaders of various European nations have met with the Dalai Lama. Europe believes it can achieve more with its smart-power approach toward China than the United States will ever achieve with its bluster and hard power. Europe sees China through the double lens of its paradoxical condition as both a large, growing major economy and a still-developing country. China is filled with contradictions and serious challenges, and its leaders are driven by the need to achieve ever more development, including more jobs, infrastructure, industry, and agricultural productivity, as well as to secure the energy and raw materials needed to fuel its growth. China badly needs trade, expertise, and development, and Europe helps to fill that gap, acting as a valuable source of high technology, investment, and know-how.

Many in the West are in awe of China's rapid development and are bullish that the Chinese system will continue to flourish. It is the new frontier where financial prospectors and "get rich quick" investors go panning for gold by speculating in some hot Chinese startup. To many awestruck pundits, China represents the future and one day will become the leader of the world. But when I visited China in August and September of 2008, in the aftermath of the Olympics, the country that I saw, whether in Shanghai, Beijing, or the rural areas, was a long, long way from being a global leader in any meaningful sense. Sure, due to the sheer size of its population—one-fifth of the world's total—China has become a global leader in economic output, trade, resource consumption, carbon emissions, and pollution. And signs of modernization and increasing affluence for a small but growing segment of the population are plain to see. But China is both a very ancient country and essentially a still-developing adolescent; it is firmly a communist one-party state, yet its economy now incorporates core elements of capitalism—what it has called "the socialist road with Chinese characteristics." It has lifted four hundred million people out of poverty, but with a population of 1.3 billion, it still has nearly a billion living in difficult conditions, with a per capita gross domestic product of $5,000 per year ($2,000 according to some estimates), which is about a sixth that of its Sino-rival Taiwan.

Two hundred million people out of a working population of nearly eight hundred million are migrants, chafing at their lowly status and rotten wages. Inequality is rampant. Returning from the rural areas to cities like Shanghai and Beijing is like a form of time travel, moving from feudal conditions where plowing is still done by water buffalo to a land of skyscrapers. For most Chinese, life is a struggle and will remain so for years to come.

Leading British economic analyst Will Hutton, author of an influential book on China called *The Writing on the Wall,* also is skeptical about China's future. Writes Hutton, "The economic model that has taken it thus far cannot take it much further. . . . it is a conflation of markets and political authoritarianism that cannot be sustained. And now the numbers are so large that China's capacity to fudge and hide reality is rapidly fading. China is everywhere broaching the limits of its capacity to continue as it has."[21]

Even before the economic crash in 2008, China's banks were overextended, with total debt of $3.7 trillion, nearly as much as China's actual gross domestic product.[22] Corruption is epidemic, whether in banks, the legal system, or the political leadership at national, provincial, and local levels, causing an estimated annual economic loss of approximately 15 percent of GDP, according to economist Hu Angang.[23] While China remains firmly communist in its basic orientation, its hybridized capitalist elements are very different from the capitalisms in Europe and the United States. It is more accurately described as a system of state corporatism, since everything in China—from business enterprises to the remotest village club—is subject to the pervasive direction, control, and ownership of the Communist Party. Politics intrudes everywhere and in everything. Hutton points out a revealing, yet usually overlooked fact: more than three-fifths of China's overall exports and nearly all its high-tech exports are made by non-Chinese, foreign companies—another indication of China's weakness. Foreign companies essentially reprocess imports of semi-manufactured goods that are then shipped to Europe and the U.S. China remains in essence a subcontractor to the West, says Hutton. "The reason why so few people can name a great Chinese brand or company despite its export success is that there are none. China needs to build them, but doing that in a one party authoritarian state, where the party second guesses business strategy for ideological and political ends, is impossible."[24]

So China has huge problems—but not all of them are economic in nature. The only thing cloudier than its economic model is the sky over its major cities, so choked with smog that when I was in Shanghai, on some days I couldn't see the high rises a few blocks away. During the run-up to the 2008 Olympics, hosted in Beijing, many were concerned that athletes would choke on the foul air. In fact, four hundred thousand people a year die of respiratory diseases caused by pollution.[25] About 500 million rural Chinese still do not have access to safe drinking water. Acid rain, caused by emissions of sulfur dioxide that belch from smokestacks of power plants, is endemic, with the state-run *China Daily* reporting that in Guangdong province—China's most prosperous region, and also its most industrialized—53 percent of its total rainfall in 2008 was acid rain.[26]

Frequent food scares, such as industrial toxins mixed into milk powder, pet food, and cough syrup, as well as the exporting around the world of toys decorated with lead paint and drywall (used in housing construction) tainted with highly toxic sulfur compounds, are additional manifestations of the amoral, corrupt, robber baron business practices that have been unleashed.[27] The 2008 earthquakes in western Sichuan province, which resulted in the collapse of over seven thousand schoolrooms and thousands of dead schoolchildren, disproportionately impacted the poor who lived in areas where corruption had resulted in shoddy construction practices. For all these reasons and more, China is plagued by seventy thousand protests per year, many of them more like riots and quite violent (including occasional bombings), and had three hundred thousand labor disputes in 2006 alone, nearly double the number reported in 2001.[28]

Young men and women I met in the cities of China had fled the third world conditions in their farming villages only to accept the yoke of working in near-sweatshop factories or as bar waitresses, earning just enough to afford to share a bedroom with three others, four to a tiny room, two to a bed. Disposable income was practically nil, life was hard, and the only hope they nurtured was that their country would one day be more affluent. Their dreams were of a distant horizon, not the present, as the ruling Communist Party drilled them in the Confucian virtues of "sacrifice." Since the crash of 2008–9, which caused an unprecedented twenty million layoffs of workers and the shuttering of thousands of Chinese businesses, many have now gone back to the farm, awaiting the next cycle of economic opportunity.

Certainly the land of "capitalist communism"—an oddball combination, to be sure—has made some impressive gains with its roaring economic growth rates and in lifting several hundred million people out of poverty. But its metrics indicate significant challenges for years to come. Prophecies of its global leadership are premature at best. The hallmark of a great power is when other nations want to emulate you. What made the United States *the* great power of the post–World War II era was not just its military might but its economic promise and freedoms, which caused people from all over the world to flock to our shores. The City on the Hill inspired people toward an ideal. But no one is banging down doors to get into China, and only the poorest of Southeast Asian countries aim to be like the People's Republic. China inspires curiosity with its ancient history and huge population, but not envy or emulation. That will not change anytime soon, and perhaps never unless China at some point opens up its political and economic system.

Given these realities and complexities that will play out over the next few years, what is the best approach to take toward China? Is it more Bush administration–type bluster? That seems extremely unlikely. Europe has adapted its bilateral policy to account for these complex realities. Practically speaking, that means the European Union has high-lighted three priorities in its relations with China: political and economic reforms; the environment and global warming; and human rights and the rule of law. The Europeans and China have launched high-level talks to discuss a full menu of issues, with more than twenty-four policy areas subject to regular meetings between representatives of both sides. The European Union is up-front about its desire to shape China's international behavior and domestic evolution according to European norms and values. Implicit in Europe's policy is that economic development and gradual modernization will lead eventually to some level of democratization. China thus provides a major test of the European strategy of long-term constructive engagement, with an approach that maintains a certain distance but stays open and leads by example. Disagreements and tensions mainly are raised behind closed doors amid efforts to engage China in practical acts of cooperation and projects of mutually shared interest. In other words, more Monnetism.

Europe's success on this front, so far, would have to be described as mixed. The Communist regime has avoided making the kind of domestic changes that are implicit in the European Union's approach, but some perceptible signs of movement are evident. While from the outside Chinese political and ideological thought looks fairly mono-lithic, from the inside signs of dissent are showing, with a "left" and a "right" emerging within Chinese political and intellectual elite circles. The dominant policy since the late 1970s has established the primacy of a state-controlled free-enterprise system and high economic growth. But today this is being challenged by a new left which advocates a gentler form of political economy. A fundamental battle of ideas is pitting the rich against the poor, the state against the free market, coasts against inland provinces, and cities against countryside.[29] A leading new left voice, Wang Hui, sounds positively European, even like a social democrat, when he says, "China is caught between the two extremes of misguided socialism and crony capitalism, and suffering from the worst elements of both. I am in favor of orienting the country toward market reforms, but China's development must be more balanced. We must not give total priority to GDP growth to the exclusion of workers' rights and the environment."[30]

The new left's philosophy, which increasingly is capturing the public mood and setting the tone for political debate, asks what should be done with China's new wealth. Should it continue accumulating in the hands of an elite, or can China foster a model of development that benefits all citizens? Those of the new left talk about developing a Chinese variant of European-like social democracy, including low-cost health care and other workfare protections, green development, and even talk about reforming property rights and enacting a degree of codetermination to give workers a say over the companies. Many Chinese officials have visited the Scandinavian countries to learn about their workfare systems, and such workfare systems have been praised in the official Chinese media.[31]

Indeed, some of the most powerful authorities in official circles appear to be listening, at least with one ear. At the end of 2005, President Hu Jintao and Premier Wen Jiabao published the "11th five-year plan," their blueprint for a "harmonious society." For the first time since the post-Mao reforms began in 1978, economic growth was not described as the overriding goal for the Chinese state. They talked instead about introducing the bare bones of a European-style workfare support system, with promises of a 20 percent year-on-year increase in pension funds, unemployment benefits, health insurance, and maternity leave. For rural China, they promised an end to arbitrary taxes and improved health and education. They also pledged to reduce energy consumption by 20 percent.

China also has begun modest experiments with electoral democracy at the local level and supplemented those with new types of deliberative democracy and public consultation exercises, as well as town hall hearings. China hired Stanford University professor James Fishkin, the political scientist who led the "Tomorrow's Europe" exercise at the European Parliament in October 2007 (see chapter 13), to draft a randomly selected, scientifically representative sample of average Chinese citizens to participate in his deliberative polling process to decide how the city of Zeguo should spend a $6 million public works budget.[32] The ruling Communist Party also has begun experimenting with a degree of internal party democracy, beginning with some competitive elections for some party posts at lower levels. Given that the Communist Party has a membership of seventy-three million people—larger than most nations—this "democratic vanguard" holds vast, yet unrealized, potential. Some are encouraged by the fact that the current president, Hu Jintao, is the first not to handpick his successor, who instead was selected as the result of a secret poll of Communist Party officials. Others have likened China's political trajectory to that of a "consultative dictatorship," in which the leaders use various public opinion technologies, combined with local democracy and deliberation, to keep their fingers on the pulse of the people, a kind of twenty-first-century version of Plato's philosopher-kings ruling for the good of society.

But the startling degree of corruption, as well as the deep involvement of the military in running businesses and controlling everything from major amounts of real estate to dealerships of ancient art and antiquities, shows the riskiness of such wishful thinking. While China has taken a few baby steps down the path of becoming more open and democratic, it still has a very long way to go. The absolute unwillingness of Communist Party authorities to tolerate any public reflection, let alone protest, during the twentieth anniversary in June 2009 of the Tiananmen Square crackdown exposes their great fear of the public, as well as the lack of self-confidence among China's rulers in either their system, their people or themselves. It remains to be seen how much of a "new China" will continue to emerge, but all these horizons certainly provide a different view of China from the one typically given by U.S. officials and media.

The U.S. policy toward China has been nothing less than schizophrenic. American companies flock to China like the gold prospectors to the hills of '49, but the politicians shake their fists toward China, bellowing that China is stealing American jobs. Yet according to a U.S. Department of Labor survey of extended mass layoffs, a total of only 28,000 jobs were lost (out of a total of 1.7 million jobs lost) as a result of out-of-country relocations between 2004 and 2006, a pitifully small number.[33] Critics also vent about America's sizable amount of indebtedness to China in the form of China's purchase of trillions of dollars' worth of U.S. Treasury notes, as well as China's undervaluing of its currency, the renminbi, but both of those policies have pluses as well as minuses, including funding the huge American debt and keeping inflation down by making Chinese imports less expensive. Nevertheless, anti-China sentiment has been rife in Washington. Congress has debated dozens of anti-China trade bills and threatened tariffs against Chinese imports, despite the spuriousness of the claim that China can be blamed for the loss of jobs and the stagnating wages of U.S. workers. While the European Union perhaps has been criticized rightly for being too weak in its human rights expectations of China, the United States has practiced its trademark bellicosity with very little gain. Speaker of the House Nancy Pelosi and other members of Congress have been vehement in their denunciation of China's human rights record, but their criticisms often seem to lack nuance and an appreciation of either China's historical context or the progress it has made.

Europe has decided that a new set of rules of engagement, a new pragmatism tempered by cold realism, is necessary to deal with such a vast land of paradoxes and contradictions. While China and Europe have their periods of disillusionment, disagreements, and even occasional rows, China "implicitly welcomes European guidance," even as it snubs American pressures regarding democratization and human rights, writes Parag Khanna. "Indeed, the state that China hopes to build is modeled on European norms of state capitalism and social democracy," he says. China's ambition is to be the anchor of an E.U.-like regional club in East Asia, with Europe as a strategic partner. Asians who once turned to the United States now turn to Europe since the European Union "makes the region more modern, prosperous, educated and professional, bolstering Asian confidence and weakening American dominance."[34] In sum, Europe's unique approach to international relations is gaining more adherents and is establishing a new and promising model—the European Way of foreign policy.

THE FUTURE OF THE INTERNATIONAL ORDER

The transatlantic partnership has been of paramount importance and will remain so in the twenty-first century. The geopolitical challenges confronting Europe and the United States are significant and similar: besides Russia, the Middle East, China, and an increasingly shaky Pakistan, other, second world nations such as India, Malaysia, Brazil, Venezuela, South Korea, Iran, Thailand, the Central Asian 'Stans, and others are elbowing for a place at the table and rightfully insisting on their inclusion in the leadership of world organizations. Global climate change and its impact on the world's resources will continue to demand our attention. Each of these carries great risk and dire ramifications if Europe, the United States, and other global leaders make the wrong choices. These are the challenges for which Europe is hoping to have a partner in its old Cold War ally across the Atlantic.

Ironically then, one of Europe's greatest foreign policy challenges is what to do about the United States of America. How does Europe, as it strives to become more united and speak with one continental voice, coax the United States to become once again like the shining City on a Hill that founded a multilateral, rules-based international order and established free markets instead of exacting vengeance after World War II?

Right now Europe is holding out hope that the City on the Hill will return under the leadership of President Barack Obama. The whole world seems to be waiting and watching to see what happens not only with America's government but also with its people, who have accepted torture, kidnappings, Abu Ghraib, Guantánamo, gutting of the Geneva Conventions, domestic surveillance, invasions under false pretenses, and other violations of the international norms of decency and human rights that the United States originally had led in establishing. Chris Patten, conservative British leader and the last British governor of Hong Kong before the handover to China, is full of both praise and criticism for his American cousins he has long admired. "The America that led the world in the post–World War II era was the 'City on the Hill,' the one everybody looked to," he told me when I interviewed him after attending a lecture he gave in 2006. "But if people in the U.S. have lost their sense of moral outrage over what their country has done, then the world is in big trouble. I mean, ideas are important in politics, in the world. I'm hoping this is a temporary departure from what America always has stood for. It's time to return to the America of 1945," he said, almost beseechingly.

In the early years of the Bush administration, Europeans would say to me kindly, "We don't blame the American people for their lousy government; we know the American people are good." But there was a shift following Bush's reelection in 2004. The day after the election, a headline in the British tabloid the *Daily Mirror* seemed to capture the new sentiment: "How can 59,054,087 people be so DUMB?" the front page blared in large bold print. In 2006, while I was in Geneva, Switzerland, an American friend of a high-ranking German embassy official to Switzerland confided a recent conversation in which this official said, "We assume that the Bush crowd probably stole a million votes in that election. But that still doesn't explain why fifty-eight million other people voted for such terrible leadership. We [the Germans] are moving on; we are so done with America; we can't wait any longer for it to get its act together."

Unfortunately this attitude has become common in Europe, indeed, around the world. America's moral and political leadership has taken a direct hit. The American dream itself has been undermined by images of the black residents of New Orleans drowning in the aftermath of Hurricane Katrina, even as government spending was being plowed into a military leviathan flouting world opinion and breaking the international rules it had helped establish. Now the metastasizing of U.S.-made toxic financial products throughout the global financial system, which brought the world's economy to the brink of disaster, has further undermined America's claims to leadership. The shining City on the Hill has suffered a fundamental erosion of the attractiveness of its narrative that once enticed the world. The election of an appealing, charismatic black president with an unusually non-Anglo-sounding name has restored some of the luster, but still, signs of its tarnishing are everywhere.

For the American power elite, as well as the American people, being on top of the world has been a way of life for over a half century. Power and global dominance have become a state of mind, a way of being. America's messianic view of itself as the "indispensable nation" seems to drive American leaders, whether left or right, as if possessed by an imperial spirit. Even President Obama's rhetoric accompanying his escalations in Afghanistan and Pakistan has been tinged with such pretensions; at times the Democrats sound like Republicans, with no alternative conceptual framework for international relations other than one based on force, strategic dominance, and an assumption of American supremacy. So any difference in foreign policy resulting from George W. Bush's exit in many ways has been one of degree, not of kind.[35] This arrogance of prerogative seems to be part of the American Way, no matter which party is at the helm.

Some Americans take pride in the fact that all the trillions of dollars that have been plowed into the military budget have succeeded in creating the strongest, most powerful military force in history. However, as we have seen, that has not translated into greater national security. Our "lone remaining superpower" moment has come and gone, and now we are in the red zone of potentially becoming the next hollowed-out post–World War II superpower. The last time anyone buzzed about Washington's "decline" came during the waning years of the Cold War, in the late 1980s, when Yale Professor Paul Kennedy authored *The Rise and Fall of the Great Powers*. Kennedy warned that the U.S. was falling into a familiar historical pattern where the combination of huge military budgets and ever larger deficits led inevitably to the kind of "imperial overstretch" that weakened once-mighty empires.[36] During the economic boom of the Internet years in the 1990s, with the U.S. astride the world as the lone remaining superpower, Kennedy's predictions seemed laughable. Now, they may turn out to be prophetic.

The United States is still a mighty power, but a new global competition has been unleashed, what economist Joseph Stiglitz has called "a worldwide battle over ideas." Writes Parag Khanna, "The world's most compelling ideology is neither democracy nor capitalism nor any other 'ism,' but *success*. Today the definition of success is up for grabs."[37] In a multipolar world, the "second world" of aspiring nations is watching closely the behaviors of the world's three superpowers, the U.S., the E.U., and China, to see which offers the best bargain. For each nation, it's a geopolitical marketplace with options to pursue toward bettering their condition. The second world nations are in effect the world's swing voters, and their affiliations will determine the shape of the new global order. In this competition between visions, the European Way is looking attractive and surprisingly nimble, while the American Way has been looking outdated and—to borrow a word from the Euroskeptics—sclerotic.

In retrospect, then, the clashing at the United Nations over the invasion of Iraq was not merely between two nations, the United States and France, each with its own national baggage—it was over the direction of the geopolitical future. The world needs to invent a new security model based on open, free-trading societies that feed from economic and political webs of interconnectedness and concentric rings of partnership and development, instead of on the model that has prevailed in the postwar era, namely, the big kid on the block with massive military might policing the smaller kids. While some criticisms of Europe's foreign policy have been valid, the value of Europe's smart power diplomacy has been underestimated. Europe does punch below its weight when it comes to wielding a military threat, but that has never been the source of Europe's power and there seems little reason to change that. Indeed, its very success with its smart power, combined with the United States's failures with its hard power, should be a wake-up call. In light of the ineffectiveness of America's unilateralist hammer approach, the world is looking for a different style of leadership during an era when the direction over the essential values needed for survival in the twenty-first century seems more crucial than ever.

Certainly it would help if Europe could accelerate its process of coalescing, and as its still-new military capabilities consolidate, it should think about what more it can do to foster international security and to step up its efforts as international peacekeeper in global hotspots. But just as Europe could step up more, America should step down and follow Europe's lead more, giving new primacy to multilateralism, diplomacy, patience, human rights, and international law, and fostering strong ties with moderate nations and with moderates within extreme nations.

Fortunately, allowing others to take the lead on the global front dovetails nicely with America's increasingly urgent need to take better care of the home front. The U.S. has its work cut out to revamp its obsolete, hyper-militarized model and provide a more balanced, European-like workfare system for U.S. families and workers. No doubt the tens of millions of Americans who lack health care and affordable higher education, and those who suffer from inequality, poverty, and declining fortunes, and those who lost their homes or their jobs or both in the economic crash, as well as those who want the United States to get serious about reducing our disproportionate contributions to global warming, would welcome this change of priorities.

The formerly tribal nations of Europe have learned a thing or two about how to advance—patiently—peace, democracy, prosperity, and sustainability, and now they are looking for a respectful partner, not a preeminence, in their transatlantic cousin. The European Way of foreign policy offers the world a way out of the dog-eat-dog turf wars that we inherited from the Cold War and that the Bush administration, having taken the bait dangled by the Koran and Talmud fundamentalists of the impoverished Middle East, seemed determined to perpetuate. Europe has devised a foreign policy and a velvet diplomacy that reflect the continent's social capitalist and multilateral impulses, which are founded on the deepest of faith in human potential and rationality. The emergence of these peaceful social capitalists is an uplifting event in human history that appears to offer the best pathway forward for a planet of over six billion people.

PART FIVE

PLURALIST EUROPE

THIRTEEN

THE LEGACY OF LUTHER AND CROMWELL

Political Democracy in Europe

Democracy is a device that ensures we shall be governed
no better than we deserve.

George Bernard Shaw

Twenty miles outside London lies a large, verdant green pasture that goes by the name of Runnymede. The River Thames winds through it, just a silver sliver this far from its mouth, but history rolls down the river from here to London and beyond. Runnymede is a hallowed place and name: it is known as one of the birthplaces of modern democracy. Here, in the year 1215, somewhere in this water meadow—the exact spot is unknown—King John put his seal to what is known as the Magna Carta, an agreement that required the king to accept that his will could be bound by laws and to respect certain legal procedures. The Magna Carta is considered one of the most important legal documents in the history of democracy, having influenced many common law documents since that time, such as the United States Constitution and Bill of Rights.

As I walked around the field at Runnymede, avoiding the cow pies and mud while lost in a contemplation of democracy's earthy roots, I saw its trajectory as if it were written across the sky. Europe's ancient cradle is scattered with nascencies and power spots that mark the ebb and flow of the democratic tide: Athens in the fifth century B.C. and its early direct democracy, in which five thousand to six thousand adult males attended mass assemblies to cast a vote;[1] the Roman Republic and its stunted attempts at representative democracy, which eventually transmogrified into dictatorship in the first century B.C.;[2] Wittenberg in eastern Germany in 1517, where Martin Luther nailed his 95 Theses to the church's door, protesting papal abuses and championing the radical notion that an individual needs no priestly intermediary between himself and God. Within months Luther's petition had spread like wildfire across Europe, sparking the Protestant Reformation against the Catholic Church hierarchy, one of the first controversies fanned by mass publication via the recently invented printing press. While Luther's name and deed loom large historically, few have recognized how his defiance of religious authority, as well as his championing of individual conscience and spiritual enfranchisement, advanced the pre-attitudes necessary for the rise of the democratic spirit. His religion was informed by a philosophy of equality, one that Alexis de Tocqueville later described as one that "proclaimed that all men are alike able to find the road to heaven."[3]

A few decades later, in Geneva, Switzerland, the austere John Calvin and sanctimonious others advanced Luther's break from papal supremacy, setting the stage for the puritanical Oliver Cromwell's rupture from a different authority a hundred years later. The Englishman Cromwell not only beheaded a king and dramatically advanced the notion of a sovereign's accountability to the people, but he also further advanced notions of individual conscience as self-determination, attitudinal milestones on the pathway to democracy.

That men like Cromwell, Calvin, and Luther—who shared much with those known today as fundamentalist Christians—acted as forefathers of Jefferson, Madison, Locke, Montesquieu, and others in the pantheon of liberal democracy's champions comes as a bit of an irony. Europe's centuries-long coalescing of the democratic spirit never was a straightforward path but rather one filled with hypocrisy, violence, and setbacks.[4] Throughout Europe's bloody history and the push-pull of revolution and counterrevolution, the forces of progress too often transmogrified into ones of empire, suppression, and violent authority.

Finally, following World War II, western Europe at long last managed to conquer most of its political demons: democracy gained firm footing, triumphing over centuries of monarchs, dictators, fascism, religious strife, and the most barbaric of internecine wars. We have seen in previous chapters how a newly democratic Europe has been able to harness capitalism's extraordinary ability to create wealth in such a way as to better support families and workers, as well as to foster ecological sustainability and a new type of global leadership based on regional networks of peace and prosperity partnerships. These are truly remarkable achievements, historic even, and one can't help but wonder with admiration, How has Europe managed to accomplish all this?

There is no single answer to that important question, but the most significant part of the answer is: democracy. Today the various European nations employ the most advanced, representative democracies the modern world has ever seen. As a reaction to their blood-soaked history, those nations have forged political institutions that foster inclusiveness, participation, authentic representation, multiparty democracy, and majoritarian policy based on a consensus of viewpoints, much more so than those of the United States or anywhere else. Europe's vibrant political democracies, and the specific institutions that have fostered their signature degree of broad pluralism, receive too little attention in my view. While economy and culture are the twin cores of our daily lives, political democracy is the means for deciding who will sit at the table of power, making policy that affects everything else. In a democracy, the political institutions must shape the economic and mediate the cultural, not the other way around, or vast inequality and ethnocentrism will result (which is particularly important as Europe grapples with immigration).

In Europe, *consensus* is a much used word, referring to the effort to find common ground among diverse and even opposing forces. Increasingly in this fractured, fractious globalized world, with so many threats, challenges, and dilemmas looming and with so much at stake in our need to work together, the ability to achieve consensus is rising in importance. The U.S. political system, still substantially rooted in its antiquated eighteenth-century origins, has shown itself to be unrepresentative, divisive, and disenfranchising. Its "winner take all" politics is founded upon electoral methods and practices that breed an adversarial clash of opposing forces and efforts by the "winners" to "take all" from the losers. But in Europe, a thriving, pluralistic, and broadly representative democracy has been the foundation for everything else that is right and good about the European Way.

WHAT TWENTY-FIRST-CENTURY DEMOCRACY LOOKS LIKE

Europe's advanced democracy is evident in fascinating ways, large and small, incorporating macro- and microinstitutions. On the little *d* democracy side, we see microinstitutions such as Question Time in

Britain, Sweden, Italy, France, and elsewhere, a weekly grilling, often televised, of the prime minister and other government officials by the opposition party. In Britain, Question Time provides great political theater, and it's informative as well. Once after delivering a lecture at Westminster to members of Parliament, I enjoyed an MP-led tour of the British Parliament buildings and had an opportunity to stand in the exact spot in the House of Commons where Prime Minister Tony Blair stood during Question Time. As I grasped both sides of Mr. Blair's podium—which I was told is exactly two sword lengths away from the opposition's, so as to prevent any rash political murders in the good ol' days—the thought struck me like a lightning bolt: What if we had Question Time in the United States? What if, once a week, George W. Bush, or any president, had to stand up and explain the rationale for his policies, under intense grilling by the opposition, all of it televised? Wouldn't that have made a difference in the rush to war in Iraq? And wouldn't that force more transparency in that hall of mirrors that is Washington DC? A small change like Question Time would probably change American politics forever, or at least alter the types of people foisted upon us as candidates.

Other microdemocratic methods in Europe are admirable. In France, no postage is necessary to mail a letter or postcard to the president. Most European nations vote on a weekend or a national holiday, making this seminal democratic ritual more revered, as well as more convenient, and providing a greater pool of poll workers for election day. Speakers' Corner in London's Hyde Park, which is a haven of free speech and is frequented by all sorts of political freaks and loudmouths, is not only an entertaining place to spend a few hours but also a quaint reminder of the importance of protecting even offensive speech in a free society. In Sweden, jailed prisoners are allowed to vote; in fact, most European democracies allow prisoners to vote, because voting is considered a human right as well as an essential part of a prisoner's rehabilitation.[5] But in the United States, only two states, Maine and Vermont, allow prisoners to vote, and most states have created byzantine procedures for restoring ex-felons' voting rights.[6]

Europe also practices what is known as "universal voter registration"— all eligible voters *automatically* are registered to vote by the government. It is done proactively, on a rolling basis, and the goal is to have 100 percent registration. A national voter database is maintained, and when a person reaches voting age she or he is welcomed into the ranks of the enfranchised. But in the United States we have an "opt-in" system in which it is left to the individual to fill out a form and register with the appropriate authorities. Registration drives often are tied to specific elections, leading to various abuses by the partisans who want to register *their* voters but prevent the other side's voters from participating.[7] This has resulted not only in lawsuits and elections decided by the courts, but also in nearly a third of eligible U.S. voters—about seventy million people—being unregistered to vote, a situation unheard of in Europe. Some states have nearly as many unregistered eligible voters as people who actually vote (nine million voters in 2006 compared with seven million eligible unregistereds in California alone). Ironically, in Iraq a higher share of adult citizens are registered to vote than in the United States because the American authorities pushed the Iraqi government to register automatically all Iraqi citizens.

What becomes obvious in observing voter registration and other practices is that Europe greatly values enfranchisement and participation, much more than does the United States. Europeans have decided to make it easy to vote and participate, whereas we in the United States have erected unnecessary barriers.

Europe's staunch belief in a pluralistic democracy is evident in other ways as well. I recall interviewing the deputy mayor of Bonn, Germany, who told me about a remarkable institution known as Children's Parliaments. Several hundred cities in Germany allow schoolchildren to elect representatives four times a year. The Children's Parliaments convene and debate issues and actually are permitted to *propose* legislation to the local city council. This was astonishing to me, because at that very moment the city of Los Angeles was establishing neighborhood councils, but the powers-that-be did not want to let even the *adults* propose legislation to their city council. It occurred to me that this was emblematic of a key difference between the United States and Europe in the practice of democracy and pluralism. In the United States, two hundred years after the founders created a political system with certain undemocratic tendencies, in which only white men of property initially could vote and institutions such as the Senate and the Electoral College were designed as a hedge against "too much democracy," we still really don't trust "we, the people" that much. Yet in Germany, as well as in the Netherlands and other European democracies, children are allowed to propose legislation to their city councils. I was fascinated by this.

I asked the deputy mayor, "What do the children propose, do they propose silly things like chewing gum in schools, or three sodas a day?"

"Oh no," she said. "They take it *very* seriously. They have proposed things like more garbage cans in the schoolyards and the transit stations, since children were throwing their wrappers and litter around. Once small pebbles were placed in the schoolyard in the play area. 'You try kneeling on that, it hurts,' said the children, so they proposed sand. They proposed moving the buttons down on the trains, which many schoolchildren use to get to school, so that small children could reach them. Very practical things. Ones that the adults would never think of. And sometimes impractical things like 'save the rain forest,' and of course the conservatives said, 'See, the children don't understand anything.' But if you think about it, there are things you can do on the local level with the rain forest, having sister city partnerships with cities there and with tropical forests, so it's a question of how to deal with it."

"So does that mean when these Children's Parliaments meet, you know that afterward you are going to receive a stack of legislation on your desk?" I asked her.

The deputy mayor nodded and groaned. "Yes, absolutely. We receive many proposals, and they are very detailed. It can be a lot of work, because they do take it seriously. And if they take it seriously, then so must we, or the children will become adults and become even more tired of politicians, having had the experience of not being taken seriously."[8]

Children's Parliaments are just one of many impressive examples of what is known as "deliberative democracy," which is practiced all . across Europe. In Rome, a representative sample of randomly selected citizens was asked to weigh in on their city government's budget priorities during a time of deficits: Should the government cut spending on hospital beds or city parks? Or increase taxes? In a town near Athens, Greece, citizens were allowed to nominate candidates to run for mayor, instead of the usual insider nomination process. In October 2007, four hundred average Europeans from the twenty-seven E.U.-member countries, who were randomly selected to form a scientifically representative sample of the European Union's half a billion residents, were brought together at the European Parliament in Brussels to deliberate about key questions related to the future of Europe.

These deliberative democracy exercises are not some nostalgic throwback to ancient Greece's direct democracy. They are a completely new and modern approach designed to create a political dialogue, a kind of "democratic agora" in search of consensus. Some of them employ technologies such as the Internet, live webcasting, keypad polling devices, and handheld computers to convene representative assemblies of average citizens who meet for one to three days of deliberation. The event often is broadcast on television, and sometimes participants in several different physical locations participate simultaneously via the Internet or closed-circuit TV. This is more than just a mere focus group or a fancy poll; participants suddenly are sitting face to face across the table or across the video link from their own worst stereotypes and political opponents, trying to find consensus. The ensuing dialogue inevitably results in a breakdown of their partisan defenses and an emergence of their more pragmatic selves. Watching them work to problem-solve and find common ground is transformative.

Europe has led the way in developing these new techniques of citizen consultation, assisted, ironically, by an American professor, James Fishkin of Stanford University. Fishkin has used his signature deliberative polling process to help Europe know what its people think, especially important in enhancing democracy and consultation in a mass society in which people often can feel alienated from politics or their governments. This is a time of great transition in Europe, and commenting on the "Tomorrow's Europe" exercise he led at the European Parliament, Fishkin told me, "We put a sample of all of Europe in the parliament building to deliberate about Europe's future. A European-wide discussion at the mass level has never existed before, but we brought it into being for the first time in the history of the world." Professor Fishkin and his collaborators have conducted similar deliberative polls in Britain, Denmark, Bulgaria, Northern Ireland, and other countries (including China), and these modern-day town halls are exciting new instruments in the toolbox of democracy.

But the various deliberative democracy exercises, Children's Parliaments and the like, while groundbreaking in their way, are merely the musical flourishes to the grand symphony of European representative democracy. From nation to nation, the real substance of Europe's consensus-seeking democracies results from multiparty representative government founded on the bedrock of specific institutions and practices that make the various European nations the most advanced representative democracies the modern world has ever seen.

REPRESENTATIVE DEMOCRACY, VERSION 2.0

I recall the first time I visited the German Bundestag to observe its parliamentary proceedings. That was in 1997, when the national parliament was still housed in Bonn, before its post–Cold War move back to the Reichstag in Berlin. The building was constructed of nearly all glass, its symbolism of transparency and accountability not lost on me. It was a beautiful modern construction, impressive in its elegance and lack of official pompousness. In certain ways, it better embodied the essence of the new modern Germany than the massive, gray neo-classical Reichstag building in Berlin, to which the capital has since returned as head of a reunited Germany.

But what was even more memorable to me than the sleek design was the parliamentary chamber itself. When you visit the chamber of the U.S. House of Representatives, left and right are plain to see—Democrats on one side, Republicans on the other—with an aisle, a dividing line, down the middle, like the line where the ocean meets the rocky shore, adversaries forever battering each other. With only two viable electoral choices, the free marketplace apparently has spread everywhere except to our politics. The U.S. House of Representatives—the People's House, as it is called—is hardly "representative" of the American people, with our vast array of ethnicities, religions, languages, geographic regions, climate zones, political philosophies, Web sites, and jazzy urban centers.

But in Germany's Bundestag, I observed several aisles and numerous sections, a different one for each political party. I had always known that Germany is a multiparty democracy rather than a two-party democracy, with five or six parties winning representation in the parliament. But seeing a visual display of that was a thrill—*that's* what democracy looks like, I remember thinking. And it also provided a shocking reminder of how lacking in actual representation the U.S. House of Representatives is.

The People's House actually doesn't look very much like "the people," since those who fill the chairs are 83 percent white and 83 percent male in a country that is 67 percent white and majority female. Also, many of the seats are filled by lawyers and businessmen (taken together, three-fourths of the House membership), and there is a plurality of millionaires; the average age is fifty-seven.[9] The Speaker of the House is a woman, but on the whole the People's House still hardly looks or thinks like the American people, and the Senate is even worse in this regard. Of one hundred senators, only five are Hispanic, black, or Asian American, only seventeen are women, the average age is sixty-three, and even greater income disparities exist between the senators and their voters than in the House. Two hundred years into our history the U.S. Congress is still a fairly patrician body, more closely resembling the ancient Roman Senate than a New England town meeting.

But in the Bundestag today, six political parties are represented: The Social Democrats and the Christian Democrats are the two main parties, one center-left and the other center-right; they are joined by the Green Party, the Free Democratic Party, the Christian Social Union, and the Left Party, a broad spectrum of public opinion, right to left, occupying the chairs of the national legislature. In addition to this broad ideological representation, 32 percent of Germany's national representatives are women (nearly twice as many as in the U.S. Congress), including the country's first ever female head of government, Chancellor Angela Merkel. A handful of Turkish-descended parliamentarians sit with their peers, the average age of representatives is forty-nine,[10] and even a nineteen-year-old was elected in recent years on the strength of votes from young Germans. These representatives from broad backgrounds, experiences, and political perspectives come together to legislate a nationwide consensus in regard to Germany's social capitalist system, to fine-tune workfare supports, and to debate Germany's place in the world and in Europe today. Given Germany's preeminent place in Europe, and Europe's influential role in the future of the planet, this parliament arguably is the most important in the world today.

Compare that with the unrepresentative U.S. Congress and its many failures to enact the types of workfare protections for the American people that are enjoyed by Germans (not to mention by themselves as members of Congress). It's pretty hard for a nation, especially one as diverse as the United States, to reach a consensus on the pressing issues of our times when so much of the nation is not seated at the table of political power. The comprehensive supports for families and workers available in Germany and other European democracies hardly even receive a debate in the U.S. Congress. And Europe's proactive policies to tackle global climate change have been approached timidly throughout this decade, even by Democrats. In the run-up to the Iraq invasion in early 2003, no anti-war party existed, nor even one that cast a discerning eye on the manipulated evidence put forward by the Bush administration. Without a multiparty democracy in which all significant points of view are represented, political debate in the United States has become stunted along increasingly narrow lines in which the best interests of the vast majority of the American people are poorly represented.

Why does Europe enjoy multiparty democracy while the United States does not? The answer is simple: Europe uses more modern political institutions than the United States does, including proportional representation electoral systems, public financing of campaigns, free media time for candidates and parties, and robust, well-funded public broadcasting that counterbalances the corporate media. The United States has none of these, instead relying on political institutions that for the most part are still rooted in their eighteenth-century origins, and on a public broadcasting sector that is too poorly funded to balance the corporate sector and too scared about its own fiscal future to engage in penetrating, incisive BBC-like journalism.

WINNER-TAKE-ALL MAKES EVERYONE A LOSER

The United States continues to be one of the last remaining advanced democracies to use a geographic-based political system that elects state and federal representatives one seat at a time, district by district. And the U.S. is the only democracy to elect its chief executive in a hodge-podge of individual state contests that turns a national election into one dominated by a handful of battleground states. In the modern era, this "winner-take-all" system, as it is called, has produced a stark landscape of legislative districts—indeed, entire states—that are little more than one-party fiefdoms. As a result, unequal treatment based on where one lives is a recurring theme in America's antiquated political system, playing out in numerous ways that will increasingly undermine majority rule and present major challenges for a nation as diverse as the United States in the twenty-first century.

Despite the excitement of the 2008 presidential election, the fact is, most elections in the United States are predictable snooze-fests. Three-fourths of races in the U.S. House of Representatives were won by lop-sided landslide margins in 2008, and over 90 percent by noncompetitive ten-point margins. Political analysts can easily predict not only which candidate is going to win but even the margin of victory, because the districts are so predictable. State legislative races are worse yet. Most statewide contests for the U.S. Senate, governor, or the Electoral College vote for president are just as noncompetitive as the U.S. House or state legislative races. The winner-take-all system has rendered whole states into partisan strongholds where one side wins most or even all the representation and all other points of view go unrepresented—that's why it's called "winner-take-all." For most voters, the "choice" where they live is not that of a two-party system but whether to ratify the candidate of the lone party that dominates their district or state. That's a level of choice we expected in the old Soviet Union.

Most American voters don't even need to show up on election day; they have been rendered superfluous, but not as a result of partisan redistricting (e.g., incumbents drawing their own legislative district lines) or campaign finance inequities, the usual reasons cited. New research shows that in most states liberals and conservatives live in their own demographic clusters, with liberals dominating in cities and conservatives dominating in rural areas and many suburbs. When those demographics cast votes via the single-seat district, winner-take-all system, the vast majority of districts are branded either Republican red or Democratic blue before the partisan line drawers even sit down at their computers and draw their squiggly lines. That means election results mostly are a by-product of partisan residential patterns (i.e., where people live), combined with the winner-take-all system. Redistricting reforms and campaign finance reform, while having their merits, will not greatly affect the defects caused by America's eighteenth-century political system based on exclusively geographic representation.

Making matters worse, the winner-take-all electoral system exaggerates the adversarial nature of American politics, making the achievement of a national consensus on the most pressing issues more difficult. Purple America—neither red nor blue—is smothered by the winner-take-all nature of the U.S. system, which forces everyone into the red or blue camp. With one side dominating entire regions and states, political monocultures have resulted where debate and discussion of innovative ideas have virtually ceased. The two sides are left bunkered in their polarized regions like combatants in a political and cultural war that has become increasingly bitter.

Given America's winner-take-all dynamics, multiparty democracy is impossible, and that has additional repercussions. Voters with widely divergent views are expected to share a single representative, an increasingly impossible task in a modern pluralistic world. Without authentic representation, many people don't bother voting, so it is hardly surprising that voter turnout in the United States is one of the lowest in the world among established democracies. For the tens of millions of "orphaned voters" living in the opposite party's lopsided districts and states there is literally nothing to vote for, even during an exciting 2008 presidential election. Only 40 percent of eligible adults voted in the 2006 congressional elections, which improved to about 53 percent in 2008 with the draw of a presidential election.[11] But even that higher figure is very low compared to other democratic nations. Currently the United States ranks 139th in the world in voter turnout, trailing Uganda, Paraguay, and Morocco in the world's rankings for national legislative elections.[12]

But it's not just elections to the U.S. Congress that are hurting American democracy. Our presidential elections suffer from problems similar to those of the House and Senate; that is, the system is geography-based, with both a stark lack of competition in nearly all states, as well as bitter regional balkanization. The vast majority of voters live in locked-up states, which, as we saw in 2000 and 2004, has produced a presidential election decided by small swathes of undecided swing voters in a handful of battleground states, notoriously led by Florida and Ohio. The 2008 presidential election, occurring during a time of economic crisis and to replace an unpopular incumbent, saw a few more states in play, but the vast majority of states were still Democratic or Republican strongholds. In most states the candidates don't actively campaign or spend any of their billion-dollar war chest since everyone knows well in advance who will win there.

Differential treatment based on where one lives plays out in alarming ways in both the Senate and the Electoral College. Both are structured to give low-population, predominantly rural states more representation per capita than higher-population states. Political scientists Frances Lee and Bruce Oppenheimer have shown that electing two senators from each state, regardless of population—a legacy of the deal struck by the constitutional founders to keep the slave-owning states from seceding from the fledgling nation—has had the effect of disproportionately favoring the low-population states when it comes to representation of interests, policy, federal spending, and even leadership positions in the Senate.[13] And because these states tend to be the most conservative in the country, that representation quota has allowed for the Republican Party's overrepresentation in the Senate in most elections since 1958.[14] It's like having a foot race in which one side starts twenty yards ahead of the other. That in turn has resulted in Democratic blue states, such as California, New York, and Illinois, heavily subsidizing GOP red states, such as Alabama, Mississippi, Alaska, and North Dakota. Billions in blue-state tax dollars end up in red-state pockets. It turns out that the most conservative states benefit from the types of redistributive government programs that American conservatives usually disdain.[15]

But it's not just federal spending that is affected by the malapportioned Senate and its anti-majoritarian tendencies. Throughout this decade conservative senators from low-population states representing a small segment of the nation have slowed down or thwarted many European-type policies involving health care reform, energy reform, campaign finance reform, labor law reform, paid parental and sick leave, and raising automobile mileage standards to a level long ago reached in Europe and Japan. One of the increasingly severe roadblocks in the Senate is its use of various arcane rules that further undermine majority rule. None of these is more arcane than what is known as the "filibuster," which requires sixty out of a hundred senators to agree to stop endless debate on a particular piece of legislation before the full Senate may vote. The filibuster, which is not a part of the Constitution, allows a mere forty-one senators, many of them from low-population conservative states and representing as little as 12 percent of the nation, to stymie what the vast majority wants.[16] Often senators from low-population states have used the power of the filibuster like a giant club to beat back unwanted legislation. In recent years Senate filibusters have been used to prevent the pullout of troops from Iraq and restrictions on war funding, to fight off cuts in huge subsidies for oil companies making obscene profits, and to water down legislative responses to global warming and automobile fuel inefficiency, despite a healthy majority of Americans supporting those positions.

No number of paeans to the founders and their constitutional creation can cover up the fact that today the United States is plagued by an unrepresentative Senate and ham-fisted filibusters that wreck majoritarian policy. These anti-majoritarian tendencies of the Senate have been with us for a long time; in fact, they are widely blamed for perpetuating slavery for decades.[17] Two of America's most revered founders, James Madison and Alexander Hamilton, opposed the creation of the Senate because of its anti-democratic tendencies and its "unjustifiable limit on national majorities."[18]

The situation with the Electoral College is similar. Low-population states, which usually are conservative, have more electoral votes per capita than the midsized and high-population states, which in turn gives an edge to election of Republican and conservative presidential candidates.[19] And because the president appoints and the Senate confirms nominees to the U.S. Supreme Court and to lower federal courts, this conservative bias is built into American courtrooms as well.[20]

Thus, a "representation subsidy" for low-population conservative states is hardwired into all three branches of government, which goes a long way toward explaining why the United States has fallen behind

Europe in so many categories. Overrepresented conservatives long have led the country in directions that are unsupported by a majority of Americans. The U.S. political system, originally created for a sparsely populated, eighteenth-century agrarian society led by wealthy slave-holders, with voters numbering no more than two hundred thousand propertied white males, is inadequate for a diverse, populated, free-trading, high-tech, twenty-first-century world. Without a major overhaul of its most basic constitutional structures, America faces a troubling future that will hurt the country and impact the rest of the world.

DEMOCRACY, EUROPEAN-STYLE

In Europe, on the other hand, proportional representation electoral systems have produced better representation, more electoral competition, and much higher voter participation rates because more voters actually have viable political choices that appeal to them. Political parties from across the political spectrum are able to compete for voters' sympathies and win their proportionate share of seats in the legislatures. There are no safe seats or locked-up regions; everywhere is competitive, and even minority points of view get elected. That's because under PR (as proportional representation is sometimes called), a political party receiving 10 percent of the popular vote wins 10 percent of the legislative seats instead of nothing, and another political party winning 60 percent of the vote wins 60 percent of the seats instead of everything.[21] Representatives are elected from multiseat districts instead of one-seat districts, making it possible for conservatives to win seats in liberal/progressive areas (like cities) and for liberals/progressives to win representation in conservative areas. This substantially reduces regional balkanization and partisan polarization. Minor parties and independent candidates can win their fair share of representation too.

In the United States third parties are discriminated against with byzantine ballot access laws and various dirty tricks played by the two major parties to maintain their duopoly. But in Europe, third parties are welcomed for the valuable role they play in a robust and confident democracy. They often act as the "laboratories for new ideas," challenging and stimulating voters, the media, and the major parties to think outside the conventional political box. Third party alternatives to the major parties often are the only hope for shaking things up a bit. Multiparty democracy creates dialogue between the political center and the margins, which in the short run can sound noisy and untidy but in the medium and long terms allows a much fuller airing of the issues and an inching toward national consensus.

Europe recognizes the importance of this dynamic, so third parties are encouraged, just like the major parties, with public financing of campaigns, free media time for advertising, and inclusion in televised debates. But only the use of proportional representation allows smaller parties to win their fair share of seats. The U.S.-style, winner-take-all electoral system using one-seat districts is notorious for preventing third parties and independent candidates from winning, so not surprisingly third-party and independent candidates in the U.S. are hardly ever elected at any level of politics. Out of 535 seats in the Congress, third parties hold none and independents hold 2; with more than 7,000 seats in state legislatures, third parties and independents held 14 seats in 2007, 6 of them in tiny, rural Vermont. As one political pundit commented, "Lightning strikes more often than that."[22]

With a much fuller marketplace of political parties and their ideas to generate voter interest, and with no balkanized, one-party districts and regions where only one party prevails, it's not surprising that Europe's multiparty democracies lead the world in voter turnout. Some nations have double the turnout of the United States.[23] Multiparty hustle and bustle have fostered more spirited debate and increased voter engagement to a degree that has been impossible in the United States, with our lopsided winner-take-all districts and states, two-party duopoly, and regional balkanization.

Some of these European democracies have constructed the electoral rules to allow a multiplicity of political parties (some say too many parties); others, such as Germany, use electoral rules that effectively limit their multiparty democracies to five or six political parties that are able to win seats in the legislature. Two of those are major parties, with a cluster of smaller parties arrayed to the left and right of them. Different types of proportional systems exist, with names like "party list," "preferential/choice voting" (also known as "single transferable voter"), "cumulative voting," "limited voting," and more. In some of these systems, voters rank candidates; in others, they vote for a political party's team of candidates. In any case, the European democracies have flourished under a multiparty/multiple-choice environment.

PR also tends to elect a far greater percentage of women to legislatures. This is important not only from a "fair representation" standpoint, but various studies have shown a strong correlation between pro-family policies enacted by legislatures and the number of women elected to those legislatures.[24] In Europe, the presence of more female legislators has brought more focus on family policies, as well as contributed to a distinctly European outlook that forms the core of its social capitalist and workfare values. With women's representation in the U.S. Congress still stuck at 17 percent—sixty-ninth in the world—Sweden leads the way with 47 percent representation by women in its national parliament, followed by Finland and the Netherlands at 41 percent, Denmark at 38 percent, Spain and Norway at 36 percent, and Belgium at 35 percent.[25] Germany presents an interesting laboratory for measuring the impact of electoral systems on women's representation, since it uses both a U.S.-style district-based, winner-take-all method to elect half of its parliamentarians and a PR method to elect the other half. The result: Women win about 13 percent of the winner-take-all seats—about the same as in the United States—and about 46 percent of the PR seats, for an overall total of 32 percent. Other nations using this "mixed member" system, such as New Zealand, Italy, Russia, and Japan, also see two to three times as many women elected to the PR seats as to the winner-take-all seats, an important factor to keep in mind as we consider the impact of women's representation on consensus-based policy making.[26]

European democracies also have led the way in electing young people to national parliaments. In addition to Germany, Sweden has also elected a nineteen-year-old in recent years. At one of my lectures I met a twenty-five-year-old member of the Danish parliament, a poised young woman representing the Conservative People's Party in Denmark. In France, 4 percent of the National Assembly is under age thirty-five, and in Germany's Bundestag the average age of representatives is forty-nine, compared with fifty-seven in the U.S. House and 63 in the Senate.[27] Says Germany's young parliamentarian Anna Luehrmann, "I was annoyed that politicians are usually elder men who don't really care about the problems and ideas of young people."[28] Surely young people in the United States feel the same, but they usually vote in extremely low numbers because in a winner-take-all system they are stuck with so few electoral choices. The unusual rise of a candidate like Barack Obama during a time of deep economic crisis is a testament to how staid the electoral choices usually are for young people. In the U.S. we are missing out on opportunities to incorporate electoral dropouts such as young people, and their unique views and brilliance, into the fabric of American politics. But in Europe's PR democracies, many countries have seen young people, from both the left and the right, elected to their national legislatures, as all political parties have incentive to broaden their appeal by including young people in their team of candidates, who then reach out to and mobilize youthful voters.

The group that has had unimpressive political representation in Europe has been ethnic and racial minorities. Racial/ethnic representation has lagged not only because of discriminatory attitudes but also because historically European countries have had small racial and ethnic minority populations. As these populations have increased, they have begun making electoral gains by winning representation in federal and state parliaments in Germany, the United Kingdom, Sweden, the Netherlands, Denmark, Switzerland, and elsewhere. While America has elected a lot more minority representatives than European nations, the 17 percent of House members and 5 percent of Senators that are racial/ethnic minority are for a national population that is *one-third* minority, compared to minority populations in Europe of around 10 percent or less. So while at first glance the United States seems to be a much better example of fairer multiracial representation, in fact America has as large a gap in the ratio of ethnic/racial representatives to population as the gaps in most European democracies. (I will say more about representation of European minorities in chapter 17.)

Europe's diversity of representation—in partisanship, gender, age, and increasingly ethnicity—only has been possible because of the use of proportional voting methods. Europe's democracies have a much greater ability to field a broader range of candidates who have a real chance of being elected, and who talk about a greater breadth of issues that attract more voters to the polls. But in America's archaic winner-take-all democracy, the connection between voters and candidates largely has been severed because most candidates are still older white guys in neckties who run in lopsided partisan districts where they don't even need to campaign to win reelection.

Because their legislatures are more broadly representative, European democracies do not suffer from the type of anti-democratic and anti-majoritarian defects that plague the U.S. political system. Europe's use of proportional voting systems ensures that all significant points of view win a seat at the table. Voters win representation on the basis of what they *think*, not where they *live*, an increasingly valuable foundation for representation in this modern, pluralistic, on-the-go world. In the antiquated U.S.-style winner-take-all democracy, next-door neighbors can have opposite political opinions, but only one of them can win representation, fostering an "If I win, you lose" adversarial politics. But in Europe's multiparty democracies the goal is to give everyone representation, no matter where they live, and bring all sides to the table, where they can hash out a consensus. In the short term, consensus building can be loud and messy, but increasingly it is proving itself to be better adapted to the challenges of the modern world than the adversarial winner-take-all tango that excludes so many of the American people from having representation at the table of decision making.

IMPACT OF EUROPE'S DEMOCRACY ON POLICY: CONSENSUS VS. EXCLUSION

It's not just in better representation and more robust political discourse that Europe's multiparty democracies outshine America's two-party duopoly. Research also has demonstrated that proportional voting systems produce legislative policy that is more responsive to the desires of the populace than winner-take-all systems. Professor Arend Lijphart from the University of California–San Diego reviewed performances of thirty-six countries, classifying them into "majoritarian" and "consensus" democracies, proxies for winner-take-all and proportional democracies, respectively. He concluded, "The consensual democracies clearly outperform the majoritarian democracies with regard to the quality of the democracy and democratic representation." They also are more likely to have enacted comprehensive workfare benefits, to have a better record on the environment, macroeconomic management, and controlling violence, and to have put fewer people in prison. They are less likely to use the death penalty and are more generous with their assistance to developing nations. And, not coincidentally, they also are more likely to elect more women.[29] Political scientists John Huber and G. Bingham Powell found similar results when they compared nearly two dozen western democracies that used either a proportional or a winner-take-all electoral system.[30]

All of this makes sense, because if you have more points of view at the decision-making table then the policies decided will be based more on a consensus of wider opinion. Some U.S. defenders have criticized European democracies as being too paralyzed by attempts to achieve this consensus. But obviously as Europe, with its social capitalism, has pulled even with and even surpassed the United States in so many economic, social, health care, workfare, energy, and transportation categories, this disparaging point of view is shown to be one not based in reality. Yes, Europe has its problems and its faults and sometimes can resemble a debating society. But something about Europe works well—extremely well—despite what the professional corps of Euroskeptics say.

Not surprisingly, given the considerable defects of the peculiar, antiquated U.S. political system, few of the world's democracies have copied it. In fact, most new democracies have copied the political institutions of western Europe and created multiparty democracy.[31] Few countries have adopted our district-based, winner-take-all system to elect their legislatures, and no countries have copied our defective Senate or our Electoral College method for electing the president. For those who have not been thoroughly dunked in the waterlogged mythologies about the alleged superiority of our system, the defects of our geographic-based political system and its outdated eighteenth-century practices are too large to ignore.

FOURTEEN

CONSENSUS BUILDING
THROUGH DYNAMIC DEMOCRACY

Besides multiparty democracy founded on the bedrock of proportional representation, another crucial component to consensus building and a thriving democracy is the means whereby average citizens and voters receive information and news. In the eighteenth century, Thomas Jefferson wrote, "Whenever the people are well-informed, they can be trusted with their own government,"[1] and things are hardly different today. In the modern age, four types of communication infrastructure are necessary to foster a vigorous democracy and robust political debate: some degree of public financing of campaigns, free media time for candidates, affordable and widespread access to high-speed broadband Internet, and a healthy public broadcasting sector that acts as a balance to the profit-driven corporate media. Of alarming note, the United States has significant shortcomings in all of these areas, while European countries have a cornucopia of all four.

THE INFRASTRUCTURE OF POLITICAL COMMUNICATION

Most European democracies award public financing of campaigns to all political parties that achieve a minimum threshold of the vote, typically 1 percent or so. Giving public money to a party with so few votes is completely alien to the American way of thinking, but in Europe a dramatic difference in philosophy exists. Europe endeavors to encourage political debate and a free marketplace of ideas as part of its consensus-seeking process. By publicly financing campaigns, Europe provides all candidates and parties with sufficient resources to communicate with voters. That allows lesser-funded candidates and parties to challenge ones that are better-funded and to raise issues that foment real debate, which in turn spurs voter engagement. But in the United States, the Democrats and Republicans have a duopoly they wish to preserve. Apparently not confident enough in the quality and vigor of their ideas, the two major parties go out of their way to prevent voters from hearing other points of view. They pass draconian ballot access laws aimed to keep third parties off the ballot, and their state bureaucracies discriminate against and even harass third parties.[2]

This loss of political debate and stifling of new ideas is one of the most insidious downsides to America's privately financed campaigns and two-party duopoly. Europeans recognize that voter information is the lifeblood of a democracy; as Jefferson implied, a misinformed electorate cannot possibly make the best decisions. Accordingly, they have chosen to provide generous public financing of campaigns for all qualified political parties, with an emphasis on inclusion. Minor parties are not legally discriminated against as they are in the United States. Consequently, even minor parties, such as the various Green parties or Libertarian-type parties in Europe, receive millions of dollars in funding that is spent not only on election campaigns but also on staff, office space, supplies, computers, photocopiers, and printers—infrastructure. The Green Party of Germany, which has never won more than 10 percent of the popular vote at the national level, occupies a large building in Berlin that is a beehive of paid staff and political leaders coming and going. But in the United States, when the editor of the volunteer newsletter of the Green Party of California took a full-time job, the newsletter died.

In addition to giving public money to candidates and political parties, another essential component of a flourishing multiparty democracy is the generous provision of free radio and television airtime for political parties and candidates. Broadcast media are the greatest expense of any candidate's campaign, especially in the biggest and most important races, so this is a valuable contribution to the quest for leveling the playing field and fomenting robust political debate and consensus seeking. In Europe, just like public financing, free media time on both TV and radio also is awarded to all political parties that achieve a minimum threshold of the popular vote, typically 1 percent or less. Parties are awarded airtime on the basis of their previous electoral performance, with the bigger parties awarded more airtime but all qualifying to receive at least a minimum of TV and radio exposure. During the campaign season, viewers see and hear ads from all the political parties, with the ad slots lasting from five to ten minutes in length, considerably longer than the thirty-second sound bites in U.S. ads. This permits a more substantive presentation of the party's issues and positions.

In the absence of public financing or free airtime, running for higher office in the United States is extremely expensive, a situation that has allowed wealthy interests as well as the corporate media to become gatekeepers of candidates' viability. Particularly for the bigger races like president, governor, and U.S. Senate, broadcasters maintain a de facto "boardroom primary" in which successful candidates are vetted by media gatekeepers, as well as by big campaign donors. The media gatekeepers also have a veto over which issues will be discussed during the electoral season. The severe effects of leaving the dissemination of public information in the hands of a private, profit-hungry corporate media industry are apparent in every election. Various studies have demonstrated that corporate broadcasters have severely restricted political coverage in recent years and shortened the length of the political sound bite heard on the news to eight seconds. The Center for Media and Public Affairs found that when presidential candidate George W. Bush went on the David Letterman talk show he had more airtime *in a single block* than he received the entire month of October 2000 from all three network newscasts combined.[3] Other studies have found that corporate broadcasters have actively gouged campaigns as Election Day approaches, with prices for TV spots doubling and tripling.[4]

So not only are political discourse and campaigns being filtered by the corporate media, but also voters are hearing only from candidates who can cough up the big bucks. This severely cramps the parameters of political debate. Barack Obama as a candidate powerfully used the Internet to raise money from millions of small donors, and to some degree circumvented the corporate media's stranglehold on information. But only time will tell if other candidates lacking in Obama's charisma can successfully employ these strategies to such an extent that they are able to tilt the playing field. Given the thousands of individual races that occur at federal and state levels, wealthy donor and corporate media gatekeepers will continue to have vast influence in the American system.

In Europe, however, the provision of free media time to all political parties ensures that voters can hear a range of views and make better decisions because they are politically well informed in the Jeffersonian sense. Legally speaking, the American public owns the airwaves; corporate broadcasters benefit from a nearly $400 billion—yes, that's billion, not million—government subsidy that has handed over control of the public's airwaves to them for free. So following Europe's lead and mandating that broadcasters provide free airtime to candidates would cost the taxpayers nothing, yet it would significantly reduce the pressure to raise gobs of money, as well as enhance political debate. While public financing of campaigns and free airtime would not dramatically change which candidates get elected—it's the winner-take-all electoral system that creates so many noncompetitive one-party fiefdoms, which is why only proportional representation will create multiparty competition—enacting European-style publicly financed campaigns and free media time would greatly open up American democracy to new voices and new ideas that would engage more voters.

THE POWER OF PUBLIC BROADCASTING

The various media institutions in Europe also differ substantially from those in the United States, with dramatic consequences. While the U.S. media market is dominated by corporate broadcasters who act as gatekeepers, reduce political coverage, and force candidates to buy ads at exorbitant rates, in Europe you see more politically diverse media and communication outlets that have fostered a flowering of public opinion, debate, and analysis. Europe enjoys the benefits of more robust public television and radio networks, as well as numerous daily newspapers with editorial slants from the right, left, center, center-right, center-left, far left, and back again. How has it managed to foster this? There are several ways.

First, Europe's public broadcasting sector is more omnipresent and popular, and for a very simple reason—it is more generously funded. Each country has its flagship public broadcaster, such as the British Broadcasting Corporation (BBC), which operates six TV and five radio stations. France's TFI, Germany's ARD, and Italy's RAI are more popular and more respected than any private media network in those countries. But in the U.S., the Public Broadcasting Service (PBS) fills a fairly small niche in a TV and radio world dominated by giant media corporations. That's because compared with Europe's public broadcasters, American public broadcasting is drastically underfunded. Public broadcasting in Sweden, Germany, and Britain has an annual budget of fifty to ninety dollars per capita, but American public broadcasting receives about three dollars per capita, a pathetic pittance in comparison.[5]

Nearly as important as the level of funding is the mechanism of public funding. In the United States, public broadcasting is funded primarily by budget allocations from Congress and donations from corporations. Public broadcasting must be careful not to bite the hands that feed it, and especially when Congress has been controlled for most of the last decade and a half by a Republican Party hostile to the mission of public broadcasting, its survival—and therefore its journalistic independence—has been in doubt. But the BBC is funded by mandatory public subscription fees, with all households required to pay a monthly amount of approximately $15, about $170 per year, much like subscribing to cable TV in the United States (but a lot cheaper, and far better quality). This gives the BBC its own funding base which is mostly independent of the government's mood swings.

That independent funding is what allows the BBC to display a level of journalistic independence from the British government that American public broadcasting can only dream about. The BBC has been noted for its hard-hitting journalism and tough interviews of political figures, even targeting sitting ministers from the Blair government during the Iraq war. But American public broadcasting is noted for its mushy, feel-good approach and puffball interviews that steer clear of controversy that could endanger its funding. As American media critic Norman Solomon has observed, "Where's the 'public' in public broadcasting?"

Germany's and Sweden's public broadcasting sectors also are funded by household monthly subscription fees. On Germany's two widely watched public broadcasting stations, one can find a full menu of choices, including the usual entertainment fare seen in the United States, but also numerous children's channels, a varied selection of educational, cultural, and political programs, and hugely popular soap operas and sitcoms that purposefully integrate controversial issues such as AIDS, immigration, gay relationships, and impending elections (with guest appearances by actual politicians starring as themselves) into their scripts and characters.

With its secure and more generous funding base, public broadcasting in Europe plays a fulcrum role in news and information sharing as well as media entertainment and is integral to the public's discourse and consensus-shaping. Meanwhile public broadcasting in the United States has a record of unfulfilled promise, and the national dialogue suffers as a result.

ENCOURAGING A VIBRANT POLITICAL CULTURE
THROUGH NEWSPAPERS

Europe also is still a place of newspaper readers. While traveling on the commuter train in Stockholm, Sweden, I noticed that I could hardly see any faces of the locals because they were buried in a newspaper. Row after row, the commuters looked like a flock of birds with large beaks, studiously pouring over their strange Swedish glyphs printed on black and white newsprint. I saw the same thing in Berlin, Rome, Paris, Brussels, indeed nearly everywhere in Europe. While the newspaper industry in the United States is hemorrhaging readers and revenue, Europe is still a place of morning headline devourers.

In Germany, there are at least thirteen national daily newspapers and tabloids, and another dozen or so regional newspapers, in a nation of eighty million people that is the size of California. The dailies include *Bild*, a conservative tabloid with a circulation of nearly four million (twice as high as the largest U.S. daily, *USA Today*); the *Süddeutsche Zeitung*, a left-leaning daily with a circulation of 600,000; *Frankfurter Allgemeine Zeitung*, a center-right daily with a circulation of nearly a half million; *Die Welt*, a conservative-leaning newspaper, circulation 350,000; *Frankfurter Rundschau* (leftish daily), *Der Tagesspiegel* (centrist daily), *Handelsblatt* (business daily), and *Berliner Zeitung* (center-left), all with circulations of about 200,000; and then a bunch of smaller circulation dailies, including *Die Tageszeitung* (lefty with attitude) and *Financial Times Deutschland* (another business daily). It's like Baskin Robbins's 31 flavors of ice cream, a colorful palette of news and entertainment on the printed page.

This flowering of newspapers is not a coincidence, but rather is spurred by conscious policy. The Europeans have made a decision to encourage a vibrant newspaper culture and a culture of reading in general. How do they accomplish that? Several factors are involved, and one of them is quintessentially European—they subsidize it. Most countries assist newspapers and periodicals with some kind of special postal rates and tax rates, but the Scandinavian countries stand out for their direct subsidies. Norway, Finland, and Sweden subsidize daily newspapers with assistance amounting to anywhere from 5 to 35 percent of their revenues (averaging around 11 percent). Newspapers that are not leaders in their markets are especially targeted for assistance as a way of encouraging disparate views. Austria also provides direct subsidies, while Britain, Germany, the Netherlands, Belgium, France, and Denmark offer indirect subsidies such as VAT exemption or reduction (given that the VAT in some countries can approach 20 percent, that can amount to a sizable subsidy).[6]

Some of these newspapers are free and designed for vulnerable and special needs populations. When I was visiting Umeå, Sweden, I saw a free newspaper for people who don't read very well, including the learning disabled, the visually impaired, the elderly, and new immigrants (who are not yet fluent in Swedish). The newspaper had real content, but in larger print and with shorter articles, simply written yet informative about the news of the day. Swedes believe that even at-risk populations need to be informed and to participate in forging the national consensus.

Newspaper reading is important, as researchers such as Robert Putnam, Henry Milner, and others have shown; it encourages literacy, and those who receive their news and information from newspapers and magazines have greater comprehension and are better informed than those who receive their news from television.[7] European policy recognizes this by encouraging a vibrant newspaper culture, and a culture of reading in general.

But in the United States the newspaper business is in a shocking state of decline. Major dailies like the *New York Times, USA Today,* the *Los Angeles Times,* and many others have suffered significant drops in daily readership and have slashed their corps of reporters and staff in response. In 2009, two dailies, the *Rocky Mountain News* and the *Seattle Post-Intelligencer,* shut their doors for good after publishing for 150 years.[8] With the explosion of the Internet and free news sources, as well as American newspapers' failure to produce a product that customers want to buy, the U.S. newspaper industry has entered an unpredictable twilight zone. While newspapers in other countries have lost some readership to the Internet, the extent has been nothing like in the U.S. You don't hear about dailies in Europe, Japan, or Australia folding or slashing tons of news staff. No, a declining newspaper industry has been a particularly American phenomenon.

That's because the U.S. newspaper industry finds itself stuck in a business model that conceives of the industry primarily as a commercial, profit-seeking enterprise that should not rely on "government handouts." While subsidizing newspapers may seem like another example of European statism throwing money at the problem, the fact is subsidizing media is as American as apple pie. As we have seen, U.S. corporate broadcasters benefit from a nearly $400 billion government subsidy that has given them the public's airwaves for free. The Public Broadcasting Service and National Public Radio also receive direct government subsidies, while the Internet has been subsidized through its creation and maintenance by the government, as well as through a federal ban on sales tax for Internet purchases. It's only newspapers and the printed media that have been conceived as strictly for-profit ventures, which has more to do with newspapers' historic development as family-owned enterprises than any sound rationale for their exclusion.

Europe's practice of subsidizing daily newspapers recognizes that newspapers and investigative journalism play a core civic role beyond that of a money-making venture. Europe's "let a thousand flowers bloom" approach works much like the Internet does, by creating a political hubbub of opinion that is enraptured with debate and fosters the most open of societies. The cacophony of voices eventually arrives at an approximate consensus, informed by the robustness of the debate. So Europe's public subsidies are not seen as a sign of media failure but part of a successful financial model. If Americans value the uniqueness of printed news and entertainment and its civic literacy qualities, they will need to throw the industry a lifeline, as the U.S. government already has done for corporate and public broadcasters, and as Europe has done.

Information permeates many other aspects of European life, whether in the form of TV screens blaring news from their mounts on subway and train interiors, or free admission and frequent evening hours at art, science, and history museums. Europe provides more generous monetary support to its artists, a recognition of the importance of the artist's role in society.[9] And Europe and Japan are way ahead of the U.S. when it comes to penetration of the Internet and broadband availability. Europe's high-speed connections are less expensive than ours and lightning fast in comparison.[10] In an Information Age, in which an informed citizenry is enhanced by its access to the democratizing aspects of the Internet, Europe is leading the way and is far ahead of the U.S., which used to lead the world but has fallen behind.

Despite the U.S. lag in broadband access, the Obama campaign for president revealed the tremendous fundraising and mobilizing potential of the Internet.[11] Nevertheless, overall Internet penetration in Europe remains much greater than in the United States, and when combined with a robust public broadcasting sector, these diverse information and media sources in Europe play an integral role in the political and cultural landscape. They establish a tone and quality that the corporate broadcasters have to compete with. But in the United States, the lack of media pluralism, especially of a well-funded public broadcasting sector and now a dwindling newspaper sector, has been leading to disastrous consequences, as we saw during the U.S. media's failure to scrutinize Bush administration claims during the buildup to the invasion of Iraq in 2003, and its failure to report on the housing and stock market bubbles and falling for Wall Street's "irrational exuberance." In all these examples, the fourth estate bombed in its mission to question official sources, investigate the truth, and inform the public. Even worse, at times it has engaged in a type of yellow journalism that was reminiscent of the days of William Randolph Hearst and his odious brand of "Remember the Maine!" patriotic boosterism.[12] Reflecting on the U.S. media's failure, *New York Times* columnist Paul Krugman commented, "[Europeans and Americans] have different views partly because we see different news. At least compared with their foreign counterparts, the 'liberal' U.S. media are strikingly conservative—and in this case hawkish."[13]

With the failure of the U.S. media in its fulcrum duty to inform the public, it has become difficult for Americans to learn what is happening in the world, or even in the United States, without consulting non-American news sources, such as the BBC and other independent media sources via the web. This is a sad commentary on the state of America's media sector. Plagued by an ailing newspaper industry, by corporate broadcasters that give little in return for the multibillion-dollar giveaway of the public's airwaves to them, and by a public broadcasting sector that is too poor and often too timid to make a difference, Americans and their democracy will continue to struggle.

CIVIC LITERACY: MAKING DEMOCRACY WORK

The robust and comprehensive nature of Europe's media and communications institutions is not some government boondoggle to line the pockets of those feeding from the public trough. Quite the contrary. Taken together, these institutions, combined with public financing, free media time for campaigns and parties, and proportional representation electoral systems, contribute to a greater degree of what political scientist Henry Milner has called "civic literacy"—the knowledge and capacity of citizens to make sense of their political world. Societies with high degrees of civic literacy are ones in which the people show an ability not only to be conversant in the politics and issues of the day but also to identify the impacts that specific policies will have upon their own interests and those of their community. Milner marshaled a wealth of data and empirical findings from numerous sources in the United States, Canada, western Europe, Australia, and New Zealand to show how civic literacy underpins effective democracies, economic performance, and social justice. Milner's thesis built on Robert Putnam's widely discussed "social capital," but Milner went beyond Putnam to draw greater attention to political and media institutions and the incentives these provide for the public to engage in activities needed to nurture and sustain individual participation and a functioning democracy.[14]

The implication of Milner's work is that, compared with that of the United States, Europe's greater level of civic literacy is much enhanced by its better-equipped political, media, and cultural institutions. Various studies have demonstrated that the peoples of Europe are the most educated and informed in the world, not only about their own domestic politics, but also about international affairs. Americans, on the other hand, consistently perform near the bottom of these measurements, whether the study gauges their knowledge of their own country's legislature, world geography, or international affairs.[15] In comparing levels of civic literacy in various countries, Milner concludes that "economic globalization adds an element of urgency to the choice confronting democratic societies. . . . Only high 'civic literacy' societies, institutionally arranged so that a substantial majority of their citizens have meaningful maps to guide them through the complexity of decisions that their community will face, will . . . be equipped to meet the challenge. Only those communities can hope to distribute fairly the costs of globalization and new information technology so as to draw optimal advantage from their benefits."[16]

The difference between the European Way and the American Way boils down to inclusion vs. exclusion and consensus building vs. power-over adversarial politics, in which one point of view tries to beat all the others. The quest for a fair economy, or better health care, or a sane energy policy, or family security, or a balanced foreign policy can be put in its proper perspective by answering a simple question: Who is to benefit? This is perhaps the single most important question that any society or political system must forge a consensus around. In Europe, this public soul searching is aided by a greater commitment to political pluralism, to a flowering of opinion and thought that finds expression in campaigns and in the legislatures, and in more politically diverse media outlets. With Europe being the land of high civic literacy and the United States lagging, it should come as no surprise that Europe's robust democracies would produce majoritarian policy that is more in tune with their populations' policy preferences and desires.

On various issues ranging from retirement pensions to immigration and militarization, one can see how Europe's democracies advance consensus building and forward-looking policy. An especially thorny issue like immigration shows how Europe's democracies can let the steam out of extremely contentious issues by giving representation and voice to various perspectives. In the November 2007 Danish elections, the usual mix of left, right, and centrist parties received their share of seats on the basis of their proportion of votes. But a brand new party, known as New Alliance, was started by a popular centrist politician of Arab descent, Naser Khader, specifically to raise a new and moderate voice regarding immigration that had been missing from the political spectrum. In its first election New Alliance was able to drive the debate about immigration, counter the influence of the right-wing Danish People's Party, and win 5 of the 179 seats in the Danish Folketing. In the U.S., a middle-ground party on immigration with such a low percentage of the vote (3 percent) would win no seats in winner-take-all elections, but in Denmark's proportional representation system, with public financing and free media time to aid in communication, such voices of moderation can find a place at the table.

Similar dynamics have occurred in the democracies of the Netherlands, Germany, Sweden, Austria, and other European nations. Multiparty democracy creates a dynamic conversation between the dominant mainstream parties and the junior parties, between the center and the flanks of the political spectrum, a valuable part of the consensusseeking process over controversial issues. A fierce debate in Europe has been raging for some time over issues of increasing inequality, the social contract, and who will benefit in an age of globalized capitalism. Whether voiced by French students and *banlieue* youth amassing in the streets with their inchoate demands, or German doctors striking like any working stiffs with their quite concrete demands, or the French and Dutch populaces voting "Non!" and "Neen!" to an E.U. treaty that many feared would render Europe more like the United States, these issues are front and center, demanding that the political system respond. And to a great degree, appearances sometimes to the contrary, Europe's multiparty democracies *are* responding.

But in the United States, government is barely responsive today.

Whether the issue is resolving the Iraq and Afghanistan wars or address-ing global climate change, growing inequality, inadequate health care, or the undermining of the social contract and economic security for most U.S. workers, America's winner-take-all system and antiquated political institutions are failing to forge a national consensus. Bedev-iled by divisive bumper-sticker politics used to win over a handful of undecided swing voters in a handful of battleground districts or states, American government and the electoral process have both failed to perform. The U.S. Congress can't even agree on something as basic and commonsensical as mandating paid sick leave so that ill people don't show up to work and infect fellow workers or customers. How-ever much the American people may yearn for more choices on election day, the winner-take-all, two-party duopoly prevents the rise of new political parties and leaders that can fill this void and raise the flag on important issues. Without a functioning democracy you cannot build an economy that works for all, and consequently more and more Amer-icans are being dragged down by the economic insecurity of our times.

CHALLENGES TO EUROPEAN DEMOCRACY

While the European democracies are well equipped for consensus build-ing and policy formation, unquestionably a continent of half a billion people has significant challenges to deal with in the years ahead. Not all the European nations always live up to the high standards that have been established. In France, the print media are known for being too cozy with the power structure, and some of the most powerful media groups have links to the Sarkozy administration.[17] One amusing inci-dent revealing this coziness occurred in August 2007, when the maga-zine *Paris Match,* owned by a Sarkozy ally, published a touched-up photograph of the shirtless French president looking manly during his U.S. vacation. But it turned out the photo had been doctored to remove unattractive rolls of flesh—"love handles"—from around his waist. The effort was exposed by a rival publication, *L'Express,* which published the original and the airbrushed photos side by side. The Battle of the Flab was all the rage for weeks.

The return of Silvio Berlusconi as prime minister of Italy presents a more serious example of democratic flat-footedness. Berlusconi is the Italian media magnate who managed to gobble up nearly all the private television media in Italy and then used that resource as a stepping-stone to a successful political career. The exquisitely dressed Berlusconi uses a campaigning method that consists of sailing up and down the Italian coast in his private yacht, pulling into ports where his TV stations cover his press conferences and beam his perennially tanned face to Italians all over the country. More damaging to Italian democracy, however, is that prime minister Berlusconi also oversees the Italian public broadcasting sector, giving him unprecedented influence over nearly all televised media in Italy. That's not how European democracy is supposed to work, and his opponents—both within Italy and in the rest of Europe—find themselves challenged to counter this impolitic figure in Europe's belly who has been in and out of government over the past sixteen years.

But Italy has long been Europe's poster child for a struggling democracy. The constantly collapsing coalition governments in Italy in the post–World War II period have provided steady fodder for finger-wagging lectures from the *New York Times,* the *Washington Post,* and the like. But it has rarely been noted that even with each new government looking like the previous one, Italy has enjoyed enough stability within its instability to have the sixth largest national economy in the world and a high standard of living. Other nations occasionally have had difficulties forming a coalition government as well. Following elections in 2007, Belgium needed an unusually protracted amount of time to compose its coalition government because of tensions over linguistic and cultural differences between the northern and southern regions. Frustration levels prompted one disgruntled Belgian to offer to sell Belgium on eBay: "For Sale: Belgium, a Kingdom in three parts."

But sales of bickering kingdoms aside, any political turmoil in the European democracies has not prevented them from prospering or enacting Europe's unique brand of social capitalism and workfare supports, which, on the whole, have continued to work remarkably well, even during times of political turmoil. Most of the criticisms leveled at European democracies—they lead to weak coalition governments,[18] or they produce welfare states in which nobody works and, paradoxically, everyone pays high taxes—have turned out to be overhyped exaggerations and stereotypes, as we have seen. Another stereotype is that European democracies elect fascists and neo-Nazis, which makes for good headlines however much it oversimplifies reality.[19] While most of the European parties and leaders that fall under the fuzzy rubric of the "far right" have strong anti-immigration views (much like the Republican Party in the United States), ironically they are to the *left* of the Democratic Party on most issues. If one actually takes the time to read the platforms or listen to the speeches of Europe's far right leaders, one is struck that, once you get past the provocative rhetoric, the far right in Europe does not question or call for the abolition of the workfare support system. On the contrary, they accept its existence to a degree even the Democrats in the U.S. don't accept today.[20]

Critics who say proportional representation gives too much influence to extremists don't recognize that with the U.S. system, small slices of the most zealous parts of the electorate ("the base") and the least informed and most detached part of the electorate ("the swing voters") acquire exaggerated power, sometimes determining which party wins the presidency or the U.S. House if they tilt the results in even one battleground state, such as Florida or Ohio, or in a handful of swing House districts. In the Senate, forty-one senators representing as little as 12 percent of the nation can stonewall legislation via filibusters.

Besides, PR systems have a fail-safe: they can handle political extremists by raising the "threshold of victory" (the percentage of the vote needed to win a seat) to a suitably high level that limits the extremists' political impact. Proportional systems and multiparty democracy are used by most of the established democracies in the world today, all of them establishing different victory thresholds to fine-tune their democracies and make them as representative—or as exclusive—as they need them to be. Among the many PR democracies, very few have the problems of Italy, Israel, or Germany's Weimar Republic in the early 1930s, the most frequently criticized examples.

In fact, Germany's political system demonstrates the possibility of creating interesting hybrids, which the United States could learn a lot from. The German electoral system combines U.S.-style single-seat, winner-take-all districts with proportional representation, offering the benefits of both. The geographic orientation of winner-take-all gives representation based on where you live, whereas proportional voting gives representation based on what you think. These are not mutually exclusive; indeed, they can be complementary. New Zealand, Italy, and Japan also use this "mixed member system," and states' bicameral legislatures in the United States provide an easy opening for such a mixed system. The United States could use geographic-based representation via winner-take-all districts in one chamber of the legislature and proportional representation in which voters win representation based on what they think in the other.

One important European institution in which criticisms of democracy are pointedly relevant is the European Union. Located in Brussels, housed in beautiful glass buildings like a modern-day emerald city, the European Parliament and the E.U.'s executive bodies (the European Commission and the European Council) preside over Europe's innovative supranational union. The glass buildings are a testimony to the European Union's attempts at transparency, as well as the fragility of that effort. The E.U., which on the whole has capably tackled the difficult job of representing twenty-seven nations, dozens of languages, and half a billion people located across a sprawling continent, nevertheless is seen by most Europeans as a distant, meddling bureaucracy. It can appear to issue directives from on high, including the enforcement of its eighty thousand pages of regulations that touch everything from air travel to household chemicals and the recipes for cheese and French bread. While the European Parliament is elected, its enumerated powers make it weaker than the major executive body, the European Commission, which is not elected by the broader European public. Thus, the European Union is seen as being too removed from electoral controls, too complex for citizens of the member states to comprehend, and generally unaccountable to its citizens. A corruption scandal under the administration of European Council president Jacques Santer led to the mass resignation of all members of the council in March 1999, further eroding public confidence.

The rather contradictory criticisms of the E.U.'s being both aloof and an overweening top-down bureaucracy, combined with concerns over its role as an advocate of economic globalization and further expansion to controversial countries such as Turkey, led French and Dutch voters to reject the 2005 treaty that sought to draw Europe into a tighter union. Irish voters rejected a scaled-back version of the treaty in June 2008 and voted again in October 2009.[21] Unquestionably, the European Union's democratic institutions have a ways to go before they match those of its national democracies, but the E.U. is a work in progress. Europeans certainly have the expertise to design a continent-wide democratic system, but what is lacking is a continent-wide consensus over how united their union should be. Questions remain over how much sovereignty each nation should cede to the supranational body.

The economic meltdown in 2008 and severe recession of 2009 exacerbated these questions over continental unity, as individual nations had to decide how much they should pool their resources and help bail each other out and cede a measure of national financial sovereignty to European authorities in Brussels and Frankfurt. Sovereignty and subsidiarity—the latter a popular notion that all government policy should

be enacted at the smallest or most immediate level of government possible (i.e., local rather than regional, regional rather than national, and
national rather than at the E.U. level)—certainly will be a subject of
ongoing negotiation, debate, and strain. Europe's innovative federalism, as well as the E.U.'s political institutions, will be forced to adapt as
its vision becomes more defined, sometimes driven by the latest crisis.
Indeed, that vision may change—dramatically—in response to future
world events and continental urgencies. It is instructive to recall that
the United States took roughly a hundred years after its founding to
congeal as a nation and nurture a broader identity that transcended
state loyalties and histories.[22] And it took the drama of a civil war
in the United States to settle some of the most divisive sectional differences and tensions. Yes indeed, the European Union is a work in
progress, so stay tuned.

TWENTY-FIRST-CENTURY DEMOCRACY

Why would any American not want quality, affordable health care, or
paid parental leave, or affordable child care, paid sick leave, generous
vacations, a low-cost university education, a generous retirement pension, and a shorter workweek? It remains one of the great unanswered
riddles why Europeans enjoy these many workfare supports but most
Americans do not.

Members of the U.S. Congress and the president and vice president
are fortunate to enjoy European-level benefits and services. They understand that having such comprehensive security for your family is a good
thing—but why would they not grant the same to their fellow Americans? Why would they not support their fellow Americans in having the
same level of health and economic security that they and their families
enjoy? The gatekeepers have closed the gate behind them, leaving millions of Americans to fend for themselves. Not even the Democrats, who
compose a majority in Congress, and who purport to stand up for average working Americans, propose to give their fellow Americans the level
of workfare benefits that are enjoyed in Europe and that they enjoy as
members of Congress. With third parties floundering on the rocks of the
winner-take-all electoral system, there simply is no viable political party
to stand up for the economic interests of the average person. Instead of
fostering informed, consensus-building national dialogue, our system
strangles new ideas and innovations in the crib. As a result, the United
States has experienced a wholesale and widespread underdevelopment

of the American people's political faculties and consciousness, contributing to an atrophied ability to find consensus.

A functioning political democracy is a prerequisite to having an economic system that works for everyone instead of just the better-off and the powerful. But in the United States we have an antiquated and unrepresentative democracy founded on eighteenth-century institutions and methods, lacking public financing of campaigns, free media time, a vibrant public broadcasting sector, and multiparty legislatures. Lacking the right institutions for the twenty-first century, the United States suffers through a sclerotic two-party, winner-take-all system. It remains stuck in gear, unwilling to try out Children's Parliaments, Citizens' Assemblies, and other forms of deliberative democracy, or Question Time, or universal voter registration. Ironically, American businesses often are extolled for innovation and modernization, yet when it comes to our basic political institutions and practices, the United States is hopelessly bogged down by stodgy tradition and special interests. Lacking a modern, vibrant democracy, Americans are falling behind their European counterparts.

While America fiddles, old Europe and its leaders have become the innovators of democracy, the Thomas Jeffersons, John Adamses, and James Madisons (or as Europeans would say, the Jean Monnets, Winston Churchills, and Konrad Adenauers) of our time.[23] European democracies are better poised to function in the mass societies and information economies that now compose the world. Ironically, just as at one time the torch of democracy was passed to the young breakaway American republic, which exhibited a popular "tumult" of political activity observed by the Frenchman Alexis de Tocqueville in his 1835 work *Democracy in America,* today it can be said that the torch has passed back across the Atlantic.[24] It is in Europe that representative democracy is better equipped to foster broad consensus among diverse populations, stakeholders, and interests about the best institutions and practices—economic, health care, workfare, energy, transportation, political, media, and foreign policy—necessary for the twenty-first century.

PART SIX

THE CONCEPT OF "EUROPE"

STICKY GLUE, SOCIAL CONTRACTS, AND FULCRUM INSTITUTIONS

In the Rijksmuseum, in Amsterdam, hangs an obscure painting that speaks volumes about the modern dilemmas of government and the natural tension between individual freedom and the ties that bind us together. The masterfully rendered work, dating from approximately 1899 by the Dutch painter Otto Eerelman, shows hundreds of soldiers costumed in the dress blues of a military parade in Amsterdam, and mounted on brawny stallions. Leading the procession are erect, square-shouldered officers in their fine, medal-adorned coats and feathery chapeaux-de-bras, with a palace looming in the background. Banners, pennants, and coats of arms are flapping in the breeze, and a few members of the public are standing at attention. The military swarm has surrounded an elegant, cream-colored carriage of royal pedigree, with the soldiers sitting atop their steeds, clutching long swords pointed skyward, at vertical attention.

What is curious about the painting is that inside the carriage are the only two females apparent in the entire male militaryscape: a young woman of eighteen, named Wilhelmina, who is about to be crowned queen of the Netherlands, and her mother, Emma, who as Queen Regent has been holding the post until her daughter came of age. The sea of soldiers and their long knives are darkly rendered, but the painter's skill has bathed the two women and their delicate carriage in a glazed light, as if the hope and aspirations of a nation are ensconced in their halo at the heart of the painting. As I stood staring at this image, what initially struck me was the frailty of these two women anchoring this muscular display. Any one of these soldiers could simply canter close to the royal barouche, say, "Good day, Your Majesty," and with a couple swings of his sword run them both through. The two women, one young and the other old, would be powerless to defend themselves.

Yet the soldiers don't do that, quite the contrary. Instead, they all hold the line, at attention while the carriage rolls past, as if all the soldiers are hypnotized by some kind of spell. Only a couple of the horses appear to buck against whatever rule is binding them to an unspoken consensus: that this vulnerable young woman shall rule over these brave hard men, indeed over an entire nation. I felt transported by the artist's skill, as if I were standing there in the Frederiksplein as the procession rolled past. The sheer incongruity of it all, of a delicate woman more powerful than all these armed men, is what entranced me.

I knew I was witnessing, from my distant perch, the social and political agreements that had bound them all to their national fate, the invisible threads of connectedness that wrap countless personal lives into a web of officialdom. Every generation, as well as every nation and political order, makes its agreements, its social contract, bonded by the "sticky glue" that holds it all together and that keeps the human heart of darkness from ripping us apart. While seeming second nature to those living under them, the rules of agreement are rooted in the past, in culture and local color, looking both backward and forward at the same time. And once you step outside the picture and observe the rules from another place or distant time, you can see that often they made sense only to those who lived under the dome of their social and political contract.

Queen Wilhelmina went on to become a popular monarch who reigned for fifty years, a symbol of national unity that inspired the Dutch people with her staunch resolve during the Second World War. But at the time of this painting, who could have known what the future held for the young queen or her nation? It made me wonder about the unwritten agreements, compromises, and social contracts we live by today. Every national paradigm, every political economy, whether the European "social capitalist" democracy, the Japanese-style "*zaibatsu* cronyism" democracy, the Iranian mullah-ocracy, the Chinese state communism or Russian feral capitalism, the previous Soviet command-style economy, or the American "Wall Street capitalism" democracy, has its rules and agreements that establish the manners and modes for the inhabitants of that time and place to live by. These rules are incorporated into certain fulcrum institutions that work as an integrated whole, which, when taken together, forms a distinctive American Way, or a European Way, or a Japanese or Chinese or Russian Way. The great historian Arnold Toynbee once wrote, "Countries have characters that are as distinctive as those of human beings,"[1] and each fulcrum institution is a component part of a greater whole that contributes to the formation of a "national character."

As in the past, different national characters exist in the world today, and while the American Way and the European Way share much in common, they also exhibit basic differences that are diverging and were leading to frequent clashes even before the U.N. rift over Iraq. It's as if we are staring at two different paintings, hung side by side, each revealing its intricate web of unwritten rules, agreements, and social contract. While it's possible to stress what Europe and America have in common, it behooves us to recognize the differences as well, and approach this divergence a bit like an art historian might approach a Da Vinci alongside a Michelangelo, straining to understand which work might be the better harbinger of the future. More than we realize is at stake: few in the world wish to emulate the Chinese or the Russian Way, stuck in their authoritarianism and low standard of living, and certainly not the Islamic fundamentalist way, which is synonymous with poverty, bloody conflict, religious intolerance, and women's oppression. But all nations, even Muslim nations, desire the wealth and quality of life of the United States and Europe. Thus, this clash between the American Way and the European Way is about the future direction over the best development model for the world during this make-or-break twenty-first century.

The American Way and the European Way have diverged in two crucial ideological areas: first, in the role and size of the military, with militarism being a core part of the American Way, as we saw in chapters 1, 4, and 11. U.S. militarism acts not only as a projection of international power but also as a stimulus of the economy, a voracious consumer of national wealth, and an indicator of societal values and priorities in a classic "guns vs. butter" tradeoff. America spends more than twice as much of our gross domestic product on the military as Europe spends, while Europe spends at least 25 percent more per capita on workfare spending than the U.S.

Second, while the American and European ways are both founded on capitalist economies, they have diverged in their conclusions regarding age-old debates about individual property rights vs. the common good, liberty vs. equality, and the role of government. These differ-

ences have led to the fashioning of distinct fulcrum institutions incorporating the laws, unwritten rules, and social contracts that guide
their respective ways. The European and American ways are deeply
rooted in old traditions, even in different branches of Christianity,
which will shape any attempts to forge a new transatlantic understanding. Exploring these origins will be instructive to a reading of
these ideological differences.

THE PURITANS AND JOHN LOCKE VS.
SAINTS AUGUSTINE AND THOMAS AQUINAS

In Europe, the ownership of property and the exercise of individual
and commercial property rights are not seen as absolutes as they are
in the United States. Rather, they are viewed as a privilege that confers
reciprocal social obligations. In the European conception, those who
own and hold property—especially the wealthy and corporations that
own lots of it—have a responsibility to contribute to the common good
for the privilege of exercising those property rights. Article 14 of the
postwar German constitution, for example, specifies that "property
imposes duties. Its use should also serve the public weal."[2]

This in turn affects attitudes toward government. Across Europe,
government fosters the conditions in which prosperity can be broadly
shared. There is a great commitment to the notion that all residents
should have an equal right to participate in economic, political, and
social life, and government is more than a safety net of last resort: it
is the fundamental vehicle for the delivery of this equality. This is the
European consensus, for the most part agreed to by all sides of the political spectrum, right, left, and center, as it was when it was conceived by
the conservative politicians of Europe following the devastation of two
world wars. They saw the European Way not as some kind of utopian
or socialist undertaking but as a pragmatic and carefully constructed
barrier against the return of economic depression, extremist politics,
and continental war, with a democratic and representative government
acting as the principal catalyst of this endeavor.[*] Today, even leading

---

*As was previously noted, the European Way does not at all amount to a singular
championing of central authority or "big government," since Europe combines this view
with another one calling for "subsidiarity," one of the defining features of European
federalism. Subsidiarity holds that government policy should be enacted at the most
immediate and local level of government possible. Nevertheless, national/central governments are conceived as having an active and significant role to play.

European conservatives such as German chancellor Angela Merkel and French president Nicolas Sarkozy support the notion that corporations have social obligations.[3] When Volkswagen, which is the largest carmaker in Europe and is 20 percent owned by the German state government of Lower Saxony (where Volkswagen is based), wanted to abolish Lower Saxony's blocking minority rights, Merkel sided with the state government, a position that would be anathema to an American conservative, or even most Democrats.[4]

In contrast, Americans prioritize the principle of protecting individual property rights and commercial interests, which is believed to be best accomplished by limiting the power of government to interfere with those rights. Government is viewed more skeptically as inefficient and inept or, even worse, as a vampire that sucks the life out of the body politic. Government regulation, seen as an infringement on individual property rights, is to be used as little as possible. Recall President Ronald Reagan, one of the most articulate proponents of this view, boldly declaring in his first inaugural address, "Government is not the solution to our problem; government *is* the problem."[5] President Bill Clinton signed up the Democrats for this detail when, with one eye on reelection, he declared in his 1995 State of the Union Address that the "era of big government is over." President George W. Bush poured it on, bashing bloated government as the excuse for enacting huge tax cuts that mostly benefited the wealthy, and as part of the rationale for deregulating the housing, banking, and financial sectors which contributed to the eventual meltdown of the U.S. and global economies.

Noted British author Will Hutton, chief executive of the Work Foundation in London, told me, "These differing attitudes between Europe and the U.S. are rooted in history and culture, even in religious beliefs. America was discovered as a wilderness by settlers who had risked all crossing the Atlantic and who, as pious Puritans rebelling against the authorities that were persecuting them, believed in their direct and individual relationship with God." They adopted a "work hard, get ahead" creed, believing fervently that industriousness was the best route to God's favor and that God had provided the land for those who could show by their diligence that they deserved it. Surviving on the New World frontier, surrounded by land that was seemingly limitless, the Puritans conceived an individualist rather than a social view of property. Their individual liberty allowed them to worship as they chose, and it also protected them from any coercive government constraint on how they used their private property.

Thus, individual liberty was the foundation of their quasi-theocratic way of life. "Property, ownership, religious freedom and the virtue of independence was thus indissolubly linked as part of God's plan," says Hutton.[6] Alexis de Tocqueville noticed this quality still present in the United States in the 1830s, commenting, "The Americans combine the notions of Christianity and liberty so intimately in their minds that it is impossible to make them conceive the one without the other."[7]

In the eighteenth century, the ideas of political philosopher John Locke were stirred into this religious stew. Locke's *Second Treatise* provided a theory and epistemology capable of justifying the claim not only that what the settlers found and created was theirs, but also that it was what the divine creator intended. According to Locke, individual property rights were conceived as "natural rights," and government was enacted by individuals to protect those property rights. "That government governs best which governs least" is how Jefferson translated Locke. Adam Smith's *Wealth of Nations* (1776), which immortalized an iconic "invisible hand of the free marketplace" as a divine economic autoregulator, next provided the intellectual rationale for extending this "laissez-faire" philosophy to commercial rights and the economy in general. By that point all the pieces were in place for a new American-minted "religion of individualism," in which individualism was worshipped simultaneously in the religious, economic, and political realms. "Nowhere," says Hutton, "was there any notion to parallel the German constitution's stipulation that property imposes reciprocal duties."[8]

The Puritans, Locke, and Smith were extremely influential with Jefferson, Madison, Washington, Hamilton, and others from the generation of 1776. The defying of royal and religious authorities and the championing of individual conscience and self-determination advanced the necessary pre-attitudes for both early America's democratic spirit and its conception of property and commercial rights. They were two sides of the same coin and became impressed into the U.S. Constitution. It's not that the early Americans didn't believe in a European-style, Rousseau-like "general welfare"; in fact, the preamble to the Constitution reads, "We the People of the United States, in Order to . . . promote the general Welfare." It's just that they believed the best way to promote the general welfare was through individual liberty and the exalting of property rights, with every man as both the king of his own castle and protected from the maraudings of rulers, aristocrats, bishops, and popes. Smith's invisible hand would take care of the rest, and this was the natural order of things.

Unquestionably, the triumph of liberty as an ideology in the new American nation resulted in an unleashing of a certain zestful entrepreneurial vitality—what George Will and John Maynard Keynes before him have called the "animal spirits"—not only economically, but also politically, indeed in virtually all nooks of early American life. The impact was transformative, recorded with a sense of wonder and admiration (though also with a few words of caution) by the French aristocrat Alexis de Tocqueville in his *Democracy in America* (1835), as well as by his philosophical colleague the German Francis Lieber. Lieber, who immigrated to the upstart young republic in 1827 and was to become one of America's leading writers and scholars on political philosophy, international affairs, and law, published *Letters to a Gentleman in Germany* in 1834, a travel narrative in which he related his impressions of political institutions and culture in his new homeland. Both Tocqueville and Lieber noted that the parvenu nation enjoyed the advantage of a society without the privileged classes found in nineteenth-century Europe's aristocratic societies, and that this contributed greatly to the unleashing of those animal spirits. But both also noted the natural tensions between liberty and equality, one colliding with the other like cold and hot air fronts. Tocqueville warned about a "tyranny of the majority" that could result if the majority's liberty ran roughshod over the rights of minorities, thus depriving them of *their* liberty. They saw that the religion of individualism had its limits and could be taken too far. The United States has been struggling with these themes ever since.

Europe, on the other hand, was founded on a feudal and Catholic value system which believed that the exercise of privilege by the wealthy came with wider social obligations beyond mere charity. Typical of this view, St. Augustine in the fifth century A.D. declared, "He who uses his wealth badly possesses it wrongfully." St. Thomas Aquinas argued that one of the duties of government was to regulate private property for the common good, and that "a Christian is obliged to make his wealth available for common needs."[9] The medieval world, despite its episodes of barbarity, fostered a tradition of *noblesse oblige* between the lord or baron and his vassals, in addition to that between the Church and its supplicants, which eventually was transferred to the state as a kind of parental overseer of its citizens' well-being. Says Hutton, "In Europe the notion persists to this day that property is held in trust for all and only delegated to individuals for as long as they accept reciprocal social obligations."[10]

Unquestionably, one can still see a certain degree of identification of the European Union with Christian social doctrine, which is ironic, since secular Europe supposedly has abandoned religion, while a more pious America mostly ignores those parts of the Christian theological doctrine of Saints Augustine and Thomas Aquinas. But it's also true that representative democracy as we know it today might never have developed if not for the influence of this seventeenth-century Puritan conception of individual property rights. The notion of the rugged individual, of Jefferson's sturdy yeoman farmers tilling their own soil in a drive toward independence and self-determination, represented an attitudinal milestone on the pathway to democracy. It was a breakthrough, especially compared with the divine right of a king.

Yet each breakthrough often contains the seeds of its own contradictions and eventual obsolescence. One contradiction emerged right away during the early years of the American Republic: the clash between one's individual property rights and enslaving a human being as one's property. As early as 1790, the newly minted U.S. Congress was wracked by heated debate over slavery's future, a controversy that would not be settled until a bitter, bloody civil war was fought seventy years later.[11] A more recent contradiction is reflected in the centrality of home ownership to the American dream. The notion of "every person owning his or her castle" has always exerted a greater pull in the United States than in Europe. But it was this same instinctual drive that contributed to the frenzy of the recent U.S. housing bubble, when historically low interest rates, unethical lenders, and media hype pumped up a land rush mentality that stoked millions of Americans to make a financial leap they could ill afford. President Bush tried to tap into these old beliefs and longings when he pushed his concept of an "ownership society," founded on an ideology not that different from Jefferson's concept of yeoman farmers or the Puritan settlers' concept of individual property rights. Nor was it that different from Herbert Hoover's use of the term *rugged individualism* as a paean to American pride, just prior to the calamity of the Great Depression, which showed millions of Americans just how on their own they really were.

Thus, this chasm between today's European Way and American Way was sown many years ago in the minds, psyches, and souls of early American settlers and was cemented into the core of American politics and culture in the form of the U.S. Constitution. Over the centuries, this difference has become magnified and distorted, with the United States very much dominated by a strict orthodoxy protecting individual rights of property and ownership. In a crucial chapter of the American story, the U.S. Supreme Court in the early and late nineteenth century handed down several key decisions that extended this ideological framework in such a way as to treat corporations as "private individuals" whose property rights also must be protected from government meddling.[12] This legally restricted government's ability to intervene in business and commerce, and did so under the guise of guarding the *public* interest via the protection of *private* property. Recent Supreme Court decisions have continued to uphold this view, displaying a clear pro-business bias, prompting one writer to rename the nine justices of the Roberts court as "Supreme Court, Inc."[13]

No doubt Jefferson would be surprised to discover that his revolutionary philosophy has been extended way beyond his sturdy yeoman farmers to include huge multinational corporations. In this age of globalization, multinationals with budgets larger than those of small and midsize nations are treated by the American legal system and politicians as private individuals whose property rights must be protected by limiting the extent of government intervention. So when more and more American corporations walk away from their part of the social contract and eliminate good jobs, health care, and retirement income for workers, they are acting wholly within this ancient narrative by exercising their individual property rights. Like Puritan leaders of yore, they feel justified in mightily resisting any attempts by government to intervene in the exercise of their private property. They feel no allegiance or responsibility to the public weal or the general welfare, especially when it affects their property or business; it's not part of their DNA. And no comparable notion has been developed in the United States of European-style codetermination, or of states like Lower Saxony having minority blocking rights over corporations.

But this is a perversion of the original doctrine—Jefferson surely would be appalled at how his "yeoman farmer" jurisprudence has provided the justification for tying government's hands while corporate agribusiness virtually wipes out American family farms. With the U.S. government on the sidelines guided by a laissez-faire philosophy, the playing field has become grossly tilted in favor of economic behemoths with few checks on their prerogative. The Puritans and Jefferson saw themselves as empowering small landowners as individual agents who were not beholden to any greater authority than themselves. They never foresaw the huge amassing of fortunes and economic power that would occur over the centuries, and they no doubt would be revolted at the way the doctrine they helped forge has been turned on its head.

In Europe, on the other hand, the idea of the social contract has been extended to the notion that companies and businesses must earn their commercial rights by operating in a socially legitimate fashion and by accepting the responsibilities that accompany ownership. In an age of globalization, this is a doctrine that has greater utility for the greatest number of people, since it provides the flexibility to fine-tune certain parts of a nation's economy. Rather than being locked into rigid and even fundamentalist notions of property and commercial rights, a nation can subject these rights to negotiation and compromise via the vehicle of a pluralistic, representative government. The *political process* then is what allows the *economic process* to be harnessed for the good of all, subject to ratification by a consensus of all sectors of society. Yet as we saw in the previous two chapters, the political process in the United States is largely broken, and the government has become unresponsive as a result of the ongoing use of antiquated institutions and practices; whereas in Europe the use of more modern methods, such as proportional representation, public financing of campaigns, free media time, universal voter registration, robust public broadcasting, and the like, has made government more responsive to the popular majority. This is a portentous transatlantic difference that has large ramifications for the future.

President Franklin Roosevelt's New Deal was the first major counterforce in the United States that tried to head in a European-like direction, crafting a second American pillar based on a social conception of the economy. In the aftermath of the Great Depression, the New Deal utilized government regulation to counter the failures of an unregulated free market system dominated by the wealthy and economically powerful. That resulted in a raft of legislation creating Social Security, a federal housing authority, the Tennessee Valley Authority, and other European-like government interventions. But it took the extremes of a depression to deliver that opportunity, and it rested on a shaky ideological foundation that left stubbornly intact the seventeenth-century "religion of individualism" ideal. Once the hard-earned lessons of economic collapse and the failure of rugged individualism had been forgotten amid the prosperity of ensuing decades, many of the New Deal provisions were eventually repealed, as was the New Deal philosophy. Some in the United States had hoped the Obama administration would be a transformative one capable of reviving this second social pillar, but these old attitudes are deeply entrenched.

Compared with Europe, the American system still regards government primarily as the protector of individual property rights, with the U.S. Supreme Court acting as the enforcer of these laissez-faire rules and agreements. That ideological framework reached a new apotheosis in the Bush-Cheney years, with Herbert Hoover's "rugged individualism" morphing into the "ownership society." Both ideologies were underpinned by the same seventeenth-century "religion of individualism," now dangerously transmogrified into a free-wheeling economic fundamentalism in which the big eat the small while government deregulates and mostly stays out of the way.

These contradictions of the American Way came crashing down in 2008, resulting in the Bush administration's near trillion dollar bailout of failing banks and financial institutions. President Bush, a free market ideologue, and his treasury secretary Hank Paulson, who was a former executive of investment banking firm Goldman Sachs, suddenly had to turn to the public sector to save the private sector. Government intervention was necessary to save the economy from the excesses of greedy corporate executives—many of them friends of the president and Paulson—but not to provide health care for forty-seven million Americans lacking it, or paid sick leave, parental leave, better retirement, or more job training. According to the ancient script of American elites, existing contracts calling for $165 million worth of bonuses to executives at AIG, the behemoth insurance company that had received $170 billion in bailout money from American taxpayers, had to be honored; but contracts with autoworkers had to be renegotiated to reduce salaries and pensions of retirees in order to save the auto industry. That kind of double standard is just one of the many signs of how much the American elite view their businesses as their individual property, and with a sense of entitlement that resists government meddling, even as they drive those businesses off a cliff.

The contradictions became utter hypocrisy when American leaders told the public that it was necessary to, in effect, privatize the gains of capitalism and socialize its losses. That is truly a radical philosophy, reminiscent of the English and French kings of old who believed in their own divine rights, paid for out of the public coffers. At the end of the day, the Bush presidency showed the tragic limitation of this antiquated American Way, as the religion of individualism reached its historical end game in a winner-take-all society that is wracked by the inconsistencies and contradictions of its internal logic. For in an era of globalized capitalism, the ownership society and its religion of individualism have become little more than euphemisms for workers and their families struggling on their own like feudal serfs, with little assistance from a government that is living by an obsolete seventeenth-century creed. A more accurate name for the "ownership society" would be the "on your own society."

The whole world is watching to see if an Obama administration will help the United States to regain its footing and its universal narrative, its sizzle and allure. The U.S. used to be the world's leading proponent of freedom and democracy, but Europe has surpassed us in those categories; we used to be the picture in everyone's head when they thought of "quality of life," but Europe and Japan have equaled us there as well; and we used to lead the world economically, extending our influence and might all over the world like an octopus, with bilateral agreements with numerous nations, but Europe has matched and in some ways surpassed us there too, with China nipping at our heels in East Asia, Central Asia, and Africa. The only arrow left in our quiver, it seems, is our military might, but the usefulness of that has been called into question. Suddenly second world countries have more choices of whom to align with—America is just one of them—and the world has fewer reasons to put up with an American Way if it is hell bent on a messianic belief in its own self-importance as the world's "indispensable nation."

The Obama administration, following on the heels of the Bush-Cheney administration's miserable failure on nearly all fronts (prompting many historians to call theirs the worst administration in U.S. history),[14] has inspired optimism for charting a new course away from the sleepwalk of the first eight years of the twenty-first century. But if it is to do so, it must begin with a reevaluation of the American mythology that has relied for too long on a seventeenth- and eighteenth-century conception of individual property and commercial rights. In its time, this ideology was a bold innovation, especially compared with the divine right of kings. It gave us democracy, a thriving economy, and an unheard of degree of self-determination for individuals and families. But today it is an ideology being used to justify the big eating the small and corporations turning their backs on their social role. Today, we live in the age of the divine rights of Wall Street, led by CEOs who stride the American landscape like the kings of old, accountable to virtually no one. Things have come full circle. In a bitter irony, the founding *ideology* of Jefferson and the Puritans is being used to undermine their founding *vision* of a roughly egalitarian society of independent agents.

The European Way's ideology, on the other hand, of a society that balances property rights with social obligation is a better fit for today's world. In the European conception, each member of the middle class (including those aspiring to the middle class) is empowered, like one of Jefferson's yeoman farmers, to act as an independent agent who is embedded within a supportive workfare structure. In Europe's social capitalist system, the individual risk of living under globalization becomes more broadly shared; it's as if the community network and economic integration of a New England township have been extended to the nation-state, and those nations have been integrated into a vast continental union. While the European Way presents a different ideology from that of Jefferson and the Puritans, it comes closest to preserving their vision and points the way forward. In short, the "sticky glue" of the European Way, the rules, agreements, and social contract that hold it all together, is best suited for this twenty-first-century world.

THE SEVEN CULTURES OF CAPITALISM

Thus, Europe's and America's attitudes toward individual property rights vs. the common good, liberty vs. equality, and the role of government and the social contract are very different, linked to distinct histories, separate Christian traditions, and diverging postures. When combined with Europe's and America's different stances toward militarism and the amount spent on related budgets, these attitudes amount to a fundamental shifting of the ground beneath the feet of the transatlantic alliance. Even more clearly now, we realize we are staring at two very different portraits showing the American and European ways, each displaying its distinctive synthesis of rules, compacts, and social agreements that provide the instinct and drive for their competing visions for the world.

Attesting to the profound depth of these differences, these attitudes are reflected not just among the general populations in America and Europe but even among the business classes. A fascinating book from the early 1990s, *Seven Cultures of Capitalism*, by two business consultants, Charles Hampden-Turner and Alfons Trompenaars, plumbed the views of entrepreneurs from both sides of the Atlantic. The authors previously had distributed questionnaires to some fifteen thousand business managers from around the world who had attended their seminars, using the results of these questionnaires to gauge how values, habits, and cultural styles affect the pursuit of economic success. Respondents in each of the "seven cultures" studied—the United States, Britain,

France, Germany, Sweden, the Netherlands, and Japan—reacted in markedly different ways. Not surprisingly, the authors found profound differences between the American respondents and those from Europe, with British respondents often straddling a line between the two.

European business managers were more disposed to communitarian values, teamwork, and long-term vision, while American managers were hyperindividualists, producing businesses that were hierarchical and narrowly focused on quarterly profit sheets. These postures also spilled over into social attitudes: entrepreneurs in the United States regarded poverty and unemployment as signs of personal failure, idleness, and disgrace; the poor are culpable. But in Germany, Austria, Scandinavia, and Japan they regarded poverty and unemployment as the consequences of workers having to adapt to the ups and downs of the economy and the ill luck of being employed in dying industries; the poor and unemployed must be retrained and assisted to make the transition. The workfare supports in the European countries were seen—by business managers no less—as a way of sharing the burden of the inevitable dislocations of capitalism and as a vehicle for getting people back to work.

French and German managers in particular scored high on the scale of communitarian values. The German managers, for example, were less inclined to fire an employee who is no longer performing satisfactorily but has a fifteen-year satisfactory service record. Only 31 percent of German managers believed this consideration shown to their workers and community to be irrelevant, compared with 77 percent of American managers. Jacques Calvet, former head of leading French automobile manufacturer Peugeot, deliberately counterpointed American business attitudes when he said, "What was good for General Motors was good for the USA? Well, I consider what is good for France is good for Peugeot."[15]

But there are signs that some influential U.S. business leaders have begun to notice that the American Way is the wrong way. In a January 2008 speech to the World Economic Forum in Davos, Switzerland, Bill Gates, Microsoft founder and the richest man in the world, sounded practically European when he told the world's business and political elites in the audience that "to harness this power [of capitalism] so it benefits everyone, we need to refine the system."[16] Gates's critique echoed those of the second wealthiest man in the world, American investor Warren Buffett, who has stated that "a market system has not worked in terms of poor people" and that the superwealthy "owe it to the rest of humanity to think about the other 99 percent." Buffett even implicitly questioned the grounding of U.S. capitalism in its seventeenth-century views when he criticized conservatives' rationalizations that say, "I'm making $80 million a year—God must have intended me to have a lower tax rate."[17] Gates and Buffett may be signaling that some of America's top business leaders are evolving toward attitudes similar to those of Europe's business leaders with their more communitarian outlook.[18]

FULCRUM INSTITUTIONS:
THE LEVERS ON WHICH EVERYTHING ELSE PIVOTS

With such different attitudes pervading even the entrepreneurial class, it's no surprise that these attitudes would be injected into the basic institutions of both the European Way and the American Way. These fulcrum institutions incorporate the unwritten rules and social contracts that guide our respective ways. While the United States focused on winning the Cold War and built up a militarized economy to match that focus, the fulcrum institutions of the European Way have been quietly incubating during the Pax Americana, particularly in the western European nations that have been leaders in its formation. Taken together these differences in fulcrum institutions have put Europe on a distinctly unique developmental path.

In particular, four fulcrum institutions form the foundation for the rest: the economic, political, media and communication, and workfare support institutions, and we have examined all of these in previous chapters. The political institutions are the means for deciding who will or will not sit at the table of power and exert authority, making policy for everyone else; the economic institutions organize the ownership and management of the economy, the means of obtaining income, and the distribution of that income, as well as the primary activity that engages most people on a daily basis; the media and communication institutions form the crucial means in a mass society for news, information sharing, and watchdog journalism, for debating pressing issues, and for fostering civic literacy, as well as for relaxation and entertainment; and the workfare institutions form the infrastructure for ensuring that workers and their families have the necessary supports to maintain themselves as healthy and productive members of society, as well as to pursue personal success and happiness. These four fulcrum institutions are the crucial ones on which everything else pivots. They work as an integrated whole, acting like the legs of a stool: change the length of any one of the legs, and the stool sits unevenly; severely shorten one of the legs, and the stool could topple.

For example, it is difficult to grasp the importance of a plethora of European media outlets, with editorial perspectives ranging from the right to the left to the center, without seeing them in the context of their multiparty democracy founded on the bedrock of proportional representation electoral systems, publicly financed campaigns, free media time for political parties and candidates, and universal voter registration. And contemplating the lack of diverging media opinion and gross underfunding of public broadcasting in the United States would be practically meaningless without recognizing America's constricted two-party, winner-take-all system as the attendant complement for such a stale media climate. Similarly, the democratization of economic authority reflected in Europe's corporate structure resulting from codetermination fits with its pluralistic political system, which fits with its pluralistic media. The famously comprehensive and universal European workfare system is much more probable in a pluralistic society in which values such as fairness, equality, and broad participation are reflected in the political, media, and economic systems. The fulcrum institutions both mold people and are molded by people. Having evolved together, they function as close-knit components, like the integrated gears of a finely tuned clock.

At this point, the American Way and its fulcrum institutions, informed by their seventeenth-century "religion of individualism" creed, are hopelessly ill-equipped for the twenty-first century. The European Way of social capitalism and its attendant institutions and underlying philosophy are better suited than the American Way of freewheeling, deregulated, Wall Street capitalism. Drawing from previous chapters, table 1 summarizes the differences in these fulcrum institutions and practices. Variations occur among the different European countries— some hew to this outline more than others—but for the most part the table recaps the fulcrum institutions of the European Way vs. the American Way, as explored in previous chapters.

These fulcrum institutions work coherently to form the sticky glue of a political economy that distinguishes the European Way from the American Way. In turn these fulcrum institutions have fostered a whole new outlook among Europeans about themselves and about the globalized world, including their relationship with the United States. T. R. Reid, author and *Washington Post* reporter covering the European

TABLE 1. THE AMERICAN WAY VS. THE EUROPEAN WAY

	European Way	American Way
Political	Proportional representation electoral systems	Winner-take-all electoral systems
	Publicly financed campaigns	Privately financed campaigns
	Free media time for political parties	No free media time, expensive to buy political ads
	Robust public TV and radio, fostering debate	Corporate media, underfunded public broadcasting, limited debate
	Multiparty legislatures	Two-party legislatures
	Political pluralism, choice for voters	One-party districts and states, "orphaned voters"
	More debate and discussion of issues	Poll-driven sound bites targeting swing voters
	Universal voter registration	70 million unregistered (eligible) voters
	Voting on a holiday or weekend	Voting in the middle of a busy workday
	High voter turnout	Low voter turnout—single digits in many races
	National election commissions and standards	Decentralized, hodgepodge election administration
	Upper legislative chambers have little power	U.S. Senate has as much power as the House
	Upper legislative chambers treat all regions the same	Senate, Electoral College give advantage to low-population, conservative states
	More trusting of democracy— Children's Parliaments, deliberative democracy, Question Time, etc.	Mistrust of democracy and "We the People"
	Foreign policy based on multi-lateralism, investment, and Marshall Plan–like development	Foreign policy based on unilateralism and preemptive strikes
Media	Diverse outlets, left/right/centrist views	Corporate media gatekeepers, constricted views
	Well-funded public broadcasting (radio and TV)	Weak, underfunded public broadcasting
	Political pluralism—promotion of ideas/debate	Loss of political ideas and debate
	Subsidized, diverse daily newspapers	Failing newspaper industry
	High level of civic literacy	Low level of civic literacy
	More people read newspapers	Fewer people read newspapers
	Better-informed citizenry	Poorly informed citizenry
Economic	Family and community values, social solidarity	Hyperindividualist values, ownership society
	Codetermination—worker represen-tatives on corporate boards of directors and works councils	Hierarchical business structures, little consultation
	Balance of stockholder and stake-holder rights	Stockholder rights are supreme
	Social contract is intact and comprehensive	Social contract is fraying and porous
	High percentage of unionized workforce	Low percentage of unionized workforce

(continued)

TABLE 1. *(continued)*

	European Way	American Way
Economic (continued)	Labor and management confer more extensively	Adversarial relations between labor and management
	E.U.-wide minimum labor standards	"Right to work" states and antiunion laws
	National referendums on joining E.U. and adopting euro	Corporate-driven free trade pacts
	Trade surpluses	Large trade deficits
	Strong euro	Weak dollar, debtor nation funded by foreign creditors
	Low unemployment in most countries, higher in Germany, France, Italy (pre-2008 economic crash)	Lower unemployment (but if prisoners included, rate is closer to Europe's)
	Unemployed have sufficient support	Unemployed can end up destitute
	Job training and retraining	Little job training or retraining
	Higher income taxes but lower out-of-pocket expenses, many more services than in U.S.	Lower taxes but much higher out-of-pocket expenses. Total tax and expense burden similar to Europe's
Energy	Increasing use of conservation, renewable energy, and new technologies	Energy inefficiency, little conservation or renewable energy
	More green energy design, green businesses, cogeneration	High CO_2 emissions, energy-wasteful businesses
	More energy-efficient autos, homes, buildings	Energy-wasteful autos, homes, buildings
	Efficient mass transit, high-speed trains, vast rail networks	Poor mass transit, sparse rail system
	First cap and trade system for CO_2 emissions	No functioning cap and trade system
	Limited use of carbon taxes to encourage conservation	No carbon taxes
Workfare	26% of $20 trillion economy spent on social benefits, 36% more per capita than U.S.	16% of $14 trillion economy spent on social benefits
	Less than 2% of GDP spent on military	More than 4% of GDP spent on military
	Universal, affordable health care for all	Patchwork health care, 47 million uninsured
	Top-ranked health care for half the cost in U.S.	Health care ranked 37th globally, spends twice per capita of Europe
	Paid parental leave following a birth	No mandatory parental leave, paid or unpaid
	Mandatory paid sick leave for all	No mandatory sick leave, paid or unpaid—workers go to work sick
	Affordable, universal child care	Sparse and unaffordable child care
	Generous vacations (avg. 4–5 weeks), more holidays	Short vacations (avg. 2 weeks), few holidays
	Shorter work hours per week	Longer work hours per week
	Comfortable retirement pension	Paltry social security retirement; some have savings
	Inexpensive university education	Escalating cost of university education
	Affordable housing, widespread nonprofit housing developers	Escalating housing costs, more homeless people

beat, succinctly captured this essential difference when he wrote, "The pan-European decision to value maternity leave over military matters is another powerful unifying element that has helped bring European countries together, and set them apart from the United States."[19]

So here, finally, we arrive at the most substantive parting of the ways. In thinking about what our two different paintings look like, imagine two figures, one portraying Europe, the other America, both peering outward toward the future. While at first they appear to look similar, upon closer inspection we can see they actually portray different habits, behaviors, colorations, and manners. Looking more closely, we can see that these figures have branched off and are leaving tracks in the sand that are clearly diverging, like two separately evolving lines of hominids. Perhaps without too much trivializing we can call them *Homo europeus* and *Homo americanus,* each following its distinctive European Way or American Way. The European Way represents a new species of human organization and social design for modern mass societies, a wholly new hybrid of political, economic, and social organization, the likes of which the world has never seen. Its impact is affecting every dimension of the lives it touches. The American Way, meanwhile, is the progenitor species, still stuck in outdated mentalities of a religion of individualism, militarism, Wall Street capitalism, and a fraying social contract, which together are embedded in antiquated, sclerotic fulcrum institutions.

In addition, the daunting ecological challenge of global climate change makes the American Way increasingly obsolete as a model for development. The emergence of populous nations such as China, India, and Brazil, among others, all of which want first-world status, ups the ante considerably. If Chindia's upwardly mobile billions adopt the individual property rights attitudes of seventeenth-century America, with each person asserting her or his untrammeled right to consume, buy, and become king of her or his own castle, human existence on planet Earth will not last long. In the next twelve years, the ranks of the middle class will swell by as many as 1.8 billion, 600 million just in China.[20] If China's resource consumption per person were the same as America's—the U.S. being by far the highest per capita polluter, greenhouse gas emitter, and resource user in the world—its 1.3 billion people would use ninety-nine million barrels of oil a day, even though the world currently produces only eighty-four million barrels daily and may never produce much more.[21] India's population is projected to surpass China's around 2031; if it were to have three cars for every four people—as in the United States, with U.S.-sized engines—billions more gas guzzlers would be on the road, belching carbon emissions and other pollutants. Or imagine hundreds of millions more homes the size of American middle-class manses, consuming electricity and emitting still more carbon. People everywhere would choke eventually on the planet Venus–like atmosphere we had created.

For all these reasons, the American system and its animating ideology have no future. The American Way is in its endgame, and another way must be found. Our future is riding in the balance, and, more than any other place, Europe is pointing us in the right direction.

"EUROPE": MORE THAN A PLACE, IT'S A CONCEPT

As Bill Gates has proposed, refining the capitalist system is precisely what Europe has been doing. The defining task of the twenty-first century is to fashion the best institutions and practices for a planet groaning under the strains of 6.5 billion people. What should be apparent at this point in our study of the European Way vs. the American Way is that "Europe" is more than a geographic place or a political economy that can be "beaten" in the global competition. Instead, Europe is a concept: it has been conceived as a place and a system that is attempting to meet head-on the challenges of trying to construct a modern mass society that can provide a comfortable, secure quality of life for billions of people in a way that is ecologically sustainable. Europe's way is based on a capitalist economy as the engine for tremendous wealth creation, but that engine has been harnessed via a robust democracy to ensure that this wealth is broadly shared, that families and individuals have sufficient support, and that the social and political agreements are steeped in values and goals such as fairness, equality, solidarity, and ecological sustainability. Europe has become the chief architect of both the crucial fulcrum institutions that form the foundation for this new "way," as well as an underlying philosophy that tries to strike a new balance between individual and commercial property rights and notions of the general welfare and the social contract.

Some have predicted that China's way might be a beacon for the future, that it one day will leave both Europe and the United States behind. Certainly China's ascent over the past thirty years from being a wretchedly poor backward country of teeming billions to a rising industrial power with a growing middle class has been impressive. But as we saw in chapter 12, China is still mostly a developing country wracked by severe economic, political, and environmental contradictions and challenges. Few people in the world are beating down the doors to get into China, and that is telling. It has a long way to go—a *long* way—before it has any meaningful claim on global leadership.

Others have proposed that South America, led by Brazil, Venezuela, Argentina, and Chile, will arise to become tomorrow's leader. Certainly Latin America has experienced a resurgence; one of the best things the Bush administration did for Latin America was to ignore it, allowing the region to solidify an identity that does not rely singularly on the United States or any other outside power. Some Americans on the left view the "people's budget" process in Porto Alegre, Brazil, and Brazil's use of alternative fuels such as ethanol, or Hugo Chávez's Bolivarian revolution and its sympathies for the poor, as examples for the rest of the world to follow. While many of these approaches have merit, any optimism should be tempered by the fact that these four countries *combined* have a smaller gross domestic product than Italy. Most people living there are still poor, many desperately so. None of these countries have so far demonstrated an economic model capable of producing a middle-class quality of life that can work for hundreds of millions of people, let alone billions.

Japan, Australia, Canada, and New Zealand come closest to matching Europe's comprehensive level of workfare supports, income equality, middle class quality of life, and people-centered system, but their capitalist economies are too small to lead by example. Only Europe has demonstrated how a capitalist economic system can be harnessed by a pluralist democracy for the good of a half billion people, while also having the sheer economic muscle to be globally influential.

In short, if Europe did not exist we would have to invent it. Now that the notions of social capitalism and workfare support have been planted, along with those of ecological sustainability and global peace and prosperity partnerships, it's up to people all over the world to nurture them and to incorporate elements of them into their own national "ways." That is the concept of Europe—a transformative vision that holds great potential and provides a new narrative for the twenty-first century, a new vocabulary and conceptual framework for moving forward. Other nations already have begun incorporating elements of this vision, and that is a hopeful sign. But their efforts are still in formation. The outcome is anything but certain.

Of course Europe itself does not always live up to this concept. The headlines regularly show ways that Europe trips up and doesn't fulfill expectations or its own lofty rhetoric. Its nations face numerous challenges and threats, and in previous chapters, I have examined some of those, including their own economic shortcomings and political contradictions, geopolitical tensions with Russia, low-wage, high-pollution economies in China and India, Middle East violence on their periphery, energy productivity and carbon emissions, and more. But two of Europe's biggest challenges are internal—first, how to cope with its aging and (in some countries) declining population, which threatens to undermine the prosperity necessary to pay for its generous workfare system; and second, how to integrate its minority populations successfully, especially first-, second-, and third-generation immigrants from North Africa, South Asia, and the Arab Mediterranean. Europe has its own dark underbelly and echoes of its ugly fascist past to contend with, and there's nothing like immigration to bring that out. When combined with its own aging populations, this package has been cause for considerable tension and anxiety, a volatile brew.

In the next three chapters I examine these latter challenges. If Europe cannot solve these internal contradictions and succumbs to a slow corrosion of its standing, the resulting deterioration will have been self-inflicted. The same old Euroskeptics and prophets of doom looking into their crystal balls naturally predict a future of decline. But they have predicted that before, and got it all wrong.

PART SEVEN

WILL EUROPE SURVIVE?

SIXTEEN

THE CHALLENGES OF
IMMIGRATION AND INTEGRATION

Meet three notorious faces that are shaping Europe's destiny. These famous faces inspire passion and opinion across the continent, leaving the Sarkozys, Merkels, Browns, Barrosos—the most powerful of leaders—playing catch-up in their wake.

The first face appeared in a large photo on the front page of the September 5, 2006, Spanish daily *El Pais*. The face is of a young boy, perhaps twelve years old, wrapped in a swaddling blanket, wet and shivering, his eyes wide with fear and confusion. His skin is black as the night sky behind him, and two large bulbous microphones from Spanish television reporters have been shoved in front of his face, incongruously, since he appears disoriented and neither capable of speech nor probably even familiar with the Spanish language. He has just washed up on the shore of Spanish territory from the impoverished African country of Ghana, like so much flotsam, after the rickety boat he was in broke apart.[1] He was hoping to find a new life, but instead he found controversy and detainment. His tale reoccurs hundreds of times a day in Spain, each episode initiating another round of national soul searching and populist protest, as well as intractable dilemmas for the Spanish government and its Catholic values: whether to ship these immigrants back or to follow the moral imperative of the Good Samaritan and lend a hand. There are no simple or quick resolutions.

The second face is masked and hooded, a menacing presence with wary eyes peering over a kerchief covering his lower face. His cropped hair is jet black, his handsome, sullen face honey brown, and that face, along with dozens of others, appeared on TV screens around the world when he and his young *banlieue* comrades burned ten thousand cars in nearly three hundred French cities in early November 2005. Contrary to stereotype, this twenty-year-old is not an immigrant; he was born and raised in France, as were his parents, whose own parents arrived in the country as part of a wave of Algerians imported for cheap labor, like any other cargo of raw material, in the early 1950s. These guest workers were never supposed to stay permanently, but many did. The only language this kid speaks is French. He is Muslim but not particularly religious, nor are his parents. Despite their long-standing roots in France, and those of most in his neighborhood, their unemployment rate is two to three times the national average; his Arab name and *banlieue* address on a résumé are the kiss of death for his prospects. Jobless, hopeless, hanging out on the streets with his homies, he is one of the *racaille*—rabble or scum, a term with implicit racial overtones, used sneeringly by then–interior minister, now president Nicolas Sarkozy to describe his young fellow Frenchmen. Sarkozy, himself the son of a Hungarian immigrant, threatened to deport the youthful rioters and even their families, but where would he deport his countrymen to?

The third important face is that of another immigrant, but this one is white-skinned with black Slavic hair. He has arrived in Britain from his native Poland, the famous "Polish plumber," taking advantage of the miracle of open borders in modern Europe to travel west in search of work. But it turns out he's not a plumber; in fact he'll do just about anything they will hire him to do. I've seen plenty dressed stiffly in colorful Elizabethan garb outside Windsor Castle, handing out adverts and using their scrambled English to lure tourists into nearby eating and drinking establishments. Some of his relatives live in Chicago—that's where ambitious Poles used to go to get ahead, but now most immigrate to London and other E.U. cities, where no visa or work permit is required, wages are relatively high, and a flight back to Warsaw takes only two hours.

But it's not always rosy in Britain, because his Slavic accent, indeed his very presence, jabs at Brits who believe he is stealing their jobs (especially during an economic downturn, when there are fewer jobs to fill). One of the idiosyncrasies of modern Europe is that an Italian football (soccer) star can play for a professional Dutch football team, or a British football star like David Beckham can play for a Spanish team, but will a Spanish worker ever be truly accepted in the Netherlands, or a Pole in Britain or Ireland, or a Romanian in Germany? Nothing bares the contradictions of this European "union" like the intracontinental peregrinations of its migrants.

Despite the inherent risks of the migrant life, this white newcomer, as well as millions more from central and eastern Europe, has fared modestly better than the brown and black immigrants from Africa or Arabia and even better than many of the second- and third-generation nationals of North African and Arab descent. Many of the initial fears about Poles stealing jobs turned out to be mostly unfounded; in fact, various studies have found that the impact of eastern and central European immigrants on Britain, Ireland, and Sweden (whose borders have been the most open in the European Union) is generally positive, with one study calling them "an elixir" for the British economy, responsible for "easing inflation, boosting output and raising tax revenue" by $600 million in 2006 and a whopping $2.5 billion in 2008.[2] These recognitions helped ease much of the pressure that had been building over intra-E.U. migration, until unemployment began rising following the recent economic crash and complaints renewed. Nevertheless, now that all national borders within the European Union have been thrown open via the Schengen agreements, more migration from east to west and back again will become a permanent feature of the landscape.

But the difference between the experiences of the white migrants from central and eastern Europe and those of the brown and black minorities in France, Germany, and elsewhere, most of whom have lived there for years, points to a dark underbelly that represents one of the greatest threats to Europe's future. While progressive Europe is leading the world in fashioning a fair and just system that harnesses capitalism for the good of the many, in discovering ecologically sustainable practices for modern societies, and in fostering a foreign policy based on regional integration, investment, and Marshall Plan–like incentives for development and peaceful coexistence, contemporaneously it is haunted by an old, old nemesis—bigoted racism.

This isn't the first time this haunting has occurred, certainly. The Nazis and the various other fascist strains that swept Europe in the 1930s were infused with sick delusions of fashioning a white master race; in the nineteenth and twentieth centuries colonialist Europe, along with an imperialist United States, justified its considerable barbarity around the world with notions of manifest destiny and "white man's burden" to uplift their "little brown brothers," whether the brown people wanted this kind of paternalism or not.[3]

Certainly the racial problems in Europe today don't come close to approaching that level of past inhumanity. You don't ever hear about official government pogroms, atrocities, or widespread or systematic human rights violations against ethnic minorities and immigrants; there are no Bull Connors and George Wallaces in Europe, no government representatives using fire hoses and police attack dogs against unarmed protesters demanding their rights.[4] And immigrant neighborhoods can't compare with sections of South Central Los Angeles or the Bronx in terms of rank destitution and violence. In part that's because European minorities, including immigrants, benefit from the same generous workfare supports that native-borns enjoy, so they don't generally sink to the desolate condition that can be found still today in many minority and immigrant communities in the United States, even among African Americans whose families arrived centuries ago.

But the dark underbelly occasionally has produced some individual brutal acts and scary headlines, echoes of the ugly past. On May 6, 2006, in pretty, picturesque Bruges, Belgium, skinheads savagely beat two men—one a French citizen of African descent—who were walking past a bar frequented by the skins. Then, on May 10, the body of a Moroccan man who had been in a fight with skinheads at an Antwerp disco was found in a nearby river. On May 11 in Antwerp, a dark-clad teenager who had been expelled from his boarding school wrote a note saying he was going to kill foreigners, shaved his head, grabbed a Winchester hunting rifle, and went on a shooting rampage. When he was finished he had critically wounded a Turkish woman and murdered a Malian babysitter and the white toddler in her care.[5]

In the English city of Manchester, a Latvian immigrant was beaten nearly to death because he spoke poor English.[6] In a suburb of Zurich—consistently ranked as one of the world's most livable cities—a thirty-seven-year-old Angolan janitor was savagely attacked at work by two masked Swiss assailants with chainsaws who shouted above the snarling machines, "We don't need Africans in our country." They slashed one arm to the bone, nearly sliced off his left thumb, and hacked his face, neck, and chest. Miraculously, he survived.[7] Such grisly scenes, while horrifying and haunting, are, thankfully, infrequent. Most minorities and immigrants don't live in fear the way African Americans did during the lynching times.

Instead, what really burdens Europe's ethnic minorities is that too many of them, while mostly well kept, suffer from a different form of humiliation—a lack of the type of dignity and respect that come with acceptance, employment, and the chance to better your lot and pass that on to your children. My American friend Denny, who has lived in France for forty years and maintains a charming blog discussing all things French, says, "The unspoken pact that France has had with its immigrés for decades has been, 'You come here, we'll greet you warmly, we'll give you free housing in suburban developments built just for you, you'll get some spending money every month, free health care, a monthly allowance for every child you bear. You, in turn, will sweep our floors and dig our trenches. *But don't even think about getting a REAL job!*'"[8]

So while the tensions unleashed by immigration have attracted gobs of garish headlines, a more precise understanding of Europe's situation reveals that, more than an immigration problem, Europe has an *integration* problem. The two are intertwined but not exactly the same.

Like so many other false alarms sounded about Europe in recent years, such as the allegedly sick, sclerotic economy and the rise of the far right (which actually has been to the left politically of the U.S. Democratic Party on most issues), the alarm over Muslim immigrants flooding Europe has been way overhyped. In the wake of September 11 and the Iraq and Afghanistan wars, commentators like Oriana Fallaci warned that a menacing flood of Muslim immigrants would soon overwhelm the continent and turn it into "Eurabia," a colony of Islam; Princeton professor Bernard Lewis gloomily predicted that by this century's end Europe will be "part of the Arabic west, the Maghreb."[9] Alarmist anti-Muslim literature has become a genre unto itself, with titles such as these gracing bookstores: *While Europe Slept: How Radical Islam Is Destroying the West from Within; The West's Last Chance: Will We Win the Clash of Civilizations?; Eurabia, the Euro-Arab Axis; Menace in Europe: Why the Continent's Crisis Is America's, Too; World War IV: The Long Struggle against Islamofascism;* and of course the grand-daddy of them all, Samuel Huntington's *Clash of Civilizations,* which drew the lines too starkly and distorted the discourse on an important subject. While some of these works have levied some thoughtful critique, increasingly the genre has resulted in a kind of shrill, pop-chart alarmism over new immigrants which, ironically, has only served to obscure the failure of Europe to integrate its longstanding ethnic minorities, most of whom are the children or grandchildren of immigrants and have resided there for years.

Certainly, the challenge of weaving a rainbow tapestry out of multiethnic Europe has been spiced by the cultural gap between Europe's largely secular ways and Islamic sympathies among many of the ethnic minorities. Over several decades, steady Muslim immigration from Africa and Arabia has brought racial, sociocultural, and religious diversity to a continent seen as homogeneously white European and Christian for over a thousand years. This in turn has resulted in social tensions with a religious bent to them, especially when compared with the United States, where religion mostly has been absent from the volatile intersection of race and immigration.

But this difference has been inflamed in the sensationalist media and by grandstanding politicians looking for political gain. More immigrants, for example, have arrived from non-Muslim countries than from Muslim; in France the largest immigrant group for the last two decades has arrived from Portugal, not North Africa. But the headlines are impervious to these sorts of complexities, as Europe tries to shield itself from its own racism, which has been better able to accommodate recent white-skinned European émigrés than darker-skinned nationals who either arrived long ago as guest workers or have descended from that group. In a perverse way, today's sensationalist headlines over an alleged Muslim flood only serve to exonerate the past by going excessively ballistic over the present.

To understand what is happening to Europe, we must back up for a moment and examine a broader context. In most ways what Europe is facing is an old, old story, a classic tale of a dominant mainstream trying to incorporate—or expel—newcomers in its midst. Ethnic minorities and immigrants have always been mistreated, across the world and down through history, and not until their sheer numbers reach a critical mass within the overall population is their condition ever addressed. At that point, a populist movement inevitably arises to deport them, only to find that it is too late to do so, since their numbers are too great and they inhabit a crucial economic niche as low-wage workers performing essential functions that native workers don't want to do. So a parallel struggle emerges over how to integrate them or at least to tolerate them, and that process plays out across decades and not always according to design. In fact, as the history of immigration and integration in the United States shows, things can get downright messy.

The United States, which has a far higher percentage of ethnic minorities than any European country has today or likely ever will have, long ago reached a demographic tipping point and began its stumbling efforts toward integration. But Europe never before has had to deal with the number of ethnic minorities who now have settled in. Only recently has that number reached this critical mass in which European nationals of North African or Arab origin not only are more visible but also are starting to push for more rights. Once the racial demographics have changed beyond a certain no-return point, the minorities' elbows become sharp enough for them to say, "Move over, I'm riding on the bus too." France, Germany, Spain, Britain, and the Netherlands, as well as many cities in other European countries, have reached this moment first, but it's just the onset of an irreversible course.

At first the smaller political parties of what is known as the "far right" pounced and called attention to these creeping demographic dilemmas. They invoked the vernacular and passion of populism to arouse the electorate. Because most European democracies use proportional representation electoral systems, in which minor parties can win their fair share of legislative seats, these far right parties and their leaders, such as Jorg Haider from Austria and Pim Fortuyn in the Netherlands, were effective—often harshly so—in moving the political center to the point at which the European center-right, center-left, and left parties were forced to deal with this crucial yet overlooked issue.

Now on the other side of the demographic tipping point, Europe increasingly is faced with some stark choices. Sealing the borders and cutting off immigration, or deporting existing immigrants, is not an option because of white Europe's own shrinking population problem and the need to counteract that with increased immigration for the good of the economy (which I will discuss in chapter 18). So that presents an even sharper dilemma: integration or apartheid. But no country that claims to be a democracy can long suppress its minorities by means of a discriminatory police state without losing its soul. So that leaves only one realistic option: integration. There simply is no other practical course. Europe, increasingly, understands this.

But the stakes are especially high, ironically, because of the fabled generosity of the European workfare state. The success of Europe's social capitalism and the extensive level of workfare securities provided to its people depend on two critical factors: first, having a steady state economy in which the wealth generated, jobs created, and tax revenue stream are sufficient to pay for the generous social benefits; and second, having a high degree of connectedness and "sticky glue" among all the individuals within the population, a sense that everyone is in the same rowboat together, what is sometimes called "solidarity." The infusion of growing numbers of minorities and immigrants from different cultures threatens to undermine that solidarity, as well as to overburden the workfare support system if sufficient jobs and resources are unavailable, making for idle hands, insecure futures, and opportunities for mischief.

Wouter Bos, a member of the Dutch parliament and leader of the center-left Labor Party in the Netherlands, outlined the high stakes in a thoughtful, soul-searching missive to his fellow social democrats across Europe. "An increasingly diverse society makes it more difficult to sustain support for solidarity," he wrote. "Solidarity thrives on common interests and common values. The tragedy in some of our Western European societies—and certainly in the Netherlands—is that these foundations of solidarity are now being challenged by migration and by failing to integrate newcomers into our societies. Taxpaying citizens may very well argue, 'Why should I make an effort for people I don't know, don't understand or who don't do things the way I would?' We have a problem, and we need an agenda to solve it."[10]

No question, Europe's back is to the wall. As Spanish Muslim leader Abdelkarim Carrasco has observed, "Either Europe develops and supports the idea of a mixed culture, or Europe has no future."[11] Europe has little choice but to figure out how to resolve its integration dilemma. Recent steps taken (presented in the next chapter) provide confidence that it will, but the resolution will take many years to accomplish— America is still at it, 400 years since the first slaves were imported to colonial America—and in the short term it will have moments of messiness.

TIPPING POINT: THE DEMOGRAPHICS OF THE DILEMMA

Part of the challenge in assessing the breadth and depth of the integration problem in Europe is the lack of good demographic data. Finding solid estimates of how many ethnic minorities—including not only recent immigrants but also the children and grandchildren of immigrants— live in each country is difficult. In the United States we can state with a degree of confidence that the population is composed of about 15 percent "Hispanics," 13 percent "African Americans," 4.5 percent "Asians and Pacific Islanders," and 1 percent "Native Americans," all of which add up to about one-third of the country being considered "ethnic or racial minority."[12] Some in these categories, especially Hispanics and Asians, are first-generation immigrants, but the vast majority are second or third generation, the children and grandchildren of immigrants. One can argue over whether these are the best categories to use, since, for example, "Hispanic" is more a cultural category that includes many white Hispanics, while the other categories are racial ones, though with significant cultural components. Unquestionably the categories used for tracking in the United States need refinement, and some experts are making sound arguments for change.[13] Yet even these flawed categories allow for the tracking of discrimination, as well as progress, and measuring the impact of policy on these minority groups across generations. For modern multiracial, multicultural societies, such tracking is a very useful device that more than makes up for the categorical shortcomings.

But the governments of Europe, by and large, don't track information this way. Instead, they track the number of "foreign-born" residents and their countries of origin, as well as a few other subcategories, but not second or later generations. This gives an imperfect snapshot at best since these measurements do not track well across generations. France is the worst in this regard, handcuffed both by lingering memories of a fascist history of genocide in which targeted populations were tracked, and ironically by its own republican tradition of *liberté, égalité, fraternité*, which fetishizes a certain concept of the French Republic in which "a citizen is a citizen" regardless of race, religion, or mother tongue. Any acknowledgment of difference is taboo and actually illegal; in fact, officially there is no such thing as a "minority," however much this sloppily defies on-the-ground reality. Like France, other nations are similarly blinded by their lack of good data, which makes this kind of demographic analysis comparable to navigating without sonar or radar.

Nevertheless, using foreign-born residents, but excluding those immigrants originating from within Europe itself (such as the Portuguese in France or Poles in Britain), as somewhat of a proxy for ethnic minority composition yields some illuminating results. Various estimates, for example, place the number of foreign-born Muslims somewhere around fifteen million people—in other words, 3 percent of Europe's population of five hundred million, a small but growing population. However, that population is concentrated more in western Europe than eastern,[14] and the proportion of Muslims is destined to increase over time since currently the Muslim birthrate in Europe is estimated to be two to three times higher than that of non-Muslim Europeans. The National Intelligence Council, a center for strategic thinking within the U.S. intelligence community, estimates that the number of Muslims in Europe likely will double by 2025.[15] Yet even if they manage to increase to 8 percent of the population, they still will constitute far less of the

European population than the total foreign-born resident share of the U.S. population today, which is at 12 percent. So in Europe, especially when compared with the United States, this is hardly an Islamic or immigrant flood, as the alarmists have claimed.

Beyond these simple population projections, the impact of Muslims in Europe is affected by the fact that not all of them are the same. They originate from dozens of countries and do not share national cultures or even languages. There is no continental phenomenon, much less a threat, that currently can be identified as "European Islam." Like Christianity, Islam has its branches and offshoots, which in Europe are even more complicated by Muslims' nations of origin. In Germany, Muslim immigrants often are described as "Turkish," but in addition to Turks they include Kurds and Moroccans, all of whom speak different languages and come from significantly different cultures. Of significance, neither the Kurds, nor the Turks, nor the Moroccans can communicate with one another in any language but German. In France, where many immigrants are from Algeria and Morocco, at least a quarter of the estimated six million North African immigrants and their descendants are Berber, who have their own language and culture and mostly don't speak the Arabic of the other Algerian or Moroccan immigrants. Many more Muslims from sub-Saharan Mali and Niger identify themselves as "blacks" rather than *beurs* (the French slang term for young Arabs). The only language most of these diverse Muslim groups can use to communicate with one another is French. Similarly in Britain, a potpourri of Muslim groups hail from Pakistan, Bangladesh (where Bengali rather than Pakistani Urdu is spoken), India, Somalia, Turkey, Nigeria, Malaysia, and Iran—yet they can communicate together only in English.[16]

Alarmist headlines obscure Muslims' motivation for living in Europe today: the vast majority go there to better themselves and to secure a brighter future for their children, not to promote a Taliban fantasy of reestablishing the Caliphate. Most Muslim immigrants, like people everywhere, simply aspire to their own version of the European dream, including its secularist-based quality of life. That's why they endured the perils of immigration to begin with.[17] Germany has one of the largest Muslim populations in Europe, but of its 3.3 million Muslims only an estimated 25 percent actually practice Islam, meaning active Muslims constitute a mere 1 percent of Germany's total population.[18] Most of the 2.6 million Turks, who account for the bulk of German Muslims, have lived there for decades and own more than seventy thousand businesses across the country, including a near monopoly on ubiquitous neighborhood falafel and doner kebab joints.[19]

According to various surveys, between 12 and 30 percent of French Muslims do not even go to a mosque. A 2004 poll found that 68 percent regard the separation of religion and state as important, and 93 percent feel the same about secular, republican values.[20] Forty-two percent of the Muslims in France think of themselves first as French (compared with only 7 percent in the United Kingdom who think of themselves as British),[21] and intermarriage rates in France are high, between 20 and 50 percent for persons of foreign origin, whether immigrants or their children or grandchildren, a powerful sign of ongoing integration.[22] In the Netherlands, which is often cited as a front line in the European "clash of civilizations," a 2005 study by the national parliament found that only 1 percent of Dutch residents of Moroccan background and 7 percent of Turkish immigrants were even registered at the more than three hundred mosques in the country. The same study found that a majority of Dutch Muslims favor a clear distinction between religion and politics and foresee an increased secularization of Dutch Muslims' religious beliefs.[23]

In short, there is just no evidence that radical, violent Islamic groups enjoy widespread support. Quite the contrary, for the vast majority of Muslim immigrants, the path to a better life takes them right smack down Main Street in whatever European country they are trying to make their new home. Your average Muslim immigrants and their second- and third-generation children are law-abiding residents, lunch-pail Ahmeds and Ameeras, looking to find their niche, aspiring to their own version of a middle-class life. While alarmist headlines have raged, little note has been taken that most Muslims in France did not rampage and burn cars, nor did more than a handful of Muslims outside France copycat the *banlieue* youth. Muslim clergy and civic leaders in Britain and Spain denounced the London and Madrid train bombings. British Muslims staged public rallies and placed newspaper ads denouncing violent extremists, calling on fellow Muslims to cooperate with police. The Spanish Muslim Council harshly denounced Osama bin Laden by name on the first anniversary of the Madrid attacks.[24] Unfortunately most Western media did not find these declarations of nonviolent faith sufficiently newsworthy to give them the same wall-to-wall coverage given to a tiny handful of violent extremists.

Even in France, contrary to media stereotype, the number of total immigrants is comparatively small, and the percentage of those from

Arab and North African regions is smaller still. From 1982 to 1999 (the last year for which demographic-phobic France bothered to track such data), more foreign-borns arrived from Portugal than from Algeria, Morocco, or Turkey.[25] Of France's foreign-born residents, who constitute 8 percent of the population (or about five million persons)—a proportion that has stayed fairly constant since 1975—more than half are from other E.U. nations. That percentage of foreign-borns is quite a bit less than that in the United States, which has risen to 12 percent; it's also quite a bit less than the percentages in Germany, Spain, Austria, and Switzerland and is comparable to those in Britain, Sweden, and the Netherlands.[26] Guillaume Duval has observed that "France is the rich country apart from Japan that has kept its borders the most hermetically sealed since 1995: the weight of immigrants in the population since then has increased 6.5 times more in Spain than in France, 4.9 times more in the United States, 3.6 times more in Great Britain, 1.8 times more in Germany."[27] Mixed into France's population of sixty-two million, these immigrants, whether Muslim or no, do not constitute a flood.

So France does not have so much an immigration problem—it's not the sheer number of people showing up on its shores or sneaking across borders that is vexing its system. The problem is more what happens to those people once they arrive and have been living there for years. France has an *integration* problem, and a very nasty one at that, since the population of domestically born, dark-skinned nationals of Arab or African stock, most of them second and third generation, is burgeoning. Best estimates say that five million to six million Muslims and two million blacks now live in France, including immigrants and their children and grandchildren—an all-time high of 13 percent of the population. With birthrates among France's minority population of two to three times that of French whites, that portends additional demographic change over the next several decades. But under no conceivable scenario will France's proportion of ethnic minorities ever be as high as that of Hispanics, Asians, and blacks in the United States, who together compose a third of the population today and are projected to reach a majority of the U.S. population by around 2040.[28]

Nevertheless, a relatively large demographic change is in store for France. Suddenly its ethnic minorities, who previously could be tucked away in an outlying suburb full of housing projects with the palliative of the generous French social system, are more visible and demanding of their fair share. As the number of darker-skinned French nationals and immigrants has reached a critical mass, white colonial France's long-standing gilded racism has bubbled to the surface. The minorities appear to be *suddenly* living in their midst, even though most have been there for decades. It's as if *suddenly* the blind can see, and they are shocked by what they have missed.

The sad fact is that in the land of *égalité* and *fraternité,* places still exist where the international French soccer star Zinedine Zidane would not be allowed into a local discotheque on a Saturday night if the bouncer at the door thought he was simply a random North African. Thanks to the beacons of burning cars, the world now knows about the *banlieues,* the segregated public housing projects adjacent to most cities, one of which is where Zidane himself grew up. But even day-to-day life in France appears to be segregated; for example, few people of color seem to be anywhere in the center of Paris (except for the errant tourist, taxi driver, or homeless person asking for change outside metro stops). The French in conversation casually categorize nonwhite folks as "the Arabs," "the *beurs*," or "the blacks" and employ a fairly constant stream of old colonialist-tinged language, using expressions like "I worked as hard as a young negress today" and calling a common round dessert dipped in chocolate and rolled in shredded coconut a *tête de nègre.* In advertising, minorities often are diminished to stereotypes, as in a fruit ad showing black soccer players brandishing bananas. Reportedly, one television commercial for a sport utility vehicle in Canada featured a black family, but in France the same commercial was redone with a white family.[29] One appalled American visitor commented to me, "I have never seen segregation like that, in terms of day-to-day life, and such overt and blatant categorization of 'otherness.'" These toxic French attitudes are still stubbornly and pervasively persistent.

One of the many mistakes that U.S. journalists make in reporting on Europe is to equate all things French with the rest of Europe, which is as unfair as it is inaccurate. No other country has erupted in riots over its failures at integration. However, while France represents the extremes of European racial turmoil, other parts of western Europe could end up in the same situation if they aren't careful. Germany in particular seems to be facing a nagging integration problem centered around its darker-skinned residents. Near Leipzig, unruly soccer fans spat on a Nigerian midfielder from the opposition's team, calling him "Shit Nigger" and "Ape" as they whooped monkey noises, an ugly scene that the great Jackie Robinson, the first American black to play major league baseball, would have recognized.[30] Once in Berlin I shared a taxi ride with a Pulitzer Prize–winning American author and his Japanese wife, who told me that she had never experienced as many racist glares and slurs and as much outright hostility as she had experienced during their year in residence there (though she did say that younger Germans were much less bigoted than the older generation). In February 2008, a suspicious blaze in an apartment building in southwestern Germany, inhabited by several Turkish families and others, resulted in nine people killed, including five children, and sixty injured. The four-story building in Ludwigshafen, which had hate graffiti scrawled on the exterior wall of a Turkish cultural center on the ground-floor level, had been the target of a Molotov cocktail attack two years prior, but no one had been hurt and the police never caught the culprits.

According to recent studies from the Organisation for Economic Cooperation and Development (OECD), Germany's young students from immigrant families have fewer opportunities than those living in any other industrialized nation. Minority pockets in cities such as Berlin see high unemployment as well as poverty levels affecting 30 to 40 percent of the minority population. Led by a small vocal cadre of reactionaries, opposition to mosques can be vociferous, racist attacks periodically resurface, and populist politicians like the conservative governor of the state of Hesse (which includes Frankfurt) continue to employ xenophobic campaigns to raise poll numbers and try to win elections (though he ended up losing instead, as many voters were alienated by his bigoted appeals).

To an outsider, it is extremely puzzling how Germany, which has been the leader of social capitalism, workfare supports, and the European Way going back to the time of Bismarck, is so backward when it comes to its racial and cultural attitudes. Its deepest national urgings often dip into a wellspring of chauvinist sentiment that can only be described as tribal. Germany still clings to a historic toxic obsession about the purity of the German people and blood line, an obsession formerly promoted by the Nazis. Until recently, Germany granted citizenship exclusively on the basis of *jus sanguinis* (Latin for "right of blood"), that is, only to those of German blood obtained from German parents. For the longest time, Turks who had lived in Germany for decades and could speak German fluently could not easily become citizens, but an ethnic German from Romania who couldn't speak a word of German but could trace parentage back to the fatherland was quickly given full citizenship rights. Austria, another Germanic country, has worked the same way, as has Switzerland, also a mostly Germanic country.

Not until 1999 did Germany join France, the United States, and many other modern democracies in granting citizenship on the basis of *jus soli* (Latin for "right of the soil"), that is, to those born on German soil, regardless of parentage. In arguing for a geographic-based notion of citizenship, then–interior minister Otto Schily proclaimed that Germans needed to rise above "the destructive principle of ethnocracy."[31] Even so, Germany has placed certain conditions around this new right of citizenship, showing that the country still clings to a tribal past that undermines its future.

Despite the many progressive aspects of Germany, France, and Europe in general, these vestiges still haunt them. More than immigrants, what Europeans have to fear is themselves. Following the destruction of World War II, Europe's states finally rejected much of their centuries-long horrific past of brutalizing one another, nation to nation and religion to religion. But this tribal fear of the "other," of the *Ausländer* (i.e., outsider), manifested as blatant discrimination against their darker-skinned minorities, is one ghost they have not yet exorcised. Truly, Germans as well as the French can look in the mirror and say, "We have met the enemy, and it is us."

MORE MARX THAN MUHAMMAD

Europe's racism and difficulties in fostering integration have led to some very predictable results. Brown and black minorities, whether immigrants or no, whether Muslims or no, have at least one thing in common: like all waves of immigrants, they start at the bottom of the economic ladder and encounter a lot of difficulty in climbing up the rungs. In Britain, where an estimated 5 percent of the population is Muslim, by 2008 around 15 percent of those Muslims were registered as unemployed, compared with 4 percent of the rest of the population. The British government's Labor Force Survey found that Muslims are more likely than any other group to be in long-term unemployment or not even seeking work. In the same survey, 31 percent of employed Muslims had no qualifications and, therefore, little prospect of advancement from menial work. In addition, Muslims are more likely than any other ethnic or religious group to reside in rented public housing.[32]

In Germany and the Netherlands, the unemployment rate for immigrants is about double that of the rest of the population. German migrants and their children account for 36 percent of the population at or near the poverty line and 29 percent of the unemployed.[33] In many ways, Turks and other ethnic minorities remain a separate and unequal population in Germany. In France, the brown and black inhabitants account for close to half of the nation's unemployed and more than half of its prison population.[34] (As alarming as that is, it's not that unusual for a minority population; in the United States in 2006, minorities constituted about 41 percent of the unemployed and 60 percent of the prison population.)[35] One study commissioned by a temp employment agency showed that white French job applicants receive three times as many offers as minority applicants with the same qualifications.[36] Most of France's minorities live in segregated ghettos of high-rise public housing towers (like the kind that American blacks used to live in until the Clinton administration had many of them torn down and replaced with scattered clusters of low townhouses). France's minorities also are saddled with poor schools and little hope that they will enjoy the prosperity of their white countrymen, another familiar story for most American minorities.

That's why the riots of the *banlieue* youth were, as French scholar Olivier Roy noted, "more about Marx than Muhammad." This was France's Rodney King moment, for after stripping away the various factors that make Europe's minority dilemma unique, such as the Islamic angle, we discover that the integration problem in Europe boils down to an age-old story after all: the confounding crossroads of racism, poverty, and lack of opportunity. Conditions in minority neighborhoods in both France and south-central Los Angeles have reminded the world of the consequences of the failure to integrate. Martin Walker, editor of United Press International, writes of Europe that when it comes to tensions with its Muslim populations, race, class, and religion "all play into a context of social and economic mobility."[37]

But these are just numbers; the data presented here cannot really illustrate the personal stories of sorrow and humiliation that accompany a statistical snapshot. While all of Europe may not be like France or even Germany, it's also true that this multiethnic, multicultural, multinational hip-hop opera points to the direction of Europe's future. Europe is on its way to becoming a melting pot, whether it wishes to or not, and it has some important decisions to make to prepare for that impending future. Europe's efforts toward integration are in the clumsy initial stages of what is going to be a long and tumultuous journey, dotted with episodes of crisis, just as it has been in the United States. Recall the recent series of crises Europe already has lived through: riots in the Arab-Muslim world in early 2006 over Danish cartoons harshly depicting the prophet Muhammad; preceded in November 2005 by the eruption of *banlieue* youth in France; preceded by a terrorist attack in July by four suicide bombers that killed fifty-two in the London subway; preceded in May and June by the French and Dutch voters rejecting the E.U. constitution, partly over concerns about losing their national identity to minorities and other forces; preceded by the November 2004 murder of Dutch filmmaker Theo van Gogh by a young Islamist fanatic unhinged over van Gogh and Ayaan Hirsi Ali's cinematic denunciation of Islamic sexism, which led in turn to retaliatory torchings of mosques and Islamic schools; preceded in March 2004 by the bombing attack in Madrid by Al Qaeda sympathizers, in which 191 people were killed on the city's trains.

Western Europe has been lurching from crisis to crisis, experiencing its Rodney King moment, its Watts riot moment, and its Selma march moment in rapid succession, causing anxiety and continental soul searching. One French friend has observed, "We are just now passing through our 1960s, '70s, '80s, and '90s phases, like you did in America—except it seems we are doing it all in one decade." Though to balance the narrative, France's youth riots in the *banlieues* were sparked by two accidental deaths originating in a police chase, but those conflagrations resulted in no other deaths, mostly just a lot of burned cars and other property damage. The level of violence, destruction, and death that France and western Europe have experienced is orders of magnitude less than what the United States suffered in its turbulent 1950s and '60s civil rights period or even during the Rodney King riots in the early 1990s.

It would be surprising if Europe did not experience additional future crises. No doubt there will be more martyrs and pariahs, and more tragedies as well as advances. And there will be more demagogues and populists, though some of the old ones like Jorg Haider and Pim Fortuyn are dead; and perhaps there will be more moves like the Berlusconi government's in 2008 when it began fingerprinting E.U. citizens who were of Roma, or Gypsy, origin as part of a wider crackdown on street crime and illegal immigration in Italy (a practice that human rights groups condemned as an "ethnic headcount"). An E.U. directive adopted in June 2008 establishing common rules for deportation of illegal immigrants was harshly criticized by civil rights advocates.[38] Perhaps a Martin Luther King is in Europe's future, a riveting figure capable of mobilizing protest marches and hunger strikes. While Europeans will experience times that try their souls, they can take hope from the fact that America *has* made advances, that racial minorities and immigrants *have* in fact contributed greatly to the American tapestry, an African American *was* elected president, remarkably so, despite howls of protests from nativists, reactionaries, and unrepentant Confederates.

There's no reason the same can't happen in Europe, no matter what the Euroskeptics, alarmists, and *jus sanguinis* conservatives might say. In the next chapter, we will see the steps that various European nations have taken to enact civil rights measures and to deal with their racism, discrimination, and immigration, and what the impacts of these steps have been.

SEVENTEEN

A EUROPEAN CIVIL RIGHTS MOVEMENT
ARISES—SORT OF

As Europeans contemplate their demographic future, more and more of them are taking a broader view and becoming better at reading the handwriting on the wall. Many governments, businesses, and nongovernmental agencies already have begun taking steps to respond to the rainbow-ization of their populations, and the mass media has played an increasingly crucial role. But a real movement—a civil rights movement—for equality is only in its nascent stage. So far no large protest marches have occurred like those seen in the United States in the 1960s, or even like the one in which two million Hispanic immigrants and their allies marched in the U.S. during the spring of 2006. Nevertheless, a stirring for equality and justice is occurring, and Europeans who support it have been slowly finding their voices.

Signs of protest have increasingly emerged, such as the one staged by a Moroccan immigrant who, seeking the right to live and work in Belgium, waged a hunger strike by gruesomely stitching his lips together. In Paris, thousands of restaurant employees and kitchen staff of African origin working *sans papiers*—that is, illegally (a common practice in that sector)—began protesting their risky status, which resulted in some of the restaurants officially sponsoring their citizenship.[1] The Muslim protests over the Danish cartoons that satirized the prophet Muhammad showed the ability of Muslims in Europe to organize and to do so nonviolently, unlike the Muslims in the Middle East, who staged violent, incendiary protests. And German voters registered an electoral protest when they handed a decisive loss to incumbent Christian Democratic governor Roland Koch in Hesse state elections following his polarizing campaign that tried to scapegoat immigrants and youth for crimes. The newspaper *Die Tageszeitung* editorialized, "The fact that this nasty populism didn't bear fruit is definitely a victory for our democratic culture. Mobilizing majorities by bashing minorities—this conservative all-purpose weapon doesn't work anymore."[2]

Even without a massive "street heat" protest movement, policies have advanced via the usual vehicles: new laws, new programs and funding, and new media and cultural awareness. In addition, Europe is starting to see the rise of new minority leaders and elected minority politicians, as well as new civil rights organizations, articulating a message of social justice and inclusion. Experimentation with large and small interventions is taking place. Hundreds of millions of euros are being poured into language classes, vocational courses, mentoring, counseling, training, and self-help for disadvantaged groups and individuals, as well as into hotlines and services offering legal and other types of advice. Sensitization and awareness campaigns are being conducted through an active use of the media, advertisements, the arts, and cultural festivals. New anti-discrimination laws have been passed in most countries (with a few notable footdraggers) as a result of a European Union directive prescribing anti-discrimination and anti-racism guidelines. While such legislation is commonplace in the United States, these are the first such laws ever passed in Europe.

Austria, once known as the stomping ground of far-right, anti-immigrant leader Jorg Haider, passed its first anti-discrimination law in 2004. "This is the beginning of a new era in outlawing discrimination in Austria," said Dieter Schindlauer, of the human rights group ZARA.[3] Like civil rights legislation in the United States, Austria's Law on Equal Treatment bans discrimination in the workplace on the grounds of race, gender, ethnic origin, sexual orientation, age, or religion. Until recently, it was common practice to state in job or housing advertisements that "no foreigners" or "only Austrians" need apply, but that has been made punishable by fine. While the law does not have as many teeth as some would like, it is a first for Austria, and other nations have joined in such efforts.

Germany's anti-discrimination legislation passed in 2006 was the first to accept the need for active measures to promote integration. Frankfurt became the first German city to create an office for multicultural affairs, which coordinates an impressive array of programs that foster integration and harmony. These include language classes and translation services, as well as help for immigrants to obtain health care and education and generally to sort out problems. Other cities have copied Frankfurt's approach. Even some conservative state governments have launched integration plans. The state of North Rhine–Westphalia's center-right coalition government empowered an "integration minister," who berated his own Christian Democratic Party for its timid efforts.[4] Most European countries have established such integration programs, especially within the major cities, spurred on by the E.U., which has provided generous funding for such efforts.

For the first time France, which has one of the worst records of integration, now has a public authority, HALDE, to act as an anti-discrimination watchdog.[5] HALDE has two principal tasks: addressing cases of discrimination and promoting equality. Unfortunately, it does not yet have much authority actually to fight concrete instances of discrimination, but even the symbolic value is a first step. Public awareness has increased, and laws and regulations are slowly changing, reflecting the shifting public mood. Now a hot line is in place to report acts of discrimination and abuse, and so is a service that records people's complaints. In addition, the Institute of Political Studies in Paris (often called Sciences Po), one of France's elite universities known as grandes écoles, has been recruiting students from minority and nonelite backgrounds by running special training programs in selected schools in economically underprivileged areas.

Nongovernmental organizations also are mobilizing. An organization known as CRAN (Conseil Représentatif des Associations Noires) is France's version of the NAACP, fighting discrimination and pushing to keep blacks and their issues visible. Just through its existence, CRAN has broken the implicit French taboo against recognizing a minority's ethnic identity, itself an important step. These new leaders and spokespeople are starting to reflect back to the French people the gap between reality and their own lofty ideals, much as civil rights leaders like Martin Luther King Jr. did in the United States. Also, monitoring of discrimination has been stepped up; in nightclubs and bars, undercover agents try to expose whether a given establishment is discriminating at the door.

Besides the government and NGO sectors, the private sector also has launched various schemes to encourage corporations to diversify their employees. While the concept of American-style affirmative action in the workplace is very controversial—in fact, as we saw previously, it's illegal to categorize people by race or religion, for reasons going back to the fascist pogroms that used such categories for horrific purposes—discreet efforts to diversify workforces have been made on a volunteer basis. An Algerian-born French business executive, Yazid Sabeg, spearheaded a campaign to counter racism in hiring after his own fourteen-year-old son was taunted with a racial epithet. Sabeg, chairman of the $520 million high-tech group CS Communication & Systèmes, said, "I am worried that we are heading for a situation like that of America in the 1960s, when frustration and anger led to violence."[6] So in 2005 he called for the introduction of affirmative action policies—called "positive discrimination" in France—to end prejudice against what he called "visible minorities," that is, French nationals of North African or Arabic origins. The proposal struck a chord, and Nicolas Sarkozy, then the finance minister, threw his support behind it. After prodding from Sabeg and others, the heads of forty large French companies, including Airbus, energy group Total, PSA Peugeot Citroën, and steel giant Arcelor, signed the Business Diversity Charter. The charter did not set hiring quotas, but companies agreed to encourage diversity and publish an annual account of the steps they had taken to promote it.

Sabeg renewed his call in the aftermath of Barack Obama's election as president, issuing a manifesto that was signed by numerous politicians. "The election of Barack Obama highlights via a cruel contrast the shortcomings of the French Republic," the manifesto read. Subtitled "Oui, nous pouvons!"—the French translation of Obama's campaign slogan, "Yes, we can!"—and supported by President Sarkozy's wife, model and actress Carla Bruni, the manifesto urged various interventions, including affirmative action programs, to turn French ideals of equality into reality for minorities.

Ironically, France's conservative president Nicolas Sarkozy has emerged as somewhat of a proponent of race-based interventions, more so than the French left, which not only clings to France's egalitarian ideal but, due to the Nazi-collaborating Vichy government's use of quotas, instinctively rejects tracking on the basis of race, religion, or other qualities. The left's paralysis has left the road wide open for Sarkozy to promote his own version of diversity and affirmative action. President Sarkozy made sure that in his first government, formed in June 2007, three women of Arab or African origin were appointed to high positions, including the minister of justice Rachida Dati, who is the first Arab and first woman of non-European immigrant background to hold a key ministerial position in the French Cabinet (which also is composed of seven women ministers out of fifteen). Sarkozy also appointed as his human rights secretary Rama Yade, a brilliant young woman and author in her early thirties who was born in Senegal into the Muslim faith and earlier had written a book about the condition of blacks in France.

While some advances certainly have been made, James Cohen, an American professor of political science teaching for many years at the Université de Paris VIII, says that after ten years of such efforts "progress so far has been slow and in many ways symbolic. There is still resistance, though more subtle than before, behind the façade of consensus over 'diversity.'" The successes that have occurred mainly have affected a small minority elite, not the broad minority working class. But they are a step in the right direction.

In Ireland, which has gone from being a virtually all white, Catholic society to one with a growing immigrant and minority population, new non-Catholic primary schools have been organized for the first time in Dublin. About 95 percent of those schools' students are Muslims and Protestants from Africa and Asia. For more than a century, the Catholic Church has been the principal administrator in Irish education, but Catholic leaders encouraged the government's move to organize non-Catholic schools as a reflection of social reality. "The Catholic Church welcomes choice and diversity within the national education system," said Bishop Leo O'Reilly, chair of the Education Commission of the Irish Bishops Conference.[7]

The Netherlands has an impressive array of macro- and microprograms to foster integration. The campaign "We Amsterdamers" tackled the Islamophobia that emerged following the assassination of filmmaker Theo van Gogh. The municipal project tries to foster integration of the city's Muslim population (about 11 percent of the city) by organizing education sessions and denouncing discrimination. Mayor Job Cohen considers religious organizations to be valid partners in this process, and the Amsterdam City Council and Muslim associations also organize various events that attract Muslims from around the city to come together to pray and eat, such as Ramadan Festival.[8]

I was most impressed by one particular Dutch program that stood out for its strategic cleverness. One way the Dutch have tried to foster empowerment for Muslim women is through a program that teaches them—ready for this?—to ride bicycles. Riding a bicycle is so very Dutch since it is the cheapest, healthiest, and most ecologically sound mode of transport, but that's not their principal reason for targeting this training at Muslim women. Learning how to operate an affordable mode of transport like a bicycle is like being given the "keys" to getting around and away from their strict, authoritarian husbands. According to some of the Dutch participants, these Muslim women's determination is uplifting to see, especially when they fall off their practice bikes at the gym, dust themselves off, and get back on, and so is the caring with which others help them. This is just one small but ingenious step toward facilitating not only affordable transportation but also cultural integration and empowerment for these women.

In some Berlin neighborhoods, such as northern Neukölln, a mainly working-class district with large Turkish and Arab populations, grassroots women known as *Stadtteilmütter,* or "neighborhood mothers," play a key role in integrating families. These are usually Turkish or Arab women who go through a six-month training course about the German educational and social welfare systems, child-rearing, sex education, and other subjects of particular interest to parents. Then each *Stadtteilmutter* visits local families and talks with them, especially the mothers, who often don't have many contacts with outsiders. Lots of immigrant kids, especially boys, do poorly in school, dropping out and sometimes ending up in the criminal justice system, and parents feel overwhelmed. The *Stadtteilmütter* is a vital part of the German strategy for influencing the family dynamic and culture that foster these problems. She brings along bilingual informational material and coloring books to occupy the kids so that she can talk to their mothers in peace. These voluntary social workers have a better chance than mostly monolingual professional German social workers of reaching women who are otherwise very isolated, and encourage them to participate more in their neighborhoods and schools, learn German, and make sure their children learn German. The *Stadtteilmütter* program is organized as part of a neighborhood management system for improving life in disadvantaged neighborhoods in Berlin.[9]

THE DOOR AJAR: POLITICAL RIGHTS AND INCLUSION

Minorities and immigrants in Europe also have been slowly winning all-important political rights. In Belgium, the center-right government of Prime Minister Guy Verhofstadt granted voting rights in 2004 to non-European immigrants who have been legal residents for five years, allowing them to participate in local elections (that's more than a "progressive" city in the U.S. like San Francisco has been willing to grant to its non-citizens). Immigrant candidates now run for local office, and in the mixed-race area of Gare du Midi, in Brussels, many of the electoral candidates who run in local elections are first- or second-generation immigrants. Some of these voters and candidates come from countries that have never known democracy, so while these rights are limited to local elections, they're an important first step. During the 2006 elections, the candidates and their colorful campaign booths were spread out in front of the Saint-Gilles Roman church on Sundays, with promotions and aromas of grilled chicken enticing a cheerful crowd gathered in the streets. Voter turnout among immigrant voters has not been high, but nevertheless retail politicking, handshaking, and door-to-door canvassing are practiced with all the enthusiasm of a New Hampshire presidential primary, establishing the rituals of democracy among these communities.[10]

Rome also has begun allowing its immigrants to vote for representatives to the local government. In the tradition of the old Roman Republic, which granted dedicated representation to its poorest citizens, Rome today allows immigrant voters to elect councillors, each of whom represents one geographic area: Africa, Europe (non-E.U. member states), Asia, and America. Those "immigrant representatives" have the right to participate at local council meetings and to make proposals on certain issues, though they are not allowed to vote with their fellow council members. Sweden also allows immigrants to vote in municipal elections. The "Time for Democracy" project encourages nontraditional candidates to run for local office, including non-Swedish citizens, young people, people with low incomes, and others. Political parties are given extra funds to recruit and prepare candidates from these backgrounds. One specific project encouraged Somali women in Sweden to participate in politics through study groups, seminars, and a program on local television. For the years 2006–8, five municipalities were granted funds to develop and test different methods of fostering the involvement of those who have not usually participated in the political process.[11]

The slow inclusion of European minorities in the political process has gradually led to a new phenomenon on the political landscape— elected minority officeholders and minority appointees to high public office. While women have been winning sizable shares of political representation for many years (leading the way in Sweden, where they constitute 47 percent of the national parliament, compared with only

17 percent of the U.S. Congress),[12] minorities also are finally beginning to see some results.

Paul Boateng was elected to Britain's House of Commons before being appointed chief secretary to the treasury in 2002, making him Britain's first black cabinet minister. Of Ghanaian heritage, he was one of fifteen black members of the British House of Commons. In Germany's Bundestag, the national parliament, five elected representatives (out of 612) are of Turkish descent. About a dozen Turkish ethnic representatives are in various state legislatures, and several more represent Germany in the European Parliament. In the Netherlands after the 2003 elections, ten elected representatives of Muslim background were among the 150 members of the national parliament. Sweden has a half dozen Parliament members who trace their ancestry to Eritrea, Ghana, Congo, Turkey, and Chile.[13]

The road has been difficult but rewarding. Lale Akgün, of the Social Democrats, has lived in Germany for more than forty years. Of Turkish descent, she won her seat representing part of the city of Cologne in 2002 after a campaign in which her opponent said, "Don't vote for the Turk, vote for me." One man at a campaign event told her, "Only people with German blood are allowed to be in the German Bundestag."

Then there's Ricardo Lumengo, the first immigrant from Africa to be elected to the Swiss parliament. Lumengo came to Switzerland in 1982, seeking asylum from war-torn Angola, became a legal scholar, and then went into politics. First he was elected locally in the city of Biel, then regionally, and now at the federal level, as a member of the Socialist Party. With about 20 percent of Swiss society foreign born, some see Lumengo's story as interesting both for his exceptional personal success and for being a harbinger of changes in Swiss society. The story the outside world often reads is about the xenophobic tendencies of the right-wing Swiss People's Party (SVP), but that focus masks what is actually going on, both in society and in politics. The SVP itself is not all made up of right-wingers like their most controversial member, Christoph Blocher, who was ousted from the Federal Council and replaced by a much more moderate member of the SVP. The political pendulum is swinging in a new direction, not always smoothly, but many observers believe Lumengo, not Blocher, is the direction of Switzerland's future. Time will tell.

Nor are the minority politicians all from the left on the political spectrum; some are from the center-right, reflecting the traditional views of many in minority communities. Coşkun Çörüz, an elected Dutch parliamentarian of Turkish descent, was courted to run by several parties that were eager to expand their support base by adding immigrants to the party slates they submitted to voters. Conservative parties' recruitment of minority candidates reflects the degree to which integrationist policies have become mainstream in certain countries. Çörüz decided to join the Christian Democratic Alliance (CDA), which he found to be most closely aligned with his conservative political views.

"I was the first Muslim in a Christian Democratic party in Europe," says Çörüz. This membership was not without its controversies. Among the other members, many had difficulties welcoming a Muslim into a party that is largely secular but has roots in the Christian church. Many weren't sure if a Muslim immigrant could be elected to the Dutch parliament as a Christian Democrat. Since his election several years ago, Çörüz has specialized in human rights issues, terrorism, and juvenile justice. He has stayed away from immigration issues to avoid being typecast as the "immigrant politician." Çörüz blames Dutch Turks for being stuck in a "ghetto" mentality and not fully assimilating. "I'm not going to deny my roots," he says, adding, "but I see myself primarily as a Dutch politician, with special antenna into the Turkish community."[14]

Minorities in France have not had as much electoral success as those in other countries. While France prides itself on being a country of *égalité*, only one nonwhite elected deputy (out of 570) is in the National Assembly, along with a handful of French senators of Arab origin. Ethnic minorities hold a few of the twenty-two seats representing France's overseas territories, but political representation is seriously lagging in France not only for minorities but for women as well, who have only 18 percent of the seats in the National Assembly (still slightly higher than the 17 percent held by women in the U.S. Congress). France is one of only two countries in Europe to use a winner-take-all electoral system rather than proportional representation to elect its national parliament, and the French variant requires that winners have a majority of the vote, which makes it very difficult for minority perspectives to win. President Sarkozy has prioritized appointing some of the diversity that France's winner-take-all system has been unable to produce, but that tactic only takes you so far.

FOMENTING A CONVERSATION ABOUT RACE

Elected and appointed minority leaders as well as minority entertainers, sports heroes, and TV news anchors have all pushed the visibility of minorities onto television screens and into living rooms, bars, and most corners of society. This in turn has fomented much public debate, as well as discussions across dinner tables within families and across backyard fences in neighborhoods. Most of the European countries have never before had such a frank, public conversation about race. This is not only virgin territory, but awkward and volatile besides.

Some of the most important dialogues occur in the "public square" through the mass media and other forums. The importance of cultural exchange through these vehicles cannot be overstated. Take, for instance, the North African origins of Zidane and several of his teammates, all heroes of the French champion soccer team that won the World Cup in 1998 and lost in the 2006 finals. The presence of these men on the team forced Le Pen–type nationalists, who have proudly cheered the French team for decades, to come face to face with their own stereotyping and bigotry (the same role that popular sports heroes such as Michael Jordan, Tiger Woods, and Magic Johnson have played in the United States). Nor was it trivial when Turkey in 2003 won the Eurovision Song Contest, which is a combination Olympics and *American Idol* in which glitzy pop singers represent their nations. The singers perform in a smorgasbord of languages, including all the European languages as well as Arab, Turkish, and Armenian, among others. It is the most-watched nonsporting event in the world, with its mostly young viewership estimated at up to six hundred million in thirty-five countries. T. R. Reid, a former London correspondent for the *Washington Post*, has written, "Eurovision has become a celebration of Europeanness," and with recent winners coming from not only Turkey but also Serbia, Ukraine, Latvia, and Estonia, the popularity of this contest has pushed the imagination of Europeans to the far eastern edges of their continent.[15]

France also has been trying quietly to diversify the talking-head newscasters the French see on their TV screens. Sometimes these unofficial affirmative action efforts have been aided by the president of France himself. Following the *banlieue* youth unrest, President Jacques Chirac met with the heads of the French media to see how the faces and spokespeople they put on television, which had always been white and Gallic, could "better reflect the French reality of today." Slowly, minority broadcasters have been appearing, such as Audrey Pulvar, who is black and in November 2005 became one of the first minority news anchors to appear regularly on French prime-time television. Television producers have also begun diversifying the ethnicity of guests and subjects treated in news and other programming.

"We're doing things quietly," says one producer, himself a French national of Algerian descent, "because if we make too much noise it will polarize people." Because affirmative action based on race or religion is effectively banned, the broadcasting companies keep no records of their efforts, no paper trail that could be used to accuse them of hiring people because of their ethnic origins. It's all done hush-hush.[16]

In Ireland, one of the country's public service broadcasters, RTÉ, has a weekly public affairs radio program hosted by a young Pole, Zbyszek Zalinski, addressing a burgeoning audience that is young, hip, and substantially composed of immigrants from central Europe, Asia, and Africa. In the Czech Republic, nonprofit media have played a key role in creating dialogue around the plight of the Roma people, one of the most discriminated-against groups in all of Europe. Some of these Czech media are run by Romani organizations, which have developed magazines, newspapers, several Internet sites, and Internet-based television and radio offered in both Czech and Romani. There is also Roma-themed broadcasting on Czech radio, accompanied by a Web site that offers news about Roma from around Europe in Czech, English, French, and German.[17]

In Germany, all public broadcasters transmit shows for immigrants on a daily basis, hiring an increasing number of journalists with an immigrant background and producing evening shows with native speakers in Turkish, Serbian, Croat, Polish, Italian, Spanish, Greek, and Russian. In 1999, the German public station Westdeutscher Rundfunk, known as WDR, launched *Broadcast House Europe,* a twenty-four-hour program in which immigrants in Germany take center stage. The broadcasts are presented by immigrants and focus on showing Germans and immigrants living together. These programs are seen as exemplary throughout Europe, having been much lauded and imitated.

Television programs such as hugely popular soap operas and sitcoms regularly confront their audiences with what makes them uncomfortable, such as interracial neighbors, Archie Bunker mentalities, and mixed marriages (since in Britain, Italy, Germany, and France, one-fifth of marriages involve a foreign-born spouse). In Germany, a popular sitcom called *Turkish for Beginners* features a dysfunctional family brought together by a German single mother and a widowed Turkish-German father, a kind of *Brady Bunch* of the new Germany. It has received critical acclaim and high ratings because of the clever way it has fun playing with ethnic clichés, subtly airing differences and real-world tensions in the process. In March 2006, a prominent nonprofit organization spearheaded a multiyear public service campaign to encourage Germans to think about what kind of society they want to live in. "Immigration = future?" one billboard asked.[18]

Back in France, nearly a fifth of the population tunes in to a nightly soap opera on a public channel, France 3, called *Plus Belle la Vie* (*Life Is So Sweet*). They are riveted to the multiracial goings-on among numerous families and characters—their disputes, love affairs, business dealings, and tragedies—that take place against the background of their cultural differences and social issues like racism, Islam, homosexuality, drugs, teenage pregnancy, and more.[19] And when France selected gigantic photographs of thirteen women to hang on the facade of the National Assembly to represent Marianne, France's historical icon portraying a national idealized female embodiment of freedom, eight of them were females of Arab or African origin.[20] From nation to nation and across the continent, Europeans are being urged in numerous and imaginative ways to participate in this ongoing dialogue about identity, integration, and race.

Discrimination flourishes when the "other" is branded as strange and foreign, so the recent rediscovery of a common heritage and history among Europeans and Arabs, Christians and Muslims, is not insignificant. Many museums have sponsored exhibits showing that the European and Arab worlds have a long-shared history dating back to Roman times, with lingering traces to this day (much like the shared history between the Confederate South and the Yankee North in the United States). Judeo-Christian civilization has been shaped by the Arab world, since historically both of them have occupied major territories on the perimeter of the Mediterranean pond. In their art, architecture, medicine, engineering, mathematics, geography, and astronomy, the European and Arab worlds have common roots in the ancient civilizations of Greece, Persia, Egypt, and Mesopotamia, as well as in the twin capitals of Constantinople and Rome. Martin Walker has written, "North Africa was a Roman province, and Egypt's Queen Cleopatra was a Greek. Southern Spain was a Muslim province for seven centuries, and the Balkans were dominated by Islam until the 19th century. . . . The Crusades were a prolonged cultural exchange from which Europe's Christians emerged enriched by 'Arabic' numerals and medicine, the lateen sail, and the table fork."[21]

Umberto Eco has written, "Greek culture would have been unthink-able without the Egyptians," and points out that St. Augustine, who was one of the most important figures in the development of western Christianity, was a North African born in a Roman provincial city in present-day Algeria.[22] The extraordinary dynamism of Arab civiliza-tion between the eighth and fourteenth centuries, sometimes known as the Islamic Golden Age, made important contributions to the worlds of science, medicine, agriculture, engineering, astronomy, technology, mathematics, physics, art, and literature. Having already benefited from the wisdom of Greece and Rome, which was mislaid by Europe in its Dark Ages, the Arab world returned it to Europe just in time for the Renaissance. Today, Spanish writers and intellectuals such as the great novelist Juan Goytisolo have played a key role in mining this rich vein, acknowledging the Arabic role in the origins of the European novel and in culture in general. In July 2008 the Louvre laid the first stone for its new Islamic wing, expected to open in 2010, which will create Europe's largest permanent exhibition of Islamic art, with ten thousand pieces from the seventh to the nineteenth century. And the Union for the Mediterranean launched by French president Nicolas Sarkozy is instituting a number of joint pan-Mediterranean projects, including a Euro-Mediterranean student exchange program, extend-ing to Arabic and Islamic nations the E.U.'s highly praised Erasmus program which has allowed over 1.5 million young people to study abroad within Europe.

The point of these initiatives and retrospectives is to reconnect the shards, showing that this latest remingling of Europe's and Islam's identities is a "back to the future" scenario that presents great oppor-tunity if the proper vision and leadership can grasp it.

PAYING FOR EQUALITY

The European Union has put real money behind all these civil rights interventions and consciousness-raising efforts, billions of euros' worth, a level of funding for civil rights interventions that, ironically, is hardly possible in the United States today. The European Social Fund (ESF), which was established to reduce differences in prosperity and living standards across E.U. member states and regions, has been targeting those regions in which development is less advanced. The ESF funds a wide variety of programs, some of them fostering better integration and reducing inequality and social exclusion of minorities, immigrants, and women. Some examples of the types of programs funded include the following: in Sweden, "Integrating immigrants into the Swedish workforce" and "Toolkits for gender equality"; in Spain, "Micro credit for business start-ups for marginalized groups" and "Opening pathways for those at risk of exclusion"; in the Netherlands, "Stepping stone to social integration"; in Germany, "Occupational integration of migrants into the German labor market," "Opening up the labor market to young immigrant school-leavers," and "Changing women's attitudes towards technology"; and in France, "Social inclusion and combating discrimination," which seeks to "draw those currently at the margins of the labour market back into work using a combination of local and individual approaches" and to counter "racial discrimination in recruitment and work."[23]

Many of the state programs are joint ventures between the government and private nongovernmental organizations. Billions already have been spent, and over the period 2007–13 the ESF will distribute a whopping $100 billion more to the E.U. member states and regions to achieve the fund's goals.[24] Besides the ESF, Europe spends billions more provided by other funds. The Integration Fund has a goal of supporting the efforts of member states in "enabling third country nationals of different economic, social, cultural, religious, linguistic and ethnic backgrounds to fulfill the conditions of residence and to facilitate their integration into the European societies." This fund is more than just benevolent-sounding words; its overall budget in 2007–13 will provide another $1.2 billion.[25]

Then there's the Programme for Employment and Social Solidarity (known by its acronym PROGRESS); the European Refugee Fund ("to support and encourage the efforts made by the Member States in receiving and bearing the consequences of receiving refugees and displaced persons"); the EQUAL Community Initiative ("combating discrimination in the workplace by promoting the awareness of employers and harnessing the support of the social partners [trade unions and employers' associations]"); and the Urban II program, with another billion euros from the European Regional Development Fund (ERDF) targeting urban renewal and redevelopment projects in seventy areas throughout Europe.[26] Indeed, the number of projects, funds, and hundreds of billions of euros that are being or will be spent are dizzying. Simply no counterpart to it exists in the United States today.

On the other hand, despite all the money spent and shoulders involved in pushing the boulder up the hill, one intervention mostly has been a no-go zone for Europe: the use of affirmative action (known as "positive discrimination"), which has been tried for years with a degree of success in the United States. Informal efforts have been made, but no country has been willing to legislate such racially based interventions. Is this really reflective of a strong concern over Europe's fascist past in using race and religion as the basis for horrible acts, or is it more evidence of Europe's racism and integration backwardness? Probably a bit of both. That past certainly provides a convenient excuse for the absence of affirmative action.

Instead of setting race-based objectives, Europeans have attempted to target efforts according to geography and socioeconomic status, but with a wink and a nod since everyone knows those are proxies for race. And interventions also have been made on the basis of gender; some nations have enacted mild forms of affirmative action to counter sex discrimination. Norway, for example, prohibits any company listed on the Norwegian stock exchange from having a board composed of more than 60 percent of one sex. Imagine the impact if such a progressive mandate were implemented in American corporations. Moreover, many political parties in most nations have taken steps to elevate women on their slates of candidates. But most nations still stubbornly refuse to adopt race-based interventions. Yet if Europe is serious about grappling with its racism, especially in employment situations, a broad degree of success without such interventions is hard to imagine. A societal consensus will have to be reached that allows well-targeted race-based goals, whether in the workplace, school admissions, home ownership, loans to small businesses, or other areas in which Europe's ethnic minorities are discriminated against.

Without question, the many European programs and policies already adopted profess lofty goals: bromides such as "ensure that ethnic minority or migrant groups have the same opportunities for employment, training and information and support as those that are available to native citizens," "fight social marginalization and discrimination based on race or ethnic origin," and "[develop] new roles and/or structures to support integration and prevent discrimination," ad infinitum. Certainly Europe is doing much to put its best foot forward—but will it be enough? These efforts are not quite in their infancy but not that far beyond the cradle either. To paraphrase Winston Churchill, it's not the end, it's not even the beginning of the end, of such efforts; but it is perhaps the end of the beginning, and time will tell if Europe will be successful ultimately.

EUROPE'S NEW MARTIN LUTHER—
OR IS IT MARTIN LUTHER KING?

As much as minorities and immigrants need a helping hand from European leaders, much of Europe is searching for a partner from the minority/immigrant/Muslim communities as well. Certainly some minorities have not made the effort to become integrated into the broader society, preferring to cling to their old culture or religion, but it's a push-pull: as long as Europe does not make its ethnic and religious minorities feel sufficiently welcome, that becomes a reason for those minority individuals or groups to stay within the comfort zone of their own ghettoized world. More minority leaders have emerged, such as those elected to the legislatures in recent years, and more athletes and entertainers have become heroes. But Europe still is awaiting a prominent figure who can articulate the minority condition, and the gap between that condition and Europe's lofty rhetoric about equality and human rights, with such riveting skill and oratory that they shame Europe into overcoming its racial conservatives and tribal ethnocentrism.

Some Europeans have proposed that one such figure may be Tariq Ramadan, a middle-aged scholar who has been described by some as a "Muslim Martin Luther," by others as Europe's Martin Luther King, and by still others as a dangerous Islamist waging a covert war against Western values. Ramadan is the leading proponent of what has been called "European Islam," a school of thought intended to create a new branch of Islam that is rooted squarely in Europe with its own traditions and rituals, rather than in ancestral lands or cultures. Ramadan believes many of the habits that Muslims display and that Europeans revile are not Islamic per se but rather are cultural traits specific to the Middle East, Africa, or Asia.

"Muslims living in Europe have an opportunity to reread our [religious] sources," he says. "From Arab Islam, or African Islam, we have to come to European Islam. . . . We are going through a reassessment, and the most important subject is women. Our experience in Europe has made it clear we must speak about equality," he says.[27] "Some scholars of Islam go on to conclude that women do not have the right to work. For me this is wrong and is against women's rights. We can actually go back to the [Islamic] scriptural sources in order to promote the struggle for women's rights."[28]

On the other hand, he adds, Europeans "must start considering Islam as a European religion, and stop building a European identity against Islam. . . . What we need is a new narrative, a new 'we,' a multicolored, multicultural European identity. Immigration is a fact whether you like it or not. Europeans need to psychologically integrate that into their world view."[29]

In his book *To Be a European Muslim,* Ramadan wrote, "Many European politicians, as well as average people, are prone to thinking that the only safe Muslims are those who neither practice their religion nor manifest their Muslim identity."[30] Ramadan rejects this kind of assimilation in favor of a European rainbow that *includes* Islam. But it is this bid to return religion closer to the core of secular Europe that has made some people uncomfortable and made Ramadan controversial.

Ramadan stirs up all sides equally. His orations in favor of uprooting Islamic principles from their cultures of origin and planting them in European soil have made him controversial among Islamic leaders as well. He was banned in Saudi Arabia, Tunisia, and Egypt after calling for a moratorium on sharia's corporal punishment, stoning, and beheading. *Time* named him one of the twenty-first century's most influential people, even as the Department of Homeland Security was revoking his visa days before he was to begin teaching at the University of Notre Dame, in Indiana. Homeland Security officials apparently found him guilty by association, since Ramadan is a grandson of Hassan al-Banna, founder of the Muslim Brotherhood, which seeks to resist Western domination and to create an Islamic state.

Despite all the controversy swirling around him, to Ramadan the calculation remains rather simple. "If Europe wants to succeed, it needs more immigrants," he says. "Who is going to do the jobs Europeans don't want to do? Who is going to pay for the welfare state? Europe is aging, and its population is shrinking." He has called for a European future based on a recognition that the Muslim presence in Europe is a "source of enrichment" which can make a "positive contribution in building a new Europe."[31]

While Ramadan's voice is vital and unique on the European landscape, comparisons to Martin Luther King are overstated. King was the leader of a cohesive constituency based in a black community whose numbers were far greater than the numbers of either Europe's Muslims or its immigrant-descended minorities. King combined strong oratory rooted in American values with street heat born of protest marches and civil disobedience. Neither Ramadan nor any other minority leader in Europe has managed to convey the moral authority that King brought to the conflict by laying his life on the line for his beliefs. No large protest marches have taken place, and few events have attracted as much attention as the French *banlieue* youth revolt did.

Another riveting public figure has been the courageous Ayaan Hirsi Ali, the Somali-born Muslim immigrant–turned–Dutch parliamentarian. Hirsi Ali, who claims she suffered horribly at the hands of Muslim male relatives (though certain parts of her personal story are in dispute), became the target of death threats from Muslim extremists when she denounced Islam's treatment of women. She challenged Dutch multicultural bromides with her fierce testimonials, declaring that Dutch acceptance of Islamic intolerance is providing a dangerous breeding ground for radicals and extremists. Some of her angry statements have been purposefully provocative and considered by some to be needlessly irresponsible, such as her claim in an interview that Muhammad would be considered a pedophile by Western standards. While Hirsi Ali's voice has been a powerful one, she does not convey King's stature either, because she challenges not Europe's racial conservatism or those parts of the power structure dependent on it, as Dr. King did in the United States, but rather a beleaguered religious minority in the heart of Europe that itself is subject to discrimination.

Europe's MLK may not have emerged yet, but Ramadan, Hirsi Ali, and other Muslims have helped to galvanize a vision of modern European Islam, indeed of modern Europe, that the continent desperately needs. These new voices represent some of the more promising currents of modern European thought and its inevitable evolution toward a multicultural society. At the same time, these Muslim leaders are putting an appropriate degree of obligation on Muslims to meet Europe halfway by laying the intellectual foundation for an independent and more liberal Islam that needs to emerge in Europe among young, educated Muslims who have been profoundly changed by modern liberal democracy.

Just as Europe still awaits its Martin Luther King, it also still awaits its President Lyndon Johnson, a political leader with the courage to meet a European civil rights movement halfway. LBJ was willing to twist some arms and step on some toes of his narrowly tribal colleagues in the South and ultimately to sign the type of civil rights legislation that significantly reduced discrimination, created more economic opportunity, and eventually turned American minorities into full, nearly equal citizens. Europe's politicians have taken some good first steps, but many more steps—and the courage to take them—are needed. At this point the future direction of the European civil rights movement is not clear: Will the conditions in Europe eventually produce a mass movement, especially as the proportion of ethnic minorities in Europe continues to rise? Or will Europe's proactive interventions release enough steam to dissipate a critical buildup of frustration? These questions are impossible to answer at this juncture.

In rising to this challenge, Europe certainly can learn something from the United States. While the United States is no paragon, and both it and Europe face daunting problems of bigotry and uneven integration of their minority and immigrant populations, America has been engaged with integration efforts for far longer and has had some success. The U.S. has assimilated many previous waves of immigrants, for the most part successfully, and Muslim immigrants have done well in the United States. (Though the U.S. has had far fewer Muslims to integrate than Europe, and no baggage of colonial history complicates the relationship as it does in Europe. Plus, America's geographic distance from Arab/Muslim lands means it attracts an immigrant who has more personal resources and abilities to begin with.) The American response to the civil rights movement, which of course has many tragic chapters to it, nevertheless is an example to Europe of how an open, progressive democracy can address the problems of integration, immigration, and civil rights, and mobilize public opinion behind specific policy goals.

The challenges ahead, however, are not simple or easy. Massive global migration is driving most countries to find ways to manage their increasingly diverse populations. Every wealthy nation faces the difficulty of coping with the world's poor arriving on its doorstep. And that implies a moral imperative to extend a charitable Good Samaritan hand, even as it sometimes conflicts with a pragmatic calculation to protect the homeland. In both the short and the long term, the Europe that is emerging will have been forever changed by this experience, just as the United States has been changed by its tumultuous journey to a multiracial, multicultural society.

But Europe should not fear this evolution, for it is natural and it is right. In today's globalized world, with revolutions occurring in telecommunications that bind us to a global fate, we are all increasingly sitting in one another's living rooms, and borders are becoming less firm. Just as Europe already has led the world—indeed, history itself—in so many areas of political, social, economic, and energy development, it must now chart a new course toward redefining human bonds and identity. Europe has a rich philosophical heritage to draw from for this purpose, filled with lofty rhetoric and ideals. It's time to live up to them.

Europe also has a younger generation—sometimes called "the Erasmus generation," after the European Union's highly praised university exchange program—with more racially open views than their parents and grandparents. Over time, they will provide the leadership of the New Europe. With the right vision and policies to support that vision, Europe has tremendous opportunities for renewal in dealing with its internalized racism. Europe in 2050 will certainly be a different place from Europe today, with a version of a European rainbow society in the offing. It is up to Europe to decide if this is the future it wants to embrace. But like it or not, that future is banging on the door and coming to dinner. It's just a matter of time.

EIGHTEEN

THE DILEMMA OF POPULATION DECLINE

"Where are all the children?"

Genoa, Italy, has been known forever as the birthplace of the explorer Columbus, an important port city, and the anchor of the Italian Riviera's charming, picturesque coastline. But lately, Genoa is acquiring a different reputation. A casual walk around the city center reveals something startling: few children are playing in the streets, few toy stores are in the malls, and a merry-go-round stands quiet in the park. Schools have closed for lack of students. For a place known for its broods of children, many Italian cities like Genoa lack the boisterous noise of kids playing. Genoa provides a glimpse into one possible future for Europe, and the challenges of an aging society combined with increased immigration.

Most native Genovese today are having few children, resulting in a birthrate (7.7 births per 1,000 people) that was about half the death rate (13.7 per 1,000) in Genoa's broader region, Liguria, in 2005. Throughout the country, a quarter of Italian women have no children, and another quarter stop at one. Twenty years ago, for every 100 people under the age of fifteen, Liguria had 70 over sixty-five; today, for every 100 people under fifteen, it has 240 over sixty-five, a graying population that is among the largest in the world.[1]

The only thing that has prevented Genoa's population of 750,000 from completely imploding is the arrival of tens of thousands of immigrants, mostly from around the southern and eastern Mediterranean regions and South America. Typical of new arrivals, the immigrants are birthing more children than the Genovese, producing more than two children per family. Fifty percent of the students in many schools in the old city are of foreign-born parentage. In the Fiumara Mall, usually the rare mother pushing a stroller is speaking Arabic, Latin American Spanish, or Albanian. Immigration has saved Genoa from experiencing the most extreme consequence of low birthrates and an aging population, providing cheap labor and filling schools that otherwise would have to be closed.

But many Genovese have begun to feel that the city is no longer theirs, a situation that has produced simmering resentment. Italians, seemingly oblivious to the consequences of their near-childless condition, complain about the loss of their culture, the sounds of strange languages filling the air, and the rise of immigrant gangs. "Some of the kids in school with my teenager don't even speak Italian," complains one Italian mother. "It's really very difficult."[2]

Genoa dramatically illustrates the twin horns of a dilemma: a declining native population being relentlessly replaced, year after year, by a swelling immigrant population. But Genoa, and Italy as a whole, are not the only places vexed by this dynamic; you could write a similar script regarding many other European cities and regions—indeed, most advanced Western countries in the world, including the United States—whose native populations all suffer from nonreplacement levels of reproduction (though some suffer more than others).[3] In much of the developed world, populations are graying, and total birthrates are at or near record lows, well below the replacement level of 2.1 children per woman. (That is the average number of births per woman necessary to maintain a stable population.)[4] The research clearly shows that as societies grow wealthier and as more and more people enter the middle class, individuals find more interesting, fun, and fulfilling things to do than have lots of children. Particularly as more women have sought careers and economic equity, fewer of them desire to have children or large families, especially if insufficient supports are in place for families so that women aren't forced to choose between a family and their career. Consequently, more women are staying childless or having fewer children, and families have gotten smaller.

While lower birthrates have positive ramifications for the ecology of a threatened planet over the long term, they have led not only to a declining population but also to an aging population as the current post–World War II baby boom generation in Europe (as well as in the United States) retires in great numbers, leaving fewer young people to replace them in the workforce. Given those demographic realities, one of the solutions to Europe's declining numbers undoubtedly must involve the devil's bargain of more immigration. But more immigration raises the chances of further cultural clashes if efforts to integrate are not accelerated. It is the height of irony that one of the current conditions that vexes Europe also contains the seeds of a solution for another of its vexations.

FALLING FERTILITY, WORLDWIDE

Birthrates (also known as fertility rates) actually are falling in most regions of the world, and over half the world's population now lives in regions with fertility rates below the replacement level. According to the United Nations, global birthrates have declined since 1972, from 6.0 to 2.8. Some read drastic, Malthusian implications into these numbers, but others take a more cautious view.

"Fertility decline is not a new phenomenon," says Alasdair Murray, director of CentreForum, a London-based think tank. "In reality, fertility in most European countries and the U.S. has been declining since the industrial revolution." Fertility rates in France, for example, peaked as early as 1800. Between 1850 and 1950, France had the oldest population in the world, "causing much soul-searching among its political elite and prompting some of the first attempts at pro-natal policies in modern times," says Murray. Seen over a long time frame, it is the postwar baby boom, "which broke a long run trend towards lower fertility rates, that looks like an aberration."[5] In other words, for the past several decades we have been living through a population bubble, and now that bubble is bursting nearly all over the world.

Some of the lowest birthrates today are in East Asia. Taiwan and South Korea have birthrates of 1.1 and 1.2 children per woman, respectively, barely half the replacement level. China, with its one-child-per-family policy, has a fertility rate of about 1.7, prompting some analysts to opine that China will "grow old before it grows rich" (and shrink to the second-largest nation, since by 2050 a faster-growing India will surpass China to become the most populous country, at nearly 1.7 billion people). Japan, with a fertility rate of 1.3, has experienced below-replacement-level fertility for decades, and some analysts project an astonishing 20 percent loss of its population by 2050.[6]

For the United States, while the native-born white population birthrate has sunk to below replacement level, births among the racial/ethnic minority populations have been the main driving force that will prevent a Japan-like population bust. Hispanics by far have the highest birthrate, with an average of 2.9 babies born to each Hispanic woman, followed by blacks (2.1), Asians (1.9), and whites (1.86).[7] In recent years Hispanics have made up nearly half the newborns.[8] By 2020 Hispanic females are projected to make up almost half (47 percent) of women ages fifteen to forty-four in California, while white females will fall to 32 percent.[9] Many other states also are seeing dramatic increases in minority birthrates. However, most of this population increase is driven by higher birthrates among the *domestic* minority populations, not by new immigrant arrivals. With a Hispanic birthrate more than 1.5 times greater than that of whites, it is the Hispanic population increases that give the United States a total fertility rate just short of replacement level, about 2.0. This means that Hispanics are destined to assume a greater and greater role in American life, much more than minorities will in Europe.

In Europe, the situation lies somewhere between those of the United States and Japan, that is, somewhere between stable and grave. The prolonged post–World War II baby boom that Europe experienced, along with the United States, Canada, and Australia, was followed by a baby bust era of low fertility rates and smaller families. The continent-wide fertility rate currently is an alarming 1.5, but there are important differences from nation to nation. Ireland and France are nearly at replacement level, about 1.9 to 2.0 children born per female, with a generous contribution of French births (about one-fourth) coming from the country's domestic minority population.[10] The Scandinavian countries and Britain are a bit below France and Ireland, with a birthrate of about 1.8 to 1.9. Germany, Italy, and Spain, even counting their immigrant and minority population increases, still have alarming birthrates of only 1.4 and are therefore slowly losing population.

But the trends become hair-raising as you sweep east. The fertility rates in the formerly communist countries of eastern and central Europe have sunk to between 1.2 and 1.3, with Russia also at 1.3, and Ukraine projected to lose more than 40 percent of its population, according to U.N. figures. Their birthrate decline closely tracks with the end of communism, when economic uncertainty and the collapse of child support structures caused women to choose to postpone births. The birthrate may rebound as prosperity and security return, and already evidence of that has appeared in the Czech Republic and Estonia, where fertility rates have been rising in recent years.[11]

While so many of Europe's indigenous white populations are shrinking, their ethnic minority populations are bursting, in part because of immigration but, as in the United States, mostly because of higher birthrates among the domestic minority populations. In two of the countries with the highest birthrates, France and Britain, about 20 to 25 percent of babies have at least one foreign-born parent.[12] Sections of cities such as Paris's suburb Evry or Berlin's Kreuzberg district contain throngs of Arab women in Muslim head scarves and veils, Arab delis, kebab vendors, mosques, and store signs announcing the permanence of a nontraditional European presence. New rituals like sheep slaughter according to Muslim's halal practice for the holy day Eid not only contravene French regulations on security and hygiene but also remind everyone of the shifting demographic picture. Even northern climes are seeing the shift: Malmö, Sweden, is estimated to have one of the highest percentages of Muslims of any European city. It is not just the addition of brown and black faces but also the simultaneous subtraction of white faces that is causing waves of general anxiety.

Yet to keep this in perspective, Europe's minorities are starting from a far lower percentage of the overall population than are minorities in the United States. By 2050 the proportion of American whites is projected to fall from 69 percent in the 2000 census to just under 50 percent; Hispanics will reach 24 percent and Asians 8 percent, and the proportion of African Americans will increase marginally to 14 percent.[13] No credible projections predict that Europe's white population will shrink to only 50 percent by 2050, so the United States is due in some ways for a more serious jolt than Europe. But at least the U.S. population will hold stable. At current fertility rates, even with high rates of immigration, the same cannot be said for Europe as a whole.

DOES POPULATION DECLINE EQUAL ECONOMIC DECLINE?

Even if these demographic shifts do not result in increased cultural clashes, Europe faces another concern with its declining population—it is thought to go hand-in-hand with economic decline. Many commentators warn that Europe's aging population will result in a workforce decline that threatens to derail national economies by blowing a hole in government budgets, wrecking pension and health care funding, reversing economic growth, and leaving European countries enfeebled in the face of competition from younger countries. Some American researchers even have charged Europe with committing "demographic suicide."[14]

Population specialist Philip Longman bluntly states, "Capitalism has never flourished except when accompanied by population growth, and it is now languishing in those parts of the world where population is stagnant."[15]

But the picture is more complex than the one demographic determinists like to portray. Europe's social capitalism has been flourishing even as its birthrates have been lagging; central and east European countries suffer from the biggest population declines, yet until the economic collapse in late 2008 they had among the fastest-growing economies in the world. China also has experienced huge growth rates along with moderately low birthrates. And after a decade-long slump, Japan's economy started growing again in the middle of this decade, even as its population has continued to fall.[16]

Still, such warnings cannot be dismissed out of hand. With fewer younger workers to pay the health and pension bills of an elderly retired population, at the very least they present a looming fiscal burden. What is known as the *dependency ratio*—the ratio of workers to retirees—is typically used to estimate the fiscal soundness of a society. Those in the workforce help pay for the retirement package of those who are retired, each generation's gift to those whose shoulders they are standing on. In recent years, the ideal dependency ratio for Western societies has been about four to one, that is, four workers for every one retiree. But by 2050, if Europe's population continues to decline, the dependency ratio is expected to halve to two workers for every one retiree, and even to one to one in Italy. With fewer workers to tax, revenue may be insufficient to continue to pay for the generous European workfare state. Or, at least, so goes the theory.

But analysts such as Alasdair Murray disagree with that pessimistic assessment. Murray is not naive about the portentousness of the numbers, but he thinks they don't tell the whole story. "Europe faces more of a labor market challenge than a demographic crisis," he says. "There is much that European governments can do to mitigate the impact of a contracting population of working age on economic growth and public finances."[17]

The emphasis on the ratio between workers and retirees gives an incomplete picture of dependency rates, says Murray. Rather than emphasizing that ratio, policy makers should pay greater attention to "total economic support ratios," which include not just the retired but also dependent children and any adults of working age not in full employment. By increasing the number of workers, as well as their productivity, and decreasing the number of dependents of any age, Europe can head off the predicted disaster.

For example, declining birthrates have resulted in a fall in dependent children, so the rise in the number of retired will be partly offset by a decline in the number of dependent children. According to Gary Burtless, a researcher at the Brookings Institution, when the decline in children is factored in, total dependency ratios in many countries in 2050 will look more like those of the 1960s, when the majority of the baby boom generation were still children, than those of the present day. In the United States, for example, the dependency ratio peaked in 1965, when there were ninety-five dependents for every hundred working adults. By 2050 the figure will be eighty dependents for every hundred workers, which, while much higher than the highly favorable figure of forty-nine dependents in 2000, will still be markedly lower than the number of dependents in 1965.[18]

But even this more comprehensive measure of total dependency fails to capture fully the balance between working and dependent populations, especially in European countries where rates of employment have been low. Many European economies have plenty of room to raise labor-force participation and rates of employment. Any adults of working age who are not working, including those who retire prematurely, can also be thought of as dependents. For starters, Murray and others say that policy makers should seek to increase the number of people who are over age sixty and still working by having people generally work longer into their elderly years. The fact is, many people retire at ages when they still could be highly productive and creative. Only about 37 percent of older European workers in the age bracket fifty-five to sixty-four are employed.[19] In Italy, 38 percent of workers retire to *la dolce vita* in their fifties.[20] Compare that with Iceland, where 81 percent of the population between the ages of sixty and sixty-four is still in the labor force in response to incentives that encourage them to continue working. In Germany only 22 percent of the population age sixty to sixty-four is still working, and only 14.5 percent in France, compared with 47 percent in the United States. Just 5.6 percent of sixty-five- to seventy-four-year-olds are working in Europe compared with 18.5 percent in the United States.[21] With the correct policy, these numbers can be increased, say Murray and other experts.

"European governments should reduce incentives to early retirement and make the transition into retirement more flexible," says Murray.[22] An increase in the effective retirement age by seven years would have the same effect as raising employment rates to 70 percent, which would substantially reduce dependency ratios and offset the negative impacts of an aging population. Some European governments already have initiated steps to increase the retirement age from the current sixty years old in most countries to sixty-five or sixty-seven. Germany has raised its retirement age to sixty-seven, to be phased in gradually by 2029. Britain has begun increasing the retirement age to sixty-eight by 2044. While politically unpopular in the short term, over the long term this is very doable, particularly as people are remaining healthier and productive for longer.

Other categories of dependents and underemployed who, with the right kinds of support services and training, could experience an increase in their labor-force participation include the long-term unemployed who have become discouraged and stopped looking for work; people on disability benefits, some of whom, with assistance, could find suitable work; and the young, especially in some categories for which entry into the labor force is delayed by excessively lengthy educational courses and other factors. In regard to the last category, the percentage of young men age fifteen to nineteen and active in the E.U. labor market has fallen from 60 percent in 1970 to around 33 percent in 2004, and for fifteen- to nineteen-year-old women the decline has been from 50 to 25 percent.[23] To Murray and others, these gaps suggest ways to improve employment rates.

But by far the most important segment of the population that must be mobilized into the workforce is women. As the next section will show, empowering European women to work is the key not only to higher employment rates and better dependency ratios but also to higher birthrates—as long as female workers are supported with sufficient pro-natal policies.

"FEMINISM IS THE NEW NATALISM"

Europe's experience indicates that many women today want to work as well as have children, and the societies that create the conditions that support women in both of those pursuits will be rewarded with higher birthrates. A greater number of women in the labor force also will affect the impending dependency ratio crisis, where there are too few workers to help pay the health and pension bills of an elderly retired population. Women's employment rates, therefore, are key to two of Europe's most daunting dilemmas.

Germany had a female employment rate of just under 60 percent in 2004, and France's was 57 percent, according to data from the Organisation for Economic Cooperation and Development (OECD). This compares with rates of 65 percent in the United States, 67 percent in Britain, and above 70 percent in Sweden, Switzerland, Denmark, and Norway. Participation rates in Italy and Spain are even lower than in Germany and France, 45 and 49 percent, respectively.[24] For the euro zone as a whole, the female employment rate was 57 percent in 2003, and the European Commission has targeted a goal of increasing this to 65 percent by 2050, which would add millions of female workers to the economy and reduce the dependency ratio.[25]

Interestingly, many of the E.U. countries that have the highest birthrates are not only the ones that have the best and most comprehensive proactive workfare policies supporting families, such as provision of child care, kiddie stipends, and generous parental leave, but also the ones that have a cultural environment that encourages women both to have children and to work. When women don't have to choose between a family and a career, the evidence suggests that this can have a positive impact on fertility rates. Europe is a virtual laboratory of experimentation, as different nations already have adopted various pro-natal policies, so to some extent we can gauge their impacts.

Some of those natal policies seek to encourage mothers and couples to have children, even paying them to do so with kiddie stipends. But encouraging women to give birth is not without controversy since, like affirmative action–type quotas, it recalls echoes of a fascist past. Italian dictator Mussolini heavily taxed single men in his Battle for Births, · Spanish dictator Franco's regime promoted policies to increase fertility, and Hitler awarded motherhood medals to women with large families in his quest for a superior German race. These fascist regimes tended to elevate motherhood to a revered cult status that also discouraged women from working, and this legacy still drags on these countries today.

Nevertheless, many European nations have set themselves on a path of encouraging families to grow. The Scandinavian countries stand out as having the best practices. Sweden and Norway have a long history of employing a range of policies designed both to help couples have more children and for women to work, including policies aimed at helping people balance their work and family life. This is part of what is known as the "Nordic model." As was detailed in chapter 4, these workfare support policies include generously paid parental leave following the birth of a child (up to sixteen months in Sweden, twelve months in Norway), subsidized public child care, paid sick leave, kiddie stipends, and flexible work schedules for parents. Women with children of preschool age are entitled to reduce their working hours without losing their place on their career ladder as a result. Fathers are included in the parental leave policy; in fact, in Norway fathers must take at least four weeks of leave or those weeks will be lost for both parents, which encourages fathers to be involved in childrearing from the earliest point in their children's lives. With Norway's and Sweden's stress on gender equality, women generally have higher pay than in other nations. The result is that Sweden and Norway both have a birthrate of around 1.8 children per woman, among the highest in Europe (though still somewhat below the 2.1 replacement level), combined with female employment levels that are among the highest in the world at 72 percent. Denmark, Finland, and the Netherlands have birthrates of around 1.7 children per woman and female employment levels at 72, 65, and 65 percent, respectively. The overarching goal in these countries is to provide a warm blanket of support around families and couples as they make decisions about having children and to help mothers remain in the workforce.

Germany, Spain, and Italy represent the flip side—places where traditional, even formerly fascist, cultures are still skeptical of women in the workforce and where, consequently, policy lags, as does the birthrate. All three countries have fairly generous paid maternity and parental leave, but they trail most of Europe in providing affordable child care and other supports. But beyond the specific natalist policies, sometimes even more significant is the cultural atmosphere surrounding women in the workforce. With roots in a Nazi past, too many traditional Germans still perceive working mothers as selfishly neglecting their family duties. Unsurprisingly, Germany's birthrate is a low 1.4 and its female employment rate a middling 60 percent. In formerly fascist Spain, a workplace bias continues against women who interrupt their careers to have children. Only in 2003 did the government introduce a national family policy to assist families and working mothers, but there is a lingering suspicion that government should not meddle in these matters, that family creation should be private. Consequently, Spain's birthrate is also a low 1.4, with a paltry 49 percent of women employed.

But patriarchal Italy wins the prize in knuckle-dragging. The job market is still dominated by the paterfamilias, the traditional male breadwinner who distributes his income to the rest of the family. The extended family is held together by a dependence on this male head of household. Italian women are expected not only to undertake the housework and child care but also to care for elderly parents; the family plays the role that government services play in other nations, as evidenced by Italy's expenditure of just 3.8 percent of its gross domestic product on child-related social spending compared with an E.U. average of around 8 percent.[26] This may sound in some ways like a desirable cozy family arrangement, but many Italian women are increasingly reluctant to fit into this old-fashioned mold and so opt out of childbearing entirely. That has resulted in a birthrate of only 1.4 children per woman and a female employment level lower than Spain's—only 45 percent.

Nikola Cordes, a thirty-three-year-old German lawyer, attests to the dual pressures of having a family and holding down a job that many European women experience. "I'd like to have children, but I can't see a way of keeping up my career and having a family," says Cordes. "In Germany, it's still not accepted at work for a woman to be successful and for her to have children at the same time."[27]

Compare that with the words of Inger Sethov, a Norwegian mother who is also a working professional. International travel is part of Sethov's work, and she says that very few of the women she meets abroad in similar jobs have children. Sethov explains, "There is just a completely different level of acceptance among employers [in Norway]. It is not uncommon to put a telephone conference on hold because you can hear a baby crying in the background."[28]

"I think many women want to combine family and work, but if society doesn't permit that, then women opt for their career," said Steffen Kroehnert, from the Berlin Institute for Population and Development. According to European Union estimates, 30 percent of German women today have not had children, an all-time high.[29]

The evidence from Italy, Spain, and Germany is that "traditional roles" within the home do not encourage women to have more babies. Quite the contrary—such roles can lead to lower birthrates. Other evidence has shown that a comprehensive level of pro-natal supports can have the desired impact; one study of twenty-one OECD countries found a positive relationship between the availability of child care and overall fertility.[30] As David Willetts, a British member of Parliament, put it, "Feminism is the new natalism."[31] That is a powerful message and one that Europe needs to embrace, especially certain countries.

Britain is an example of how changes in government policy can lead to dramatic increases in birthrates in a short period of time. In 2001, the United Kingdom had a fertility rate of 1.6. The Blair government implemented pro-natal policies, including maternity and paternity pay (new mothers are provided six months' paid leave and an option of six months' more unpaid leave), more free early education placements, free part-time nurseries for children from the age of four, and stronger provisions for more flexible working hours.[32] Beyond the policies themselves, the Blair government's emphasis led to a general change of attitude, say experts, such as Clem Henricson, director at the National Family Planning and Parenting Institute. The result? By 2006, the United Kingdom's fertility rate had risen to 1.9, a twenty-six-year high and nearly at replacement level. Interestingly, a sizable portion of that 15 percent increase occurred among women over forty, who nearly doubled their number of births as a result of the better climate that allowed working women to embrace both family and career.[33] And the country was able to do this even as it maintained a high level of women in the labor force with a female employment rate of 67 percent, higher than in the United States. Britain's experience so far is testimony to sound government policy leading to the desired pro-natal outcome.

But it's not a sure thing that having progressive, pro-natalist policies always will lead to higher female employment. France has some of the best pro-natalist policies, including having some of the most extensive state-funded child care in Europe. France also allows mothers to take sixteen weeks' paid maternity leave for the first child, rising to twenty-six weeks for the third child, and the government also pays kiddie stipends as well as a cash incentive for the birth of each child, with even more money paid for a third child as France tries to encourage larger families. Yet while France's birthrate is a high 1.9, its female employment rate is only 57 percent, not much higher than Ireland's, and lower than the OECD average.

Ireland is a contradictory case, because it has the highest birthrate in Europe, 2.0 children born per woman, yet it does not offer the high level of supports for mothers and families that one sees in France and Scandinavia (though it does offer substantially more than the United States does). Mothers get twenty-six weeks of paid maternity leave, but child care is underdeveloped and expensive. Most attribute Ireland's high fertility rate to its Catholic culture, which emphasizes women's motherhood role, but Italy is another highly Catholic country, as are Poland and Spain, yet they all have low birthrates. Poland in particular has gone through many economic and political shocks over the last twenty years since the fall of communism, and the ensuing uncertainty has not been conducive to population growth. Its population has declined, including by half a million in the first six years of this decade, and the birthrate is only 1.3, prompting this staunchly Catholic country to pass legislation that will pay a woman for each child she bears.[34] In any case, the effect that increased religion might have on Europe's birthrate, when combined with other factors, is unclear and does not appear to be determinative.

The take-home lesson here is that the correct pro-natal policies hold great potential to foster an increase in birthrates, as well as an increase in women's labor-force participation. That in turn will help maintain Europe's ratio of workers to economic dependents. That's a win-win-win. But introducing more women into the workforce will require not only comprehensive policies that support families but also sufficient job training and assistance finding work, as well as the creation of enough jobs. Perhaps most important, it will require a more open attitude regarding women's empowerment, as well as a recognition of how Europe's success depends on it. The right government policy certainly can play a positive role, such as Norway's to require companies to fill 40 percent of their corporate board seats with women, with heavy penalties, including a threat to shut down companies, if they do not comply.[35]

Women have made more gains in the last fifty years than in the previous five thousand years, but the struggle for equality and employment is not over. Germany, Italy, Spain, and other countries need a new generation of women's liberation, founded on freeing women to be both mothers and workers—working mothers. Fortunately, successful models already exist in neighboring Scandinavia and Britain.

OTHER POLICY OPTIONS

Several other policy options have been proposed to cushion the impacts of a declining workforce and Europe's aging population. These include pension reform, an increase in productivity growth, and the use of technology to improve the lives of elderly people, which could help extend their working years.

Besides rolling back the age for pension eligibility as previously discussed, pension reform is likely to entail at some point the introduction of small private pensions to supplement state pensions. Sweden has been the most innovative on this score, having created supplemental private accounts during the mid-1990s that require workers to contribute 2.5 percent of their pay, which is invested through government-approved investment managers. Germany has done something similar, and most countries will likely follow suit at some point (though in the wake of the stock market crash of 2008, a renewed sense of caution has made this policy less favored).

Productivity growth also holds the potential to foster more favorable dependency ratios. It is the single most important factor in wealth creation, because it allows workers to produce more of their products or services per hour, generating more income from the same amount of time worked. The natural tendency of businesses to spur innovation, automation, and other efficiencies will be redoubled if an aging population and declining workforce lead to labor shortages that drive up wages. Already aging Japan has pioneered widespread use of intelligent robots that boost productivity in many occupations; with more than a fifth of its population sixty-five or older, Japan is banking on robots to replenish its workforce. Once the stuff of science fiction, Japan is perhaps the closest to a future where humans and intelligent robots routinely exist side by side. Japan is already an industrial robot powerhouse where robots are taken for granted in Japanese factories. Over 370,000 robots worked at factories across Japan in 2005, about 40 percent of the global total and 32 robots for every 1,000 Japanese manufacturing employees. Today robots make sushi, they plant rice and tend paddies, they serve as receptionists, can vacuum office corridors, and can spoon-feed the elderly. They serve tea, greet company guests, and chatter away at public technology displays. "Soon, robots could even replace low-cost workers at small firms, greatly boosting productivity," says Eimei Onaga, CEO of Innovation Matrix Inc., a company that distributes Japanese robotics technology in the U.S.[36]

Europe likely will follow this path. More productivity-driven wealth will mean greater tax revenues to pay for social benefits and services, as it has historically. Political analyst Michael Lind has argued that "productivity growth can solve much or all of the pension funding problem," and as proof of that he points out that if the ratio of workers to retirees goes from four to one today to two to one in the future, that is quite minor compared with the shift from a ratio of eighteen workers to one retiree in 1950 to four to one today—a shift made smooth and painless by technology-driven productivity growth over the past half century.[37]

However, as the postwar baby boom generation enters its senior years, the aging of the population will become ever more prominent.

So Europe also is taking innovative steps to use technology to improve the lives of older people and to assist them in staying healthy, productive, and employed longer. The European Commission has outlined plans for a $1.5 billion research program to develop new directed technologies, including ways that will help seniors take advantage of accessible online services that could support their needs, and to create more personalized health and workfare services. Currently only 10 percent of seniors use the Internet, and vision, hearing, or dexterity problems leave many frustrated in their efforts to engage with modern technology. So the use of technology is seen by the European Union as helpful in allowing older people to remain active, productive, and independent for more years, as well as an opportunity to spur new investment and research, creating opportunities for European industry.[38]

No single intervention will allow Europe to reverse the threat of a declining population, unfavorable dependency ratios, and the risk of future underfunding of pensions and social services. But together these many interventions compose a potent, multipronged approach that presents to Europe an opportunity to manage its dilemma. It is deeply ironic that a substantial part of the response to the continent's dilemmas hinges on two solutions: less sexism and less racism. More immigration and better integration will help reverse the population decline and increase employment, which will positively affect dependency ratios; more women's equality also will increase employment and the dependency ratio, and could lead to a higher birthrate. At this point Europeans really have no choice. No amount of holding their fingers in the dike will prevent the sheer demographics from gradually flooding the cozy corners of old mind-sets. Europe needs to redouble its civil rights efforts with a goal of expanding opportunities for both its minority populations and its women.

While Europe has its work cut out for it, the situation is not nearly as bleak as some of its critics make it out to be. Many of the Europessimists lose sight of the fact that the challenge is not one of solving these dilemmas in the short term, but rather of managing them over the long term. Without a long-term view, these discussions often become twisted with a sense of urgency to the point of hysteria. Fortunately some of the European countries already have begun taking steps in the right direction, with real progress being made that can serve as models for those that are lagging behind. And here again, the younger generation, the Erasmus generation, which has a more open and progressive attitude, will lead the way.

CONCLUSION

The Make or Break Century

Having lost the comfort of our geographical boundaries,
we must in effect rediscover what creates the bond between
humans that constitute a community.

Jean-Marie Guéhenno,
French diplomat and United Nations official

I recall the time I sat in the public gallery of the European Parliament
in Brussels, observing a heated debate among hundreds of members of
the European Parliament (or MEPs, as they are called). It was October
2005, and the MEPs had come from all across the European continent, representing a half billion people. In typical European fashion
the debate was being translated simultaneously into twenty-two different languages, including the usual English, French, Italian, Spanish,
German, Swedish, and Dutch, but also Magyar, Romani, Maiti, Latvian, and Czech, among others.

The MEPs sat with their headsets on, listening intently to the trans-
lations, as one by one they sparred over pressing political and economic
issues that, at the time, you would have heard only faint echoes of in the
halls of the United States Congress. Yet, once the American economy
collapsed three years later in the fall of 2008, dragging the rest of the
world into its vortex, these issues suddenly were center stage all across
the globe, framed by the following questions: To what extent should
a capitalist economy and its core institutions—the banks, the finan-

cial institutions, the corporations—be regulated to maintain stability as well as sufficient economic growth? How do you harness global capitalism so that it not only produces wealth but also contributes to a broadly shared prosperity? How does an economy ensure that employers provide high enough wages and sufficient workfare security so that people can live a good life, but without squashing entrepreneurship and damaging the competitiveness of the economy itself? Finally, how do you make that kind of dynamism ecologically sustainable in a world staring into the face of global climate change, burgeoning populations, and finite natural resources? These and other questions weighed heavily on the minds of the MEPs.

To an unfamiliar American, this debate would have sounded like the age-old one of socialism vs. capitalism, but nothing was further from the truth. As we have seen, all of the various European nations have capitalist economies and vibrant, competitive businesses. But while it's true that free market forces and global trade have lifted millions of people out of poverty, it also is true that in the short term the "creative destruction" of global capitalism produces both winners and losers.

So Europe's parliamentarians knew a lot was at stake; it was as if they were anticipating the crash to come. MEP after MEP stood and delivered with passion, each followed by ripples of applause. This was no idle conversation; the future of Social Europe was wavering in the balance. In fact, the post–World War II consensus—the social contract itself—was in play. I listened to the English translation through my headset, marveling that this continent which had fought two horrific wars in the previous century now was leading the world in debating the best way to enact a peace founded on the three pillars of broadly shared prosperity, economic security, and ecological sustainability. Disagreements abounded, but even the "conservative" MEPs were less conservative than the Democratic Party in the United States, which remained too timid after retaking Congress in the 2006 elections to raise substantive debate about rampant inequality in the United States, a speculative housing bubble, global climate change, or a failing health care system.

Europe's intense debate, which now is occurring all around the world, sheds important light on one of the preeminent challenges of the twenty-first century. The overarching task today is to fashion institutions and practices that are capable of fostering a desirable quality of life for a burgeoning global population of over six billion people. The addition of global climate change—the prospect of an overheating atmosphere, rising sea levels, tumultuous weather patterns, and subsequent mass dislocation—to the usual mix of geopolitical tensions has resulted in an even greater sense of urgency. If we don't succeed, the future of our world is in jeopardy. We are living in a make or break century.

Unfortunately this sophisticated level of discussion was quite beyond the American conversation during the George W. Bush years, and barely has begun under the Obama administration. But Europeans have been confronting it head on for some time now. As this book has shown, the various nations of Europe and their unique adaptations and institutions have much to offer as we attempt to chart a steady course during an anxious and insecure twenty-first century. Our transatlantic cousins are showing the world a new face, a new way of structuring the economy, work, health care, family values, energy, transportation, democracy, foreign policy, and other crucial sectors that, on balance, augur the best future for the world.

Let's review some of the ground we have covered. We looked at the following five key areas where the European Way is fomenting a quiet revolution.

1. SOCIAL CAPITALIST EUROPE

Europe's social capitalism and workfare system, misnamed a "welfare state" by detractors, is driven by a powerful capitalist economic engine that powers the largest, wealthiest economy in the world, nearly a third of the global economy and almost as large as the economies of the U.S. and China combined. Capitalist Europe has a lot more Fortune 500 companies than the U.S., Japan, or China (179 in Europe vs. 140 in the U.S.), and its national economies are regularly rated among the most competitive in the world. Yet this economic powerhouse also is more responsive to social needs because of numerous countervailing institutions and practices, such as codetermination, supervisory boards, works councils, flexicurity, and effective trade unions. Its capitalist engine has been harnessed to channel its tremendous wealth into funding Europe's comprehensive workfare support system, which includes universal health care, low-cost higher education, adequate retirement pensions, paid parental leave, child care, kiddie stipends, generous vacations, a shorter workweek, paid sick leave, affordable housing, elder care, efficient mass transportation, and more. This social capitalism ensures that Europe's wealth is broadly shared and that families and individuals have the support they need to enjoy healthy and productive lives.

The Euroskeptics' claim that Europe is stuck in a crippled, low-growth economy, with higher unemployment and higher taxes than Americans experience, turns out to be a stereotype that masks a more complex reality. In normal economic times, Europe's "steady state" economy does not need to grow as fast as America's because Europe is better at spreading its wealth around, while America's economy is substantially more "trickle down." And in any case, the Euro zone's per capita economic growth rate was slightly higher than that of the United States over the ten years prior to 2008.

In terms of unemployment rates, prior to the economic crash of 2008–9, Europe had not been the land of "double digit" unemployment for many years and in fact had been enjoying record low unemployment, contrary to stereotype. After the crash, the U.S. shed many more jobs than Europe did, until unemployment on both sides of the Atlantic became identical. But even beyond the ups and downs of the economy, unemployment rates are affected greatly by what exactly is being measured. For example, unemployment rates don't count those who are in prison, and because the U.S. has an incarceration rate that is seven to ten times higher than the rates of European nations, it means including prisoners would have the effect of increasing the U.S. unemployment rate by about 1.2 percent compared to Europe's. That would have made the true unemployment rates in America and Europe much closer to equal throughout the 2000's; and it means America's unemployment was even higher than Europe's after the crash.

In terms of taxes, it turns out Europeans don't pay any more than most Americans if we factor in the entire tax burden of federal, state, local, real estate, and social security taxes, as well as the out-of-pocket fees, deductibles, premiums, and tuition that Americans pay *in addition to* their taxes in order to receive the same level of workfare supports that Europeans have. Many of the things Europeans receive for their taxes—health care, a university education, a decent retirement, child care, and parental leave, for example—are hardly discretionary; they are necessary in order to enjoy a basic level of security and comfort. But Americans have to pay extra for those services and benefits. In short, when you sum up the total balance sheet you discover that many Americans pay out just as much as Europeans, but we receive a lot less for our money.

The Europeans recognize that, in today's risky world, a middle-class standard of living is not only about income levels but also about adequate workfare supports for individuals and families. That is central to their way of ensuring life, liberty, and the pursuit of happiness.

The sheer breadth and depth of these workfare securities is impressive, especially compared with the miserly system that Americans are used to. Europe's social contract is steeped in the values of fairness, equality, and solidarity, forming the backbone of its considerable economic success. Much more than America, Europe is based on real "family values," and unlike America it is not timid or stingy about spending its wealth to support those values. Indeed, Europe spends at least 25 percent more *per capita* than the U.S. on workfare supports, and three times more on families, according to OECD figures.

In effect, the European workfare support system creates vehicles to help individuals and families better plan for more insecure times in their lives, whether resulting from economic downturn, sickness, disability, old age, or tragic accident. It ensures that people invest in their own future, channeling the funds necessary to pay for the workfare infrastructure that provides a lot more for its middle, working, and poor classes while still maintaining the highest standard of living. And as we have seen, Europe accomplishes all this without undermining its economic competitiveness or the success of its businesses.

2. HEALTHY EUROPE

We saw how Europe's formal and informal health care systems produce quality universal care for a lot less money than the United States spends on our patchwork system, which has left forty-seven million Americans without insurance and has neglected tens of millions more. The U.S. is ranked thirty-seventh in the world in health care, while France is ranked first and most European countries are ranked in the top twenty. Yet contrary to stereotype, many successful nations such as Germany, France, Belgium, Switzerland, and others have health care systems that do not use government-run, single payer, or "socialized" medicine. Instead, they have devised clever "shared responsibility" plans that apportion the financing of health care among employers, employees, and the government, all paying a fair share. They mostly use private doctors and hospitals, they have freedom of choice for patients, and they have private insurance companies too, but with two essential differences compared to America: First, these private insurance companies are *nonprofit* organizations. You don't see mammoth health care corporations like UnitedHealth Group, whose CEO is paid a staggering hundred million dollars in annual compensation. Second, they negotiate prices and fees among all the various health care stakeholders, which keeps the costs down, just as Medicare does.

In short, Europe has wrung the profit motive out of health care and produced a less expensive and more efficient system in the process. This in turn is good for European businesses because it does not expose them to the soaring health care costs that have plagued American businesses and created so much bitter strife between business owners and their employees as owners try to push health care costs onto their employees.

Besides this formal health care system, Europe's approach to better health includes an informal sector composed of a vast network of bicycle and walking paths for transportation and exercise, plus features such as "slow food," organic agriculture, saunas, and a culture that prioritizes health. With all these advantages, Europeans, especially in the west, live longer and have better health than Americans.

3. SUSTAINABLE EUROPE

We explored the many ways Europe is leading the world in figuring out how today's mass societies can enjoy prosperity and freedom in energy-efficient ways that don't harm our environment and endanger the future. Compared with the United States, Europe is preparing better for the coming low carbon emission society and peak oil transitions. Some of the new renewable energy and transportation technologies deployed in Europe—solar, wind, ocean, hydrogen, biofuels, "sea snakes," electric cars, high-speed trains, and more—seem like something straight out of a sci-fi fantasy. But most European improvements have been more mundane; they are just better ways of boosting energy conservation through more efficiency, better mass transportation, and the incorporation of "green" principles into everything from building design and the size of automobile engines to urban planning and the design of toilets. This in turn has made Europe's "ecological footprint" about half that of the United States for the same standard of living. Not only is this new horizon essential for human survival, it also has been a boon to the European economy, creating jobs and new industries that are poised for expansion as the impacts of global climate change deepen.

4. GLOBAL EUROPE

We have seen how a continent that for centuries was wracked by bloody and bitter war has become the leading proponent of a new pragmatic "smart power" approach to peace and sustainable development. This smart power is based on the promotion of regional economic and political unions, with Marshall Plan–like aid, trade, investment, and development. The European Union itself is the best example of this, with its continent of half a billion people having become a remarkably civil place, where formerly bitter enemies who fought against each other for centuries have become "peace and prosperity" partners. Clustered around the European Union are a host of other countries for whom Europe has become the biggest trading partner. All told, the Eurosphere's orbit has pulled countries with two billion inhabitants—nearly a third of the world's population—into concentric rings of economic and political engagement and development.

With America's "hard power" looking increasingly flat-footed, now Europe has begun applying its principles and methods to hot spots around the world, such as China, the Middle East, Russia, and Central Asia. Time will tell if these latter efforts will bear similar fruit, but lessons learned from Europe's bloody history have produced not only an outlook that recognizes what's at stake but also the temperament to bring the many countries of the world together around the challenges of the twenty-first century.

5. PLURALIST EUROPE

We examined how the European Way is founded on unique political, media, and communication institutions that have produced the most advanced, representative democracies the modern world has ever seen. As a reaction to its blood-soaked history, Europe has forged institutions and methods that foster inclusiveness, participation, authentic representation, multiparty democracy, and majoritarian policy based on a consensus of viewpoints. These methods include proportional representation electoral systems, public financing of campaigns, free media time for candidates and parties, universal voter registration, Children's Parliaments, deliberative democracy, and other techniques that foster pluralism and consensus building.

Having multiple parties in their legislatures has ensured that a broad cross section of viewpoints is at the table of political power, participating in the formation of policy. Sometimes the political process can sound like endless bickering, but in the end that debate has produced a broad European consensus that has resulted in a widely shared prosperity. This process has been aided by Europe's various media and communications institutions, which are centered around a well-financed and robust public broadcasting sector (television and radio), a still vibrant newspaper industry, as well as widespread, affordable access to speedy broadband Internet. These in turn have produced the most informed public in the world, which helps ensure that a breadth of opinion is represented in the legislatures, which in turn fosters majoritarian policy that enjoys broad public support.

But the United States is plagued by an antiquated winner-take-all system in which most legislative districts—indeed, entire states—have become one-party fiefdoms with little competition or choice for voters. Low-population and usually conservative states receive vastly more representation per capita in the Senate and in presidential elections, and sensible policy proposals with nationwide support get strangled by Senate filibusters led by conservative senators representing a small proportion of the nation's population. Adding insult to injury, the corporate media vets which candidates and issues the public will hear about, the newspaper industry is on shaky ground, and public broadcasting is poorly funded and lacking in visibility or hard-hitting, BBC-like journalism. Any of these factors acting singly would be worrisome toward the goal of robust and representative democracy; combined, they are deadly, acting as a barrier to the enactment of pragmatic and future-oriented policy.

Consequently, Europe's democracies are better adapted than America's democracy for the demands of representation and policy formation in the twenty-first century. Indeed, Europe's thriving, pluralistic, consensus-seeking democracy is the single most important reason Europeans have been able to harness their capitalist economy for the good of all. It has been the foundation for everything else right and good about the European Way. While the various political institutions of the European Union are lacking in the type of relevancy and transparency exhibited by Europe's national democracies, they are relatively new and very much a work in progress. Whatever their shortcomings, they have not prevented Europe from advancing its social capitalism agenda. Indeed, in their own way they have contributed to it.

Properly understood, all these different components that I have just outlined are intricately linked, like different sides of the same cube. These components, and the values inherent in them, have been incorporated into key fulcrum institutions that have been incubating over the last sixty years. The European system is not a nanny or welfare state, as it has been derided by its critics; it truly is a "workfare state"—it's designed for working people and families who form the backbone of this successful system. There is something intriguing and even uplifting about Europe's ingenious framework for a mass society constructed around a new form of capitalism—what I have called social capitalism—where the steady state economy, the comprehensive workfare supports, and the consensus-seeking democracy function as a single unit, marching in step, to keep as many people as possible productive and enjoying unprecedented levels of economic security and prosperity. Because they have the right democratic institutions to ensure representative government, robust public debate, an informed citizenry, and ultimately policy formation based on a broad consensus of viewpoints, the powerful European economic engine has been harnessed: it produces the wealth that pays for the most advanced human-centered system in the world.

Certainly Europe's prosperity and the funding for its comprehensive workfare supports always are subject to the dips and bumps of the global economic cycle, as they are anywhere, including the United States. No more dramatic example of that was needed than the severe economic crisis that sent the world into a tailspin in the fall of 2008. And it is well known that Europe has its dark underbelly and still has echoes of its ugly fascist past to contend with. As we have seen, the continent faces numerous challenges and threats, including unpredictable energy costs, geopolitical tensions with Russia, Iran, Pakistan, and the Middle East, and competition from low-wage, high-pollution countries such as China and India. Domestically, Europe is trying to cope with integration of its ethnic minorities, immigration, Muslim extremism, and its aging and in some nations declining population. But most national governments have begun enacting various policies to cope with these tensions, tearing a few pages from the 1960s era in the United States. Only time will tell if these efforts let the steam out of the kettle.

No question, at times Europe can look quite messy, lurching from one apparent crisis to another, sometimes resembling a fractious debating society that is more disunited than united. But generally speaking, at the end of the day, Europe gets the job done, and that has been the most salient feature, the most impressive credential, over the past sixty years. Europe has been rising, with innumerable past obstacles and challenges now barely visible in the rearview mirror.

Indeed, comparing Europe with the United States raises fundamental questions: Has America overmilitarized its political economy, becoming the world's RoboCop, spending our nation's bounty on the most powerful war machine in the history of the planet, only to see other nations surpass us in quality of life for their people? Have we geared American society, our citizens, our politics, and our productive capacity toward vanquishing the enemy abroad, even as we fall behind in the battle at home? Have we deregulated our economy too much, resulting in an economic meltdown of historic proportions, and contributing to vast inequality and increasing economic insecurity for tens of millions of Americans? Have we clung too long to a seventeenth-century conception of individual property rights and laissez-faire government that treats wealthy corporations as private individuals, whose property is protected at the expense of the "general welfare"? While the American Way may have been a useful system for the twentieth century, wracked by two world wars followed by the Cold War, will that militarized, deregulated, hyperdrive economy best serve Americans going forward in the twenty-first century, during an age of increasing economic insecurity and an overheating atmosphere?

The United States and Europe face many of the same challenges today, as do all other nations, but the major difference is that Europe has the right institutions to deal with these challenges, while the United States does not. Europe has the transformative institutions necessary to harness capitalism's tremendous capacity to produce wealth and foster a more sustainable, fair, and equitable outcome. Social Europe has struck a new, twenty-first-century balance among liberty, equality, property, justice, and solidarity. But in the United States the social contract has become increasingly moth-eaten, stuck to the flypaper of antiquated institutions, ossified beliefs about the "religion of individualism," and its deregulated Wall Street casino capitalism.

In short, the European Way's model of development, centered around its finely tuned balance of economic and political power and ecological sustainability, has arrived none too soon in this make or break century.

THE NEW "CITY ON THE HILL"

During the ten years I traveled back and forth to Europe to research this book, I sometimes had surprising encounters with perfect strangers who, in their own way, led me further down the path of my discoveries. One day I had such an encounter as I was relaxing in a *platz* in Salzburg, Austria, surrounded by leisurely Europeans settled at tables with festive sunbrellas and colorful tablecloths. Accordion music was wafting through the air along with the sounds of glasses clinking, and the sunlight was streaming through the many pints of different-colored beers and ales, ruby and amber reds, dark rooty browns, and hefeweizen yellows. On this day I was seated in Salzburg's Hagenauerplatz, gazing contemplatively at Mozart's *Geburtshaus*—birthplace—a short distance away, mulling over history, music, the history of music, the wonder of a three-year-old wunderkind playing the harpsichord and composing by the time he was six . . . when my reverie was interrupted by an older, dark-haired gentleman with a Ronald Reagan haircut, slight paunch, big St. Bernard eyes, perhaps in his early sixties.

"American, right?" he said to me in his thick, German-tinged English.

How do they always know, I wondered. I nodded and smiled cordially, hoisting in salute my glass of hefeweizen with a lemon wedge. He was friendly in a gruff sort of way and within minutes had offered his opinions on all manner of subjects. Since this was May 2003, only a few weeks after the U.S. invasion of Baghdad, the conversation soon drifted there. In fact, I had the feeling that's where he had intended it to go all along.

"Who could object to getting rid of Saddam?" he said. "And a half-dozen others like him? But U.S. cannot do it alone. Big mistake."

He puffed on a cigarette with a heavy, curling lower lip. It turned out his name was Matthias. His English was halting but good, and I was later to find out he had learned a lot of his English growing up close to a U.S. military base near Frankfurt, interacting with the soldiers who shopped in his family's store. The conversation soon moved on to other topics, steered by me and my perennial probing of all things European. I was in a philosophical mood, spurred in part by the splendid afternoon, with its sunlight reflecting off the bright yellow of Mozart's house at Number 9 Getreidegasse, and glinting off the fashionable patrons strolling along the bustling alleyway that makes the Hagenauerplatz a great place to people-watch. I tossed Matthias the big question.

What do you think, I asked him, is the main difference between Austrians and Americans?

He kind of laughed, a thick guttural snort. He pulled on his cigarette, his lips gripping the filter, pausing thoughtfully before he responded.

"You know what the difference is, the main difference?" he said. "Between you Americans and Austrians, and Germans and French and Italians too?" He paused dramatically, again drawing heavily on his cigarette.

"As an American, I wonder if you can even imagine what it must be like to live in a country where every person has health care. And a decent retirement. And day care, parental leave, sick leave, education, vacation, job retraining. For every plumber, carpenter, taxi driver, waitress, executive, sales clerk, scientist, musician, poet, nurse, of all ages, income, race, sex, whatever, not worrying about those basic arrangements. Can you imagine what that is like?"

At first I didn't see where he was going with this. He spoke with such passion to point out the obvious. But then suddenly the lightbulb went on. I had never really thought about it before: what impact does it have on an individual's psyche—and by extension on all of society and our feeling of extended family, which is after all the "sticky glue" that holds us all together—to know that certain basics will always be taken care of because you are a stakeholding *member* of that society, entitled to certain benefits? Certainly it is hard for an American, raised as an atomized individual in the "ownership" (i.e., "on your own") society, to step into the shoes of a European and imagine what that sense of security and support must feel like and how it affects your overall outlook.

Matthias squinted his eyes and nodded his head.

"In America, you are so rich," he said. "Why don't you have these things for your people?"

He stared at me with his big St. Bernard eyes, and I suddenly felt defensive. I searched for a response, muttered something about Americans being against big government. But in truth, I didn't have a good response. I often wondered that same thing myself. But Matthias's next point was even more profound.

"Don't you think this has something to do with why America is so violent?"

My blank stare caused him to laugh.

"Look, when everything is taken care of, don't you see how that decreases each person's anxiety and aggression? And how that has an overall effect on all of society?"

A lightbulb went on again. It made complete sense. All these workfare supports aiding individuals and families would lessen not only inequality but also individual anxiety and aggression and, sure, the anxiety and aggression of the overall society as well. And a society in which more individuals have a stake, an investment in its future, is a society in which nonviolence is logical. A society in which so many are not stuck on the lower rungs, and in which individuals on the middle rungs don't have to constantly scamper so fast up the ladder to maintain their place in the world, is a society that can be built more on cooperation, nonviolence, and solidarity. That psyche becomes the foundation for a more consensual society instead of the winner-take-all, "if I win, you lose," dog-eat-dog society we have in the United States.

Not surprisingly, the United States has become plagued by the steady corrosion of its unequal society. Various studies have demonstrated that unequal societies tend to result in more violence, lower levels of trust, less involvement in community life, and more racial and gender discrimination. No wonder the United States is the world's leader in murders and other violent crimes, suicides, and incarceration rates.[1] We spend more money on constructing prisons than we do on universities. In the United States, violence of all kinds—street violence, domestic violence, entertainment violence, official state-sanctioned military violence—has become a way of life, the sea in which we swim.

Later when I reflected on this conversation, I realized what an epiphany it had been. That's when it really struck me what a failure the American Way is. Here we are, the lone remaining superpower, the wealthiest nation in the history of the world, with the most powerful military the world has ever seen, and yet we have not figured out how to ensure that the lives of Americans are not so filled with anxiety and fear. Despite all our wealth and military power, for too many Americans there is no security.

Europeans, meanwhile, have a more stress-free attitude that perhaps can be summed up best in one word, a Danish word—*hygge* (pronounced *hooga*)—which describes a relaxed state of conviviality that involves close friendships and family bonds. One American expat who has lived in Denmark for more than thirty years tried to explain the sentiment. "The gist of it is that you are not supposed to have anything to do except let go," she said, describing a nearly zen timelessness where the present doesn't worry so much about the future.[2] Wrote another American who had been living in the Netherlands, "To comprehend this system is to enter a different state of mind."[3]

Matthias crushed out his cigarette, as if to underscore his final words: "Europe has the right system for its people . . . it's what all nations should strive for . . . to take care of their people. Isn't that obvious?"

His point had penetrated deeply. He had touched on the core of something important, but my defensive comments only served to absolve the United States of any responsibility for having failed to live up to this European standard. In truth, whether and how to take care of its people is a fundamental choice about values and budget priorities that every society has to grapple with. The fact that we have not yet figured out how to extend things like health care, child care, paid parental leave, adequate retirement benefits, paid sick leave, sufficient vacation time, and free (or nearly free) university education to tens of millions of Americans is a sign that something is very askew about the American dream. It shows something warped about our idea of "family values." And when you factor in that Europeans really don't pay more than Americans to receive all of these benefits—and that only the president, members of Congress and their families, and employees of the most prosperous U.S. businesses receive the full range of European-level workfare supports—the tragedy becomes perverse. Just a fraction of the bloated U.S. military budget would pay for all of this. Why is this so hard? What's an economy for, anyhow?

Flash forward to February 2008, to a day I was visited by two leaders of Sweden's Liberal Party, one of the four parties in the governing center-right coalition, which achieved a majority in the 2006 election. They sat in my living room and we had a freewheeling discussion about American politics and the differences between Sweden and the United States. Many Europeans had been following the U.S. presidential primaries with great interest. Barack Obama had generated excitement in Europe, as he had in the United States. One of my Swedish guests remarked about how exciting American politics seemed compared with Sweden's, since the night before he had watched Obama and Hillary Clinton on TV, slugging it out over the merits of their health care proposals.

"Both of them put forward their views, and there was a passion there, a spark, that often is missing from our politics and our politicians," complained Per.

But then his brow scrunched up. "Of course, we don't debate health care in Sweden like you do here, because we already *have* health care. There's not so much to debate there in any major way."

His colleague Peter chimed in. "I guess that's true of most of the political issues you fight about here in the U.S. We in Sweden already *have* what you are still fighting to get. I guess our politicians just don't have as much to fight over, so compared to you, our politics seem dull."

"Nothing like lousy politicians and unpopular policies like an expensive war in Iraq to drive up voter interest," laughed Per.

No question, the political leaders of Europe tend not to be flashy like some American leaders; they don't have the soaring oratory of Barack Obama, the stirring themes of Ronald Reagan, or the vitality of a JFK—they just get the job done. For decades now, they have made sure that all their countrypeople enjoy a level of economic security that only a handful of Americans ever achieve. That's something no American president has ever accomplished.

Yet despite Europe's impressive accomplishments, many Europeans don't view themselves as riding some global crest. I have found a fair number of them, especially the Germans and the French, to be prone to excessive bouts of gloominess and pessimism whenever they experience cutbacks in their extremely generous benefits, however slight, rather than counting their remaining blessings. What psychologists know as "loss aversion" makes people more fearful of what they might lose than satisfied with what they have. Nevertheless, the European consensus has coalesced around a broad agreement over the foundations of the European Way. What's left to do is to fine-tune that consensus and incorporate it into the various levels of fulcrum institutions, engaging in what President John F. Kennedy once called the "practical management of a modern economy" in "keeping a great economic machinery moving ahead." That involves adjusting and tinkering with their steady state economy to grow not too fast but not too slowly. That's a rather technocratic, unglamorous job, one fit more for an engineer, a systems designer, or an economist than a charismatic political evangelist. Sure enough, that's how many of Europe's politicians come off, as some kind of bland technocrats, which does not exactly stir the public and leads to much griping about faceless government bureaucrats and their directives.

But those politicians, standing on the mighty shoulders of giants like Monnet, Churchill, and Adenauer, have produced the most successful human-centered system the world has even known. The United States set the original standard, giving birth in the post–World War II era to the middle class and the sunny prospect of an enjoyable life, and people all around the world tried to follow our lead. Now Europe has taken that torch and ascended with it to a new mountaintop. In reaching this pinnacle, Europe has settled many of the questions and doubts that continue to plague the United States, as well as most of the rest of the world. Just as the 1776 generation in America gave birth to an idea, the most innovative and exciting "way" of the late eighteenth and early nineteenth centuries that was chronicled by Tocqueville, Lieber, and others and was destined to spread and revolutionize the world, so too has Europe given birth to a new revolution: the next stage of development for a modern mass society. Europe has been the chief architect of the crucial fulcrum institutions that form the foundation for this new "way," injected with a new understanding of the necessary human-centered priorities of the twenty-first century. It has set a new standard that now other nations will try and emulate.

In 1970, French intellectual iconoclast Jean-François Revel defied convention and the European left by declaring, "The revolution of the twentieth century will take place in the United States. It is only there that it can happen."[4] At the time, his polemic raised eyebrows as well as hackles. Now, over thirty years later in the twenty-first century, things have come full circle. The quality-of-life advances in the areas important to most people's lives are taking place in Europe. Indeed, it is no exaggeration to say that the hope of tens of millions of Americans currently frozen out of the American dream lies in the adoption of an American version of the European Way. It's not always clear that Europe is even aware of its new leadership role, or wants it or is ready for it; but Europe's reluctance is part of its appeal, especially compared with America's messianic impulses and China's regular bouts of clumsy thuggery. But make no mistake about it, when it comes to finding solutions to the twenty-first-century problems that plague our world—economic insecurity, global climate change, health care, political disenfranchisement, geopolitical posturing, the divide between rich and poor—Europe is the brightest beacon penetrating the chiaroscuro of the storm. In short, *Europe is the new City on the Hill.*

So now, whenever I am in Europe, whether in Paris, Amsterdam, Brussels, Stockholm, London, Rome, Prague, Oslo, Berlin, Vienna, Barcelona, Ljubljana, Budapest, Zagreb, or elsewhere, at some point in my journey I always make a point to stand on a street corner and stop and look around me at all the people milling about. I watch them for a few minutes, take a deep breath, and remembering Matthias's words, I think to myself, "Everyone I see, all those people walking by, no matter their age, gender, religion, or income, has the right to go to a doctor whenever they are sick. And all those I see have a decent retirement pension waiting for them, and parents can bring their children to day care, or stay home to take care of themselves or their sick loved one, and get paid parental leave and job retraining if they need it, and an affordable university education." Of course, not every European country, or every region or city within each country, lives up to every aspect of this menu 100 percent of the time, particularly since economic fluctuations will always result in contractions and expansions of the social agenda. That's to be expected. But all of them, even the poorer countries among them, achieve a far higher level of success than the United States can muster, and the arc of their trajectory is clear.

That is the "concept" of Europe, and you have to admit that's a pretty wonderful thing, a tremendous act of love and commitment between all of the European peoples and their governments.

As Matthias said that day, sure, we can argue over the future and whether it's sustainable. And we can continue to debate whether Europeans pay more in taxes or Americans pay less or whether Americans just don't get as much as Europeans for all the out-of-pocket expenses and taxes we pay. But at the end of the day, the clever Europeans have crafted a pretty amazing and beautiful scene, something that we have not yet figured out how to do in the United States. Their social contract is still vibrant and durable, and that's worth contemplating as I stand on street corners in Europe, with the memory of Matthias's words ringing in my ears: "In America, you are so rich—why don't you have these things for your people?"

Notes

PREFACE

1. Leigh Phillips, "Merkel and Sarkozy Call for Global 'Economic Security' Council," *EU Observer,* January 9, 2009, http://euobserver.com/9/27373; Emma Vandore, "Sarkozy, Merkel, Blair Call for New Capitalism," Associated Press, January 8, 2008.

2. Bruce Crumley, "Europe's Conservatives Pooh-Pooh the Free Market," Time.com, September 26, 2008, www.time.com/time/world/article/0,8599 ,1844919,00.html?xid=rss-world.

3. Bruce W. Jentleson and Steven Weber, "America's Hard Sell," *Foreign Policy,* November–December 2008, 44.

4. The members of the G-20 are Argentina, Australia, Brazil, Britain, Canada, China, France, Germany, India, Indonesia, Italy, Japan, Mexico, Russia, Saudi Arabia, South Africa, South Korea, Turkey, and the United States. The European Union is also a member, represented by the rotating council presidency and the European Central Bank.

5. Douglas Rediker, "Obama Must Lead the Way on Global Financial Reform," *European Affairs,* Winter 2009.

6. Online interview with Bruce W. Jentleson and Steven Weber, *Foreign Policy,* December 2008, www.foreignpolicy.com/story/cms.php?story_id=4528.

7. Joellen Perry, "Europe Basks as U.S.-Style Capitalism Draws Fire," *Wall Street Journal,* January 30, 2009, http://online.wsj.com/article/SB123327936 218431707.html.

8. See, for example, Herman Daly, *Toward a Steady-State Economy* (New York: W.H. Freeman, 1973), and Herman Daly, *Beyond Growth: The Economics of Sustainable Development* (Boston: Beacon Press, 1997). Daly has written: "The facts are plain and uncontestable: the biosphere is finite, nongrowing, closed (except for the constant input of solar energy), and constrained

by the laws of thermodynamics. Any subsystem, such as the economy, must at some point cease growing and adapt itself to a dynamic equilibrium, something like a steady state. Birth rates must equal death rates, and production rates of commodities must equal depreciation rates." Herman Daly, "Economics in a Full World," *Scientific American* 293, no. 3 (September 2005), http://sef.umd.edu/files/ScientificAmerican_Daly_05.pdf.

INTRODUCTION

1. In 2007, Europe spent $319 billion on military spending, compared to China's $58 billion (a figure that is disputed; some experts believe China spends twice that amount) and U.S. expenditure of $547 billion. But the U.S. figure does not include spending for operations in the Iraq and Afghan wars, which amounts to another estimated $1 to $3 trillion, nor does it include huge expenditures by the Department of Homeland Security, the National Security Agency, the CIA, the Veterans Administration, or the parts of NASA and the Department of Energy for military-related activities.

2. Joby Warrick and Walter Pincus, "Reduced Dominance Is Predicted for U.S.," *Washington Post,* September 10, 2008.

3. Fareed Zakaria, *The Post-American World* (New York: W. W. Norton, 2008). Jim Hoagland, "A Gates-Style Thaw," *Washington Post,* December 16, 2007. Also see Parag Khanna, *The Second World: Empires and Influence in the New Global Order* (New York: Random House, 2008); Fred Kaplan, *Daydream Believers: How a Few Grand Ideas Wrecked American Power* (New York: Wiley, 2008); Nancy Soderberg, *The Superpower Myth* (New York: Wiley, 2005); Roger Burbach and Jim Tarbell, *Imperial Overstretch: George W. Bush and the Hubris of Empire* (London: Zed Books, 2004); and Charles Kupchan, *The End of the American Era: U.S. Foreign Policy and the Geopolitics of the Twenty-first Century* (New York: Alfred A. Knopf, 2002).

4. Jesse Drucker, "Richest Americans See Their Income Share Grow," *Wall Street Journal,* July 23, 2008.

5. *Chindia* is a portmanteau word used by various analysts and pundits to refer to China and India together, since they embody many similar qualities, including rapidly growing low-wage, high-pollution economies. See, for example, Jagdish N. Sheth, *Chindia Rising* (New Delhi: McGraw Hill India, 2007), and Peter Sondergaard, "Do You Have a 'Chindia' Strategy?" *Forbes,* August 13, 2007, www.forbes.com/opinions/2007/08/05/india-gartner-chindia-oped-cx_psg_0813chindia.html.

6. Robert Frank and Philip Cook, *The Winner-Take-All Society* (New York: Free Press, 1995).

7. Jeffrey Kopstein and Sven Steinmo, eds., *Growing Apart? America and Europe in the Twenty-first Century* (Cambridge and New York: Cambridge University Press, 2008), 13n13.

8. Alexis de Tocqueville, *Democracy in America* (New York: D. Appleton and Co., 1904), vol. 1: 241.

ONE. THE RISE OF THE EUROPEAN WAY

1. Khanna, *The Second World*, 312.

2. The ten countries that joined the European Union in 2004 are Poland, Hungary, the Czech Republic, Slovakia, Lithuania, Latvia, Estonia, Cyprus, Slovenia, and Malta. In 2007, Romania and Bulgaria joined.

3. Andrew Moravcsik, "Rumors of Europe's Demise are Greatly Exaggerated," *Washington Note,* June 8, 2006, www.thewashingtonnote.com/archives/001452.php.

4. Charles Kupchan, "The End of the West," *Atlantic Monthly,* November 2002, 42.

5. David Wessel, "As Rich-Poor Gap Widens in the U.S., Class Mobility Stalls," *Wall Street Journal,* May 13, 2005; also see *The Economist,* "Middle of the Class," July 14, 2005.

6. Doug Bandow, "Defense Budget Black Hole," Center for Defense Information, February 20, 2007, www.cdi.org/program/issue/document.cfm?DocumentID=3840&IssueID=98&StartRow=1&ListRows=10&appendURL=&Orderby=DateLastUpdated&ProgramID=37&issueID=98. According to CDI, "American expenditures are roughly twice those of the rest of NATO, 4.5 times those of China, and 8.5 times those of Russia. Washington spends as much as the next 20 countries combined, most of which are allies and friends. Indeed, the U.S. devotes almost three times as much to the military as do all of its potential adversaries combined: China, Russia, North Korea, Iran, Syria, Burma, Venezuela, and a handful of others."

7. Many military experts and defense spending critics say that the United States military is increasingly ill-prepared for the types of wars that will most likely be fought in the future, namely insurgencies led by nonstate actors, as in Afghanistan and Iraq. For years the Department of Defense has been squandering staggering levels of military appropriations on aircraft, ships, and futuristic weapons systems that have little relevance to America's national defense. The United States has 761 military bases in other people's countries, and the Navy, with its eleven large aircraft-carrier battle groups, is, as conservative defense critic William Lind has written, "still structured to fight the Imperial Japanese Navy." Chalmers Johnson, "The Looming Crisis at the Pentagon: How Taxpayers Finance Fantasy Wars," TomDispatch.com, February 2, 2009.

8. In the aftermath of 9/11, the Bush administration increased defense spending by about 15 percent per year. Just the increase in U.S. defense spending—about $45 billion annually—was greater than the total annual defense budget of either France or Britain, the two biggest military spenders in Europe. T. R. Reid, *The United States of Europe: The New Superpower and the End of American Supremacy* (New York: Penguin Press, 2004), 180.

9. The Iraq war has cost at least $1.5 trillion and eventually will cost over $3 trillion, according to Nobel laureate economist Joseph Stiglitz. See Joseph E. Stiglitz, "The Economic Consequences of Mr. Bush," *Vanity Fair,* December 2007, www.vanityfair.com/politics/features/2007/12/bush200712, and Joseph Stiglitz and Linda Bilmes, "The Three Trillion-Dollar War," *Times of London,* February 23, 2008.

10. Reid, *The United States of Europe,* 180.

11. According to the Congressional Budget Office, U.S. expenditure for Social Security is about 4.4 percent of GDP, and Medicare and Medicaid combined are about 4.2 percent of GDP. See www.cbo.gov/ftpdoc.cfm?index=5530 &type=0&sequence=1 and "The Medicare Fiscal Time-Bomb," *Washington Times* editorial, July 16, 2007, www.washingtontimes.com/article/20070716/ EDITORIAL/107160002/1013/editorial. Also see Tom Curry, "Long-Term Budget View May Surprise You," MSNBC, February 5, 2007, www.msnbc.msn .com/id/16928315. Military watchdog groups claim that the share of the budget consumed by the military is actually much higher because of hidden costs, such as expenditures for the military portion from other federal departments like Homeland Security, Department of Energy expenditures on nuclear weapons, and the like, as well as annual expenditures on "past military," such as veterans benefits and the interest paid on the national debt that can be attributed to past military spending. Using calculations like these, the War Resisters League has estimated military outlays to be 54 percent of the annual federal budget. See "Where Your Income Tax Money Really Goes," War Resisters League, www.warresisters.org/piechart.htm.

12. David Leonhardt, "What $1.2 Trillion Can Buy," New York Times, *New York Times,* January 17, 2007, http://www.nytimes.com/2007/01/17/ business/17leonhardt.html?_r=1&ei=5090&oref=slogin. The figures are contained in accompanying graphic at http://www.nytimes.com/imagepages/2007/ 01/17/business/20070117_LEONHARDT _ GRAPHIC.html.

13. Andrew Revkin, "Budgets Falling in Race to Fight Global Warming," *New York Times,* October 30, 2006.

14. Chalmers Johnson, "The Looming Crisis at the Pentagon: How Taxpayers Finance Fantasy Wars," TomDispatch.com, February 2, 2009.

15. Khanna, *The Second World,* xxiv.

16. WWF, "Living Plant Report," World Wildlife Fund, Gland, Switzerland, October 2008, http://assets.panda.org/downloads/living_planet_report_2008.pdf.

17. *Codetermination* is an economic arrangement that is used to some degree in most European countries and that brings a level of democratic representation and accountability to corporations that Americans can scarce imagine. Codetermination consists of two basic components: supervisory boards and works councils. *Supervisory boards* require anywhere from a third to half of the boards of directors of major corporations to be elected by workers; *works councils* are quasi-labor organizations that allow workers to have significant input at the workplace level into their wages, benefits, amount of vacation time, and working conditions. *Flexicurity* is the economic system used in Denmark and increasingly in other European economies that combines an "easy hire—easy fire" policy with massive investment in job retraining so that workers dislocated by declining industries can be quickly transitioned into new employment. *Proportional representation* is a classification of electoral systems that foster multiparty democracy and give European voters a range of political choices unknown to frustrated American voters. This in turn tends to result in higher voter turnout, because voters have more meaningful choices to vote for at the ballot box.

18. Leonard, *Why Europe Will Run the 21st Century,* 4. When Mark Leonard made this point in his book in 2005, only four million entries came up, so the number of joint references to "Europe" and "crisis" has grown exponentially in just a few years.

19. Steven Pearlstein, "Old Europe Unprepared for New Battles," *Washington Post,* July 21, 2004; Robert Samuelson, "The End of Europe," *Washington Post,* June 15, 2005; Fareed Zakaria, "The Decline and Fall of Europe," *Washington Post,* February 14, 2006; George Weigel, "Is Europe Dying? Notes on a Crisis of Civilizational Morale," History News Network, hnn.us/articles/12295.html, August 15, 2005; Steven Pearlstein, "Western Europe Is Cursed by Philosophy of Economy," *Washington Post,* July 8, 2005; "The Decline of France," *Wall Street Journal,* March 21, 2006; Naomi Klein, "The Rise of the Fortress Continent," *The Nation,* February 3, 2003; Floyd Norris, "Europe Isn't Working, but Investors Are Not as Worried as the Politicians," *New York Times,* May 17, 2005; Peter Gumbel, "Will Europe Ever Work?" *Time* (Europe), April 9, 2006; Associated Press, "Reforms in Europe Needed, Most Say," *St. Petersburg Times,* April 3, 2006; Frida Ghitis, "Europe's Long Vacation Is Ending," *Philadelphia Inquirer,* June 11, 2006; "Impasse in German Politics Reflects 'Political Crisis' Paralyzing Europe," interview with Charles Kupchan by Bernard Gwertzman, Council on Foreign Relations, www.cfr.org/publication/8924/kupchan.html, September 28, 2005; Fareed Zakaria, "What's Wrong with Europe," *Newsweek,* June 13, 2005; Charles Kupchan, "Europe Turns Back the Clock: The Dream of a European Union Is Imperiled by a Surge in Nationalism," *Los Angeles Times,* May 30, 2006; Niall Ferguson, "Why America Outpaces Europe (Clue: The God Factor)," *New York Times,* August 11, 2003.

20. The article kept out of the U.S. print edition was Emily Flynn Vencat, "The Great Job Machine: Despite Its Laggard Reputation, Europe Continues to Grow Faster, and Create More Jobs, than America." *Newsweek International,* www.msnbc.msn.com/id/15674093/site/newsweek, November 20, 2006.

21. The article kept out of the U.S. print edition was Kerry Capell, "Is Europe's Health Care Better?" BusinessWeek.com, June 13, 2007, www.businessweek.com/globalbiz/content/jun2007/gb20070613_921562.htm?chan=globalbiz_europe+index+page_economics+%2Bamp%3B+policy.

22. Overblown alarms about Europe's imminent decline are reminiscent of the "yellow peril scare" in the American media during the early 1990s, when Japan supposedly was the future and the United States was written off. Yet the menace of the Rising Sun turned out to be only so much political and Hollywood bunk, since within a few years Japan plunged into a decade-long recession.

23. Richard E. Smith, "Economy Slumps to 'the Razor's Edge,'" *International Herald Tribune,* April 1, 1992, www.iht.com/articles/1992/04/01/econ.php. The *International Herald Tribune* is published by the *New York Times* and republishes many *Times* articles.

24. Ibid.; Brandon Mitchener, "Economy Likely to Remain Sluggish: Optimism in Germany May Prove Unfounded," *International Herald Tribune,* January 14, 1994, www.iht.com/articles/1994/01/14/uphill.php.

25. Thomas Grose, "Sluggish EU Economies Foil Euro," *USA Today*, June 8, 1999.

26. Perhaps no American journalist or columnist has so consistently missed the mark as the *Washington Post*'s Steven Pearlstein. In various columns throughout 2004–5 he ranted about "the undeniable crisis in the European economy," stating, "The economies of Western Europe are cursed"; crowed about "the latest victory for Anglo-American capitalism over the more civilized 'social market' preferred by Western Europe"; and ridiculously tut-tutted, "The thing you have to understand about the French is that they brush their teeth in the kitchen sink. They simply don't have the material things we have." The latter preposterous claim unleashed a firestorm of responses on French blogs refuting his claim, with one respondent tartly replying, "Places where I have seen homes without plumbing include North Carolina, Mississippi and Louisiana. 1.95 million people in the U.S. do not have such plumbing." See http://superfrenchie.com/?p=671. As Europe's economy rebounded and refuted his claims, Pearlstein went unrepentingly quiet on the subject. See Pearlstein, "Old Europe Unprepared for New Battles"; and Pearlstein, "Western Europe Is Cursed by Philosophy of Economy."

TWO. THE CAPITALIST ENGINE
THAT HUFFED AND PUFFED . . .

1. All gross domestic product figures and some population figures are from the International Monetary Fund's World Economic and Financial Surveys, World Economic Outlook Database, April 2009 edition, www.imf.org/external/pubs/ft/weo/2009/01/weodata/index.aspx.

2. Tim Hepher and Emmanuel Jarry, "Sarkozy Tackles Hu on Yuan and Human Rights," Reuters, November 26, 2007. The European Union surpassed the United States and Japan as China's largest trading partner in 2004, and China is the union's second largest trading partner after the United States. The European Union imports more from China than anywhere else, with trade volumes with China doubling since 2003. Linda Yueh, "Reflections on the EU-China Economic Relationship," *Social Europe Journal*, Spring 2008.

3. Dan O'Brien and Aurore Wanlin, "Reasons to Be Cheerful about Europe," *Financial Times*, November 24, 2006.

4. Quoted in Stephen Foley, "Anguish on Wall Street as European Stock Markets Push US Off Pole Position," *The Independent* (U.K.), April 4, 2007.

5. "Europe and America: An Economic Union," *E.U. Focus* (special E.U. advertising supplement of the European Union), July 2005, 1.

6. While there are twenty-seven member nations in the European Union, only sixteen of these nations use the euro as their currency. Those sixteen are Austria, Belgium, Cyprus, Finland, France, Germany, Greece, Ireland, Italy, Luxembourg, Malta, the Netherlands, Portugal, Slovakia, Slovenia, and Spain. These countries comprise the "Eurozone" or "Euro Area," which together have some 326 million people. In addition, over the next several years many of the new E.U. countries from central and east Europe will also begin using the euro.

7. According to the *Wall Street Journal*, a Goldman Sachs report found that from 1998 to 2008, gross domestic product growth in the euro currency zone averaged 2.2 percent per year, a bit less than the U.S.'s 2.6 percent though well above Japan's 1.1 percent. But when measured on a *per capita* basis—a more refined measurement of actual growth—euro-zone growth was greater than U.S. growth over that period, coming in at 1.8 percent per year compared with the U.S., at 1.6 percent. Joellen Perry, "Europe Basks as U.S.-Style Capitalism Draws Fire Article," *Wall Street Journal*, January 30, 2009, http://online.wsj.com/article/SB123327936218431707.html. Also see Jack Ewing, "Europe's Locomotive Is Back on Track," BusinessWeek.com, www.businessweek.com/globalbiz/content/oct2006/gb20061010_457604.htm ?campaign_id=eu_Oct11&link_position=link34, October 10, 2006; and John Schmitt, "Whatever Happened to the American Jobs Machine?" Center for Economic and Policy Research, Issue Brief, October 2006. On productivity, see Dean Baker, "Productivity: Is the Boom Over?" *In These Times*, March 15, 2007; and Simon Kennedy, "Trichet, Like Greenspan, May Be Aided by Productivity," *Bloomberg News*, October 16, 2007, www.bloomberg.com/apps/ news?pid=20601085&sid=aOEGFx.hBXWM&refer=news. Productivity is notoriously difficult to calculate, but economist Dean Baker reported in 2007 that the U.S. rate of productivity growth had declined dramatically from 2.5 percent per year to 1.5 percent, the lowest in more than a decade. Morgan Stanley economists calculated that productivity increased in the dozen Euro-nations at an annual rate of 2.6 percent in the first half of 2006, double the pace of the prior six years. On trade imbalances, see Report from the European Policy Centre, "European Growth and Jobs in 2007," January 18, 2007, www.theepc.be/ en/er.asp?TYP=ER&LV=293&see=y&t=2&PG=ER/EN/detail&l=&AI=668. Also see Robert J. Samuelson, "The Economy's Rebalancing Act," *Washington Post*, December 20, 2006.

8. World Economic Forum, "Global Competitiveness Report 2008–2009," www.weforum.org/pdf/gcr/2008/rankings.pdf. The top ten rankings were: the United States, Switzerland, Denmark, Sweden, Singapore, Finland, Germany, the Netherlands, Japan, and Canada.

9. All business rankings are taken from *Fortune* magazine's Global Fortune 500 rankings, 2009, located at http://money.cnn.com/magazines/fortune/ global500/2009/index.html.

10. "Europe and America: An Economic Union," 1, 4, 8.

11. Tim Reason, "America for Sale," *CFO Magazine*, February 2, 2006, www.cfo.com/article.cfm/5435380/c_8435337.

12. Figure provided by the International Air Transport Association. David Armstrong, "Ryanair's Proposal Could Lower Fares," *San Francisco Chronicle*, April 13, 2007.

13. Neil King Jr., Greg Hitt, and Jeffrey Ball, "Oil Battle Sets Showdown over China," *Wall Street Journal*, June 24, 2005; and Howard W. French and Norimitsu Onishi, "Economic Ties Binding Japan to Rival China," *New York Times*, October 31, 2005.

14. According to data from the U.S. Bureau of Labor Statistics, private employers in the United States spent on average 9.9 percent of payroll on health

insurance contributions in 2006, and if you include the cost of contributions to Medicare hospital insurance, that figure rises to 11.3 percent. But anywhere from 40 to 50 percent of all private employers do not provide health insurance for their employees, so when those uncovered workers are excluded, the average cost per worker in firms that offer health insurance is 11.5 percent of payroll (not including Medicare contributions). Also, many workers in firms that offer health insurance are not eligible for health insurance or do not enroll. So when these workers are excluded as well, the average cost per enrolled worker is 18.3 percent of payroll. Len M. Nichols and Sarah Axeen, "Employer Health Costs in a Global Economy: A Competitive Disadvantage for U.S. Firms," a study by the New America Foundation, Health Care program, May 2008, 8, www.newamerica.net/files/EMPLOYER%20HEALTH%20COSTS%20IN%20A%20GLOBAL%20ECONOMY.pdf.

15. Ibid. The percentage of payroll for each country follows: Germany, 6.7 percent; the United Kingdom, 1.9 percent; France, 12.8 percent; Canada, 4.5 percent; and Japan, 3.7 percent. The gap between the United States and these other countries is actually even greater than it looks. For example, the French rate finances much more than just health benefits; it also pays for sick leave, maternity leave, disability, and survivor benefits. Similarly, the German rate also finances sick leave and maternity leave.

16. Nick Carey, "US Companies Seen Warming to Idea of Health Reform," Reuters, June 4, 2007. See also Lee Hudson Teslik, "Healthcare Costs and U.S. Competitiveness," Council on Foreign Relations Backgrounder, May 14, 2007; and Jonathan Cohn, "What's the One Thing Big Business and the Left Have in Common?" *New York Times Magazine*, April 1, 2007.

17. William Drozdiak, "A Culture of Shared Sacrifice," *New York Times*, from "Europe's Solution: Take More Time Off," March 29, 2009, http://roomfordebate.blogs.nytimes.com/2009/03/29/europes-solution-take-more-time-off.

18. Guardian Unlimited, "New M&S Stores Powered by Windmill," September 10, 2007, http://business.guardian.co.uk/story/0,,2166110,00.html?gusrc=rss&feed=networkfront.

19. David Roberts, "Ikea: Who Says Big Retail Can't Be Good for the Environment?" *Grist Magazine*, March 1, 2007, www.alternet.org/envirohealth/48578/.

20. Cogen Europe, "What Is Cogeneration?" www.cogen.org/about/what_is_CHP.htm; also see "Cogeneration," by UNEP Division of Technology, Industry and Economics—Energy and Ozone Action Unit, www.cogen.org/Downloadables/Publications/Fact_Sheet_CHP.pdf.

21. "Ikea—Carugate Outlet," Heat and Power: Continuous Generation of Heat and Electric Power, www.heat-and-power.com/en/referenze_7.htm.

22. "World Survey of Decentralized Energy, 2006," World Alliance for Decentralized Energy (WADE), 31, www.localpower.org/documents_pub/report_worldsurvey06.pdf.

23. Stanley Reed, "Would $100 Oil Slam the Global Economy?" *BusinessWeek*, July 27, 2006, www.businessweek.com/globalbiz/content/jul2006/gb20060726_793734.htm?campaign_id=eu_Aug2&link_position=link21.

24. Jack Ewing, "Making Good Money Out of Old Plants," *BusinessWeek,* November 20, 2006, 50.

25. Gail Edmondson, "Detroit East: Eastern Europe Is Becoming the World's Newest Car Capital," *BusinessWeek,* July 25, 2005, www.business week.com/magazine/content/05_30/b3944003.htm?campaign_id=nws_europ_jul19& link_position=link1.

26. Katinka Barysch, "Europe's New Division of Labour," Centre for European Reform, *CER Bulletin* 48 (June/July 2006), www.cer.org.uk/arti cles/48_barysch.html.

27. David Rocks, Katerina Zachovalova, and Nichola Saminather, "The Chinese Discover Central Europe," BusinessWeek.com, December 28, 2006, www.businessweek.com/globalbiz/content/dec2006/gb20061228_552972 .htm?campaign_id=eu_Jan4&link_position=link23.

28. Marion Kraske and Jan Puhl, "Poland Is the New Germany," Spiegel Online, November 28, 2005, http://service.spiegel.de/cache/international/spie gel/0,1518,387922,00.html.

29. Barysch, "Europe's New Division of Labour."

30. Ibid.

31. Ralph Atkins, "Germany Sees Surge in Exports to East Europe," *Financial Times,* June 8, 2004.

32. The gross domestic product figure is from the International Monetary Fund's World Economic and Financial Surveys, World Economic Outlook Database, September 2006 edition, www.imf.org/external/pubs/ft/weo/2006/02/data/index.aspx.

33. "Pay in Europe 2007: Pay Gap between Europe's Richest and Poorest Countries Has Fallen Significantly over the Last Six Years," *Finfacts Ireland,* March 27, 2007, www.finfacts.com/irelandbusinessnews/publish/article_100 09569.shtml.

34. Carol Matlack, "Scared Of China? Not Europe," BusinessWeek.com, February 9 2004, www.businessweek.com/magazine/content/04_06/b38690 72_mz054.htm.

35. Carter Doughtery, "Europe May Thrive Despite the U.S.," *New York Times,* December 26, 2006, www.nytimes.com/2006/12/26/business/world business/26euroecon.html?ex=1167800400&en=8c4b562707094d07&ei=5040 &partner=MOREOVERNEWS.

36. Richard Milne, "Germany's Engineering Groups Shrug Off Financial Crisis," *Financial Times,* April 23, 2008.

37. Jeremy Rifkin, *The European Dream: How Europe's Vision of the Future Is Quietly Eclipsing the American Dream* (New York: Jeremy P. Tarcher/Penguin, 2004), 69.

38. "La Vie Impossible," *BusinessWeek,* August 14, 2006, www.business week.com/magazine/content/06_33/b3997064.htm?campaign_id=eu_Aug9& link_position=link20.

39. See the Web site of the World Economic Forum, www.weforum.org; for the world rankings 2008–9, see www.weforum.org/pdf/gitr/2008/Rankings .pdf. The top ten rankings were held by Denmark, Sweden, the United States,

Singapore, Switzerland, Finland, Iceland, Norway, the Netherlands, and Canada.

40. Kerry Capell, "A Midnight Sun for Biotech," August 17, 2007, Spiegel Online, www.spiegel.de/international/business/0,1518,500438,00.html.

41. Bill Rigby, "Airbus CEO Dropped Trousers for Plane Deal: Book," Reuters, January 15, 2007; also see Reid, *The United States of Europe*, 135.

42. Reid, *The United States of Europe*, 134–35.

43. Douglas Rediker and Heidi Crebo-Rediker, "Don't Pick on Sovereign Wealth," *Wall Street Journal Europe*, July 17, 2008.

44. Reid, *The United States of Europe*, 134–35.

45. David Holley, "France Wins Contest to Develop World's First Fusion Power Reactor," *Los Angeles Times*, June 29, 2005.

46. Reid, *The United States of Europe*, 123–24.

47. Bernhard Winkler, "Europe's Space Probe Wings by Mars," Reuters, February 24, 2007. In February 2007 the ESA's Rosetta probe swooped past Mars, gathering important data and completing a key maneuver in its ten-year mission to meet a distant comet to gather data on the origins of the universe. Another Martian probe actually landed on the surface, digging up some Martian soil and returning it to Earth for analysis.

48. Because of Galileo's potential military applications, especially with China's involvement, the Defense Department threatened at one point to shoot Galileo satellites out of the sky if they were suspected of putting American lives at risk. But that has only cemented European determination, now treating Galileo as a matter of its own sovereignty. See Ambrose Evans-Pritchard, "EU Dispute as China Arms Ban Stays in Force," *Telegraph*, December 9, 2004; and Reid, *The United States of Europe*, 142.

49. S. Derek Turner, "Broadband Reality Check II: The Truth behind America's Digital Decline," *Free Press*, August 2006, 8, www.freepress.net/docs/bbrc2-final.pdf; John Borland, "Estonia Sets Shining Wi-Fi Example," CNet News.com, November 1, 2005, http://news.com.com/Estonia+sets+shining+Wi-Fi+example/2010–7351_3–5924673.html?tag=html.alert.

50. Blaine Harden, "Japan's Warp-Speed Ride to Internet Future," *Washington Post*, August 29, 2007, www.washingtonpost.com/wp-dyn/content/article/2007/08/28/AR2007082801990_pf.html; Esme Vos, "100 Mbps for 30 Euros in Paris," Muniwireless.com, August 31, 2007, www.muniwireless.com/article/articleview/6367/1/2. France, Japan, and other nations are offering broadband access with typical speeds of 100 megabytes per second, whereas in the U.S. typical speeds are 2.5 to 3.0 megabytes per second.

51. Paul Krugman, "The French Connections," *New York Times*, July 23, 2007.

52. Personal communication.

53. Heidi Crebo-Rediker and Douglas Rediker, "Financing America's Infrastructure: Putting Global Capital to Work," a policy brief of the Global Strategic Finance Initiative, New America Foundation, June 8, 2008, 6, www.newamerica.net/files/Financing_America_Infrastructure.PDF.

54. Ibid. Under covered bonds, "loans are made by a bank to fund infrastructure projects such as roads, hospitals, schools or utilities. These loans

are pooled and sold to investors as a large, liquid covered bond, which is then traded on the markets with other such bonds." This allows a small amount of government money to leverage huge amounts of private capital.

55. In fact, while large private U.S. investors often remain on the sidelines of the U.S. municipal markets, they have been big investors in public sector covered bonds issued by European banks like Depfa Bank.

56. Crebo-Rediker and Rediker, "Financing America's Infrastructure."

57. Many U.S. banks already actively participate in the European covered bond markets through their European operations. Some U.S. banks, such as Washington Mutual and Bank of America, have issued their own covered bonds backed by their U.S. mortgage portfolios and sold them in the European market.

58. American Society of Civil Engineers, *Report Card for America's Infrastructure* (Reston, VA: ASCE, 2005), www.asce.org/reportcard/2005/index_2005.cfm.

59. Irwin Stelzer, "US regulators run to catch up with EU," *Financial Times,* May 27, 2009, http://www.ft.com/cms/s/0/a0a5cb5c-4b02-11de-87c2-00144 feabdco.html.

60. Lyndsey Layton, "Chemical Law Has Global Impact: E.U.'s New Rules Forcing Changes by U.S. Firms," *Washington Post,* June 12, 2008.

61. Quoted in Mark Schapiro, "Toxic Toys," *The Nation,* November 5, 2007, www.thenation.com/doc/20071105/schapiro.

THREE. EUROPE'S SECRET ADVANTAGE

1. Jonas Pontusson, *Inequality and Prosperity: Social Europe vs. Liberal America* (Ithaca, NY, and London: Cornell University Press, 2005), 115.

2. According to German law, any company with more than five hundred employees must set aside one-third of the seats on its supervisory board for employee representatives. In the coal and steel industries, companies with more than a thousand employees must set aside half of the seats for employee representatives; in other sectors, employing two thousand or more workers triggers 50 percent representation. Ibid., 115, 117.

3. Ibid., 116-17.

4. Dmitri Iglitzin and Steven Hill, "No Friend of Labor," *Los Angeles Times,* December 13, 2006.

5. Sarah Anderson, "The Equity Factor and Free Trade: What the Europeans Can Teach Us," *World Policy Journal* 20, no. 3 (Fall 2003).

6. David Bacon, "German Unions and Social Democrats—Coming to Blows?" LaborNet, May 25, 2003. This is an interview with Wolfgang Mueller, labor organizer for the German union IG Metall, Nuremberg, Germany, www.labornet.org/viewpoints/dbacon/germun.htm.

7. "BMW's Dream Factory," BusinessWeek.com, October 16, 2006, www.businessweek.com/magazine/content/06_42/b4005072.htm?campaign_id=eu_Oct11&link_position=link26.

8. Pontusson, *Inequality and Prosperity,* 117–18.

9. The majority of the E.U.-15 member states have statutory provisions for employee representation on the boards of directors or supervisory boards of some types of companies. Such participation is relatively widespread in Germany, Austria, Denmark, France, Luxembourg, the Netherlands, Norway, Finland, and Sweden, and is restricted to some public-sector organizations in Greece, Spain, and Ireland. It is also present in various forms in most of the new E.U. member states that joined in May 2004, including the Czech Republic, Cyprus, Hungary, Malta, Poland, Slovakia, and Slovenia. In 2004, the E.U.'s first legislation in the form of a directive that deals with board-level employee representation went into effect. The directive establishes the "employee involvement provisions" to apply to European companies, with involvement constituting the information and consultation of employees and, in some cases, board-level participation—defined as "the influence of the body representative of the employees and/or the employee's representatives in the affairs of a company by way of: the right to elect or appoint some of the members of the company's supervisory or administrative organ, or the right to recommend and/or oppose the appointment of some or all of the members of the company's supervisory or administrative organ." See Mark Carley, "Board-Level Employee Representatives in Nine Countries: A Snapshot," edited by Kevin O'Kelly and Norbert Kluge, published in *Transfer* (Brussels, European Trade Union Institute, 2005), www.seeurope-network.org/home pages/seeurope/europeancompany/publications.html. Also see "The European Company—Prospects for Worker Board-Level Participation in the Enlarged E.U.," edited by Norbert Kluge and Michael Stollt, published by Social Development Agency and European Trade Institute for Research, Education and Health and Safety, Brussels, 2006, www.seeurope-network.org/homepages/ seeurope/file_uploads/booklet2006.pdf. For country by country descriptions of codetermination institutions, see "Workers' Participation at Board Level in the EU-15 Countries," edited by Rolf Simons and Norbert Kluge, Hans Boeckler Foundation/European Trade Union Institute, Brussels, 2004.

10. "Merkel Asks CDU to Start Soul-Searching," *Deutsche-Welle,* February 21, 2006, www.dw-world.de/dw/article/0,2144,1911223,00.html; and EUobserver, "Berlin to Push Revival of EU Social Model," published on Businessweek .com, October 17, 2006, www.businessweek.com/globalbiz/content/oct2006/ gb20061018_998903.htm?campaign_id=eu_Oct19&link_position=link29.

11. Barry Eichengreen, *The European Economy since 1945* (Princeton, NJ: Princeton University Press, 2006), 6.

12. Katrin Bennhold, "Europe's Economy/Work or Play? Continent Guards Its Right to Leisure," *International Herald Tribune,* July 19, 2004.

13. "Flexicurity," *The Economist,* September 7, 2006.

14. Thomsen quoted in Marcus Walker, "For the Danish, a Job Loss Can Be a Learning Experience," *Wall Street Journal,* March 21, 2006.

15. Robert Kuttner, "The Copenhagen Consensus: Reading Adam Smith in Denmark," *Foreign Affairs,* March/April 2008, www.foreignaffairs.org/2008 0301faessay87207/robert-kuttner/the-copenhagen-consensus.html.

16. Katinka Barysch, Simon Tilford, and Philip Whyte, "The Lisbon Score-

card VIII: Is Europe Ready for an Economic Storm?" Centre for European Reform, February 2008, www.cer.org.uk/pdf/p_806_lisbon08.pdf.

17. Heinz Werner and Werner Winkler, "Unemployment Compensation Systems: A Cross-Country Comparison," Institute for Employment Research of the Federal Employment Services, Germany, *IAB Labour Market Research Topics*, no. 56 (2004): 9, Figure 3, http://doku.iab.de/topics/2004/topics56 .pdf. According to this study, the United States spends a mere 0.15 percent of GDP on unemployment benefits/assistance compared with 0.36 percent in the United Kingdom, 0.51 percent in Austria, 1.24 percent in Germany, 1.31 percent in France, 1.37 percent in Sweden, and 1.55 percent in the Netherlands, the last of which is ten times as high as in the United States.

18. "EU 'Temps' Granted Equal Rights," BBC News, October 22, 2008, http://news.bbc.co.uk/2/hi/europe/7684389.stm.

19. Sarah Anderson, "The Equity Factor and Free Trade: What the Europeans Can Teach Us," *World Policy Journal* 20, no. 3 (Fall 2003).

20. OECD Standardized Unemployment Rates, August 2009, 2, www.oecd .org/dataoecd/32/24/42134775.pdf. Even France's unemployment rate of 7.7 percent in 2008 was its lowest in decades, as was Germany's 7.3 percent.

21. John Schmitt, Hye Jin Rho, and Shawn Fremstad, "U.S. Unemployment Now as High as Europe," Center for Economic and Policy Research, May 2009, www.cepr.net/documents/publications/US-EU-UR-2009-05.pdf.

22. Simon Briscoe, "Youth at Work," *Financial Times,* March 18, 2006. Official figures put French youth unemployment at 22 percent, compared with 11, 12, and 13 percent, respectively, in the United Kingdom, the United States, and Germany. But the *Financial Times*'s chief statistician, Simon Briscoe, showed that only 7.8 percent of all those under twenty-five were actually out of work in France, only slightly more than 7.4 percent in the United Kingdom, and 6.5 percent in Germany, and about the same percentage as in the United States. It turns out the official numbers were misleading, because France has a much greater percentage of young people attending university full time, and they are not considered part of the labor force. This makes the "available labor force" much smaller, so the percentage of that labor force that is unemployed appears much greater. The higher percentage of French youth in college, in fact, could be viewed as a very good thing. On the other hand, some critics claim that more French youth go to school to delay entering the job market because job prospects aren't so bright, and there seems to be some truth to that as well. In any case, the unemployment situation among young people in France clearly was distorted due to nothing more than the methodology used.

23. The U.S. has an incarceration rate of 750 prisoners per 100,000 in population, the highest in the world, compared with Britain's 148, Germany's 93, Belgium's 91, France's 85, Sweden's 79, and Italy's and Denmark's 67. Even Turkey has an incarceration rate much lower than that of the U.S.: 112 prisoners per 100,000 population. See International Centre for Prison Studies, "Entire World—Prison Population Rates per 100,000 of the National Population," http://www.prisonstudies.org/.

24. The U.S. Department of Justice in June 2008 reported 2,310,984 prisoners held in federal and state prisons and in local jails (www.ojp.usdoj.gov/

bjs/prisons.htm). In 2008 the civilian labor force was 154,287,000 with an official unemployment rate of 5.8 percent, or approximately 8,924,000 unemployed (Bureau of Labor Statistics, ftp://ftp.bls.gov/pub/special.requests/lf/aat1.txt). If we include the prison population, that increases the civilian labor force to 156,597,984 and the unemployed to 11,234,984, for an unemployment rate of 7.2 percent—not 5.8 percent, a difference of 1.4 percent.

25. Robert Gordon, "Two Centuries of Economic Growth: Europe Chasing the American Frontier," Discussion Paper no. 4415, London, Centre for Economic Policy Research, June 2004, cited in Leonard, *Why Europe Will Run the 21st Century*, 84.

26. Rifkin, *The European Dream*, 52.

27. Peter Meiksins and Peter Whalley, "Labor and Leisure: Should Europe Work More, or America Less?" *International Herald Tribune*, August 11, 2004.

28. "Dents in the Dream: 85% of U.S. Unhappy with Economy," *Time*, July 28, 2008, 40–41.

29. David Charter, "Power Supergrid Plan to Protect Europe from Russian Threat to Choke Off Energy," *Times of London*, November 13, 2008, http://business.timesonline.co.uk/tol/business/industry_sectors/natural_resources/article5142622.ece.

30. Michael Hume, John Dew, and Sila Sepping, "Building the New Europe," Lehman Brothers, April 28, 2004, cited in Leonard, *Why Europe*, 82.

FOUR. FAMILY VALUES, EUROPEAN STYLE

1. Reid, *The United States of Europe*, 180.

2. OECD Social Expenditure Statistics, 2005, http://stats.oecd.org/Index.aspx?datasetcode=SOCX_AGG. The degree of Europe's greater workfare spending compared to America's probably has been underestimated due to limitations in the spending categories used in the OECD database.

3. See *Welcome to Swedish Social Insurance Agency*, brochure on the Web at www.forsakringskassan.se/sprak/eng/engelska.pdf.

4. Wouter Bos, "Europe's Social Democrats, Solidarity and Muslim Immigration," The Globalist.com, December 9, 2005, http://theglobalist.com/StoryId.aspx?StoryId=4976.

5. David Crary, "US Family-Oriented Job Policies Weak," Associated Press story in the *Washington Post*, February 1, 2007, www.washingtonpost.com/wp-dyn/content/article/2007/02/01/AR2007020100214.html.

6. The Family Medical Leave Act in the U.S. provides twelve weeks of unpaid leave to new or adoptive parents and to caregivers of elderly relatives, but this applies only to firms with fifty or more workers, which excludes most workers in the United States and disproportionately affects women who tend to work for small companies or earn low wages.

7. Michael Skapinker, "Paid Maternity Leave Is a Win-Win Formula," *Financial Times*, March 2, 2009, www.ft.com/cms/s/0/0c869d0e-075d-11de-9294-000077b07658.html.

8. Lawrence Mishel, Jared Bernstein, and Heather Boushey, "The State

of Working America, 2002/2003," 420–21, quoted in Rifkin, *The European Dream,* 43.

9. "EU Seeks More Time Out for Working Mothers," *Agence France Presse,* October 3, 2008.

10. Russell Shorto, "Going Dutch," *New York Times Magazine,* April 29, 2009, www.nytimes.com/2009/05/03/magazine/03european-t.html?em.

11. "Europe in Figures—Eurostat Yearbook 2006–07," chapter 2, Education, 84, 86, http://epp.eurostat.ec.europa.eu/cache/ITY_OFFPUB/KS-CD-06 -001-02/EN/KS-CD-06-001-02-EN.PDF.

12. Jeremy Cliffe, "From Macho Italians to Progressive Swedes," Cafebabel .com, January 8, 2005, www.cafebabel.com/en/article.asp?T=A&Id=1358.

13. "The Price of Parenthood," BBCNews.com, February 6, 2002, http:// news.bbc.co.uk/2/hi/europe/1804390.stm.

14. In France, child care facilities are subsidized by the government, and younger children are entitled to placement in full-day child care programs *(crèches).* France and several other continental European countries employ a dual system of public child care, one for the under-threes and another from three until school age. For most medium-range earners, the cost for two-year-old children in preschool programs amounts to about $130 per month, and this includes lunch. Quality standards are set by national policy, and teachers in these *écoles maternelles* have the equivalent of graduate training in early education and earn wages that are above the national average for all employed women. In fact, as in Sweden, staff compensation is high, particularly for professionals working with children over age three. The staff members are generally well-trained, meeting educational standards that are comparable to those of public school teachers, particularly for those working with three- and four-year-old children. See Marcia K. Meyers and Janet C. Gornik, "The European Model: What We Can Learn from How Other Nations Support Families That Work," *American Prospect,* November 2004; and "Map: Parenthood Policies in Europe," BBC News.com, March 24, 2006, http://news.bbc.co.uk/2/hi/ europe/4837422.stm#spain.

15. "German Coalition Backs More Childcare," *Expatica,* February 26, 2007, www.expatica.com/actual/article.asp?channel_id=4&story_id=36963; Nicholas Kulish, "Falling German Birthrate Dispels Baby Miracle Myth," *International Herald Tribune,* September 23, 2007, www.iht.com/articles/2007/09/ 23/news/germany.php.

16. Isabelle de Pommereau, "Hot Campaign Issue in Germany: Working Moms," *Christian Science Monitor,* July 11, 2002, www.csmonitor.com/2002/ 0711/p01s02-woeu.html?s=widep.

17. Regarding SCHIP, see Crary, "US Family-Oriented Job Policies Weak"; and Paul Krugman, "An Immoral Philosophy," *New York Times,* July 30, 2007. Regarding state child care assistance, see Ruth Rosen, "The Child Care Crisis," TomPaine.com, October 03, 2006, www.tompaine.com/articles/2006/ 10/03/the_child_care_crisis.php.

18. Q&A with Judith Warner, http://www.perfectmadness.net/qa.html.

19. Quoted in Reid, *The United States of Europe,* 153.

20. Crary, "US Family-Oriented Job Policies Weak."

21. A report published by the European Trade Union Institute compared the pitifully low amount of vacation received by Americans with that received by Europeans and stated, "The United States is in a class of its own. It is the no-vacation nation." The report highlighted that this situation in Europe resulted from a conscious decision to ensure more free time. See "Europe Heads to Beach, America Heads to Work," Reuters, July 5, 2007, www.reuters.com/article/domesticNews/idUSL0522341220070705. Also see "Numbers," *Time,* July 2, 2007, 18.

22. Rebecca Ray and John Schmitt, "No-Vacation Nation," a report from the Center for Economic and Policy Research, May 2007, 1–3.

23. Rifkin, *The European Dream,* 51.

24. Crary, "US Family-Oriented Job Policies Weak." Also see "The Cost of Staying Home Sick," *New York Times* editorial, May 4, 2009, www.nytimes.com/2009/05/05/opinion/05tue3.html?scp=3&sq=paid%20sick%20leave&st=cse.

25. Since 1993 the Family and Medical Leave Act has required employers to provide up to twelve weeks of unpaid leave a year, but even that does not cover all workers. Stephen Singer, "States Push Laws Requiring Paid Sick Days," Associated Press, August 20, 2008.

26. Shorto, "Going Dutch."

27. Kevin Sack, "Many Eligible for Child Health Plan Have No Idea," *New York Times,* August 22, 2007; "World's Best Medical Care?" *New York Times* editorial, August 12, 2007; Christopher Swann, "More Americans Lack Cover for Ill-Health," *Financial Times,* August 30, 2005, http://news.ft.com/cms/s/090ffe88–198e-11da-804e-00000e2511c8.html.

28. Reuters, "One-third of U.S. Lacked Health Insurance: Survey," September 20, 2007, http://today.reuters.com/news/articlenews.aspx?type=healthNews&storyid=2007–09-20T232639Z_01_N20467584_RTRUKOC_0_US-INSURANCE-USA.xml; transcript of President Bush's speech in Cleveland, Ohio, July 10, 2007, www.whitehouse.gov/news/releases/2007/07/20070710-6.html.

29. A study by the Institute of Medicine documented that uninsured Americans get about half the medical care of those with insurance. For example, uninsured women with breast cancer have a 30 to 50 percent higher risk of dying than insured women. Uninsured car crash victims receive less care in the hospital and have a 37 percent higher mortality rate than privately insured patients. Holly Sklar, "Time for Health Care for All," *Progressive Populist,* September 1, 2005. Also see Paul Krugman, "The Waiting Game," *New York Times,* July 16, 2007.

30. For American figures, see "Social Security Provides a Foundation on Which to Build Retirement Security," Social Security Administration, http://www.ssa.gov/pubs/10055.html. Also see Edmund L. Andrews, "Germany Clears Way for Pension Reform," New York Times Service, published in the *International Herald Tribune,* May 12, 2001; and "Germany's Pension Reform," *The Economist,* May 10, 2001.

31. "Go Private, Says the State," *The Economist,* May 10, 2001.

32. Beth Shulman, "Retirement Insecurity," TomPaine.com, April 24, 2006, www.tompaine.com/articles/2006/04/24/retirement_insecurity.php; Jonathan

Peterson, "Study: Grim Retirement Awaits Many," *Los Angeles Times,* June 7, 2006, www.latimes.com/business/la-fi-retire7jun07,0,4348386.story; Eileen Alt Powell, "Workers Have Retirement 'Overconfidence.'" Associated Press, April 3, 2006, http://news.yahoo.com/s/ap/20060404/ap_on_bi_ge/retirement _confidence.

33. Dale Fuchs, "In Europe, Care for the Elderly Is Being Transformed," *International Herald Tribune,* April 13, 2007, www.iht.com/articles/2007/ 04/13/business/wbelder.php; R.B. Saltman, H.F.W. Dubois, and M. Chawla, "The Impact of Aging on Long-Term Care in Europe and Some Potential Policy Responses," *International Journal of Health Services* 36, no. 4 (2006): 719–46.

34. Tim Ferguson, "EC Launches Tech Plan for Seniors," BusinessWeek .com, June 15, 2007, www.businessweek.com/globalbiz/content/jun2007/ gb20070615_383702.htm.

35. Mike Baker, "How to Pay for Universities?" BBC.com, June 27, 2003, http://news.bbc.co.uk/2/hi/uk_news/education/3027204.stm.

36. See online brochure of Deutsches Studentenwerk, *What Are the Fees I Have to Pay Each Term at University?* www.internationale-studierende.de/en/ prepare_your_studies/financing/cost_of_education.

37. Tuition costs cited are from the Web site of College Board, "2007–2008 College Costs," www.collegeboard.com/student/pay/add-it-up/4494.html.

38. Gretchen Morgenson, "Given a Shovel, Americans Dig Deeper into Debt," *New York Times,* July 20, 2008.

39. About 30 percent of students put tuition on their credit cards, up from 24 percent in 2004, according to a study conducted by private lender Sallie Mae. Students who used credit cards for tuition, books, and other direct college expenses in 2008 charged an average of $2,200, up from $942 in 2004, according to the survey. See Scott Travis and Missy Diaz, "More Students Paying College Costs with Credit Cards," *Chicago Tribune,* April 15, 2009, www .chicagotribune.com/business/chi-tc-biz-wed-student-credit-04apr15,0,58 42177.story. Also see Tamara Draut and Javier Silva, "Generation Broke: The Growth of Debt among Young Americans," Demos, Borrowing to Make Ends Meet Briefing Paper no. 2, October 2004, 7, 10, www.demos-usa.org/pubs/ Generation_Broke.pdf.

40. Patrick M. Callan, "The 2008 National Report Card: Modest Improvements, Persistent Disparities, Eroding Global Competitiveness," writing about "Measuring Up 2008: National Report Card on Higher Education," a report by the National Center for Public Policy and Higher, http://measuringup2008 .highereducation.org/commentary/callan.php.

41. Hunter L. Johnson, "Europe's Affordable Housing Standard," *San Francisco Chronicle,* January 7, 2004.

42. CECODHAS Exchange: Special Housing Europe Exhibition Guide, Winter 2005, no. 1, 6. CECODHAS is the European Union's Liaison Committee for Social Housing.

43. Christian Lindner, "Pragmatism Beats Idealism among Squatters," August 28, 2006, http://cafebabel.com/en/article.asp?T=T&Id=7894.

44. Steven Hill and John Bartlett, "Cracks in the Foundation," *Guard-*

ian Unlimited (U.K.), April 24, 2008, http://commentisfree.guardian.co.uk/steven_hill_and_john_bartlett/2008/04/cracks_in_the_foundation.html.

45. Derrick Z. Jackson, "An Unlivable Minimum," *Boston Globe,* July 28, 2007, www.boston.com/news/globe/editorial_opinion/oped/articles/2007/07/28/an_unlivable_minimum/; Nathan Glazer, "Why Americans Don't Care about Income Inequality," paper presented at the Inequality and Social Policy Seminar Series, February 11, 2002, 3–4, quoted in Rifkin, *The European Dream,* 43.

46. David R. Howell and Mamadou Diallo, "Charting U.S. Economic Performance with Alternative Labor Market Indicators: The Importance of Accounting for Job Quality," paper published by the Schwartz Center for Economic Policy Analysis (SCEPA), New School for Social Research, June 29, 2007. For the U.S. in 2005, the OECD's measure of low-wage workers (defined as those paid less than two-thirds of the median weekly earnings for full-time workers) was 24 percent in the United States. This compares with 20.7 percent for the U.K., 15.9 percent for Australia, 15.8 percent for Germany, and just 6.4 percent for Sweden (OECD 2007, Statistical Annex, table H).

47. The U.S. spends 0.3 percent of GDP compared with 0.56 percent in the United Kingdom, 1.02 percent in Austria, 1.89 percent in Germany, 1.38 percent in France, 1.33 percent in Sweden, and 2.11 percent in the Netherlands. Heinz Werner and Werner Winkler, "Unemployment Compensation Systems: A Cross-Country Comparison," IAB Labour Market Research Topics, Institute for Employment Research of the Federal Employment Services, Germany, no. 56, 2004, 9, http://doku.iab.de/topics/2004/topics56.pdf.

48. The U.S. is on the bottom in terms of the duration that unemployment compensation may last, only six months, the same as the United Kingdom but less than Austria (nine months), Germany (twelve months), Sweden (fourteen), the Netherlands (twenty-four), France (thirty), and Denmark (forty-eight). Benefit rates—the percentage of the last income earned—differ substantially: 50 percent in the United States, 74 percent in Germany, 83 percent in Britain, 86 percent in France, and 90 percent in Sweden, the Netherlands, and Denmark. However, some countries cap the maximum amount per month: $1,800 in the United States (specifically California), $1,900 in Germany, $1,816 in Sweden, and $2,200 in Denmark. In France, benefits are cut by 15 percent after four months of unemployment compensation. Werner and Winkler, "Unemployment Compensation Systems," 12–13; Reid, *The United States of Europe,* 148–49.

49. Heather Boushey, "How to Help the Economy, and Families," *New York Times,* from "Europe's Solution: Take More Time Off," March 29, 2009, http://roomfordebate.blogs.nytimes.com/2009/03/29/europes-solution-take-more-time-off.

50. Anton Troianovski, "Majority of Jobless in U.S. Don't Get Benefits," *Wall Street Journal,* July 29, 2008.

51. Reid, *The United States of Europe,* 149.

52. Sandra Block and Julie Appleby, "Firms Fear Health Costs May Rise," *USA Today,* February 20, 2009.

53. Ray and Schmitt, "No-Vacation Nation," 1–3. In the Netherlands, the

vakantiegeld—vacation money—totals 8 percent of a worker's annual salary. Shorto, "Going Dutch."

54. Susan Neiman, "Germans Have Rights, Not 'Benefits,'" *New York Times,* from "Europe's Solution: Take More Time Off," March 29, 2009, http://roomfordebate.blogs.nytimes.com/2009/03/29/europes-solution-take-more-time-off.

55. Crary, "US Family-Oriented Job Policies Weak."

FIVE. THE MYTH OF THE OVERTAXED EUROPEAN

1. To view the Tax Misery Index for 2008, see Jack Anderson, "The Forbes Tax Misery Index," *Forbes,* April 7, 2008, http://www.forbes.com/global/2008/0407/060_2.html.

2. Russell Shorto, "Going Dutch," *New York Times Magazine,* April 29, 2009, www.nytimes.com/2009/05/03/magazine/03european-t.html?em. Also, critics forget that the Dutch do not have a flat personal income tax, so 52 percent is actually the highest tax rate and (just as with income tax brackets in the U.S.) an individual pays tax at a given bracket only for each dollar earned that is above the threshold for qualifying for that highest bracket and is within that bracket's range. The practical effect is that, in fact, no one pays a 52 percent income tax on 100 percent of their income, just as no one in the United States pays the top 35 percent income tax on 100 percent of their income.

3. As we saw in chapter 4, in Europe the state pensions are worth some 70 to 80 percent of a worker's average salary and provide 80 to 85 percent of overall retirement income (depending on the country), compared to U.S. Social Security payments of only 40 percent of average working salary and which provide only 45 percent of an individual's overall retirement income.

4. Out of pocket expenses were for prescription drugs, hospital care, physicians' costs, clinical services, and nursing home care. See Centers for Medicare and Medicaid Services, "Sponsors of Health Care Costs: Businesses, Households, and Governments, 1987–2007," 2008, 1, 2, table 3 on p. 7, www.cms.hhs.gov/NationalHealthExpendData/downloads/bhg07.pdf.

5. Shannon Brownlee and Ezekiel Emanuel, "Five Myths about Our Ailing Health Care System," *Washington Post,* November 23, 2008.

6. Jacob Hacker, "There Goes the Rug," *Los Angeles Times,* January 15, 2006.

7. Ibid.

8. Nick Timiraos, "Moderate Earners Increasingly Lack Health Coverage," *Los Angeles Times,* April 26, 2006.

9. Kaiser Family Foundation and Health Research and Educational Trust, "Employer Health Benefits: 2007," cited in Sarah Axeen and Elizabeth Carpenter, "The Employer Health Care Burden," New America Foundation, Health Policy Program, Issue Brief, May 2008, pg. 3, www.newamerica.net/files/Employer%20Burden%20-%20issue%20brief.pdf.

10. Hacker, "There Goes the Rug"; also see Jacob Hacker, *The Great Risk Shift* (New York and Oxford: Oxford University Press, 2006).

11. Robert Reich, "Finally a Progressive Budget," Robert Reich's Blog, February 26, 2009, http://robertreich.blogspot.com/2009/02/finally-progressive-budget.html.

12. Claudia Goldin and Larry Katz, *The Race between Education and Technology* (Cambridge, MA: Belknap Press, 2008), cited in Chrystia Freeland, "The Lesson of US Income Inequality," *Financial Times,* August 25, 2008. Goldin and Katz found that the top 1 percent of income earners received 24 percent of the growth in income, nearly double the 13 percent that went to the bottom half of U.S. income earners.

13. For the U.S. figure, see Current Population Survey (CPS), Annual Social and Economic (ASEC) Supplement 2007, a joint effort between the Bureau of Labor Statistics and the Census Bureau, table POV01: Age and Sex of All People, Family Members and Unrelated Individuals Iterated by Income-to-Poverty Ratio and Race: 2007, Below 100% of Poverty—All Races, http://pubdb3.census.gov/macro/032008/pov/new01_100_01.htm. For the European figures, see D. Bradley, E. Huber, S. Moller, F. Nielson, and J.D. Stephens, "Determinants of Relative Poverty in Advanced Capitalist Democracies," *American Sociological Review* 68, no. 3 (2003): 22–51. Also see Christopher Swann, "More Americans Lack Cover for Ill-Health," *Financial Times,* August 30, 2005. Also see David Leonhardt, "U.S. Poverty Rate Rose in 2004, Even as Economy Grew," *New York Times/International Herald Tribune,* September 1, 2005.

14. Organization for Economic Cooperation and Development (OECD), "Growing Unequal? Income Distribution and Poverty in OECD Countries," COUNTRY NOTE: UNITED STATES (2008), www.oecd.org/dataoecd/47/2/41528678.pdf. By way of comparison, here are other child poverty rates: Sweden, 4.2 percent; Germany and Austria, 10.2 percent; the United Kingdom, 15.4 percent; Italy, 16.6 percent; and Mexico, 27.7 percent. See "The State of the World's Children, 2006," a report by UNICEF, 2006, www.unicef.org/sowc06/pdfs/figure2_4_2005.pdf (see www.unicef.org/sowc06 for the full report). Also see Economic Policy Institute, "The State of Working America 2004/2005." The "International Comparisons" chapter compares the economic performance of the United States with the nineteen other rich, industrialized countries that also belong to the OECD. See a summary at www.epinet.org/books/swa2004/news/swafacts_international.pdf.

15. Infant mortality rates come from the Centers for Disease Control and Prevention, reported in Gardiner Harris, "Infant Deaths Drop in U.S., but Rate Is Still High," *New York Times,* October 15, 2008. The U.S. rank in infant mortality is equal to 7 deaths per 1,000 live births, substantially higher than the proportion in Japan (3.4 deaths), Sweden (3.4 deaths), France (4.3 deaths), Germany (4.5 deaths), the Czech Republic (4.6 deaths), and even Cuba (6.4 deaths). Life expectancy figures come from the World Health Organization, World Health Statistics 2005, www.who.int/healthinfo/statistics/en/index.html. And the U.S. life expectancy, seventy-seven years, lags behind Japan's eighty-two years, Italy's and Sweden's eighty-one, France's and Spain's eighty, and Germany's seventy-nine, but is a little ahead of South Korea's seventy-six years and is equal to Cuba's.

16. Chris Giles, "Two Percent Hold Half of World's Assets," *Financial Times*, December 5, 2006.

17. Tony Judt, "Europe vs. America," *New York Review of Books* 52, no. 2, February 10, 2005. Also see Steven Hill and Dmitri Iglitzin, "A Fair Way to Shrink the Wealth Gap," *Christian Science Monitor*, January 24, 2007. In fact, the top twenty CEOs of U.S. companies made three times more than the top twenty CEOs of European companies, even though the European CEOs had booked higher sales numbers in 2006 than their U.S. counterparts. Jeanne Sahadi, "CEO Pay: 364 Times More than Workers," CNNMoney.com, August 29 2007, http://money.cnn.com/2007/08/28/news/economy/ceo_pay _workers/index.htm?section=money_topstories.

18. Christopher Swann, "More Americans Lack Cover for Ill-Health," *Financial Times*, August 30, 2005. Also see Leonhardt, "U.S. Poverty Rate Rose in 2004."

19. Gretchen Morgenson, "Given a Shovel, Americans Dig Deeper into Debt," *New York Times*, July 20, 2008. As of July 2008, Americans carried $2.56 trillion in consumer debt, up 22 percent since 2000 alone, according to the Federal Reserve Board. Also see Associated Press, "Economy Rebounds with 4.8% Annual Growth Rate in Q1; Inflation Weakens," *USA Today*, April 28, 2006, which reported that Americans' personal savings as a percentage of after-tax income had dipped to *negative* 0.5%.

20. See Kirstin Downey, "Basics, Not Luxuries, Blamed for High Debt," *Washington Post*, May 12, 2006; and Peter S. Goodman, "Economy Fitful, Americans Start to Pay as They Go," *New York Times*, February 5, 2008.

21. Harper's Index, *Harper's Magazine*, April 2006.

22. David Wessel, "As Rich-Poor Gap Widens in the U.S., Class Mobility Stalls," *Wall Street Journal*, May 13, 2005; also see "Middle of the Class," *The Economist*, July 14, 2005.

23. John Vidal, "Wealth Gap Creating a Social Time Bomb," *The Guardian* (U.K.), October 23, 2008.

24. The gross domestic product has been criticized by some experts as "a calculating machine that can only add, not subtract." The GDP doesn't differentiate between transactions that add to the well-being of a country and those that diminish it. Thus, a dollar spent sending a kid to prison adds as much to the GDP as a dollar spent sending a kid to college. The wrongdoings of Enron contributed up to $1 billion to the U.S. GDP, in the form of legal fees, jail time, media frenzy, and associated payouts. The massive cleanup effort of the oil spill from Exxon's ship *Valdez* adds to the GDP, but the GDP cannot measure the environmental destruction of the oil spill, since it doesn't show up as a negative anywhere on the balance sheet. Ted Halstead and Jonathan Rowe, "If the GDP Is Up, Why Is America Down?" *The Atlantic*, October 1995.

25. Richard Wilkinson, "Social Corrosion, Inequality, and Health," in Anthony Giddens and Patrick Diamond, eds., *The New Egalitarianism* (Cambridge: Polity, 2005), 191.

26. Katrin Bennhold, "Europe's Economy/Work or Play? Continent Guards Its Right to Leisure," *International Herald Tribune*, July 19, 2004.

27. In the United States, wealth and retirement savings are much more tied

up in the stock market, with a majority of people owning at least a modest stake. By contrast, only 13 percent of German households, 20 percent of British, and 24 percent of French households own shares, according to 2006 figures compiled by the European Savings Institute. In Europe, pensions are still largely state-driven, not 401(k)-style investment accounts, which are the trend in the United States. Katrin Bennhold, "In Europe, Crisis Revives Old Memories," *International Herald Tribune,* October 26, 2008, http://iht.com/articles/2008/10/26/business/bury.php.

28. Judy Harris, "Letter from Rome: Prodi's Contradictions," February 26, 2007, DIreland blog, http://direland.typepad.com/direland/2007/02/letter_from_rom.html.

29. Reuters, "Milking Germany's Generous Welfare System," *Taipei Times,* September 8, 2003.

30. Anne-Laure Murier, "A Capital That Can't Grow Up," Cafebabel.com, August 29, 2007, http://cafebabel.com/en/article.asp?T=T&Id=11969&utm_source=NL_EN&utm_medium=email. Also see "Kinderarmut hat mit Hartz IV Rekordniveau erreicht," at www.kinder-armut.de/hartz-iv.html, for a demographic map of child poverty in Germany.

31. For two examples of such university rankings, see the Shanghai Academic Ranking of World Universities, http://ed.sjtu.edu.cn/rank/2007/ARWU 2007Methodology.htm, and Mines-Paris Tech Professional Ranking of World Universities, www.ensmp.fr/Actualites/PR/EMP-ranking.html.

32. Marc Zimmer, "Are American Scientists an Endangered Species?" Inside Higher Ed, July 2, 2007, http://insidehighered.com/views/2007/07/02/zimmer.

33. There were 583,000 international students enrolled in 2006–7 in American universities. Juliana Barbassa, "More Foreign Students at U.S. Schools," Associated Press, December 5, 2007.

34. Prepared remarks for U.S. Secretary of Education Margaret Spellings before the Senate Health, Education, Labor, and Pensions Committee, February 9, 2006, www.ed.gov/news/pressreleases/2006/02/02092006.html.

35. "Final Report, National Geographic–Roper Public Affairs: 2006 Geographic Literacy Study," National Geographic Education Foundation, National Geographic Society, May 2006, 6, www.nationalgeographic.com/roper2006/pdf/FINALReport2006GeogLitsurvey.pdf.

36. See the report issued by former secretary of state Colin Powell's America's Promise Alliance. Associated Press, "High School Graduation Rates Plummet below 50 Percent in Some U.S. Cities," FoxNews.com, April 1, 2008, www.foxnews.com/story/0,2933,344190,00.html.

37. The "early school leavers" in 2005 for the E.U.-25 were 15.2 percent. See "EUROPE IN FIGURES—Eurostat Yearbook 2006–07," chapter 2, Education, table 2.2: Youth Education and Early School Leavers, 87, http://epp.eurostat.ec.europa.eu/cache/ITY_OFFPUB/KS-CD-06-001-02/EN/KS-CD-06-001-02-EN.PDF.

38. "Two Unamalgamated Worlds," *The Economist,* April 3, 2008, www.economist.com/world/europe/displaystory.cfm?story_id=10958534.

39. Eric J. Lyman, "Italians Moderate Traditional Month-Long Vacation," *USA Today*, August 24, 2006.

40. See Daniel Kahneman and Amos Tversky, "Prospect Theory: An Analysis of Decisions under Risk," *Econometrica*, 47, 313–27, quoted in Jacob Hacker, "It's Not the Economy, Stupid," *Washington Post*, October 30, 2006.

SIX. THE ECONOMIC CRASH OF 2008–9

Epigraph: Francis Fukuyama, "The Fall of America, Inc.," *Newsweek*, October 13, 2008, www.newsweek.com/id/162401.

1. Milton Friedman, *Capitalism and Freedom* (Chicago: University of Chicago Press, 1962), preface. On disaster capitalism, see Naomi Klein, *The Shock Doctrine* (New York: Metropolitan Books, 2007).

2. Joellen Perry, "Europe Basks as U.S.-Style Capitalism Draws Fire," *Wall Street Journal*, January 30, 2009, http://online.wsj.com/article/SB1233 27936218431707.html.

3. Jonathan Stempel, "Warren Buffett Sees U.S. Economy in Shambles," *International Herald Tribune*, February 28, 2009, http://www.iht.com/arti cles/reuters/2009/02/28/business/OUKBS-UK-BERKSHIRE-BUFFETT.php.

4. Perry, "Europe Basks as U.S.-Style Capitalism Draws Fire."

5. Leigh Phillips, "Merkel and Sarkozy Call for Global 'Economic Security' Council," *EU Observer*, January 9, 2009, http://euobserver.com/9/27373.

6. Reuters, "German Upper House Approves Bank Takeover Law," *New York Times*, April 3, 2009.

7. Nelson D. Schwartz, "Suddenly, Europe Looks Pretty Smart," *New York Times*, October 18, 2008.

8. Parmy Olson, "Europe's Ticking Time Bomb," *Forbes*, February 12, 2009, www.forbes.com/2009/02/12/banks-eastern-europe-markets-equity-02 12_writedowns_31.html?partner=contextstory; William Drozdiak, "Europe, Breaking Up Is So Easy to Do," *Washington Post*, March 1, 2009; John Vinocur, "Tomorrow's Europe: Not Necessarily Influential," *International Herald Tribune*, December 1, 2008, www.iht.com/articles/2008/12/01/europe/ politicus.php; Czech News Agency, "Spirit of Divided Europe Back on Scene in Spite of EU," *Prague Daily Monitor*, March 13, 2009, http://praguemonitor .com/2009/03/13/reflex-spirit-divided-europe-back-scene-spite-eu; Liaquat Ahamed, "Subprime Europe," *New York Times*, March 7, 2009; Paul Krugman, "A Continent Adrift," *New York Times*, March 16, 2009; Philippe Alfroy, "Divided Europe Holds Financial Crisis Summit," *Agence France Press*, October 4, 2008; Anthony Faiola, "Economic Malaise Threatens to Undermine European Unity," *Washington Post*, August 12, 2008; Brian Till, "Tremors of European Financial Collapse Will Be Felt Worldwide," *Las Vegas Sun*, March 7, 2009; Stephen Castle, "East-West Divide Plagues Europe," *International Herald Tribune*, February 27, 2009, www.iht.com/articles/2009/02/27/europe/union .php; Steven Erlanger and Stephen Castle, "Growing Economic Crisis Threatens the Idea of One Europe," *New York Times*, March 1, 2009.

9. Douglas Rediker, "Obama Must Lead the Way on Global Financial Reform," *European Affairs,* Winter 2009.

10. Steve LeVine, "G-20: Big Role for a Low-Profile Regulator," Business Week.com, April 3, 2009, www.businessweek.com/globalbiz/content/apr2009/gb2009042_612425.htm.

11. Ibid.

12. Simon Johnson, "The Last European: Why the G-20 Was a Success," *New York Times* blog Economix, April 3, 2009, http://economix.blogs.nytimes.com/2009/04/03/why-the-g-20-was-a-success-obamas-initiative.

13. Nelson D. Schwartz, "Europe Faulted on Too-Tepid Stimulus," *New York Times,* March 11, 2009.

14. Krugman, "A Continent Adrift."

15. Nicholas Kulish, "Europe, Aided by Safety Nets, Resists U.S. Stimulus Push," *New York Times,* March 26, 2009.

16. Harold Meyerson, "Rendezvous with Inertia," *Washington Post,* April 1, 2009.

17. Nelson D. Schwartz, "In Europe, 'Cash for Clunkers' Drives Sales," *New York Times,* March 31, 2009, www.nytimes.com/2009/04/01/business/global/01refunds.html?_r=1&ref=business.

18. Kulish, "Europe, Aided by Safety Nets, Resists U.S. Stimulus Push."

19. William Drozdiak, "A Culture of Shared Sacrifice," *New York Times,* in "Europe's Solution: Take More Time Off," March 29, 2009, http://roomfordebate.blogs.nytimes.com/2009/03/29/europes-solution-take-more-time-off.

20. From 1973 to 1985, the financial sector never earned more than 16 percent of domestic corporate profits. By the 1990s that level was oscillating between 21 and 30 percent, higher than it had ever been in the postwar period. But in this decade it shot through the roof, reaching 41 percent. Pay rose just as dramatically. Average compensation in the financial sector from 1948 to 1982 ranged between 99 percent and 108 percent of the average for all domestic private industries. By 2007, it had reached 181 percent. Simon Johnson, "The Quiet Coup," *Atlantic,* May 2009, www.theatlantic.com/doc/200905/imf-advice. Over the past sixty years, the U.S. financial sector has grown from 2.3 percent to 7.7 percent of GDP, more than a tripling in size. At the end of 2008, according to the Federal Reserve Board, total debt in the financial sector came to $17.2 trillion, or 121 percent of the size of the gross domestic product of the United States. That was $1 trillion more than a year earlier, when the total came to 115 percent of GDP. Half a century earlier, financial sector debt was $21 billion, which came to just 6 percent of GDP. Floyd Norris, "Who's Most Indebted? Banks, Not Consumers," *New York Times,* April 3, 2009, www.nytimes.com/2009/04/04/business/economy/04charts.html.

21. As of January 31, 2009, the end of the first month of the Barack Obama administration, there were 12.7 million manufacturing jobs in the United States. As of January 31, 2001, the end of the first month of the George W. Bush administration, there were 18.2 million manufacturing jobs in the United States (source: Department of Labor).

22. Norris, "Who's Most Indebted?"

23. Robert Kuttner, "How Europe Avoided Our Mess," *Boston Globe,* April 30, 2008.

24. Harold Meyerson, "Building a Better Capitalism," *Washington Post,* March 12, 2009, www.washingtonpost.com/wp-dyn/content/article/2009/03/11/AR2009031103218.html?wprss=rss_opinions.

25. Jordan Stancil, "Old Europe, New Again," *The Nation,* April 3, 2009, www.thenation.com/doc/20090420/stancil?rel=hpbox.

26. Kuttner, "How Europe Avoided Our Mess."

27. Meyerson, "Building a Better Capitalism."

28. Chrystia Freeland, "Salvation, Like the Sin, Will Emerge from US," *Financial Times,* March 11, 2009, www.ft.com/cms/s/0/b7433198-0e6b-11de-b099-0000779fd2ac.html.

29. Ibid.

30. Ian Traynor, "G20 Nations Edge towards Agreement," *Guardian,* March 30, 2009, http://www.guardian.co.uk/world/2009/mar/30/g20-europe-uk-us.

31. James Quinn, "G20 Summit: Timothy Geithner Calls for Global Regulation," *Telegraph,* March 27, 2009, www.telegraph.co.uk/finance/financetopics/g20-summit/5057267/G20-summit-Timothy-Geithner-calls-for-global-regulation.html.

32. Michael Hirsh, "Wall Street Digs In," *Newsweek,* April 10, 2009, www.newsweek.com/id/193360.

33. Stancil, "Old Europe, New Again."

34. Ibid.

35. Schwartz, "Suddenly, Europe Looks Pretty Smart."

36. Mario Monti, "How to Save the Market Economy in Europe," *Financial Times,* April 5, 2009, www.ft.com/cms/s/0/4e78b1f0-220d-11de-8380-00144feabdco.html.

37. Pierre Calame, "A Structural Crisis Demands a Comprehensive Solution," *Le Monde,* March 17, 2009, www.lemonde.fr/opinions/article/2009/03/17/a-crise-structurelle-reponse-globale-par-pierre-calame_1169019_3232.html.

38. See Oxford Analytica, "The E.U. Will Weather Economic Crisis," March 26, 2009, www.forbes.com/2009/03/25/integration-european-union-business-oxford.html?partner=relatedstoriesbox.

39. Carter Dougherty, Nelson Schwartz, and Floyd Norris, "Europe Tested by Financial Crisis," *New York Times,* October 6, 2008.

SEVEN. THE EUROPEAN WAY OF HEALTH

1. John Pucher, Ph.D., and Lewis Dijkstra, Ph.D., "Promoting Safe Walking and Cycling to Improve Public Health: Lessons from the Netherlands and Germany," *American Journal of Public Health* 93, no. 9 (September 2003): 1509–16. Also see John Pucher and Lewis Dijkstra, "Making Walking and Cycling Safer: Lessons from Europe," Department of Urban Planning, Rutgers University, February 2000, http://www.vtpi.org/puchertq.pdf.

2. Angelique Chrisafis, "'The City's Gone Cycling Mad,'" *The Guardian,*

August 16, 2007, www.guardian.co.uk/environment/2007/aug/16/ethicalliving
.france.

3. Some have proposed that shopping malls are the new town square, but malls exist mostly for a single purpose—to shop. Other activities, whether political, theatrical, or social (except for teenagers hanging out), are actively discouraged, making malls a negation of the multiple purposes served by European plazas.

4. Other traffic-calming features include speed humps, pedestrian refuges or small islands in the middle of the street, pedestrian zones created by closing streets to auto traffic, cul-de-sacs and dead-end streets created by closing intersections, reduced speed limits near institutions such as schools and hospitals, vehicle-activated signs that react with a message if they detect a vehicle exceeding a particular speed, among others.

5. Robert P. Walzer, "A Driving Force to Change Paris," *International Herald Tribune*, January 23, 2009, www.iht.com/articles/2009/01/22/business/wbspot24.1-411196.php.

6. Among the worst practices of animal cannibalism in North America is weaning calves on milk formula containing "raw spray dried cattle blood plasma," even though scientists have known for many years that blood can transmit diseases of the mad cow type. John Stauber, "Mad Cow USA: The Nightmare Begins," AlterNet.org, December 30, 2003.

7. This revolving door between government and industry has existed for many years. In the Bush administration, former Monsanto employees held positions as cabinet members and positions with the Food and Drug Administration and the Environmental Protection Agency and have even sat on the U.S. Supreme Court. Secretary of Agriculture Ann Veneman was on the board of directors of a Monsanto subsidiary, EPA deputy chief Linda Fisher was a Monsanto executive, and Justice Clarence Thomas is a former Monsanto attorney. In previous administrations, Michael Friedman, former FDA commissioner, became a senior vice president for a Monsanto subsidiary; Mickey Kantor, former secretary of commerce and former U.S. trade representative, became a member of Monsanto's board of directors; William Ruckelshaus, former chief of the EPA, also became a member of Monsanto's board; and Clayton Yeutter, former secretary of agriculture and former U.S. trade representative, became a member of the board of directors of Mycogen Corporation, a subsidiary of the Dow Chemical Company.

8. Figures for 2007 were produced from updated but unpublished figures provided by Helga Willer, from Helga Willer and Minou Yussefi, eds., "The World of Organic Agriculture: Statistics and Emerging Trends, 2005," a report by the International Federation of Organic Agriculture Movements (IFOAM), Bonn, Germany, 7th ed., revised and slightly abridged, July 2005, http://org prints.org/4297/01/1365-world-of-organic-agriculture.pdf. Also see Organic Europe at http://www.organic-europe.net/.

9. See "Organic Agricultural Lands and Farms in Europe, December 31, 2006," Research Institute of Organic Agriculture FiBL, www.organic-europe .net/europe_eu/statistics-europe.htm.

10. Leo Hickman, "Is Organic Worth It?" *The Guardian,* March 31, 2006, www.guardian.co.uk/g2/story/0,,1743510,00.html.

11. Anna Muoio, "We All Go to the Same Place. Let Us Go There Slowly," *Fast Company* 34 (April 2000): 194.

12. Carolyn Jones, "Dry Times for Swimming Pool," *San Francisco Chronicle,* August 7, 2006.

13. See "Livet med brystkreften," *Verdens Gang (VG),* September 30, 2005, cover story.

EIGHT. *LA SANTÉ D'ABORD*

1. Kevin Sack, "Many Eligible for Child Health Plan Have No Idea," *New York Times,* August 22, 2007; "World's Best Medical Care?" *New York Times* editorial, August 12, 2007; Christopher Swann, "More Americans Lack Cover for Ill-Health," *Financial Times,* August 30, 2005, http://news.ft.com/cms/s/090ffe88-198e-11da-804e-00000e2511c8.html.

2. Nicholas Kulish, "$1.85 Fee to See a Doctor? Some Say It's Too Much," *New York Times,* May 27, 2008.

3. The U.S. has fewer physicians, nurses, and hospital beds per person and fewer MRI and CT scanners than the average for other advanced nations; see Holly Sklar, "Time for Health Care for All," *Progressive Populist,* September 1, 2005; Organization for Economic Cooperation and Development (OECD) Health Data 2005, "How Does the United States Compare?" http://www.oecd.org/dataoecd/15/23/34970246.pdf. The United States has the highest rate of medical errors (receiving the wrong medication, incorrect test results, a mistake in treatment, or late notification about abnormal results), and Americans have more difficulty than Europeans in obtaining quick appointments with physicians or care after hours. Americans generally have easier access to specialists and shorter waits for elective surgery than Canadians and Britons, though longer waits than Germans. Gaps in coverage and high out-of-pocket costs hinder U.S. patients' access to care, with nearly a third of them reporting spending more than a thousand dollars in out-of-pocket expenses, far outpacing all other nations. (Canada and Australia came next, with only 14 percent of patients spending that much.) In large part because of high out-of-pocket expenses, Americans also were much more likely than residents of the other nations to skip recommended follow-up care, fail to fill prescriptions, or even forgo doctors' visits, even though a lack of timely care can exacerbate health problems and lead to more expensive treatment down the road, preventable suffering, and even death. Rob Stein, "For Americans, Getting Sick Has Its Price," *Washington Post,* November 4, 2005; Paul Krugman, "Pride, Prejudice, Insurance," *New York Times,* November 7, 2005. The U.S. ranking in life expectancy and the number of years expected are discussed in chapter 5 and its notes, along with comparative statistics for other countries.

4. The World Health Report 2000—Health Systems: Improving Performance, World Health Organization, Geneva, 2000, annex table 1, 152, www.who.int/whr/2000/en/whr00_en.pdf.

5. Kerry Capell, "Is Europe's Health Care Better?" BusinessWeek.com, June 13, 2007, www.businessweek.com/globalbiz/content/jun2007/gb200706 13_921562.htm?chan=globalbiz_europe+index+page_economics+%2Bamp %3B+policy.

6. Quoted in "Government Adds Another 45 Million to the Sick List," *New York Times*, May 14, 2003.

7. Dmitri Iglitzin and Steven Hill, "A Fair Way to Shrink the Wealth Gap," *Christian Science Monitor*, January 24, 2007.

8. See the listing for UnitedHealth Group in *Fortune* magazine's Global Fortune 500 rankings, 2007, http://money.cnn.com/magazines/fortune/global 500/2007.

9. Just examining the profit sheets of one of Blue Cross Blue Shield's thirty-nine state franchises is telling. In 2007, the profit of "nonprofit" NC Blue Cross Blue Shield, North Carolina's largest health insurer, was $190 million, and CEO Bob Greczyn made a salary of $3.1 million. Greczyn's salary had risen 261 percent from 2000–2007, even as the average North Carolina worker had seen a 1.7 percent drop in yearly wages over the same period of time. Adam Searing, "Time for Blue Cross to Act Like a Non-Profit," *The Carrboro Citizen*, March 29, 2007, www.carrborocitizen.com/main/2007/03/29/ flux-up-yonder.

10. "OECD Health at a Glance—How France Compares," Organisation for Economic Cooperation and Development (OECD) Policy Brief, October 2003.

11. Capell, "Is Europe's Health Care Better?"

12. For French employers, the cost for health care per worker is 12.8 percent of payroll, while for American employers that provide health care the cost per enrolled worker to provide health care is 18.3 percent of payroll. However, the rate for France also pays for sick leave, maternity leave, disability, and survivor benefits. Len M. Nichols and Sarah Axeen, "Employer Health Costs in a Global Economy: A Competitive Disadvantage for U.S. Firms," a study by the New America Foundation, Health Care program, May 2008, 8, 10. www .newamerica.net/files/EMPLOYER%20HEALTH%20COSTS%20IN%20A%20 GLOBAL%20ECONOMY.pdf. See the expanded discussion of this in chapter 2 and its notes.

13. Victor G. Rodwin and Simone Sandier, "Health Care under French National Health Insurance," *Health Affairs* 12, no. 3 (1993): 111–31, www .nyu.edu/projects/rodwin/french.html.

14. PBS *Frontline*, "Q&A with Correspondent T.R. Reid," April 15, 2008, www.pbs.org/wgbh/pages/frontline/sickaroundtheworld/etc/notebook.html.

15. Martin Sipkoff, "Do We Really Have the Best Health Care in the World?" *Managed Care*, April 2004, www.managedcaremag.com/archives/ 0404/0404.worldsbest.html.

16. Ulla Schmidt (German federal minister of health), "Health Policy and Health Economics in Germany," speech given at the conference "The American Model and Europe: Past—Present—Future," organized by the Friedrich Ebert Foundation, Washington DC, January 27, 2006. For the full text of

the speech, see www.germany-info.org/relaunch/politics/speeches/012706_1 .html.

17. One study found that for German employers the cost for health care per worker was 6.7 percent of payroll, while for American employers that provide health care the cost per enrolled worker to provide health care was 18.3 percent of payroll. However, the rate for Germany also pays for sick leave and maternity benefits. Nichols and Axeen, "Employer Health Costs in a Global Economy."

18. In Germany, workers making over $4,700 per month have the option of purchasing health care through a private insurance company. Most don't choose that option, but it has led about 8 percent of Germans to opt out of the SIFs and receive coverage from private insurers.

19. Paul Krugman, "Keeping Them Honest," New York Times, June 5, 2009.

20. Commonwealth Fund, "Massachusetts Health Care Reform—On Second Anniversary of Passage, What Progress Has Been Made?" April–May 2008, http://www.commonwealthfund.org/Content/Newsletters/States-in-Action/2008/Apr/April-May-2008/Feature/Massachusetts-Health-Care-Reform—On-Second-Anniversary-of-Passage-What-Progress-Has-Been-Made .aspx.

21. Pam Belluck, "Massachusetts Sets Health Plan for Nearly All," New York Times, April 5, 2006; and Steffie Woolhandler and David Himmelstein, "Massachusetts' Mistake," TomPaine.com, April 7, 2006, http://www.tompaine.com/articles/2006/04/07/massachusetts_mistake.php.

22. Phillip Longman, "The Best Care Anywhere," Washington Monthly, January 1, 2005.

23. Schmidt, "Health Policy and Health Economics in Germany."

24. PBS Frontline, "Q&A with Correspondent T.R. Reid."

25. Steve Lohr, "How to Make Electronic Medical Records a Reality," New York Times, February 28, 2009.

26. Quoted in Longman, "The Best Care Anywhere."

27. Kaiser Family Foundation and Health Research and Educational Trust, "Employer Health Benefits: 2007," cited in Sarah Axeen and Elizabeth Carpenter, "The Employer Health Care Burden," New America Foundation, Health Policy Program, Issue Brief, May 2008, 3, www.newamerica.net/files/Employer%20Burden%20-%20issue%20brief.pdf.

28. Doctors in Europe don't make nearly as much money as their American counterparts; general practitioners make an annual salary of about $110,000 in the United Kingdom and Germany, $100,000 in France, and $65,000 in Spain and Italy, compared with at least $150,000 in the United States. In fact, occasionally you hear about doctors in France or Germany going on strike for higher pay and better working conditions, just like any other working stiff. They are not part of the financial elite, as they are in the United States. "UK GPs Top European Pay League," BBC News, September 2, 2005, news.bbc.co.uk/1/hi/health/4205616.stm.

29. Guy T. Saperstein, "Medicare for All: The Only Sound Solution to Our Healthcare Crisis," AlterNet, January 16, 2007, www.alternet.org/story/46550.

30. Americans of ages fifty-five to sixty-four have significantly higher rates of diabetes, heart disease, stroke, lung disease, and cancer than Britons in the same age group, even after controlling for income levels, race, and ethnicity. These middle-aged Britons have much better health than Americans, even though the United States spends $5,274 per head on medical care compared with the United Kingdom's $2,164. Clive Cookson, "England Beats US in Health Stakes," *Financial Times,* May 2, 2006, http://news.ft.com/cms/s/6c9dee06-d9ff-11da-b7de-0000779e2340.html; *USA Today* editorial, "Why Are Brits Healthier?" May 5, 2006.

31. Sipkoff, "Do We Really Have the Best Health Care in the World?"

32. Associated Press, "Lawmakers Far Outpace Most Americans in Benefits," *USA Today,* April 19, 2006, http://www.usatoday.com/news/washington/2006–04–19-congressbenefits_x.htm.

33. Lindsey Tanner, "U.S. Newborn Survival Rate Ranks Low," Associated Press story in the *Houston Chronicle,* May 9, 2006, http://www.chron.com/disp/story.mpl/ap/health/3850137.html.

34. Kim Housego, "Europe Struggles to Count Dead from Heat Wave," Associated Press, August 22, 2003.

35. "Krauts and Cancer Sticks," Spiegel Online, April 6, 2006, http://service.spiegel.de/cache/international/0,1518,410123,00.html.

36. *Health and Consumer Voice,* newsletter on food safety, health, and consumer policy from the European Commission's Health and Consumer Protection DG, special edition, May 2005, 3–4. Smoking among men has fallen from 54 to 39 percent in Poland, from 51 to 30 percent in Denmark, from 50 to 36 percent in France, from 35 to 26 percent in the United Kingdom, and from 30 to 16 percent in Sweden.

37. Richard Woodman, "Breast Cancer Diagnosed Late in Europe," Reuters Health, March 3, 2003; "Global Action against Cancer," World Health Organization, Geneva, Switzerland, 2003, available at http://www.uicc.org/index.php?id=497.

38. Reuters, "Milking Germany's Generous Welfare System," *Taipei Times,* September 8, 2003.

39. "Germany Weighs Difficult Healthcare Cuts," *Deutsche Welle,* June 18, 2003, http://www.dw-world.de; Michael Gavin, "Falling Out in 'Union': Seehofer Call to Make Everyone Pay into Health Funds Rejected," *Frankfurter Allgemeine Zeitung,* June 20, 2003; Kristina Merkner, "Health Funds Plan Alternative to Fee," *Frankfurter Allgemeine Zeitung,* April 23, 2004.

NINE. WINDMILLS, TIDES, AND SOLAR BESIDES

1. Bruno Giussani, "A Concrete Step toward Cleaner Air," BusinessWeek.com, November 8, 2006, www.businessweek.com/innovate/content/nov2006/id20061108_116412.htm?campaign_id=eu_Nov15&link_position=link40; Mike Remmert, "The 1.5 Liter Car Is Here! 100 Kilometers with 1.5 Liters

or 157 Miles a Gallon: German Engineering Does the Trick," *German World,* June 2007, www.german-world.com/articles/e_200706_Car.htm.

2. Carsten Volkery, "Europe Takes the Lead in Fighting Climate Change," Spiegel Online, www.spiegel.de/international/0,1518,470926,00.html. The energy mix includes power for electricity, heat, transportation, and other uses. The percentage of renewable energy sources does not include hydropower produced by large power dams. The United States produces 6 percent of its total energy (including electricity and transportation) from renewable energy sources, but electricity from large hydrodams makes up 45 percent of that capacity. See "American Energy: The Renewable Path to Social Security," Worldwatch Institute, Center for American Progress, September 2006, 7, http://images1.americanprogress.org/il80web20037/americanenergynow/ AmericanEnergy.pdf.

3. Kevin Morrison, "Fears for Growth Push Energy Efficiency up Global Political Agenda," *Financial Times,* September 27, 2005; Janet Wilson, "U.S. Emits Half of Car-Caused Greenhouse Gas, Study Says," *Los Angeles Times,* June 28, 2006.

4. Kenneth Chang, "As Earth Warms, the Hottest Issue Is Energy," *New York Times,* November 4, 2003; Diana Farrell et al., "Curbing Global Energy Demand Growth: The Energy Productivity Opportunity," McKinsey Global Institute, May 2007, 30. Also see the United Nations Millennium Development Goals Indicators, which lists the United States as having more than twice the per capita carbon dioxide emissions as either Germany, the United Kingdom, or Japan, more than three times the emissions of France or Sweden, six times greater than those of China, and seventeen times greater than India's. See http://mdgs.un.org/unsd/mdg/Data.aspx.

5. "Setting the Target," *The Economist,* February 8, 2007, www.economist.com/displayStory.cfm?story_ID=8670957. The average engine capacity in the U.S. is 3.4 liters, compared with 1.8 liters in Germany and Britain, 1.7 in France, and 1.6 in Italy.

6. Daniel C. Esty, Marc A. Levy, Tanja Srebotnjak, Alexander de Sherbinin, Christine H. Kim, and Bridget Anderson, "Pilot 2006 Environmental Performance Index," appendix A, policy category tables and maps, 51, 52, 55, Yale Center for Environmental Law and Policy, New Haven, CT, 2006. The Environmental Peformance Index (EPI) ranks 149 countries according to twenty-five indicators tracked across six established policy categories: environmental health, air pollution, water resources, biodiversity and habitat, productive natural resources, and climate change. In 2006, the United States was ranked twenty-eighth for overall environmental performance and twenty-third out of twenty-nine OECD countries. In 2008, the U.S. was ranked thirty-ninth overall, just ahead of Belarus and Cuba. See http://epi.yale.edu/CountryScores.

7. WWF, "Living Planet Report," World Wildlife Fund, Gland, Switzerland, October 2008, 36–38, http://assets.panda.org/downloads/living_planet _report_2008.pdf.

8. Los Angeles Times Wire Services, "Greenhouse Gas Emissions Shock Scientists," *Los Angeles Times,* September 26, 2008.

9. It wasn't just the Bush administration that was an obstacle to dealing

with America's environmental gluttony; Democratic Party leaders also have played a role. Before Al Gore became a Nobel laureate and an Academy Award winner for his Paul Revere role in sounding the alarm about climate change, as vice president he let the fuel economy standards lapse. The Clinton administration failed to push through climate change legislation, even though it knew America's leadership was crucial. Democrats voted for Enron-led energy deregulation in states all across America, which, contrary to the promises of cheap energy, led to soaring utility rates and regional blackouts. Michigan's two Democratic senators, Carl Levin and Debbie Stabenow, as well as the powerful Democratic chairman of the House Energy and Commerce Committee, Michigan's John Dingell, have protected their home state's auto industry by watering down proposals for higher fuel standards, in Dingell's case for decades. See John M. Broder, "A Power Duo, Dingells Battle on Two Fronts," *New York Times*, November 15, 2008.

The American media also largely were asleep at the wheel, failing to report accurately on global climate change. In the ten-year period prior to 2004, 928 studies on global warming were published in juried scientific journals, and all of the studies agreed not only that global warming was a reality but also that humans were the primary cause. See *Science* 306, no. 5702 (December 3, 2004): 1686, www.sciencemag.org/cgi/content/full/306/5702/1686. During that same time period, 636 news articles were published in the popular press about global climate change, yet 53 percent of those articles insinuated that global warming was only a theory with no scientific consensus. Jules Boykoff and Maxwell Boykoff, "Journalistic Balance as Global Warming Bias: Creating Controversy Where Science Finds Consensus," November/December 2004, FAIR, www.fair.org/index.php?page=1978. A warped version of journalistic "balance" gave the impression that the scientific community was embroiled in a rip-roaring debate over whether humans were contributing to global warming, yet that debate already had been settled. Europe, Japan, and other countries already had begun taking necessary steps, based on the science, to ease the problem. But in the United States the bipartisan consensus, fed by a somnambulant media, was to maintain the "do nothing" status quo.

10. Steve Hargreaves, "Fuel Efficiency and the American Driver," CNN Money.com, December 1, 2007, http://money.cnn.com/2007/12/01/news/economy/fuel_efficiencysat/index.htm; Juliet Eilperin, "150 Global Firms Seek Mandatory Cuts in Greenhouse Gas Emissions," *Washington Post*, November 30, 2007.

11. Ibid.

12. Leah McDonnell, "Germany Leads with Wind Power," *Deutsche Welle*, October 26, 2006, www.dw-world.de/dw/article/0,2144,2214648,00.html.

13. The Climate Group, "In the Black: The Growth of the Low Carbon Economy," May 2007, 7, 12. Also see Robert Collier, "Germany Shines a Beam on the Future of Energy," *San Francisco Chronicle*, December 20, 2004.

14. "Germany Plans 30 Offshore Wind Farms," Spiegel Online, July 7, 2008, www.spiegel.de/international/germany/0,1518,564274,00.html.

15. Charles Clover, "Windfarms to Power a Third of London Homes," *The Telegraph*, December 20, 2006, www.telegraph.co.uk/news/main.jhtml;jsession

id=BMRYVNCKZPTCNQFIQMGSFFOAVCBQWIVO?xml=/news/2006/12/19/
nwind19.xml; Laura Cohn, Carlta Vitzhum, and Jack Ewing, "Wind Power Has
a Head of Steam," www.businessweek.com/magazine/content/05_28/b39420
79_mz054.htm?campaign_id=nws_europ_jul5&link_position=link3, July 11,
2005.

16. "New Record: Wind Powers 40 Percent of Spain," MetaEfficient.com,
March 26, 2008.

17. Carol Matlack, "Portugal Makes Waves in Alternative Energy," Business
Week.com, May 3, 2006, www.businessweek.com/globalbiz/content/may2006/
gb20060503_258443.htm?campaign_id=eu_May10&link_position=link24.

18. The Climate Group, "In the Black," 12.

19. Steve Jacobs, "Farming for Energy," BusinessWeek.com, September 7,
2006, www.businessweek.com/globalbiz/content/sep2006/gb20060906_2936
90.htm; Barnaby Feder, "Alternative Energy: A Small but Growing Option,"
International Herald Tribune, May 29–30, 2004.

20. The Climate Group, "In the Black," 15.

21. Matthew Wald, "U.S. Grid Slows Wind Use," *International Herald
Tribune,* August 28, 2009.

22. Collier, "Germany Shines a Beam on the Future of Energy."

23. The Climate Group, "In the Black," 12.

24. "EU Almost on Track in Reaching Its 2010 Renewable Electricity
Target," Europa, Gateway to the European Union, January 10, 2007, http://
europa.eu/rapid/pressReleasesAction.do?reference=MEMO/07/12&format
=HTML&aged=0&language=EN&guiLanguage=en.

25. "World's Largest Solar Photovoltaic Power Plant to Be Built with GE
Investment and PowerLight Technology," PowerLight Corporation press
release, April 27, 2006, http://www.powerlight.com/company/press-releases
/2006/04.27.06_Serpa_Portugal_Worlds_Largest_Solar_Power_Plant.shtml.

26. Margot Roosevelt, "Bill Heats Up Talk of Solar Water Systems," *Los
Angeles Times,* May 29, 2007.

27. David Case, "Cleaner than Cows," *Progressive Populist,* March 15,
2001, 11.

28. Justin Hibbard, "Bright Days for NanoSolar," BusinessWeek.com,
June 26, 2006, www.businessweek.com/technology/content/jun2006/tc2006
0626_804634.htm?campaign_id=eu_Jun27&link_position=link25.

29. The Climate Group, "In the Black," 12.

30. Jane Burgermeister, "Renewable Energy Jobs Soar in Germany," Renew
ableEnergyWorld.com, April 8, 2008, www.renewableenergyworld.com/rea/
news/story?id=52089; "German Environment Minister Wants to Triple 'Renewables,'" *Deutsche Welle,* February 27, 2007, www.dw-world.de/dw/article/0,21
44,2366959,00.html.

31. McDonnell, "Germany Leads with Wind Power"; The Climate Group,
"In the Black," 12.

32. Alvaro Sanchez, "Solúcar: Renewable Energy Platform in Andalusia,"
EU Debate 2009, July 16, 2008, www.eudebate2009.eu/eng/article/25586/
trans-solucar-el-sol-es-el-futuro.html.

33. Ian Johnston, "Wave Farm Points Way Ahead for Scotland," *The Scots-*

man, February 20, 2007, http://news.scotsman.com/index.cfm?id=271042007; Michael Strauss, "Harnessing the Power of Sea Will Demand Economic Muscle," *International Herald Tribune*, September 12, 2006; Jacobs, "Farming for Energy."

34. "The World's First Underwater Windmill Starts Turning," *Deutsche Welle*, June 17, 2003, www.dw-world.de/english/0,3367,1446_A_895835_1_A,00.html.

35. Reuters, "UK Approves World's Biggest Biomass Power Plant," November 21, 2007.

36. Douglas Fischer, "Denmark Paves Way for Freedom from Big Oil," *Oakland Tribune*, June 5, 2006.

37. "EU Almost on Track in Reaching Its 2010 Renewable Electricity Target."

38. Burgermeister, "Renewable Energy Jobs Soar in Germany."

39. Katinka Barysch, Simon Tilford, and Philip Whyte, "The Lisbon Scorecard VIII: Is Europe Ready for an Economic Storm?" Centre for European Reform, February 2008, 107, www.cer.org.uk/pdf/p_806_lisbon08.pdf.

40. "EU Almost on Track in Reaching Its 2010 Renewable Electricity Target."

41. Reuters, "UK Must Aim for Near Carbon-Free Power by 2020—PM," November 19, 2007.

42. "Germany to Massively Invest in Energy Sector," *Deutsche Welle*, April 4, 2006, www.dw-world.de/dw/article/0,2144,1953512,00.html; World Business Council for Sustainable Development, "German Firms to Step Up Renewables Spending," *Environment Daily*, April 4, 2006, www.wbcsd.org/plugins/DocSearch/details.asp?type=DocDet&ObjectId=MTg2ODQ.

43. "Portugal Opens Major Solar Plant," BBC News, March 28, 2007, http://news.bbc.co.uk/2/hi/europe/6505221.stm.

44. In the 2007 fiscal year, the Energy Department planned to spend $159 million on solar R&D, $303 million on nuclear energy R&D, and $427 million on coal R&D, nearly triple the amount spent on solar, as well as $167 million on other fossil fuel R&D. See Andrew Revkin and Matthew Wald, "Solar Power Captures Imagination, Not Money," *New York Times*, July 16, 2007.

45. Alok Jha, "'Wave Snakes' Switch on to Harness Ocean's Power," *The Guardian*, September 24 2008, http://www.guardian.co.uk/environment/2008/sep/24/renewable.wave.energy.portugal.

46. Off the coast of Wales, a Danish company has deployed a "wave dragon" that scoops water into a basin and then releases it through outlets with turbines that spin and generate electricity. Paul Davidson, "Marine Energy Can Be Forecast," *USA Today*, April 18, 2007, www.usatoday.com/tech/science/2007-04-18-wave-power_N.htm. Also see Remmert, "The 1.5 Liter Car Is Here!"

47. Quoted in Morrison, "Fears for Growth Push Energy Efficiency up Global Political Agenda."

48. Lisa Margonelli, "Myths about That $3.18 per Gallon," *Washington Post*, June 3, 2007, www.washingtonpost.com/wp-dyn/content/article/2007/06/01/AR2007060101838_3.html. The United States has not always ignored

conservation and energy efficiency. Today it uses 43 percent less energy and 50 percent less oil per dollar of real GDP than it did in 1975, which explains why the U.S. economy has been able to weather paying sixty to sixty-five dollars per barrel of oil so well.

49. Farrell et al., "Curbing Global Energy Demand Growth."

50. "The Climate Group Partners with HSBC on US$100 Million Programme to Combat Climate Change World-wide," press release from the Climate Group, May 30, 2007, http://theclimategroup.org/index.php/news_and _events/news_and_comment/the_climate_group_partners_with_hsbc_on_ us100_million_programme_to_combat_c/.

51. Mike Davis, "Home-Front Ecology: What Our Grandparents Can Teach Us about Saving the World," *Sierra Magazine*, July–August 2007; Stan Cox, "Big Houses Are Not Green: America's McMansion Problem," AlterNet.org, September 8, 2007, www.alternet.org/environment/61523.

52. The Climate Group, "In the Black," 20.

53. Helena Spongenberg, "EU Could Ban Incandescent Bulbs," Business Week.com, June 22, 2007, www.businessweek.com/globalbiz/content/jun2007/ gb20070622_706666.htm?chan=globalbiz_europe+index+page_energy+%2 Bamp%3B+environment.

54. Farrell et al., "Curbing Global Energy Demand Growth," 15, 33, 44; Cogen Europe, "What Is Cogeneration," www.cogen.org/about/what_is_CHP .htm; also see UNEP Division of Technology, Industry and Economics—Energy and Ozone Action Unit, "Cogeneration," www.cogen.org/Downloadables/ Publications/Fact_Sheet_CHP.pdf.

55. Leila Abboud, "How Denmark Paved Way to Energy Independence," *Wall Street Journal*, April 16, 2007.

56. Thomas Casten and Phillip Schewe, "Getting the Most from Energy," *American Scientist*, January–February 2009, Figure 5 and Figure 7, 30–31.

57. Elisabeth Rosenthal, "No Furnaces but Heat Aplenty in 'Passive Houses,'" *New York Times*, December 26, 2008, www.nytimes.com/2008/ 12/27/world/europe/27house.html.

58. Alok Jha, "Warm Welcome for House Powered by Hydrogen Fuel Cell," *The Guardian* (U.K.), October 10, 2008.

59. Sara Kugler, "16 Cities to Go Green under Clinton Plan," Associated Press, May 16, 2007.

60. "The Rise of the Green Building," *The Economist Technology Quarterly*, December 4, 2004, 17.

61. "Drawing on Energy in a 'Passive' Way," *Deutsche Welle*, January 16, 2003, www.dw-world.de/english/0,3367,1430_A_751589,00.html.

62. "The Rise of the Green Building," 18.

63. Gwladys Fouché, "Sweden's Carbon-Tax Solution to Climate Change Puts It Top of the Green List," *The Guardian* (U.K.), April 29, 2008.

64. Nicolai Ouroussoff, "Why Are They Greener than We Are?" *New York Times*, May 20, 2007, www.nytimes.com/2007/05/20/magazine/20europe-t .html.

65. Kugler, "16 Cities to Go Green under Clinton Plan."

66. Quoted in Ouroussoff, "Why Are They Greener than We Are?"

67. Farrell et al., "Curbing Global Energy Demand Growth," 34.

68. Ouroussoff, "Why Are They Greener than We Are?"

69. The Climate Group, "In the Black," 20.

70. James Kanter, "Group Says European Cap-and-Trade System Reduced Emissions," *New York Times,* Green Inc. blog, February 16, 2009, http://greeninc.blogs.nytimes.com/2009/02/16/group-says-european-cap-and-trade-system-reduced-emissions.

71. James Kanter, "In London's Financial World, Carbon Trading Is the New Big Thing," *New York Times,* July 6, 2007.

72. Helena Spongenberg, "EU Carbon Trading Hailed as Success," Business Week.com, May 29, 2007, www.businessweek.com/globalbiz/content/may2007/gb20070529_879251.htm?chan=search.

73. Steven Mufson, "Companies Gear Up for Greenhouse Gas Limits," *Washington Post,* May 29, 2007.

74. Lorne Cook, "EU Seal Deals on Economy, Climate Packages," Agence France-Presse, December 12, 2008.

TEN. REVOLUTION ON WHEELS

1. Jad Mouawad, "The Big Thirst," *New York Times,* April 20, 2008, see graphic accompanying article at http://www.nytimes.com/imagepages/2008/04/20/weekinreview/20mouawad-graphic-1.html.

2. "France Launches New High-Speed Trains," *International Business Times,* June 10, 2007.

3. Steve Jacobs, "High-Speed Trains of Europe," BusinessWeek.com, June 13, 2006, www.businessweek.com/globalbiz/content/jun2006/gb20060613_790699.htm?campaign_id=eu_Jun20&link_position=link30; and Steve Jacobs, "Europe on a Fast Track," June 13, 2006, http://images.businessweek.com/ss/06/06/fasttrains/index_01.htm.

4. Christian Wüst, "Is France's Energy-Guzzling TGV Prototype the Right Answer?" Spiegel Online, April 4, 2007, www.spiegel.de/international/business/0,1518,475641,00.html.

5. Jacobs, "Europe on a Fast Track."

6. European Commission, "The Social Situation in the European Union," May 22, 2002, cited in Rifkin, *The European Dream,* 75.

7. "Setting the Target," *The Economist,* February 8, 2007, www.economist.com/displayStory.cfm?story_ID=8670957. The average engine capacity in the U.S. is 3.4 liters compared to 1.8 liters in Germany and Britain, 1.7 liters in France, and 1.6 liters in Italy.

8. John M. Broder, "A Power Duo, Dingells Battle on Two Fronts," *New York Times,* November 15, 2008.

9. Ken Livingstone, "Congestion: Europe at a Crossroads," *E!Sharp,* February 2004, 12; "Stockholm Voters Approve Contentious Traffic Congestion Toll," Associated Press, September 18, 2006; "The Greening of Paris," *Ode Magazine,* http://odemagazine.com/news.php?nID=524; Neal Peirce, "London's

Gearing Traffic Move: Successful, but Right for Us?" Washington Post Writers Group, May 18, 2003.

10. Martin LaMonica, "Better Place Denmark to Plug Electric Cars by 2011," January 27, 2009, http://news.cnet.com/8301–11128_3–10150716–54.html.

11. Christopher Knight, "New Alchemy: Grass into Fuel," *International Herald Tribune,* September 18, 2006, 12.

12. Diana Farrell et al., "Curbing Global Energy Demand Growth: The Energy Productivity Opportunity," McKinsey Global Institute, May 2007, 15, 44.

13. Stanley Reed, "Would $100 Oil Slam the Global Economy?" Business Week.com, July 27, 2006, www.businessweek.com/globalbiz/content/jul2006/gb20060726_793734.htm?campaign_id=eu_Aug2&link_position=link21.

14. Michael Fitzgerald, "Hotbed," *Fast Company,* April 2008, 99.

15. Ibid.

16. For a comprehensive vision of the hydrogen economy, see Jeremy Rifkin, "A Grand Idea for a Grand Coalition: Will Germany Lead the Way to the Hydrogen Era and a Third Industrial Revolution?" March 2006, www.foet.org/activities/HydrogenProposalChancellorMerkelFinal.pdf; and Jeremy Rifkin, *The Hydrogen Economy: The Creation of the Worldwide Energy Web and the Redistribution of Power on Earth* (New York: Tarcher/Penguin, 2003).

17. Fitzgerald, "Hotbed," 99.

18. Gwladys Fouché, "Sweden's Carbon-Tax Solution to Climate Change Puts It Top of the Green List," *The Guardian* (U.K.), April 29, 2008.

19. Elisabeth Rosenthal, "Europe Turns to Coal Again, Raising Alarms on Climate Change," *New York Times,* April 23, 2008. Fifty is not a huge number of plants, and the coal-fired plants will be "cleaner" than most, employing the latest technology for that purpose. But as one critic stated, "There's no such thing as clean coal."

20. Erik Kirschbaum, "Germany Shows Contradictions on Climate Change," Reuters, December 2, 2007, www.reutersinteractive.com/Carbon/83453.

21. Pierre Noël, "Beyond Dependence: How to Deal with Russian Gas," a report from the European Council on Foreign Relations, November 2008, http://ecfr.eu/page/-/documents/Russia-gas-policy-brief.pdf.

22. David Charter, "Power Supergrid Plan to Protect Europe from Russian Threat to Choke Off Energy," *Times of London,* November 13, 2008, http://business.timesonline.co.uk/tol/business/industry_sectors/natural_resources/article5142622.ece.

23. Fouché, "Sweden's Carbon-Tax Solution."

24. Clifford Krauss, "Oil Is So Last-Century: Now Wind's the Thing," *International Herald Tribune,* February 25, 2008, 15.

25. Ibid.

26. Peter Foster, "India to Shun G8 Demands on Gas Emissions," *The Telegraph* (U.K.), May 30, 2007.

ELEVEN. THE RELUCTANT SUPERPOWER

1. Central Asia consists of the five former Soviet republics of Kazakhstan, Kyrgyzstan, Tajikistan, Turkmenistan, and Uzbekistan, plus Afghanistan and northeastern Iran, and western parts of China such as Xinjiang. Also included by some analysts are Mongolia, northern Pakistan, Tibet, Inner Mongolia, and southern parts of Siberia, all in all a vast region.

2. Josh Kurlantzick, "Crude Awakening," *New Republic,* September 25, 2006, www.carnegieendowment.org/publications/index.cfm?fa=view&id=18739&prog=zch,zgp,zru&proj=zme.

3. Prune Antoine and Julia Mills, "Barroso: I Have No Doubt That Portugal's Integration Has Been a Success," Cafebabel.com, January 2, 2006, http://cafebabel.com/en/article.asp?T=A&Id=1592.

4. Fernando Navarro, "EU, Hormone for Economic Growth," Cafebabel.com, January 2, 2006, http://cafebabel.com/en/article.asp?T=T&Id=5520.

5. The gross domestic product figure is from the International Monetary Fund's World Economic and Financial Surveys, World Economic Outlook Database, September 2006 edition, www.imf.org/external/pubs/ft/weo/2006/02/data/index.aspx.

6. David Crossland, "Man Awakes to Moaners and Mobiles after 19 Years," *Times of London,* June 3, 2007, www.timesonline.co.uk/tol/news/world/europe/article1878225.ece.

7. Metropolitan Chicago, with a population of more than nine million, has more than eight hundred thousand residents of Polish descent. But the number of Poles in the Chicago area who were granted permanent resident status in 2005 fell to 5,575, a 5.3 percent drop from 2004, when Poland joined the European Union, according to the U.S. Department of Homeland Security. Poles in Chicago say their culture, influence, and businesses are declining there, along with their numbers. Joe Carroll, "In Expanded EU, Poles No Longer Flock to the U.S. for a Better Life," Bloomberg News, *International Herald Tribune,* March 8, 2007, http://iht.com/articles/2007/03/08/business/zloty.php.

8. Quoted in Parag Khanna, "The Metrosexual Power," *Foreign Policy,* July/August 2004, 67.

9. "Pay in Europe 2007: Pay Gap between Europe's Richest and Poorest Countries Has Fallen Significantly over the Last Six Years," *Finfacts Ireland,* March 27, 2007, www.finfacts.com/irelandbusinessnews/publish/article_10009569.shtml.

10. Christopher Torchia, "Turkey's Ruling Party Wins Election," Associated Press, July 22, 2007.

11. Christopher Power, "The Transformation of Turkey," BusinessWeek.com, January 26, 2007, www.businessweek.com/globalbiz/content/jan2007/gb20070126_615103.htm?campaign_id=eu_Feb1&link_position=link37.

12. Andrew Moravcsik, "Rumors of Europe's Demise Are Greatly Exaggerated," The Washington Note, June 8, 2006, www.thewashingtonnote.com/archives/001452.php.

13. *Milenio,* one of Mexico's national newspapers, reported 2,773 killings related to organized crime and drug trafficking in 2007, up 24 percent from 2,241 in 2006. The death toll included 261 policemen, 35 soldiers, and

21 public officials. These figures are quoted in *Mexico, Politics and Policy,* a newsletter prepared by Zemi Communications, December 18–January 7, 2007.

14. Niall Ferguson, "Dollar Diplomacy: How Much Did the Marshall Plan Really Matter?" *New Yorker,* August 27, 2007, www.newyorker.com/arts/critics/books/2007/08/27/070827crbo_books_ferguson.

15. Parag Khanna, "The Metrosexual Power," *Foreign Policy,* July–August 2004, 67. For 2003, the European Union gave about $36.5 billion in development aid, compared with the United States, which gave only $13.3 billion. The United Nations has set a standard that developed countries should give 0.7 percent of their gross domestic product each year in foreign aid; the only countries that pass that test are European, with Denmark giving 0.96 percent; Sweden giving 0.83 percent; and the Netherlands giving 0.81 percent. France gives only 0.38 percent, yet that is still three times greater than the U.S. proportion at 0.13 percent. See Reid, *The United States of Europe,* 189–90. However, U.S. spending on the military, the wars in Iraq and Afghanistan, and military aid to targeted allies such as Israel and Egypt has been astronomical, exceeding U.S. foreign development aid by more than ten times; see Anatol Lieven, "Spend More on Making Wealth Not War," *Financial Times,* June 26, 2007.

16. Angela Charlton, "43 Nations Creating Mediterranean Union," Associated Press, July 13, 2008.

17. "EU Forges New Eastern Partnership in Prague," Deutsche Welle, May 8, 2009, www.dw-world.de/dw/article/0,,4235133,00.html.

18. See Mark Leonard, "Europe: The New Superpower," *Irish Times,* February 18, 2005, for further elucidation of this view.

19. The ten Southeast Asia member countries of ASEAN are Singapore, Thailand, Vietnam, Malaysia, Brunei Darussalam, Cambodia, Indonesia, Laos, Myanmar, and the Philippines. In past years, relations between China and ASEAN members were troubled, but in recent years the relationship has become more constructive and substantive.

20. Stephen Castle, "A 'World of Continents' Emerges," *International Herald Tribune,* January 23, 2008.

21. Sakurada Jun, "On the Historically Significant Agreement on Joint Development of Gas Fields between Japan and China," *Council on East Asian Community (CEAC) E-Letter* 1, no. 6 (September 5, 2008), www.ceac.jp/e/index.html.

22. Edward Wong, "China and Taiwan Expand Accords," *New York Times,* November 4, 2008.

23. Khanna, *The Second World,* xviii.

24. Quoted in Patten, *Cousins and Strangers,* 94–95.

25. The legacy of Neville Chamberlain, British prime minister from 1937 to 1940, is marked by his policy of appeasement toward Nazi Germany regarding the concession of Austria and Czechoslovakia to Adolf Hitler, the latter marked by the Munich Agreement in 1938.

26. Anatol Lieven, "Defusing EU-Russia Tension," *International Herald Tribune,* May 23, 2007.

27. Charles Kupchan, "The End of the West," *Atlantic Monthly*, November 2002, 42.

28. James Madison and Thomas Jefferson fought strongly against what they called "consolidation," which they considered to be an ideological cousin to "monarchy," both terms "suggesting a threatening aggregation of political power reminiscent of the tyrannical British government that the American colonies had defied and then overthrown. . . . Madison described the aggregation of power by the federal government as an ominous second coming on American soil of the British monster that the American Revolution had supposedly banished forever." This mistrust affected the creation of the Supreme Court and federal court system, federalization of the national debt, the creation of banks, the slavery issue, Indian policy, indeed virtually any embodiment of federal power which was suspected of undermining the principles of the Revolution itself. All of these and more quickly became potent flashpoints for ideological struggle between the Jeffersonians and the Hamiltonians. Washington was perceptive and understood this, and therefore "fashioned a kind of Fabian presidency that had sustained the credibility of the federal government by avoiding political battles" that would raise even more suspicions by pushing greater federal sovereignty. Joseph J. Ellis, *His Excellency: George Washington* (New York: Alfred A. Knopf, 2004), 200, 204–5, 214, 218.

29. Madeleine Albright, secretary of state under President Bill Clinton, said, "If we have to use force, it is because we are America. We are the indispensable nation. We stand tall. We see further into the future." Madeleine K. Albright, interview on NBC-TV's "The Today Show" with Matt Lauer, Columbus, Ohio, February 19, 1998, as released by the Office of the Spokesman, U.S. Department of State, http://secretary.state.gov/www/statements/1998/980219a.html.

30. Joby Warrick and Walter Pincus, "Reduced Dominance Is Predicted for U.S.," *Washington Post*, September 10, 2008.

31. Peter Spiegel, "Defense Chief Gates Wants to Spend More on U.S. Diplomacy," *Los Angeles Times*, July 16, 2008.

32. Andrew Moravcsik, "Rumors of Europe's Demise Are Greatly Exaggerated," The Washington Note, June 8, 2006, www.thewashingtonnote.com/archives/001452.php.

TWELVE. THE EUROPEAN WAY OF FOREIGN POLICY

1. "Russia 'Backed Litvinenko Murder,'" BBC News, http://news.bbc.co.uk/2/hi/uk_news/7494142.stm, July 8, 2008.

2. Josh Kurlantzick, "Crude Awakening," *New Republic*, September 25, 2006, www.tnr.com/doc.mhtml?i=20061002&s=kurlantzick100206.

3. Anatol Lieven, "To Russia with Realism," *American Conservative*, March 26, 2007.

4. Ibid.

5. The State Department's 2007 Human Rights Report found "serious problems" with Georgia's human rights record and notes "excessive use of force to disperse demonstrations"; "impunity of police officers"; and declining

respect for freedom of speech, freedom of the press, freedom of assembly, and political participation. Pro-democracy advocates in Georgia have described how Saakashvili acted quickly after entering office to empower the executive branch at the expense of parliament and to strengthen the government by "stifling political expression, pressuring influential media and targeting vocal critics and opposition leaders"—including by using law enforcement agencies. "Saakashvili is far from the morally pure democrat he would have the West believe he is. Georgia's internal realities help make clear that the fighting erupted not primarily because of what the country represents but because of its government's actions. Tbilisi could have avoided the confrontation by deferring its ambitions to subjugate South Ossetia and pursuing them through strictly peaceful means." Paul J. Saunders, "Georgia's Recklessness," *Washington Post,* August 15, 2008.

6. Michael Dobbs, "'We Are All Georgians'? Not So Fast," *Washington Post,* August 17, 2008.

7. Mark Deen and Reed V. Landberg, "Russia's War with Georgia May Revive U.S.-Europe Rift," Bloomberg News Service, August 15, 2008.

8. Ibid.; Denis Corboy, William Courtney, and Kenneth Yalowitz, "Europe, Not the US, Can Get Russia to Behave," *Christian Science Monitor,* November 7, 2008; Nicholas Kulish, "Germany Aims to Guide the West's Ties to Russia," *New York Times,* December 1, 2008, www.nytimes.com/2008/12/02/world/europe/02germany.html?_r=1&hp. Indeed, in 2007 German exports alone to Russia totaled $36 billion, more than five times the $6.7 billion exported from the United States to Russia. Some 4,600 German companies invested $13.2 billion, building factories and delivering machinery to Russians.

9. Parag Khanna, "Waving Goodbye to Hegemony," *New York Times Magazine,* January 27, 2008.

10. Joschka Fischer, "Missiles, Oil, and Europe Re-divided," March 2007, www.project-syndicate.org/commentary/fischer11.

11. Flynt Leverett and Hillary Mann Leverett, "Wrong on Russia," National Interest Online, August 20, 2008.

12. However, in Germany public criticism of Israeli policies toward the Palestinians has been on the rise, and Germany has become one of the single largest contributors to the Palestinian Authority as part of its policy toward supporting a two-state solution to the Israeli-Palestinian conflict. See Paul Belkin, "Germany's Relations with Israel: Background and Implications for German Middle East Policy," *Congressional Research Service Report for Congress,* January 19, 2007.

13. Reuters, "India Says No Quid Pro Quo over U.S. Nuclear Pact," August 2, 2007.

14. Robert Burns, "Abizaid: World Could Abide Nuclear Iran," Associated Press, September 17, 2007.

15. Several years later, Secretary of State Condoleezza Rice, who at the time of the Iranian proposal was head of the NSC, said she couldn't recall having ever seen such an Iranian proposal, a claim that Leverett dismissed as preposterous. Glenn Kessler, "2003 Memo Says Iranian Leaders Backed

Talks," *Washington Post,* February 14, 2007; also see Reuters, "Ex-Aide Says Rice Misled U.S. Congress on Iran," February 14, 2007.

16. Anne Gearan, "US Has Two-Part Strategy with Iran," May 27, 2007, Associated Press story at Forbes.com, www.forbes.com/feeds/ap/2007/05/27/ap3761892.html.

17. David E. Sanger, "U.S. May Drop Key Condition for Talks with Iran," *New York Times,* April 13, 2009.

18. Linda Yueh, "Reflections on the EU-China Economic Relationship," *Social Europe Journal* (Spring 2008): 135. In 2007, the European Union imported $320 billion worth of goods from China ("EU-China Trade in Facts and Figures," EUBusiness.com, September 23, 2008, www.eubusiness.com/China/eu-china-trade.08), and the United States imported $233 billion worth of goods from China (US-China Business Council, "US-China Trade Statistics and China's World Trade Statistics," table 8: China's Top Export Destinations 2007, www.uschina.org/statistics/tradetable.html).

19. In 2006, the European Union invested in 2,738 projects in China, with the contract value amounting to US$10.58 billion and the realized value of US$5.39 billion. Including previous years through the end of 2006, the E.U. had accumulatively invested in 25,418 projects in China, with the contract value reaching US$97.95 billion and the realized value of US$53.18 billion, making up 8 percent of the amount of foreign capital actually introduced to China. In addition, by the end of 2006, China had signed 24,108 technology contracts with E.U. member countries, valued at US$98.66 billion. "China Now EU's Biggest Import Market," *People's Daily,* January 31, 2007, http://english.peopledaily.com.cn/200701/31/eng20070131_346408.html.

20. Khanna, *The Second World,* 307.

21. Will Hutton, "Will China Dominate the 21st Century?" *Social Europe Journal* (Spring 2008): 132; Will Hutton, *The Writing on the Wall: Why We Must Embrace China as a Partner or Face It as an Enemy* (New York: Free Press, 2006), 87.

22. Hutton, *The Writing on the Wall,* 149.

23. Ibid., 31, 120–21. Chinese researcher Sun Yan has written that the number of arrests of senior Communist Party members for corruption quadrupled between 1992 and 2001. At the level of the central government, corruption has been debilitating and helps set the national tone. High-level officials, including the mayor of Beijing, a vice-chairman of the National People's Congress, the former president of the Bank of China, the vice-governor of the People's Bank of China, and the director of China's foreign exchange administration, were arrested and imprisoned for embezzlement and fraud. One of them eventually was executed, and another leaped to his death. To put that in perspective, it would be as if the mayor of New York, the Speaker of the House of Representatives, and the chief executives of Goldman Sachs and Citibank, along with a governor of the Federal Reserve, were all imprisoned for fraud, were executed, or committed suicide. China's leadership has taken steps to crack down. Punishments have been increased, and tougher laws have been passed. Officials now are forbidden to enter business relationships with family members. Audits

and anti-corruption screenings have been introduced. But China's corruption likely will remain at epidemic levels for many years to come.

24. Will Hutton, "Don't Expect China to Get the West Out of This Mess," *The Observer*, October 26, 2008, www.guardian.co.uk/commentisfree/2008/oct/26/china-global-economy?commentpage=1.

25. Hutton, "Will China Dominate the 21st Century?" 132.

26. Zhan Lisheng, "Guangdong Faces Acid Rain," *China Daily*, September 6, 2008.

27. Steven Hill, "China's Robber-Baron Ways," *International Herald Tribune*, September 23, 2008.

28. Antoaneta Bezlova, "China Grapples with Labor Dragon," *Asia Times*, April 4, 2006. On reports of bombings, see Jim Yardley, "At Least Two Die in Blasts on Chinese Buses," *New York Times*, July 22, 2008.

29. Mark Leonard, "China's New Intelligentsia," *Social Europe Journal* (Spring 2008): 142. Also see Mark Leonard, *What Does China Think?* (New York: Public Affairs, 2008).

30. Leonard, "China's New Intelligentsia," 142.

31. Daniel A. Bell, *China's New Confucianism: Politics and Everyday Life in a Changing Society* (Princeton, NJ: Princeton University Press, 2008), 6.

32. Professor Fishkin and other practitioners of deliberative democracy use a completely new and modern approach designed to create a political dialogue and consensus, employing technologies such as the Internet, handheld computers, keypad polling devices, and closed-circuit TV to convene representative assemblies of average citizens.

33. Hutton, "Will China Dominate the 21st Century?" 133–34.

34. Khanna, *The Second World*, 261–62.

35. Philip S. Golub, "The Politics of Absolute Power," *Le Monde Diplomatique*, October 2007, http://mondediplo.com/2007/10/05absolute. This article also was published as "The Sun Sets Early on the American Century," *Eurozine*, October 16, 2007, www.eurozine.com/articles/2007–10–16-golub-en.html.

36. See Paul Kennedy, *The Rise and Fall of the Great Powers* (New York: Random House, 1987). Also see Jim Lobe, "Can the US Brace Its Fall?" Anti war.com, February 18, 2008, www.antiwar.com/lobe/?articleid=12380.

37. Parag Khanna, *The Second World: Empires and Influence in the New Global Order* (New York: Random House, 2008), xxiv.

THIRTEEN. THE LEGACY OF LUTHER AND CROMWELL

1. No proper population censuses were taken in ancient Athens, but the most educated modern guess puts the total population of fifth-century Athens, including its home territory of Attica, at around 250,000 men, women, and children, free and unfree, enfranchised and disenfranchised. Of those 250,000, some 30,000 adult males of Athenian birth were eligible to vote. Of those 30,000, perhaps 5,000 might have regularly attended one or more meetings of the popular Assembly, of which there were at least forty a year

in Aristotle's day. Women, even Athenian women, were totally excluded; this was a men's club. Foreigners, especially unfree slave foreigners, were excluded formally and rigorously. The citizen body was a closed political elite with a small electorate. Paul Cartledge, "The Democratic Experiment," BBC.com, 3, www.bbc.co.uk/history/ancient/greeks/greekdemocracy_01.shtml.

2. While the early Roman Republic had a limited representative democracy dominated by wealthy families, in one way it was more democratic than our own republic: it granted a "representation quota" to its poorest citizens. In the Centuriate Assembly all male citizens of military age were enrolled in one of five voting groups based on economic class, with the poorest classes able to have their say (however, the voting in the Centuriate Assembly was weighted in such a way that the wealthier elements could always outvote the poorest). In the middle Roman Republic the poorer classes exclusively elected ten high-level leaders, called the tribunes of the plebeians, who could use their office to take up the causes of the poor. Even in the oligarchic Roman Republic, class was distinctly recognized and formally incorporated into the voting practices and institutions, but today the idea of such affirmative action along class lines is ridiculed. Instead, poor people pretty much have opted out, since there are no class quotas, no tribunes like the Gracchi brothers to speak for them, and little hope that a viable political party might arise that can represent their interests. William G. Sinnigen and Arthur E.R. Boak, *A History of Rome to A.D. 565* (New York: Macmillan, 1977), 68, 70, 71-72, 78.

3. Tocqueville, *Democracy in America,* Introduction, 28.

4. Cromwell, for example, was a devout anti-papist who massacred thousands of Catholics at Drogheda and Wexford.

5. In October 2005 the European Court of Human Rights ruled that Britain's banning of prisoners from voting had breached the basic right to free elections, writing, "[The] removal of the vote . . . runs counter to the rehabilitation of the offender as a law-abiding member of the community." BBC News, "Q&A: UK Prisoners' Right to Vote," October 6, 2005, http://news.bbc.co.uk/2/hi/uk_news/4316148.stm.

6. Kentucky and Virginia actually permanently ban felons from voting, even after they have served their time and finished parole. Vanessa Gezari, "Go to Jail, Get to Vote—in Maine or Vermont," *St. Petersburg Times,* August 6, 2004; Justin Mason, "Vermont's Voting Laws Are Unique in Nation," *Vermont Brattleboro Reformer,* September 9, 2004; "Felony Disenfranchisement Laws in the United States," Sentencing Project, April 2007, www.sentencingproject.org/Admin/Documents/publications/fd_bs_fdlawsinus.pdf; Ann Louise Bardach, "How Florida Republicans Keep Blacks from Voting," *Los Angeles Times,* September 26, 2004.

7. In the 2004 presidential election, a Republican-linked voter registration firm in Nevada and Oregon was caught throwing out forms collected from voters registering as Democrats. In Milwaukee and Chicago, Republicans accused Democratic urban machines of registering dead people to vote, though no actual cases were ever proved. David Paul Kuhn, "Voter Fraud Charges Out West," CBS News.com, Oct. 14, 2004, http://www.cbsnews.com/stories/2004/10/14/politics/main649380.shtml.

8. Interview with Dr. Dorothea Staiger, deputy mayor of Bonn, Germany, 1997, translation by Karin Knöbelspies.

9. See Mildred Amer, "Membership of the 111th Congress: A Profile," CRS Report for Congress, December 31, 2008, http://assets.opencrs.com/rpts/R40086_20081231.pdf.

10. For the German figure, see "German Parliament Sports Young Face," Deutsche Welle, Sept. 24, 2002, www.dw-world.de/english/0,3367,1430_A_642760_1_A,00.html. For the U.S. figure, see Associated Press, "A Numeric Profile of the New Congress," Fox News, January 4, 2007, www.foxnews.com/story/0,2933,241441,00.html. Forty-two senators are sixty-five or older; while the average American is thirty-seven, no senators are in their thirties. Intelligence Report, *Parade,* November 25, 2007, 12.

11. U.S. voter turnout figures taken from the United States Election Project, http://elections.gmu.edu/voter_turnout.htm.

12. See statistics published by the Institute for Democracy and Electoral Assistance (IDEA), http://idea.int/vt/survey/voter_turnout_pop2.cfm.

13. Frances E. Lee and Bruce I. Oppenheimer, *Sizing Up the Senate: The Unequal Consequences of Equal Representation* (Chicago: University of Chicago Press, 1999), 4–5.

14. Throughout the 1990s and into the 2000s, the Democrats and a Vermont independent represented a total of 240 million adult Americans (if one counts the total adult population of a state once for each senator representing that state), and Republicans represented a total of 190 million adults—yet the Republicans had the majority. In 2004, 52 percent of the two-party vote was cast for Democratic senatorial candidates, yet Republicans elected nineteen of the thirty-four contested seats (56 percent). Richard Winger, "2006 Vote for U.S. Senate," *Ballot Access News* 22, no. 9 (January 1, 2007): 4; Matthew Shugart, "Filibuster Protects the Majority—of Voters," *San Diego Union Tribune,* May 18, 2005; Hendrik Hertzberg, "Nuke 'Em," *New Yorker,* March 14, 2005.

15. In 2004 Alaskans received from the federal government $1.87 for every dollar they pay in federal taxes, Mississippians received $1.77, and North Dakotans $1.73. California and New York, with large urban areas and some of the neediest of residents, received only $0.79, and Illinois received even less, a mere $0.73. See the tax table "Federal Outlays to States per Dollar of Tax Revenue Received," in *The World Almanac and Book of Facts, 2007* (New York: World Almanac Books, 2007), 390.

16. Jean Edward Smith, "Filibusters: The Senate's Self-Inflicted Wound," *New York Times,* 100 Days blog, March 1, 2009, http://100days.blogs.nytimes.com/2009/03/01/filibusters-the-senates-self-inflicted-wound. By 2050 as little as 5 percent of the population could have majority power in the Senate. According to the Census Bureau, by 2025 our four largest states, California, Texas, New York, and Florida, will be nonwhite majority containing a combined 25 percent of the nation's population, yet these four states will have the same representation in the Senate as sparsely settled Wyoming, Montana, Idaho, and North Dakota, which all together have less than 1 percent of the

nation's population. A similar, though not as drastic, malapportionment will prevail in the Electoral College.

17. Between 1800 and 1860, eight anti-slavery measures passed the House, only to be killed in the anti-majoritarian Senate. It took a bloody, fratricidal civil war to resolve what an unrepresentative Senate could not. Barry R. Weingast, "Political Stability and Civil War: Institutions, Commitment, and American Democracy," in *Analytical Narratives*, ed. Robert H. Bates, Avner Greif, Margaret Levi, Jean-Laurent Rosenthal, and Barry R. Weingast (Princeton, NJ: Princeton University Press, 1988), 148–93, 166, table 4.3, 168. James Madison and Alexander Hamilton correctly foresaw that awarding two senators per state, regardless of population, could result in a minority of voters winning a majority of Senate seats, which would become a real barrier to enacting policies supported by a majority of Americans. Hamilton wrote in Federalist Paper no. 22 that bestowing representatives on the basis of equal representation rather than population "contradicts the fundamental maxim of republican government, which requires that the sense of the majority should prevail." See Michael Lind, "75 Stars: How to Restore Democracy in the U.S. Senate (and End the Tyranny of Wyoming)," *Mother Jones,* January–February 1998, 47; and Dahl, *How Democratic Is the American Constitution?* 13–14.

18. Dahl, *How Democratic Is the American Constitution?* 13.

19. For example, in the 2000 presidential election, George W. Bush won most of the states that had three, four, or five electoral votes, and that small-state padding explained the difference between the Electoral College vote (won by Bush with a lean 271–267 margin) and the national popular vote (won by Al Gore with a half million more votes).

20. For example, in 1991, the fifty-two senators confirming Clarence Thomas for a lifetime appointment to the Supreme Court represented only 48.6 percent of the nation's population, seven million fewer people than were represented by the senators who voted against Thomas. Also, two-thirds of the justices are Republicans, yet less than half the nation identifies as Republican. For a full exploration of how "unrepresentative" the U.S. Supreme Court is of the views of most Americans, see Steven Hill, *10 Steps to Repair American Democracy* (Sausalito, CA: PoliPoint Press, 2006), chapter 9: "Reform the Supreme Court."

21. In PR systems, the percentage of votes it takes to win one seat is dependent on the "victory threshold" of representation, which is derived by making each contested seat in a multiseat district equal to the same proportion of votes. That is, if ten seats are being elected at once from a multiseat district, each seat will be worth 10 percent of the vote in that ten-seat district. Winning 30 percent of the vote will gain three out of the ten seats, 60 percent of the vote will gain six out of the ten seats, and so on. By adjusting the victory threshold, you can fine-tune your democracy and decide how inclusive or exclusive you want it to be. See the Web site of FairVote (www.fairvote.org) for additional resources about proportional representation. But generally speaking, PR creates multiparty democracy, and winner-take-all creates two-party democracy. In fact, half a century ago a French political scientist named Maurice Duverger proposed what became known to political scientists as Duverger's Law: winner-

take-all electoral systems tend to result in a two-choice/two-party political system. See Maurice Duverger, *Political Parties: Their Organization and Activity in the Modern State* (New York: John Wiley, 1954), 217. This observation has since been seconded by leading American political scientists and theorists such as Robert Dahl, Arend Lijphart, Anthony Downs, and Douglas Amy, among others.

22. Richard Winger, "Candidates Elected to State Office Who Weren't Major Party Nominees," *Ballot Access News* 23, no. 8, December 1, 2007, 5.

23. Italy tops the list with 93 percent participation. Belgium, Austria, and the Netherlands have 85 percent; Sweden, Denmark, and the Czech Republic, 83 percent; Germany, 81 percent. In the 2006 elections for the U.S. House of Representatives, voter turnout was a paltry 40 percent.

24. Arend Lijphart, *Patterns of Democracy: Government Forms and Performance in 36 Countries* (New Haven, CT, and London: Yale University Press, 1999), 281–82.

25. See statistics on women's representation worldwide, published by the Inter-parliamentary Union, at http://www.ipu.org/wmn-e/classif.htm. Women's representation in other European democracies includes Iceland at 33 percent, Switzerland and Portugal at 28 percent, Austria at 27 percent, Bulgaria, Estonia, Italy, and Croatia at 21 percent, Poland and Britain at 20 percent, and France at 18 percent.

26. Sweden, with 47 percent representation by women, demonstrates why PR democracies elect more women. A few years ago, Swedish women from several political parties, both right and left, were dissatisfied with the number of female legislators elected to the national parliament and threatened to bolt their parties and start a woman's party. Such a threat is credible in Sweden's proportional democracy, in which a party needs only 4 percent of the vote to win representation, especially when combined with full public financing of campaigns and free air time for parties. To prevent this, many of the political parties agreed to promote more female candidates, quickly resulting in Sweden's having one of the highest percentages of female legislators in the world. Meanwhile, when women leaders from the National Organization for Women and the Feminist Majority in the United States threatened to create a woman's party, no one took them seriously because it is so notoriously difficult for third parties to succeed in a winner-take-all system. To this day, fair female representation remains an elusive dream in the U.S. but a reality in Sweden and many other European democracies.

27. For the French figure, see Léna Morel, "Dan Jorgensen (32): 'I'm Lucky to Be a Politician So Early on in My Life,'" Cafebabel.com, January 16, 2008, http://cafebabel.com/en/article.asp?T=T&Id=13529. For the German figure, see "German Parliament Sports Young Face," *Deutsche Welle*, September 24, 2002, www.dw-world.de/english/0,3367,1430_A_642760_1_A,00.html. For the U.S. figure, see Associated Press, "A Numeric Profile of the New Congress," Fox News, January 4, 2007, www.foxnews.com/story/0,2933,241441,00.html.

28. Quoted in Seven McDonald, "Baby Greens," *LA Weekly*, January 15, 2003, www.laweekly.com/news/features/baby-greens/3235/?page=1.

29. Lijphart, *Patterns of Democracy*, 275, 280–82, 301–2.

30. John D. Huber and G. Bingham Powell, Jr., "Congruence between Citizens and Policymakers in Two Visions of Liberal Democracy," *World Politics* 46 (April 1994): 291–326; and G. Bingham Powell, Jr., *Elections as Instruments of Democracy: Majoritarian and Proportional Visions* (New Haven, CT: Yale University Press, October 2000). Huber and Powell assessed the extent to which a government achieves "policy congruence"—that is, does it do what its citizens want it to? They found that policy passed by governments elected by proportional representation were more responsive to the desires of the populace than policy passed by governments elected by winner-take-all methods. That was because the coalition building that occurs often in governments elected by PR has a positive impact on policy, since "giving some (but not too much) policymaking weight to the opposition will typically increase congruence." Huber and Powell concluded, "Proportionate Influence systems are on average significantly closer to the median voter than are governments in the Majority Control systems. . . . On average the failures of electoral competition in the Majority Control . . . systems seem more serious for congruence. . . . The winning parties in the Majority Control systems are often not very close to the median." Powell updated and expanded this research in his book, in which he examined over 150 elections in twenty democracies over a quarter century. Once again, Powell laid out how the two models of democracy—majoritarian vision and proportional vision—dealt with voters' intent and desires. While both political systems have their merits, Powell concluded, the proportional vision produces greater policy congruence between what the public wants and actual government policy. Proportional vision systems have outperformed the majoritarian ones by better reflecting the populace's needs and better representing the voters' wishes.

31. The former Soviet bloc nations in eastern and central Europe now use proportional voting and a parliamentary government structure, not winner-take-all or an eighteenth-century Electoral College system for electing the president. Even our own national progenitor, Great Britain, from whom our founders adopted many of our eighteenth-century practices, is midstream in a remarkable political transformation, having adopted PR for electing representatives to the European Parliament, the London City Council, the Scottish and Wales regional assemblies, and Scottish local councils.

FOURTEEN. CONSENSUS BUILDING THROUGH DYNAMIC DEMOCRACY

1. Thomas Jefferson to Richard Price, 1789, from *The Writings of Thomas Jefferson,* Memorial Edition, ed. Andrew A. Lipscomb and Albert E. Bergh, 20 volumes (Washington DC: Thomas Jefferson Memorial Association, 1904), vol. 7: 253.

2. Presidential candidate Ralph Nader filed numerous lawsuits against the Democratic National Committee for mounting what Richard Winger, editor of *Ballot Access News,* called an unprecedented and massive legal effort to remove Nader from the ballot. Winger wrote that "past efforts [by the Demo-

crats to remove third-party candidates] were confined to one or two states," but "the 2004 Democratic efforts [to remove Nader] were massive, existing in almost half the states." Richard Winger, "Nader Sues Dems," *Ballot Access News* 23, no. 8, December 1, 2007, 3. Richard Winger's *Ballot Access News* is the most authoritative source in the United States on ballot access laws for third parties and independent candidates. For a gripping insider's view on Democrats' dirty tricks used against Nader, see Theresa Amato, *Grand Illusion: The Myth of Voter Choice in a Two-Party Tyranny* (New York: New Press, 2009), which is an account of Nader's runs for president in 2000 and 2004 by his national campaign manager.

3. *The Political Standard* (newsletter of the Alliance for Better Campaigns) 3, no. 9, December 2000, 2.

4. "Gouging Democracy: How the Television Industry Profiteered on Campaign 2000," a study by the Alliance for Better Campaigns, www.better campaigns.org, 6.

5. See "Review of Public Service Broadcasting around the World," a report by McKinsey and Company, London, September 2004, http://www.ofcom.org .uk/consult/condocs/psb2/psb2/psbwp/wp3mck.pdf.

6. Henry Milner, *Civic Literacy: How Informed Citizens Make Democracy Work* (Hanover, NH, and London: University Press of New England, 2002), 108.

7. See Robert Putnam, *Bowling Alone: The Collapse and Revival of American Community* (New York: Simon and Schuster, 2001); and Milner, *Civic Literacy*, 90–104.

8. Richard Pérez-Peña, "As Cities Go from Two Papers to One, Talk of Zero," *New York Times*, March 11, 2009, www.nytimes.com/2009/03/12/ business/media/12papers.html?hp. In May 2007 the *San Francisco Chronicle* slashed its number of staff reporters by 25 percent and six months later slashed its staff again. The *Los Angeles Times* axed nearly a hundred of its editorial staff and reporters, including Pulitzer Prize–winning journalists. Newspapers across the country, including the *New York Times,* the *Philadelphia Inquirer,* and the *Boston Globe,* terminated a chunk of their news staffs, in most cases reducing or eliminating their investigative reporting departments.

9. I am always fascinated by the small TV screens you see mounted high in many European buses and subways, blaring the latest news or human interest stories, keeping Europeans up to date and well informed. In Paris, one way the French encourage reading is by selling books via sidewalk vending machines— Baudelaire and Homer available 24/7, side by side with more practical fare such as *The Wok Cookbook* and *100 Delicious Couscous,* for only $2.45 per book. Associated Press, "Vending machines serve up helping of books," MSNBC .com, August 26, 2005, www.msnbc.msn.com/id/9005718/. To further contribute to worldly knowledge, many national museums and even some private museums have free or low-cost admission (much like the Smithsonian museums in Washington DC, among the few free museums in the United States) and frequent evening hours so that working people can attend (a rarity in American museums, in my experience). Germany and Austria have created an Artists' Social Fund (*Künstlersozialkasse*), which assists any freelance musician, writer,

translator, dancer, actor, or visual artist in affording health care, social security, and private nursing insurance. France has long been known for its support of artists and freelancers, including generous unemployment benefits and access to the broad array of French social supports. Ireland also provides generous tax breaks for artists. Compare that with the United States, where the vast majority of artists live hand to mouth without access to health care or any kind of safety net, and under several presidents more federal funding was appropriated for military marching bands than for the entire National Endowment for the Arts.

10. Blaine Harden, "Japan's Warp-Speed Ride to Internet Future," *Washington Post,* August 29, 2007, www.washingtonpost.com/wp-dyn/content/article/2007/08/28/AR2007082801990_pf.html; Esme Vos, "100 Mbps for 30 Euros in Paris," Muniwireless.com, August 31, 2007, www.muniwireless.com/article/articleview/6367/1/2. France, Japan, and other nations are offering broadband access with typical speeds of 100 megabytes per second, whereas in the U.S. typical speeds are 2.5–3.0 Mbps. Also see Paul Krugman, "The French Connections," *New York Times,* July 23, 2007.

11. The Obama campaign raised hundreds of millions of dollars over the Internet, mostly from small donors, allowing Obama to circumvent to some degree the influence that the corporate media and wealthy donors have on the U.S. political process. Team Obama also took advantage of YouTube for free advertising and message dissemination and embraced social networking sites like MySpace and Facebook. Some are saying that Obama's use of this relatively new medium will change politics the way John F. Kennedy's use of television did, though it remains to be seen if future candidates can replicate this success. Since assuming office, the Obama administration has drawn on the high-tech organizational tools that helped elect him and has applied those tools to the earliest stages of governing. European politicos have been earnestly studying the Obama Internet campaign to see what they may learn from it. See Steven Hill, "The World Wide Webbed: The Obama Campaign's Masterful Use of the Internet," *Social Europe Journal,* April 8, 2009, www.newamerica.net/publications/articles/2009/world_wide_webbed_12862.

12. After the rupture at the United Nations, American media suddenly turned on our transatlantic allies, transmogrifying them overnight into double-crossers, an "axis of weasels," and "cheese-eating surrender monkeys," to quote that erudite political analyst, Bart Simpson. During the U.N. tussle over the Iraq invasion, the front page of Rupert Murdoch's *New York Post* showed the graves of Normandy with the headline "They Died for France but France Has Forgotten." Leading intellectuals in the United States, such as Thomas Friedman, George Will, and Christopher Hitchens, among others, apparently drawing inspiration from Bart and Murdoch, piled it on, saying France should be removed from the Security Council (Friedman), that it had retreated "into incoherence" (Will), and that the French president Jacques Chirac was "the rat that tried to roar" (Hitchens). Gary Younge and Jon Henley, "Wimps, Weasels and Monkeys—the US Media View of 'Perfidious France,'" *The Guardian,* February 11, 2003, www.guardian.co.uk/world/2003/feb/11/pressandpublishing.usa.

13. Paul Krugman, "Behind the Great Divide," *New York Times,* February 18, 2003. A notable exception to America's poor-quality journalism has been Pacifica Radio's *Democracy Now!* but the audience is relatively small.

14. Milner, *Civic Literacy;* Putnam, *Bowling Alone.*

15. Participants in these tests typically are asked questions to see if they can find Iraq on a map of the Middle East, or if they can identify the name of the U.N. secretary general, or if they know the name of the president or prime minister and other high government officials. Milner, *Civic Literacy,* 55–65.

16. Ibid., 189.

17. See Augustin Scalbert, "Who Controls the Media in Europe?" *Rue89,* November 5, 2007, www.rue89.com/2007/11/05/qui-controle-les-medias-en-europe. According to Scalbert, the most-watched station in France, TF1, belongs to Bouygues, a building and public works group that signs contracts with the government daily. Arnaud Lagardère, an important shareholder in the aeronautics group EADS, with which the French government also is involved, controls the empire that bears his name and consequently controls *Europe 1, Paris Match,* the *Journal du Dimanche,* 25 percent of *Parisien-Aujourd'hui,* 17 percent of *Le Monde,* and half of the biggest newspaper distributor, the NMPP. Serge Dassault, who is trying to sell his Rafale aircraft with the French government's help, is the owner of *Le Figaro.* Bernard Arnault—owner of *La Tribune,* was the witness to Nicolas Sarkozy's first marriage.

18. Critics of proportional representation voting systems usually stereotype them by saying that they lead to "dozens of small political parties" that cause collapsing governments. Yet this is demonstrably false; the number of political parties is purely a function of the "victory threshold" used, which is chosen by those designing the electoral system. If you use a low victory threshold for which, say, only 1 percent of the vote is needed to win a legislative seat, you will likely see the "flowering effect" of numerous political parties. However, if you use a higher threshold, for instance, the 5 percent threshold used by Germany, you will see what is called "moderate proportional representation," with approximately four to six political parties with any chance of getting elected, and two of these will be major parties (one center-right and one center-left), with two to four smaller parties that wax and wane in influence depending on the issues of the day. If you want it to be extremely inclusive (and perhaps a bit fractious, with numerous parties that may not get along well), use a 1 percent threshold, as Israel used for many years. If you want your democracy to be exclusive, with few parties and few choices for voters, use a U.S.- or British-style winner-takes-all system, with victory thresholds of 60 percent or higher for most legislative races. But experience around the world suggests a happy medium is possible, somewhere around Germany's 5 percent victory threshold.

19. Some American critics contend that a proportional representation electoral system was responsible for bringing Adolf Hitler to power in Germany in the early 1930s. When I posed this question to a midlevel leader of the conservative Christian Democratic Union in Germany, he just laughed and dismissed such an idea as preposterous, citing numerous other aspects of the Weimar Republic that were far more significant in the rise of Nazism. In fact, some

scholars contend that if the Weimar Republic had used a U.S.-style winner-take-all electoral system, its "sweep effect" would have magnified the electoral impact of the Nazi Party, causing them to win even more seats than they won under proportional representation. Interview with Tom Schlatmann, chief of staff for CDU parliamentarian Andrea Schmitt, Bonn, Germany, 1997.

20. For example, some of the far right parties have found electoral success by promising to impose longer waiting periods (up to seven years in Denmark) before new arrivals can enter the country's cradle-to-grave welfare system. Imagine how many natural-born Americans would be overjoyed at the prospect of waiting a mere seven years to attain the level of workfare benefits bestowed upon Danish immigrants. Indeed, most Democratic Party candidates or leaders who espoused the pro-workfare policies of the European far right would be hounded by conservative Democrats into a backbench seat or retirement.

21. Interestingly, in the scaled-back E.U. treaty one of the anti-democratic features targeted for reform was the U.S. Senate–like awarding of greater representation to low-population member countries, which sometimes has thwarted the formation of an E.U.-wide majoritarian policy. The European Union does not want to be held back as America has been by anti-majoritarian tendencies in its most basic institutions.

22. Charles Kupchan, "The End of the West," *Atlantic Monthly,* November 2002, 42.

23. In addition to Jean Monnet, Robert Schuman, Winston Churchill, Altiero Spinelli, and Konrad Adenauer, any list of the founders of modern Europe comparable to the Washington-Jefferson-Adams-Madison-Franklin-Hamilton lineup would include a second generation of European leaders composed of Jacques Delors, Helmut Schmidt, François Mitterand, Willy Brandt, and Helmut Köhl, among others. Winston Churchill gave a speech at the University of Zürich in September 1946 calling for a "United States of Europe."

24. Wrote Tocqueville about the still-young United States of America circa 1832, "The political activity that pervades the United States must be seen in order to be understood. No sooner do you set foot on American ground than you are stunned by a kind of tumult." Tocqueville, *Democracy in America,* pt. 1, 108.

FIFTEEN. STICKY GLUE, SOCIAL CONTRACTS, AND
FULCRUM INSTITUTIONS

1. Arnold Toynbee, *East to West: A Journey Round the World* (New York: Oxford University Press, 1958), 199.

2. Hutton, *The World We're In,* 50.

3. American conservatives hailed the election of Nicolas Sarkozy as France's return to a more U.S.-style free market enterprise, but that was a gross misreading of the French president's views. While Sarkozy has tried to liberalize the French economy to some extent, he also has stated, "Rigidities of ideology limit your choices when the best solutions might involve a mix: more liberalism where best, intervention when necessary." When the financial markets melted

down in September 2008, Sarkozy called for sweeping regulation and "moralization" of international finance and declared that the era "of the market always being right is over." During one speech, Sarkozy attacked those who had created the unfolding financial crisis. "A certain conception of globalization has closed out: [one that] imposed its own logic on the entire economy and helped pervert it." Bruce Crumley, "Europe's Conservatives Pooh-Pooh the Free Market," Time.com, September 26, 2008, www.time.com/time/world/article/0,8599,1844919,00.html?xid = rss-world.

4. George Frey, "Germany's Merkel Backs 'Volkswagen Law,'" Associated Press story in *San Francisco Chronicle*, September 24, 2008.

5. Ronald Reagan, First Inaugural Address, January 20, 1981.

6. Hutton, *The World We're In*, 55.

7. Tocqueville, *Democracy in America*, vol. 1: 241.

8. Hutton, *The World We're In*, 58.

9. Ibid., 54.

10. Ibid., 61–63.

11. For a fascinating discussion of the congressional debates over slavery in the early years of the republic, see Joseph J. Ellis, *Founding Brothers: The Revolutionary Generation* (New York: Vintage Books, 2002), 81–119.

12. In *Dartmouth College v. Woodward* (1819), the Supreme Court ruled that any state that had given a corporation the right to enter into contracts had no more right to interfere in its affairs under the contract clause. In *Lawton v. Steel* (1894), the Supreme Court ruled that "the Legislature may not, under the guise of protecting the public interest, arbitrarily interfere with private business, or impose unusual and unnecessary restrictions upon lawful occupations." In its *Pollock v. Farmers Loan and Trust Company* decision in 1895, the Supreme Court also declared unconstitutional the levying of an income tax, necessitating the passage of the Sixteenth Amendment in 1916, making income tax legal. Cited in Hutton, *The World We're In*, 59.

13. See Jeffrey Rosen, "Supreme Court Inc.," *New York Times*, March 16, 2008, in which Rosen documents the clear pro-business bias in recent high court decisions. Writes Rosen, "Though the current Supreme Court has a well-earned reputation for divisiveness, it has been surprisingly united in cases affecting business interests. Of the 30 business cases last term, 22 were decided unanimously, or with only one or two dissenting votes."

14. See opinion pieces by historians Eric Foner, "He's the Worst Ever," *Washington Post*, December 3, 2006; and Sean Wilentz, "The Worst President in History?" *Rolling Stone*, April 21, 2006, www.rollingstone.com/news/coverstory/worst_president_in_history. Author Michael Lind rated Bush as "only" the fifth worst; Michael Lind, "He's Only Fifth Worst," *Washington Post*, December 3, 2006. In April 2008 the History News Network took an unofficial poll of U.S. historians who were asked to rank the presidency of George W. Bush in comparison to those of the other forty-one U.S. presidents. More than 61 percent of the historians concluded that the Bush presidency was the worst in the nation's history. See Robert S. McElvaine, "HNN Poll: 61% of Historians Rate the Bush Presidency Worst," History News Network, April 1, 2008, http://hnn.us/articles/48916.html.

15. Charles Hampden-Turner and Alfons Trompenaars, *The Seven Cultures of Capitalism: Value Systems for Creating Wealth in the United States, Japan, Germany, France, Britain, Sweden and the Netherlands* (New York: Currency Doubleday, 1993), 340.

16. See text of Bill Gates's speech to the World Economic Forum, Davos, Switzerland, January 24, 2008, www.gatesfoundation.org/MediaCenter/ Speeches/Co-ChairSpeeches/BillgSpeeches/BGSpeechWEF-080124.htm.

17. For Buffet quotes, see Stephen J. Dubner, "Warren Buffet Swats the Invisible Hand," *New York Times,* June 27, 2006, http://freakonomics.blogs .nytimes.com/2006/06/27/warren-buffet-swats-the-invisible-hand/; and Tom Bawden, "Buffett Blasts System That Lets Him Pay Less Tax than Secretary," *Times of London,* June 28, 2007, http://business.timesonline.co.uk/tol/business/ money/tax/article1996735.ece.

18. This stance would not be as unusual as it might seem, since it was enlightened business leaders of the late nineteenth century, including the French industrialist Leon Harmel (who established sick funds and a social insurance fund for his workers to which he contributed half) and the German industrialist Franz Brandts, both of whom bucked their own fellow capitalists to assist in the formation of the first vestiges of European social capitalism. Hutton, *The World We're In,* 63–64.

19. Reid, *The United States of Europe,* 178.

20. Moisés Naím, "Can the World Afford a Middle Class?" *Los Angeles Times,* February 8, 2008, www.latimes.com/news/opinion/la-oe-naim8febo8 ,0,3322827.story.

21. Lester R. Brown, "A New World Order," *The Guardian,* January 25, 2006.

SIXTEEN. THE CHALLENGES
OF IMMIGRATION AND INTEGRATION

1. The photo of the boy appeared on the front page of *El Pais,* September 5, 2006, English edition with the *International Herald Tribune.*

2. See Agence France-Presse, "Immigration from East Europe Is 'Elixir' for British Economy, Experts Say," April 23, 2006; and Susie Mesure, "Immigrants Have Boosted UK Growth, Says Study," *The Independent,* April 23, 2006, http://news.independent.co.uk/business/news/article359850.ece.

3. "The White Man's Burden" is a poem by the English poet Rudyard Kipling, originally published in the popular magazine *McClure's* in 1899, with the subtitle "The United States and the Philippine Islands," in the aftermath of the U.S. conquest of the Philippines and other former Spanish colonies. Kipling presents a Eurocentric view of the world in which non-European cultures are seen as childlike, proposing that white people have an obligation to rule over these other people until they can take their place in the world by fully adopting Western ways. While Kipling's paean to Western empire was mixed with sober warnings of the costs involved in empire building, Western imperialists latched

on to the phrase "white man's burden" as a justification that rationalized their murderous policies as a noble enterprise.

4. Governor George Wallace later rehabilitated his reputation to some degree, so the public tends to forget his early extreme bigotry. Among other things, during a time when lynchings and church bombings occurred on a regular basis, he campaigned by saying, "What this country needs is a few first-class funerals, and some political funerals too." He was a fund-raiser for Ku Klux Klan causes, blamed the "nigras" themselves for bombings of their own homes and churches, and appeared in public with Klan leaders, such as convicted church bomber Robert Chambliss, a local legend for his remorseless savagery. And of course Wallace defied a federal court order to integrate Alabama's public schools and university. For his hate-mongering policies, Wallace was a hero and cultivated a fervent constituency among racists throughout the nation. Compared with Wallace, Europe's far-right leaders, such as Jean Marie Le Pen and Jorg Haider, are relative lightweights. See Diane McWhorter, *Carry Me Home: Birmingham, Alabama: The Climactic Battle of the Civil Rights Revolution* (New York: Simon and Schuster, 2001).

5. John Ward Anderson, "Belgians Seek Roots of Racist Crimes; String of Attacks on Foreigners Feeds Fears about Political Appeal of Intolerance," *Washington Post,* Washington Post Foreign Service, May 20, 2006, www.washingtonpost.com/wp-dyn/content/article/2006/05/19/AR2006051901782.html.

6. Ian Herbert, "'We Muslims Stick Together so We Aren't Given as Much Stick,'" *The Independent,* September 22, 2005.

7. Molly Moore, "Swiss Fury at Foreigners Boiling Over," *Washington Post,* Washington Post Foreign Service, October 9, 2007.

8. See Denny Adelman's blog at http://blog.cocagne.com.

9. The late Italian journalist Oriana Fallaci sold more than a million copies of her 2004 book *The Force of Reason,* in which she warned against the impending Islamic invasion. In addition to Bernard Lewis's foreboding prediction, Middle East specialist Daniel Pipes has predicted that "grand cathedrals will appear as vestiges of a prior civilization—at least until a Saudi-style regime transforms them into mosques or a Taliban-like regime blows them up." Martin Walker, "Europe's Mosque Hysteria," *Wilson Quarterly,* Spring 2006, www.wilsoncenter.org/index.cfm?fuseaction=wq.essay&essay_id=178659.

10. Wouter Bos, "Europe's Social Democrats, Solidarity and Muslim Immigration," The Globalist.com, December 9, 2005, http://theglobalist.com/StoryId.aspx?StoryId=4976.

11. Quoted in Richard Bernstein, "Despite Minor Incidents, Chance of Large-Scale Riots Elsewhere in Europe Is Seen as Small," *New York Times,* November 8, 2005.

12. U.S. Census Bureau, 2006 estimated data, http://quickfacts.census.gov/qfd/states/00000.html.

13. See Gregory Rodriguez, *Mongrels, Bastards, Orphans, and Vagabonds: Mexican Immigration and the Future of Race in America* (New York: Pantheon, 2007).

14. One exception to the western European concentration of Muslims is in Bulgaria, where Muslims make up about 12 percent of the Balkan coun-

try's 7.6 million people. Bulgaria is the only European Union member country where Muslims are not recent immigrants, since most are descendants of ethnic Turks who arrived during five centuries of Ottoman rule that ended in 1878. Bulgarian Muslims mostly are secular, having lived alongside Christians in a culture known as "komshuluk," or neighborly relations. Bulgaria has won praise for avoiding ethnic clashes after the end of the Cold War, in contrast to the former Yugoslavia, which borders it to the west and which was wracked by bloody Muslim-Christian strife. Still, Bulgaria's intolerance of its Muslim minority occasionally flares up. Anna Mudeva, "Cracks Show in Bulgaria's Muslim Ethnic Model," Reuters, May 31, 2009.

15. Farooq Kathwari and Lynn M. Martin, cochairs, "Strengthening America: The Civic and Political Integration of Muslim Americans," Report of the Task Force on Muslim American Civic and Political Engagement, the Chicago Council on Global Affairs, 2007, 36.

16. Walker, "Europe's Mosque Hysteria."

17. Ibid.

18. Katja Heise, "More Muslims, More Mosques in Europe," Cafebabel .com, October 1, 2007, www.cafebabel.com/en/article.asp?T=A&Id=2766& utm_source=NL_EN&utm_medium=email.

19. "Two Unamalgamated Worlds," The Economist, April 3, 2008, www .economist.com/world/europe/displaystory.cfm?story_id=10958534.

20. Matt Carr, "You Are Now Entering Eurabia," Race and Class 48, no. 1 (July 2006): 1–22.

21. Christian Rioux, "La citoyenneté n'est pas une formalité," Le Devoir, July 18, 2008.

22. The percentages are quoted from Justin Vaisse, coauthor of Integrating Islam: Political and Religious Challenges in Contemporary France, by Jonathan Laurence and Justin Vaisse (Washington DC: Brookings Institution Press, August 1, 2006), in a panel discussion on September 13, 2006, transcript at www.brookings.edu/~/media/Files/events/2006/0913islamic%20world/2006 0913islam.pdf, 6.

23. Carr, "You Are Now Entering Eurabia."

24. Caryle Murphy, "U.S. Muslim Scholars to Forbid Terrorism," Washington Post, July 28, 2005.

25. See demographic information for France and other countries at the Web site of the Migration Policy Institute, www.migrationinformation.org/ datahub/countrydata/data.cfm.

26. According to the Migrant Integration Policy Index at www.integration index.eu/integrationindex/2377.html, France has 8.1 percent "foreign-borns," but only 3.8 percent are "third country nationals," which are immigrants from outside the E.U. Those percentages are quite a bit lower than Germany's (12.9 percent foreign-borns and 5.6 percent third country nationals; see www .integrationindex.eu/integrationindex/2556.html), Spain's (8.6 percent foreign-borns, 7.2 percent third country nationals; see www.integrationindex.eu/inte grationindex/2531.html), Austria's (13 percent foreign-borns, 7.1 percent third country nationals; see www.integrationindex.eu/integrationindex/2299.html), and Switzerland's (23.5 percent foreign-borns, 8.3 percent third country nation-

als; see www.integrationindex.eu/integrationindex/2553.html), and are comparable to Britain's (9.3 percent foreign-borns, 3.5 percent third country nationals; see www.integrationindex.eu/integrationindex/2583.html), Sweden's (12.2 percent foreign-borns, 2.9 percent third country nationals; see www.integrationindex.eu/integrationindex/2549.html), and the Netherlands's (10.6 percent foreign-borns, 2.9 percent third country nationals; see www.integrationindex.eu/integrationindex/2468.html).

27. Guillaume Duval, *Sommes-nous des paresseux?* [Are we lazy?] (Paris: Seuil, 2008), 15, quoted in Frederic Lemaitre, "Inevitable, Indispensable Immigration," *Le Monde*, January 22, 2008.

28. The U.S. Census calculates that "by 2042, Americans who identify themselves as Hispanic, black, Asian, American Indian, Native Hawaiian and Pacific Islander will together outnumber non-Hispanic whites. Four years ago, officials had projected the shift would come in 2050." The main reason for the accelerating change is the significantly higher birthrates among immigrants. Another factor is the influx of foreigners, rising from about 1.3 million annually today to more than 2 million a year by mid-century, according to projections based on current immigration policies. "No other country has experienced such rapid racial and ethnic change," said Mark Mather, a demographer with the Population Reference Bureau, a research organization in Washington DC. Sam Roberts, "In a Generation, Minorities May Be the U.S. Majority," *New York Times*, August 14, 2008, p. A1, http://www.nytimes.com/2008/08/14/washington/14census.html.

29. Craig S. Smith, "France Is Trying, Discreetly, to Integrate Television a Bit," *New York Times*, November 16, 2005.

30. Eva Lodde, Mike Glindmeier, and Jens Todt, "Player Silences German Racists with Hitler Salute," *Spiegel*, April 3, 2006, http://service.spiegel.de/cache/international/0,1518,409517,00.html.

31. Gregory Rodriguez, "What It Means to Be German," *Los Angeles Times*, May 28, 2006.

32. Walker, "Europe's Mosque Hysteria."

33. "Two Unamalgamated Worlds," *The Economist*, April 3, 2008.

34. Walker, "Europe's Mosque Hysteria."

35. For U.S. unemployment figures sorted by race, see Bureau of Labor Statistics at http://www.bls.gov/cps/home.htm, specifically the statistical tables at ftp://ftp.bls.gov/pub/special.requests/lf/aat6.txt and ftp://ftp.bls.gov/pub/special.requests/lf/aat5.txt. For prison population figures sorted by race, see U.S. Department of Justice, "Prisoners in 2006," Bureau of Justice Statistics Bulletin, December 2007, NCJ 219416, table 8, 7, www.ojp.usdoj.gov/bjs/pub/pdf/p06.pdf.

36. John Rossant, "Liberte, Egalite, Affirmative Action," BusinessWeek.com, January 31, 2005, www.businessweek.com/magazine/content/05_05/b3918104_mz054.htm.

37. Walker, "Europe's Mosque Hysteria."

38. One of the controversies with the E.U. directive was the length of detention of illegal immigrants that it would allow. Until then the duration varied considerably between E.U. countries, from the harshest policy in Sweden and

the Netherlands, allowing unlimited detention, to the policy in France, of only thirty-two days' detention. The E.U. directive fixed it at a maximum of six months in all European countries, with an extension to twelve months if cooperation from the prisoner or his or her country of origin is insufficient.

SEVENTEEN. A CIVIL RIGHTS MOVEMENT ARISES— SORT OF

1. John Lichfield, "Kitchen Staff Stage Sit-in at Champs-Elysées Bistro," *The Independent,* May 27, 2008.

2. The *Die Tageszeitung* editorial is quoted in Josh Ward and David Crossland, "Koch Gets Face Slapped for 'Nasty' Campaign," *Spiegel,* January 28, 2008, www.spiegel.de/international/germany/0,1518,531422,00.html.

3. Agence France-Presse, "Equal Treatment Law in Austria," *International Herald Tribune,* May 29, 2004.

4. "Multicultural Hysterics," *The Economist,* April 20, 2006, www.econo mist.com/World/europe/displayStory.cfm?story_id=6837182.

5. HALDE is the Haute Autorité de Lutte contre les Discriminations et pour l'Égalité, which is French for the High Authority on the Fight against Discrimination and for Equality. Its main decision-making body consists of eleven members who are designated jointly by the president, the prime minister, the presidents of the assemblies, and the social and economic council, as well as the vice-president of the Council of State and the first president of the Court of Cassation. The board puts in place an advisory committee composed of eighteen persons, which allows it to recruit qualified experts to its work. Finally, HALDE has administrative services at its disposal, as well as a limited number of regional delegates.

6. Quoted in John Rossant, "Liberte, Egalite, Affirmative Action," Business Week.com, January 31, 2005, www.businessweek.com/magazine/content/05 _05/b3918104_mz054.htm.

7. Shawn Pogatchnik, "Ireland to Open Non-Catholic Schools in Dublin," *USA Today,* Associated Press story, December 14, 2007.

8. Mariona Vivar Mompel, "Muslims against the Grain," Cafebabel.com, September 6, 2006, www.cafebabel.com/en/article.asp?T=T&Id=7964.

9. Pamela Selwyn, personal e-mail sent to author, January 16, 2008.

10. Prune Antoine, "Foreigners Shun Polling Stations in Brussels," Cafebabel .com, October 12, 2006, www.cafebabel.com/en/article.asp?T=T&Id=8364.

11. Henry Milner, "Youth Electoral Participation in Canada and Scandinavia," published in Peter Levine and James Youniss, eds., *Engaging Young People in Civic Life* (Nashville, TN: Vanderbilt University Press, 2009).

12. See statistics on women's representation worldwide, published by the Inter-parliamentary Union at http://www.ipu.org/wmn-e/classif.htm. Women's proportion of representation in other European democracies includes Finland and the Netherlands at 41 percent, Denmark at 38 percent, Spain and Norway at 36 percent, Belgium at 35 percent, Iceland at 33 percent, Switzerland and

Portugal at 28 percent, Austria at 27 percent, Bulgaria, Estonia, Italy, and Croatia at 21 percent, Poland and Britain at 20 percent, and France at 18 percent.

13. Keith B. Richburg, "Europe's Minority Politicians in Short Supply," *Washington Post*, April 24, 2005, www.washingtonpost.com/wp-dyn/articles/A12396–2005Apr23.html.

14. Ibid.

15. Reid, *United States of Europe*, 198.

16. Craig S. Smith, "France Is Trying, Discreetly, to Integrate Television a Bit," *New York Times*, November 16, 2005.

17. Gwendolyn Albert, "Racism in the Czech Republic," *ENAR Shadow Report 2006* (Brussels: European Network against Racism, 2007), www.enar-eu.org/en/national/czechrep/Czech_Republic_2006.pdf.

18. Gregory Rodriguez, "What It Means to Be German," *Los Angeles Times*, May 28, 2006.

19. Steven Erlanger, "Melting Pot of Melodrama Enthralls French Nightly," *New York Times*, March 2, 2009.

20. Smith, "France Is Trying, Discreetly, to Integrate Television a Bit."

21. Martin Walker, "Europe's Mosque Hysteria," *Wilson Quarterly*, Spring 2006, www.wilsoncenter.org/index.cfm?fuseaction=wq.essay&essay_id=178659.

22. Umberto Eco, *Turning Back the Clock* (New York: Harcourt, 2007), 271.

23. See the Web site for the European Commission, specifically the European Commission's European Social Fund, at http://ec.europa.eu/employment_social/esf/discover/esf_en.htm.

24. Ibid. Also see "European Social Fund 2007–2013: Integration of Migrants in the Labour Market," Brussels, November 2006, http://ec.europa.eu/employment_social/esf/docs/migrants_en.pdf.

25. See "European Social Fund 2007–2013: Integration of Migrants in the Labour Market," Brussels, November 2006, 4, http://ec.europa.eu/employment_social/esf/docs/migrants_en.pdf.

26. Tiziana Sforza, "EU Plays 'Urban Governance' Card," Cafebabel.com, November 21, 2005, http://cafebabel.com/en/article.asp?T=T&Id=5274.

27. Peter Ford, "Europe's Rising Class of Believers: Muslims," *Christian Science Monitor*, February 24, 2005, www.csmonitor.com/2005/0224/p10s01-woeu.html.

28. Ehsan Masood, David Goodhart, and Adair Turner, "Tariq Ramadan: An Interview," *Prospect* no. 124, July 2006, www.prospect-magazine.co.uk/article_details.php?id=7571.

29. Katrin Bennhold, "Two Personalities Clash on European Immigration," *International Herald Tribune*, January 15, 2008, www.iht.com/articles/2008/01/15/europe/debate.php.

30. Quoted in Ford, "Europe's Rising Class of Believers."

31. Matt Carr, "You Are Now Entering Eurabia," *Race and Class* 48, no. 1 (July 2006): 1–22.

EIGHTEEN. THE DILEMMA OF POPULATION DECLINE

1. Elisabeth Rosenthal, "Empty Playgrounds in an Aging Italy," *International Herald Tribune*, September 5, 2006.

2. Ibid.

3. Author and demographic analyst Joel Kotkin writes, "No advanced Western country—America, Canada, Australia, Britain, Germany, France or Japan—produces enough new children to keep them from becoming granny nation-states by 2050." Joel Kotkin, "Vintage Radicalism May Emerge in Protest," *Arizona Republic*, April 30, 2006. Joel Garreau, writing in *Smithsonian Magazine*, says, "Nearly half the world's population lives in countries where the native-born are not reproducing fast enough to replace themselves. This is true in Western Europe, Eastern Europe, Russia, Japan, Canada and the United States. It's also true in much of East Asia, pockets of Latin America and such Indian megacities as New Delhi, Mumbai (Bombay), Kolkata (Calcutta) and Chennai (Madras). Even China is reproducing at levels that fall short of replacement." Joel Garreau, "300 Million and Counting," *Smithsonian Magazine*, October 2006, www.smithsonianmagazine.com/issues/2006/october/presence.php.

4. The replacement fertility rate, 2.1 children per woman, includes 2 children to replace both parents, but one of those children must be a female child who survives long enough also to give birth to a female child, and so on for succeeding generations. An average of two children will "replace" all mothers and fathers but only if the same number of girls as boys are born and all female children survive into reproductive age and also reproduce. However, those two ideal conditions cannot prevail because of the premature mortality of some girls. So that means the replacement-level fertility rate is actually a little higher than 2.0; it's 2.1. See Office for National Statistics in the United Kingdom, "Population Trends," no. 119, Spring 2005, 16, www.statistics.gov.uk/downloads/theme_population/PT119v2.pdf.

5. Alasdair Murray, "Growing Old Gracefully: How to Ease Population Ageing in Europe," EU2020 essay, published by the Centre for European Reform (CER), January 2008, 5–6, www.cer.org.uk/pdf/e790_17jan08.pdf.

6. All figures for total fertility rates come from the United Nations report *World Population Prospects*, 2006 revision, for the period 2005–10, table A.15, using the medium variant. See www.un.org/esa/population/publications/wpp2006/WPP2006_Highlights_rev.pdf. Also see Hans P. Johnson, "Birth Rates in California," *California Counts: Population Trends and Profiles* (a publication of the Public Policy Institute of California) 9, no. 2, November 2007, 3–4 (available online at www.ppic.org/main/publication.asp?i=777).

7. Rob Stein, "U.S. Fertility Rate Hits 35-Year High, Stabilizing Population," *Washington Post*, December 21, 2007, www.washingtonpost.com/wp-dyn/content/article/2007/12/20/AR2007122002725.html.

8. Bulletin Board, "300 Million and Counting," *AARP Bulletin,* October 2006, 3.

9. Johnson, "Birth Rates in California," 1, 7. Hispanic females make up a large and growing share of California's women. In 2005, Hispanic females

made up 38 percent of women ages fifteen to forty-four; whites, 40 percent; Asians, 13 percent; and African Americans, 6 percent.

10. Agence France-Presse, "France Has a Baby Boom," *International Herald Tribune*, May 13, 2005, 1.

11. Murray, "Growing Old Gracefully," 9–10.

12. Rosenthal, "Empty Playgrounds in an Aging Italy"; David Batty, "25% of UK Babies Have a Foreign Parent," *Guardian Unlimited*, August 22, 2007.

13. Ed Pilkington, "300 Million and Counting . . . US Reaches Population Milestone," *The Guardian*, October 13, 2006, www.guardian.co.uk/usa/story/0,,1921310,00.html.

14. George Weigel, *The Cube and the Cathedral: Europe, America, and Politics without God* (New York: Basic Books, 2005).

15. Philip Longman, "The Global Baby Bust," *Foreign Affairs*, May–June 2004.

16. Murray, "Growing Old Gracefully," 19.

17. Ibid., 21.

18. Gary Burtless, "Does Population Aging Represent a Crisis for Rich Societies?" Brookings Institution, January 2002, 3, www.sprc.unsw.edu.au/seminars/SPRC%20Burtless%20Crisis.pdf.

19. Natascha Gewaltig, "How Europe Can Age Gracefully," BusinessWeek.com, January 23, 2006, www.businessweek.com/investor/content/jan2006/pi20060123_5208_pi001.htm.

20. An astonishing 38 percent of Italians in the fifty-to-fifty-four-year-old bracket are already retired and out of the labor force, and hardly anyone in Italy between sixty and sixty-four still works. Sylvester J. Schieber, "Paying for It," *Wilson Quarterly*, Spring 2006, www.wilsoncenter.org/index.cfm?fuseaction=wq.essay&essay_id=178670.

21. European Commission, "Economic and Financial Consequences of Ageing Populations," *European Economy Review*, November 2002.

22. Murray, "Growing Old Gracefully," 22.

23. European Commission, *Report of the High Level Group on the Future of Social Policy in an Enlarged European Union* (Brussels: May 2004).

24. See "Percent of Men and Women of Working Age in Employment," in *OECD Factbook: Economic, Environmental and Social Statistics* (Paris: OECD, 2006), www.oecd.org/dataoecd/22/34/38181941.xls.

25. Gewaltig, "How Europe Can Age Gracefully."

26. "Map: Parenthood Policies in Europe," BBC News.com, March 24, 2006, http://news.bbc.co.uk/2/hi/europe/4837422.stm#spain.

27. "Dwindling Germans Review Policies," BBC News.com, March 28, 2006, http://news.bbc.co.uk/2/hi/europe/4852040.stm.

28. "Norway's Welfare Model 'Helps Birth Rate,'" BBC News.com, March 28, 2006, http://news.bbc.co.uk/2/hi/europe/4786160.stm.

29. "Dwindling Germans Review Policies."

30. Francis Castles, "The World Turned Upside Down: Below Replacement Fertility, Changing Preferences and Family Friendly Policy in 21 OECD Countries," *Journal of European Social Policy* 13, no. 3 (2003).

31. David Willetts, *Old Europe? Demographic Change and Pension Reform* (London: Centre for European Reform, 2003), 57.

32. Olivia Ekert-Jaffe et al., "Fertility, Timing of Births, and Socioeconomic Status in France and Britain: Social Policies and Occupational Popularisation," *Population* 57, no. 3 (May–June 2002).

33. "Fertility at 26 Year High," a video report by the BBC, June 7, 2007, viewed at http://news.bbc.co.uk/player/nol/newsid_6730000/newsid_6732300/6732343.stm?bw=nb&mp=wm&news=1&nol_storyid=6732343&bbcws=1.

34. "The EU's Baby Blues," BBC News.com, March 27, 2006, http://news.bbc.co.uk/2/hi/europe/4768644.stm.

35. Sharon Reier, "In Europe, Women Finding More Seats at the Table," *New York Times*, March 22, 2008.

36. Hiroko Tabuchi, "Japan Looks to a Robot Future," Associated Press, March 1, 2008. A 2007 national technology roadmap by the Trade Ministry calls for one million industrial robots to be installed throughout the country by 2025.

37. Michael Lind, "A Labour Shortage Can Be a Blessing, Not a Curse," *Financial Times*, June 9, 2006.

38. Tim Ferguson, "EC Launches Tech Plan for Seniors," BusinessWeek.com, June 15, 2007, www.businessweek.com/globalbiz/content/jun2007/gb20070615_383702.htm.

CONCLUSION

1. Adam Liptak, "1 in 100 Americans Are behind Bars, Study Says," *New York Times*, February 28, 2008. One recent study revealed that the United States, with 2.3 million people incarcerated, now imprisons triple the number it did in 1987 and is far ahead of the more populous China, which is in second place with 1.5 million people in prison. The U.S. prisoners per capita rate, 750 per 100,000 people, is also far ahead of Russia's second-place rate (628 per 100,000) and is nine times higher than the E.U.'s rate (only 87 prisoners per 100,000). (Note 23 in chapter 3 presents more of these comparative statistics.) Russia figure cited in David Crary, "Report: 1 in Every 100 Americans behind Bars," Associated Press story in *Houston Chronicle*, February 28, 2008; European Union figure cited in Tony Judt, "Europe vs. America," *New York Review of Books* 52, no. 2, February 10, 2005; also see International Centre for Prison Studies, "Entire World—Prison Population Rates per 100,000 of the National Population," http://www.prisonstudies.org/.

2. Matt Mabe, "There's Something about Denmark," *BusinessWeek*, August 20, 2008, www.businessweek.com/globalbiz/content/aug2008/gb20080820_005351.htm.

3. Russell Shorto, "Going Dutch," *New York Times Magazine*, April 29, 2009, www.nytimes.com/2009/05/03/magazine/03european-t.html?em.

4. Jean-François Revel, *Without Marx or Jesus* (Garden City, NY: Doubleday, 1970), 1.

Selected Bibliography

Alesina, Albert, and Edward L. Glaeser. *Fighting Poverty in the U.S. and Europe.* Oxford: Oxford University Press, 2004.

Alesina, Albert, and Enrico Spolaore. *The Size of Nations.* Cambridge, MA: MIT Press, 2003.

Bacevich, Andrew J. *The New American Militarism: How Americans Are Seduced by War.* New York: Oxford University Press, 2005.

Bell, Daniel A. *China's New Confucianism: Politics in Everyday Life in a Changing Society.* Princeton, NJ: Princeton University Press, 2008.

Carley, Mark. "Board-Level Employee Representatives in Nine Countries: A Snapshot." In *Transfer,* ed. Kevin O'Kelly and Dr. Norbert Kluge. Brussels: European Trade Union Institute, 2005.

Century Foundation. *National Health Insurance: Lessons from Abroad.* New York: Century Foundation Press, 2008.

Cooper, Robert. *The Breaking of Nations: Order and Chaos in the Twenty-first Century.* New York: Atlantic Monthly Press, 2003.

Dahl, Robert. *How Democratic Is the American Constitution?* New Haven and London: Yale University Press, 2002.

Diamond, Patrick, et al. *The Hampton Court Agenda: A Social Model for Europe.* London: Policy Network, 2006.

Downs, Anthony. *An Economic Theory of Democracy.* New York: Harper and Row, 1957.

Fallaci, Oriana. *The Force of Reason.* New York: Rizzoli, 2006.

Faux, Jeff. *The Global Class War.* Hoboken, NJ: Wiley and Sons, 2006.

Ferguson, Niall. *The War of the World: History's Age of Hatred.* London: Penguin, 2006.

Franck, Dan. *Bohemian Paris.* New York: Grove Press, 1998.

Frank, Robert H., and Philip J. Cook. *The Winner-Take-All Society.* New York and London: Free Press, 1995.

Friedman, Thomas. *The Lexus and the Olive Tree: Understanding Globalization.* New York: Anchor, 2000.

———. *The World Is Flat: A Brief History of the 21st Century.* New York: Farrar, Straus and Giroux, 2005.

Fukuyama, Francis. *The End of History and the Last Man.* New York: Avon Books, 1992.

———. *State Building: Governance and World Order in the Twenty-first Century.* Ithaca, NY: Cornell University Press, 2004.

Gallagher, Michael, Michael Laver, and Peter Maier. *Representative Government in Modern Europe.* 2nd ed. New York and London: McGraw-Hill, 1995.

Garton Ash, Timothy. *Free World: America, Europe and the Surprising Future of the West.* New York: Random House, 2004.

Goldfein, Alan. *Europe's Macadam, America's Tar.* Heidelberg: American Editions, 2004.

Gopnik, Adam. *Paris to the Moon.* New York: Random House, 2000.

Hacker, Jacob. *The Great Risk Shift.* New York: Oxford University Press, 2006.

Hamilton, Alexander, James Madison, and John Jay. *The Federalist Papers.* New York: New American Library, 1961.

Hampden-Turner, Charles, and Alfons Trompenaars. *The Seven Cultures of Capitalism: Value Systems for Creating Wealth in the United States, Japan, Germany, France, Britain, Sweden and the Netherlands.* New York and London: Currency Doubleday, 1993.

Hertsgaard, Mark. *The Eagle's Shadow: Why America Fascinates and Infuriates the World.* New York: Picador, 2002.

Herzog, Todd, and Sander L. Gilman, eds. *A New Germany in a New Europe.* New York and London: Routledge, 2001.

Hill, Steven. *Fixing Elections: The Failure of America's Winner Take All Politics.* New York and London: Routledge, 2002.

———. *10 Steps to Repair American Democracy.* Sausalito, CA: PoliPoint Press: 2006.

Hirsi Ali, Ayaan. *Infidel.* New York: Free Press, 2007.

Hockenos, Paul. *Joschka Fischer and the Making of the Berlin Republic: An Alternative History of Postwar Germany.* London: Oxford University Press, 2007.

Huntington, Samuel P. *The Clash of Civilizations: Remaking of World Order.* New York: Touchstone Books, 1996.

Hutton, Will. *The World We're In.* London: Little, Brown, 2002.

———. *The Writing on the Wall: Why We Must Embrace China as a Partner or Face It as an Enemy.* New York and London: Free Press, 2006.

Judt, Tony. *Postwar: A History of Europe Since 1945.* New York: Penguin, 2005.

Kagan, Robert. *Of Paradise and Power: America and Europe in the New World Order.* New York: Alfred A. Knopf, 2003.

Kaplan, Robert D. *Balkan Ghosts: A Journey through History.* New York: Picador, 1993.

Kennedy, Paul. *The Rise and Fall of the Great Powers.* New York: Random House, 1987.

Khanna, Parag. *The Second World: Empires and Influence in the New Global Order.* New York: Random House, 2008.

Kluge, Dr. Norbert, and Michael Stollt, eds. "The European Company— Prospects for Worker Board-Level Participation in the Enlarged E.U." Brussels: Social Development Agency and European Trade Institute for Research, Education and Health and Safety, 2006.

Kopstein, Jeffrey, and Sven Steinmo, eds. *Growing Apart? America and Europe in the Twenty-first Century.* Cambridge and New York: Cambridge University Press, 2008.

Kotkin, Joel. *The City: A Global History.* New York: Modern Library, 2005.

Kupchan, Charles. *The End of the American Era: U.S. Foreign Policy and the Geopolitics of the Twenty-first Century.* New York: Alfred A. Knopf, 2002.

Lee, Frances E., and Bruce L. Oppenheimer. *Sizing Up the Senate: The Unequal Consequences of Equal Representation.* Chicago and London: University of Chicago Press, 1999.

Leonard, Mark. *What Does China Think?* New York: Public Affairs, 2008.

———. *Why Europe Will Run the 21st Century.* London and New York: Fourth Estate, 2005.

Levinson, Klas. "Codetermination in Sweden: Myth and Reality." *Economic and Industrial Democracy* 21 (2000): 457–73.

———. "Employee Representatives on Company Boards in Sweden." *Industrial Relations Journal* 32, no. 2 (2001): 264–74.

Lewis, Bernard. *The Crisis of Islam: Holy War and Unholy Terror.* New York: Modern Library, 2003.

Lieven, Anatol, and John Hulsman. *Ethical Realism: A Vision for America's Role in the World.* New York: Pantheon, 2006.

Lijphart, Arend. *Patterns of Democracy: Government Forms and Performance in 36 Countries.* New Haven, CT, and London: Yale University Press, 1999.

Lind, Michael. *The American Way of Strategy: US Foreign Policy and the American Way of Life.* New York: Oxford University Press, 2006.

www.longitudes.org.

Longman, Phillip. *Best Care Anywhere: Why VA Health Care Is Better Than Yours.* Sausalito, CA: PoliPoint Press, 2007.

Lynn, Barry C. *End of the Line: The Rise and Coming Fall of the Global Corporation.* New York: Doubleday, 2005.

Magris, Claudio. *Danube.* London: Harvill Press, 1989.

Milner, Henry. *Civic Literacy: How Informed Citizens Make Democracy Work.* Hanover, NH, and London: University Press of New England, 2002.

Moravcsik, Andrew. *The Choice for Europe: Social Purpose and State Power from Messina to Maastricht.* Ithaca, NY: Cornell University Press, 1998.

———. *European Union and World Politics.* New York and London: Routledge, 2009.

———. *Europe without Illusions: The Paul-Henri Spaak Lectures, 1994–1999.* Lanham, MD: University Press of America, 2005.

Mumford, Lewis. *The City in History.* New York and London: Harcourt, 1961.

Nye, Joseph. *Soft Power: The Means to Success in World Politics.* New York: Public Affairs, 2004.

Patten, Chris. *Cousins and Strangers: America, Britain, and Europe in a New Century*. New York: Henry Holt, 2006.

Pejovich, Svetozar. *The Economics of Property Rights: Towards a Theory of Comparative Systems*. Dordrecht, Boston, and London: Kluwer Academic Publishers.

Pontusson, Jonas. *Inequality and Prosperity: Social Europe vs. Liberal America*. Ithaca, NY, and London: Cornell University Press, 2005.

Ramadan, Tariq. *Western Muslims and the Future of Islam*. New York: Oxford University Press, 2004.

Reid, T. R. *The United States of Europe: The New Superpower and the End of American Supremacy*. New York: Penguin Press, 2004.

Revel, Jean-François. *Without Marx or Jesus: The New American Revolution Has Begun*. New York: Doubleday, 1970.

Richie, Rob, and Steven Hill. *Whose Vote Counts*. Boston: Beacon Press, 2001.

Rifkin, Jeremy. *The European Dream: How Europe's Vision of the Future Is Quietly Eclipsing the American Dream*. New York: Jeremy P. Tarcher/Penguin, 2004.

———. *The Hydrogen Economy*. New York: Jeremy P. Tarcher/Penguin, 2002.

Rossmann, Witich. "Globalization, Economic and Monetary Union in Europe and the Trade Union Strategies for Employment and Workers' Rights." Paper presented at the IMF-JC International Labor Seminar, Cologne, Germany, July 10–12, 1997.

Russell, James. *Double Standard: Social Policy in Europe and the United States*. Lanham, MD: Rowman and Littlefield, 2006.

Schwenninger, Sherle. "Revamping American Grand Strategy." *World Policy Journal* 20, no. 3 (Fall 2003): 25–44.

Simons, Rolf, and Dr. Norbert Kluge. "Workers' Participation at Board Level in the EU-15 Countries." Brussels: Hans Boeckler Foundation/European Trade Union Institute, 2004.

Tocqueville, Alexis de. *Democracy in America*. New York: New American Library, 1956.

Wilensky, Harold L. *Rich Democracies: Political Economy, Public Policy and Performance*. Berkeley and London: University of California Press, 2002.

Willets, David. *Old Europe? Demographic Change and Pension Reform*. London: Centre for European Reform, 2003.

Yergin, Daniel, and Joseph Stanislaw. *The Commanding Heights: The Battle for the World Economy*. New York: Simon and Schuster, 1998.

Yu Keping. *Democracy Is a Good Thing*. Washington, DC: Brookings Institution Press, 2009.

Zakaria, Fareed. *The Post-American World*. New York: W. W. Norton, 2008.

Acknowledgments

European writers were among the earliest analysts of the new American nation, trekking from state to state and city to city like political tourists, studying the vanguard democratic republic across the Atlantic. Alexis de Tocqueville's *Democracy in America,* published in 1835, was the most famous of the political travelogues that emerged from this time, but there were others. The German Francis Lieber, who immigrated to the upstart young republic in 1827 and was to become one of America's leading writers and scholars on political philosophy, international affairs, and law, published *Letters to a Gentleman in Germany* in 1834, a travel narrative in which he related his impressions of political institutions and culture in his new homeland. Many historians have mined these seminal works for their own understanding of America's early years.

So in writing this book I was cognizant of following not only in the enormous footsteps of two intellectual giants but also a rich tradition and literary genre that I dubbed "political tourism." I have always been inspired by political travel writers who, not content with accepting conventional wisdom, struck out on their own either to discover new worlds or to see an old world with new eyes. Besides Lieber and Tocqueville, I have admired Marco Polo, John Reed, Rebecca West, Arnold Toynbee, V. S. Naipaul, and Claudio Magris, to name just a few who have inspired me with their intellect, bravery, crisp and vivid writing, and the sense of significance that pervades their works. In recent years, Robert Kaplan and Peter Hessler have maintained the quality of the genre, and Parag Khanna has reinforced the nobleness of it when practiced with vision.

My own European travels and research—both geographic and intellectual peregrinations—would not have been possible had I not been aided by many people who opened doors for me, including their front doors and in some cases their lives. I now count so many of them as colleagues and friends, and I feel greatly enriched for having made so many personal connections. This includes a most hospitable and insightful network of Americans living in Europe, some of them for decades. They generously gave me their time and insights, and sometimes their couch or spare bedroom, and from them I have learned so much. The number of people who helped me along my way are too many to list, but I would be remiss if I didn't single out a few.

In the United Kingdom, I am especially grateful to Will Hutton from the Work Foundation, in London; Mark Leonard, formerly with the Centre for European Reform and now with the European Council on Foreign Relations; Henning Meyer, editor of *Social Europe* magazine; Jenny Jones, vice-mayor of London; Noel Lynch, London Assembly member; Ken Ritchie, from the Electoral Reform Society; Peter Facey, from the New Politics Network; Carol Grose and her husband, Jeffrey D'Souza; Diana Clark; MPs Richard Burden (Labour) and Paul Tyler (Liberal Democrat); and many others too numerous to name.

In Germany, special thanks to Eva Altemolles for her friendship, cultural shepherding, and intellectual camaraderie, as well as savory muesli on the Bodensee; Karin Knöbelspies, media policy advisor for the Green Party Group in the German parliament, who opened some important doors for me and provided valuable commentary on Germany and the United States; and Paul Nellen, a diligent journalist who stays up late at night worrying about the state of the peak oil world and is my coeditor at www.Longitudes.org. Also thanks to Dr. Dorothea Staiger, deputy mayor of Bonn; Dr. Witich Rossman, trade union secretary with IG Metall; Tom Schlatmann, chief of staff for a Christian Democratic Union parliamentarian; Gunter Gworkek and Malti Taneja, policy advisors for the parliamentary Green Group; MP Andrea Nahles (Social Democratic Party); Jason Kirkpatrick; Harry Ernst; Donald Griffith and his Fountainhead Tanz Theatre / Black International Cinema in Berlin; Jakob Köllhofer and the German American Institute in Heidelberg for sponsoring my lecture there; John McQueen; Pam Selwyn; Peter Johnson; Susan Haug; and others.

In France, I particularly want to thank Meredith Wheeler, a lion of an archangel who coordinated two speaking tours to sixteen cities, which allowed me to make contact with hundreds of Europeans and Americans living in Europe. I also wish to thank her husband, Robin Ellis, the sweetest Poldark of a man who makes omelettes so light they float off your plate. Also thanks to Professor James Cohen, from Université de Paris VIII, who guided my understanding of immigration in France and Europe and gave invaluable feedback on the manuscript; the late, great journalist Daniel Singer for his warmth and collegiality; and Charles Steiger, Denny Adelman, Angela Shaw, Connie Borde, journalist Guillaume Serina, Kathy Coit, Lois Grjebine, and others.

In Belgium, many thanks to Ralph Mono, Arnold Cassola, and Ann Verheyen with the European Federation of Green Parties in Brussels for giving me (temporarily) the keys to the European Parliament, and also MEPs Monica Frassoni, Carl Schlyter, Frithjof Schmidt, Rebecca Harms, Juan Behrend, and Danny Cohn-Bendit, as well as Niki Kortvelyessy and Niels Fischer. In addition, I wish to thank Kevin Prager for his hospitality, Simon O'Connor and the Centre for sponsoring two of my lectures, Sandrine Dixson-Decleve, and Vincent Van Quickenborne.

In Sweden, I wish to express my profound gratitude to Professor Henry Milner, a Canadian who teaches in both Canada and Sweden and understands the world as well as anyone I know. Henry gave an important critique of the manuscript, and his own book *Civic Literacy* is a gem to which I am greatly indebted. Also special thanks to Klas Levinson and the former National Institute for Working Life; Professor Anders Lidström and his colleagues at Umeå University; and Professor Ben Reilly, Andrew Ellis, and Frances Lesser, currently or formerly with the Institute for Democracy and Electoral Assistance (IDEA) in Stockholm. I also extend an especially warm thanks to Brad Delange for his hospitality and friendship.

In Austria, affectionate thanks to Erich Fröschl and the Renner Institut for sponsoring my lecture in Vienna; MP Brigid Weinzinger; Austrian Broadcast Corporation journalists Eugen Freund and Jill Zobel; and Kristin Smeral and Michael Platzer, especially for the delicious *Sturm*. In the Netherlands, many thanks to Ivo Hartman from the Instituut voor Publiek en Politiek (Dutch Centre for Political Participation); Robbie Checkoway and his partner Chris for their hospitality; Lynette Hart for a memorable boat tour of the Amsterdam canals; and Linda Deak, in memoriam. In Italy, thanks to Professors Roberto D'Alimonte, Gianfranco Baldini, and Stefano Bartolini, and to Grazia

Francescato and Mariagrazia Midulla from the Green Party. In the Czech Republic, warm thanks to Gwen Albert, Vincent Farnsworth, Arie Farnam, and Rob Hyde. In Norway, thanks to Olee Olsen, Barbara Ødegård, and Caroline Lorgen, not only for your hospitality but for directing me to the magnificent Vigeland sculptures. In Switzerland, many thanks to Kim and Paul Polman and Caitlin Kraft-Buchman. In Spain, thanks to Andrew Davis and Professor Josep Colomer.

In China, a special note of gratitude to Professor Yu Keping, deputy director of the Centre of the Central Compilation and Translation Bureau for his gracious hospitality, goodwill, and richly textured conversation; to Professor Yang Yao, deputy director of the China Center for Economic Research and editor of the *China Economic Quarterly,* for being the scholar "with the numbers" that refute conventional wisdom; to Tang Feng Qiong for her trustworthy tour guiding around the rural areas and for her poignant insights regarding life for farming families; to Professor Pan Wei from Peking University; Professor Daniel Bell from Tsinghua University; Jim Fallows, from the *Atlantic,* for making some connections for me; Professors Joseph Chan and Mirana May Szeto at the University of Hong Kong; journalist Adam Minter; and Professor Daniel Guttman.

In the United States, a special affectionate thank you to my oldest friend in the world, Chris Siemer, and his wife, Anne, and children William and Cara for hosting me in Brussels, Kuala Lumpur, and Shanghai, and for the worldly discussions, guitar picking, and friendship (I look forward to wherever you end up next); to Mike Feinstein, former mayor of Santa Monica and Green Party leader, for introducing me to his far-flung international network and for his camaraderie, humanity, adventurous spirit, and late-night discussions; to economist Dean Baker for his clarity and feedback (and for seeing the housing bubble before Alan Greenspan!); to Vahdet Avci for his insights on Turkey; to Lisa Margonelli from the New America Foundation and Diana Farrell from McKinsey Global Institute for their insights on energy productivity and conservation; to Professors Andrew Moravcsik, Arend Lijphart, and Robert Dahl for their inspiration and counsel; to Sherle Schwenninger from the New America Foundation for his insights regarding the growth of a global middle class; to Rob Richie and Richard Winger for their scholarship and collegiality; to economist Jeffrey Mitchell, my longtime friend, for helping me to hone some of my economic arguments; and to another longtime friend, Emily McFarland, for reading and providing helpful criticism for parts of the manuscript.

I also would like to thank my agent, Barbara Moulton, and my editor at the University of California Press, Naomi Schneider. Each of them in turn steered this project into its final form, and I am thankful for their efforts and guidance.

Finally, I would like to thank my parents, Pat and Jack Hill, and my in-laws, Barbara and Jim Colvin, for their love and support. And most of all, words can hardly express my gratitude to my partner, Lucy Colvin, for, first, her invaluable feedback on the manuscript, spirited discussions, assistance with some of the interviews, and tag-team traveling around the world, and, second, her love, patience, and encouragement while I ground this one out. I owe you quite a few weekends.

Index

About the Author

Steven Hill is director of the Political Reform Program at the New America Foundation (www.newamerica.net). His articles and commentaries have appeared in dozens of newspapers and magazines, including the *New York Times, Washington Post, Los Angeles Times, Wall Street Journal, Roll Call, Christian Science Monitor,* Salon.com, *The Nation, Ms., American Prospect, Sierra, American Scientist, New York Daily News, San Francisco Chronicle, Miami Herald, Baltimore Sun, Chicago Tribune, Houston Chronicle,* and many others in the United States, plus the *International Herald Tribune, Prospect, The Guardian, Social Europe Journal, Italy Daily, Prague Post,* Cafebabel.com, The Globalist.com, *Hürriyet Daily News* (Turkey), *Taiwan News,* and other publications abroad.

His previous books include *10 Steps to Repair American Democracy* (2006, www.10Steps.net) and *Whose Vote Counts* (2001). His book *Fixing Elections: The Failure of America's Winner Take All Politics* (2002, www.FixingElections.com) has been called "the most important book on American democracy that has come out in many years." He has lectured widely in the United States and Europe and has appeared on C-SPAN, Fox News, National Public Radio, and numerous other radio and TV programs across the nation. He also has made radio and television appearances in various European nations and in Dubai, United Arab Emirates. He is cofounder of FairVote/Center for Voting and Democracy (www.fairvote.org).